Algeria
a country study

Federal Research Division
Library of Congress
Edited by
Helen Chapin Metz
Research Completed
December 1993

On the cover: A typical village scene, with market and houses in the foreground and mosque in the background

Fifth Edition, First Printing, 1994

Library of Congress Cataloging-in-Publication Data

Algeria: a country study / Federal Research Division, Library of Congress; edited by Helen Chapin Metz.—5th ed.
    p. cm.—(Area handbook series, ISSN 1057–5294) (DA Pam; 550–44)
    "Supersedes the 1986 edition of Algeria: A Country Study edited by Harold D. Nelson."—T.p. verso.
    "Research completed December 1993."
    Includes bibliographical references (pp. 295–311) and index.
    ISBN 0–8444–0831–X
    1. Algeria. I. Metz, Helen Chapin 1928– . II. Library of Congress. Federal Research Division. III. Series. IV. Series: DA Pam; 550–44
DT275.A5771 1994   94–43019
965–dc20   CIP

Headquarters, Department of the Army
DA Pam 550–44

For sale by the Superintendent of Documents, U.S. Government Printing Office
Washington, D.C. 20402

Foreword

This volume is one in a continuing series of books prepared by the Federal Research Division of the Library of Congress under the Country Studies/Area Handbook Program sponsored by the Department of the Army. The last two pages of this book list the other published studies.

Most books in the series deal with a particular foreign country, describing and analyzing its political, economic, social, and national security systems and institutions, and examining the interrelationships of those systems and the ways they are shaped by cultural factors. Each study is written by a multidisciplinary team of social scientists. The authors seek to provide a basic understanding of the observed society, striving for a dynamic rather than a static portrayal. Particular attention is devoted to the people who make up the society, their origins, dominant beliefs and values, their common interests and the issues on which they are divided, the nature and extent of their involvement with national institutions, and their attitudes toward each other and toward their social system and political order.

The books represent the analysis of the authors and should not be construed as an expression of an official United States government position, policy, or decision. The authors have sought to adhere to accepted standards of scholarly objectivity. Corrections, additions, and suggestions for changes from readers will be welcomed for use in future editions.

> Louis R. Mortimer
> Chief
> Federal Research Division
> Library of Congress
> Washington, D.C. 20540–5220

Acknowledgments

The authors wish to acknowledge the contributions of the writers of the 1985 edition of Algeria: A Country Study, edited by Harold D. Nelson. Their work provided general background for the present volume.

The authors are grateful to individuals in various government agencies and private institutions who gave of their time, research materials, and expertise in the production of this book. These individuals include Ralph K. Benesch, who oversees the Country Studies—Area Handbook program for the Department of the Army. The authors also wish to thank members of the Federal Research Division staff who contributed directly to the preparation of the manuscript. These people include Sandra W. Meditz, who reviewed all drafts and served as liaison with the sponsoring agency; Marilyn L. Majeska, who managed editing and production; Andrea T. Merrill, who edited tables and figures; Ramón Miró, who assisted with bibliographic research; Barbara Edgerton and Izella Watson, who did word processing; and Stephen C. Cranton and David P. Cabitto, who prepared the camera-ready copy.

Also involved in preparing the text were Mimi Cantwell, who edited chapters; Catherine Schwartzstein, who performed the prepublication editorial review; and Joan C. Cook, who compiled the index.

Graphics were prepared by David P. Cabitto, and Tim L. Merrill, assisted by Thomas Hall, prepared map drafts. David P. Cabitto and the firm of Greenhorne and O'Mara prepared the final maps. Special thanks are owed to Teresa Kamp, who prepared the illustrations on the title page of each chapter and the cover art.

Finally, the authors acknowledge the generosity of the Algerian Embassy in Washington and the other government and private bodies and individuals who allowed their photographs to be used in this study.

Contents

Foreword iii
Acknowledgments v
Preface xiii
Table A. Selected Acronyms and Contractions xv
Country Profile xvii
Introduction xxvii

Chapter 1. Historical Setting 1
Anthony Toth
PREHISTORY OF CENTRAL NORTH AFRICA 4
NORTH AFRICA DURING THE
   CLASSICAL PERIOD 7
      Carthage and the Berbers 7
      The Roman Era 8
      Vandals and Byzantines 10
ISLAM AND THE ARABS, 642–1830 11
      Fatimids 13
      Almoravids 14
      Almohads 15
      Zayanids 16
      Marabouts 17
      European Offensive 17
      Privateers 18
      Ottoman Rule 19
      Relations with the United States 21
FRANCE IN ALGERIA, 1830–1962 22
      Invasion of Algiers 22
      The Land and Colonizers 23
      Opposition to the Occupation 24
      Abd al Qadir 25
      Colonization and Military Control 27
      Hegemony of the Colons 32
      Algerian Nationalism 34

Polarization and Politicization	40
War of Independence	44
INDEPENDENT ALGERIA, 1962–92	56
Aftermath of the War	57
Ben Bella and the FLN	58
Boumediene Regime	60
Chadli Benjedid and Afterward	61

Chapter 2. The Society and Its Environment 67
Mary-Jane Deeb

PHYSICAL SETTING	69
Geographic Regions	72
Climate and Hydrology	74
Terrain	75
POPULATION	76
Demographic Profile	76
Migration	78
Urbanization and Density	79
ETHNIC GROUPS AND LANGUAGES	81
The Peoples	81
Languages: Arabic and Berber	86
Arabization	87
STRUCTURE OF SOCIETY	91
Preindependence Society	91
The Revolution and Social Change	95
Toward a Modern Society	96
THE INDIVIDUAL, THE FAMILY, AND THE SEXES	99
Family and Household	100
Men and Women	101
Family Code	104
Family Planning	105
ISLAM	106
Early History	107
Tenets of Islam	108
Islam and the Algerian State	109
RELIGIOUS MINORITIES	111
EDUCATION	112
HEALTH AND WELFARE	118
Health	118
Social Welfare	121
Housing	121

Chapter 3. The Economy 127
                        Boulos A. Malik
DEVELOPMENT PLANNING 130
GOVERNMENT ROLE 131
PUBLIC FINANCES................................ 134
    Budget...................................... 135
    External Debt and Payments 136
    Currency and Exchange Rates................... 137
    Foreign Aid.................................. 138
    Investments 139
SERVICES 142
    Banking..................................... 142
    Tourism..................................... 142
LABOR AND EMPLOYMENT 143
NATURAL RESOURCES AND ENERGY 145
    Hydrocarbons 145
    Minerals 148
    Electric Power 149
INDUSTRY....................................... 150
    Manufacturing................................ 151
    Construction 151
AGRICULTURE................................... 152
    Land Tenure and Reform....................... 153
    Crops 157
    Livestock.................................... 158
    Forestry 160
    Fishing..................................... 160
TRANSPORTATION AND TELECOMMUNI-
    CATIONS.................................... 160
    Transportation................................ 160
    Telecommunications 166
TRADE.. 167
    Trading Partners.............................. 168
    Exports and Imports 169
    Balance of Payments........................... 170
    Trade Account................................ 170
TRENDS 171

Chapter 4. Government and Politics 173
                John P. Entelis with Lisa Arone
POLITICAL ENVIRONMENT 176

Postindependence Politics and the
Socialist Tradition............................ 176
The Revolutionary Period and
Independence 177
The "Heroic" Stage: Ben Bella's
Regime, 1962-65............................ 177
Boumediene and the Socialist Experiment 178
Recent Political Events 181
POLITICAL STRUCTURE AND PROCESSES 192
Structure of the National Government........... 192
Role of Political Parties........................ 195
Judicial System 198
Local and Regional Government 202
EFFECTIVE INSTITUTIONS 204
Political Configuration: The Army-Party-State
Triangle................................... 204
The Elite..................................... 205
Military Dictatorship 206
The Islamist Factor 207
CIVIL SOCIETY..................................... 210
Algerian General Workers' Union and
the Workers' Movement 211
Youth and Student Unions 212
The National Union of Algerian Farmers 213
The Entrepreneurial Class...................... 214
Socialist Vanguard Party....................... 214
The Women's Movement...................... 215
The Press 218
The Arabization Movement.................... 220
FOREIGN POLICY 221
General Trends............................... 221
Africa.. 222
Arab and Middle East Affairs................... 227
The West 228

Chapter 5. National Security....................... 235
Jean R. Tartter
EXTERNAL SECURITY PROBLEMS AND
POLICIES....................................... 238
Security Interests Outside the Maghrib 239
Security Problems with Neighboring States....... 241

Strategic Perspectives	244
DOMESTIC SECURITY CONCERNS	245
Islamic Opposition	247
Berber Separatism	249
THE MILITARY HERITAGE	250
THE ARMED FORCES	256
Army	259
Air Force	262
Navy	263
Uniforms, Ranks, and Insignia	265
Personnel and Recruitment	265
Conditions of Service	268
THE DEFENSE BURDEN	270
FOREIGN MILITARY ASSISTANCE	272
INTERNAL SECURITY	277
Gendarmerie Nationale	278
Sûreté Nationale	279
Intelligence Agencies	279
Criminal Justice System	280
Prison Conditions	283
Appendix. Tables	285
Bibliography	295
Glossary	313
Index	317
Contributors	339

List of figures

1 Administrative Divisions of Algeria, 1993	xxvi
2 Roman North Africa, Fourth Century B.C. to Third Century A.D.	6
3 French Algeria, 1845–1962	28
4 Topography and Drainage	70
5 Population by Age and Gender, 1987	80
6 Oil and Gas Industry, 1993	146
7 Economic Activity, 1993	150
8 Transportation System, 1993	162
9 Balance of Power in the Maghrib, 1993	246
10 Organization of National Defense, 1993	258
11 Military Regions, 1993	260

12 Commissioned Officer and Enlisted Personnel
   Ranks and Insignia, 1993 266

Preface

This edition of *Algeria: A Country Study* replaces the previous edition published in 1985. Like its predecessor, the present book attempts to treat in a compact and objective manner the dominant historical, social, economic, political, and national security aspects of contemporary Algeria. Sources of information included scholarly books, journals, and monographs; official reports and documents of governments and international organizations; and foreign and domestic newspapers and periodicals. Relatively up-to-date economic data were available from several sources, but the sources were not always in agreement.

Chapter bibliographies appear at the end of the book; brief comments on some of the more valuable sources for further reading appear at the conclusion of each chapter. Measurements are given in the metric system; a conversion table is provided to assist those who are unfamiliar with the metric system (see table 1, Appendix). The Glossary provides brief definitions of terms that may be unfamiliar to the general reader. A list of acronyms and contractions also has been provided to assist the reader.

The literature on Algeria is frequently confusing because of the tendency of writers to mix English and French transliterations of Arabic words, personal names, and place-names. For the most part, the authors of this study have attempted to reduce this confusion by adhering to the system of French transliteration, inasmuch as that is the form used among French speakers in Algeria and by most Western scholars. In transliterating place-names, again with minor exceptions, the authors followed a modified version of the system adopted by the United States Board on Geographic Names and the Permanent Committee on Geographic Names for British Official Use, known as the BGN/PCGN system; the modification entails the omission of most diacritical markings and hyphens. In some instances, however, the names of places are so well known by another spelling that to have used the BGN/PCGN system may have created confusion. For example, the reader will find Algiers rather than Alger.

The body of the text reflects information available as of December 1993. Certain other portions of the text, however, have been updated. The Introduction discusses significant events that have occurred since the completion of research, and the Country Profile includes updated information as available.

Table A. Selected Acronyms and Contractions

Acronym or Contraction	Organization
ACDA	United States Arms Control and Disarmament Agency
ALN	Armée de Libération Nationale (National Liberation Army)
AML	Amis du Manifeste et de la Liberté (Friends of the Manifesto and of Liberty)
ANP	Armée Nationale Populaire (People's National Army)
APC	Assemblée Populaire Communale (Communal Popular Assembly)
APN	Assemblée Populaire Nationale (National People's Assembly)
APW	Assemblée Populaire de Wilaya (Popular Wilaya Assembly)
BNP	Banque Nationale de Paris (National Bank of Paris)
CCN	Conseil Consultatif National (National Consultative Council)
CNDR	Comité National pour la Défense de la Révolution (National Committee for the Defense of the Revolution)
CNRA	Conseil National de la Révolution Algérienne (National Council of the Algerian Revolution)
DGDS	Délégation Générale de Documentation et Sûreté (General Delegation for Documentation and Security)
EPÉ	Entreprises Publiques Économiques (Public Economic Enterprises)
FFS	Front des Forces Socialistes (Front of Socialist Forces)
FIS	Front Islamique du Salut (Islamic Salvation Front)
GPRA	Gouvernement Provisoire de la République Algérienne (Provisional Government of the Algerian Republic)
HCÉ	Haut Conseil d'État (High Council of State)
HCS	Haut Conseil de Sécurité (High Security Council)
MDA	Mouvement pour la Démocratie en Algérie (Movement for Democracy in Algeria)
MNA	Mouvement National Algérien (National Algerian Movement)
MTLD	Mouvement pour le Triomphe des Libertés Démocratiques (Movement for the Triumph of Democratic Liberties)
OAS	Organisation de l'Armée Secrète (Secret Army Organization)
OAU	Organization of African Unity
OECD	Organisation for Economic Co-operation and Development
OPEC	Organization of the Petroleum Exporting Countries
OS	Organisation Spéciale (Special Organization)
PAGS	Parti de l'Avant-Garde Socialiste (Socialist Vanguard Party)
PCA	Parti Communiste Algérien (Algerian Communist Party)
PLO	Palestine Liberation Organization
Polisario	Frente Popular para la Liberación de Saguia el Hamra y Río de Oro (Popular Front for the Liberation of Saguia el Hamra and Río de Oro)
PPA	Parti du Peuple Algérien (Party of the Algerian People)
PRS	Parti de la Révolution Socialiste (Socialist Revolution Party)
SADR	Saharan Arab Democratic Republic
SM	Sécurité Militaire (Military Security)
Sonatrach	Société Nationale pour la Recherche, la Production, le Transport, la Transformation, et la Commercialisation des Hydrocarbures (National Company for Research, Production, Transportation, Processing, and Commercialization of Hydrocarbons)

Table A. Selected Acronyms and Contractions

Acronym or Contraction	Organization
UDMA	Union Démocratique du Manifeste Algérien (Democratic Union of the Algerian Manifesto)
UGTA	Union Générale des Travailleurs Algériens (General Union of Algerian Workers)
UMA	Union du Maghreb Arabe (Union of the Arab Maghrib)
UNÉA	Union Nationale des Étudiants Algériens (National Union of Algerian Students)
UNFA	Union Nationale des Femmes Algériennes (National Union of Algerian Women)
UNJA	Union Nationale de la Jeunesse Algérienne (National Union of Algerian Youth)
UNPA	Union Nationale des Paysans Algériens (National Union of Algerian Farmers)

Country Profile

Country

Formal Name: Democratic and Popular Republic of Algeria.

Short Form: Algeria.

Term for National(s): Algerian(s).

Capital: Algiers.

Date of Independence: July 5, 1962, from France.

Note—The Country Profile contains updated information as available.

Geography

Size: 2,381,741 square kilometers, more than four-fifths desert.

Topography: Sharp contrast between relatively fertile, mountainous, topographically fragmented north and vast expanse of Sahara in south; northern Algeria dominated by parallel ranges of Saharan Atlas mountain system; no navigable rivers.

Climate: Mediterranean climate in coastal lowlands and mountain valleys; mild winters and moderate rainfall. Average temperatures and precipitation lower in intermountain Hauts Plateaux. Hot and arid in desert; little seasonal change in most of country but considerable diurnal variation in temperature.

Society

Population: Estimated at 27.4 million in 1993, increasing at an annual rate of 2.8 percent and expected to reach 32.5 million by 2000. Majority of population lives in predominantly urban coastal lowlands and adjacent mountain valleys, with population density dropping sharply toward interior; desert regions uninhabited except for isolated nomadic and sedentary communities. High urbanization rate of 5.6 percent annually, resulting from natural population growth and internal migration.

Ethnic Groups: Population a mixture of Arab and indigenous Berber, largely integrated with little or no social stratification along racial or ethnic lines; several other ethnic groups present in small numbers. Arabs constitute about 80 percent of total.

Languages: Arabic official language and spoken by vast majority; French widely spoken; bilingualism and trilingualism common. Berber spoken in a few isolated Saharan communities and in Tell hill villages.

Religion: Islam official state religion; observance of Sunni (see Glossary) Islam nearly universal. Unofficial militant Islam gaining strength and challenging Western practices in legal and political systems. Non-Muslim minorities include about 45,000

Roman Catholics, small number of Protestants, and very small Jewish community.

Education: Free public education at all levels, including nine-year system of compulsory basic education. In 1991–92 enrollments in basic education totaled almost 5.8 million. Three-track system of secondary education offers placement in general, technical, or vocational instruction.

Literacy: United Nations Educational, Scientific, and Cultural Organization estimates 1990 adult literacy rate at 57.4 percent, up from less than 10 percent in 1962; male literacy rate 69.8 percent; female literacy rate 45.5 percent.

Health and Welfare: Major transformations in health care system reflected in improving health conditions. Infant mortality rate reduced from 154 per 1,000 live births in 1965 to sixty-seven per 1,000 live births in 1990. In 1990 life expectancy at birth sixty-five years for males and sixty-six for females. Tuberculosis, trachoma, and venereal infections most serious diseases; gastrointestinal complaints, pneumonia, diphtheria, scarlet fever, and mumps relatively common. Typhoid fever, cholera, dysentery, and hepatitis also widespread among all age-groups. National health care system based on universal, almost free health care. Network of hospitals and clinics organized into health districts providing services to 90 percent of population. Modified social security system inherited from French colonial administration, expanded in 1971 to provide sickness and disability insurance, old-age pensions, and family allowances to all workers in formal economy. Acute housing shortage worsening despite growth in public housing.

Economy

Salient Features: State-directed economic system undergoing market-oriented structural adjustment and decentralization. Central government retains ownership of more than 450 state-owned enterprises. Economy dominated by hydrocarbon sector, mainly oil, but diversifying into natural gas and refined products. Underinvestment in agriculture and other nonoil sectors.

Gross Domestic Product (GDP): In 1992 estimated at US$42 billion. GDP grew at average annual rate of 6.5 percent during

1970s and 4.5 percent during first half of 1980s, largely as result of increasing oil revenues. Economy contracted sharply during latter half of 1980s and early 1990s; per capita GDP declined from US$2,752 in 1987 to US$1,570 in 1992.

Minerals: Hydrocarbon sector, mainstay of economy and main source of exports, constituted 23 percent of GDP in 1990. Exports include crude oil, refined petroleum products, and gas. Nonfuel minerals include high-grade iron ore, phosphate, mercury, and zinc.

Energy: Electricity supplied mainly by gas-powered plants. Overall energy consumption quadrupled between 1970s and early 1990s.

Industry: Manufacturing constituted 10 percent of GDP in 1990. Investment concentrated in state-owned heavy industry, mainly steel.

Agriculture: Variably estimated to account for 7 to 11 percent of GDP in 1990 and employing more than 22 percent of labor force. Arable land restricted mainly to coastal strip in north; pastoral agriculture dominant farther south. Production mainly grains, dominated by wheat and barley. Other main crops include grapes, citrus fruits, vegetables, olives, tobacco, and dates. Livestock and poultry production significant but heavily dependent on imported feed. Local consumption heavily reliant on food imports. Landholding, agricultural marketing, and distribution undergoing gradual decentralization and reprivatization.

Foreign Trade: Total exports US$12.7 billion in 1990, of which 96 percent hydrocarbons. Nonhydrocarbon exports include wine, metals and metal products, phosphates, fruits and vegetables, and iron ore. Total imports US$9.8 billion in 1989; include foodstuffs, semifinished goods, industrial and consumer goods.

External Debt: US$26 billion in 1992, mainly held by public sector. Debt service exceeded US$7 billion in 1991. International Monetary Fund standby agreement negotiated in

May 1994.

Currency and Exchange Rate: Algerian dinar (DA); US$1 = DA40.7 in October 1994.

Fiscal Year: Calendar year.

Transportation and Telecommunications

Railroads: 4,060 kilometers total; 2,616 kilometers standard gauge (1.435 meters); 1,188 kilometers 1.055-meter gauge; 256 kilometers 1.000-meter gauge; 300 kilometers electrified; 215 kilometers double track. System carries passengers but used mainly for freight.

Ports: Nine major ports at Algiers, Oran, Annaba, Mostaganem, Arzew, Bejaïa, Skikda, and Jijel. Three largest ports handled 71 percent of traffic in 1991.

Roads: More than 90,000 kilometers total; 58,868 kilometers paved; 31,163 kilometers gravel, crushed stone, or unimproved earth. Network unevenly distributed, more developed in northern coastal region; south served by limited number of national roads, mainly trans-Saharan highway.

Airports: International airports at Algiers, Oran, Annaba, and Constantine; more than 100 secondary and minor airfields, fifty-three with permanent surface runways.

Telecommunications: High-capacity radio-relay and coaxial cable trunk routes linking all major population areas along northern coast. Sahara linked by satellite ground stations to major population centers. Extensive international service based on satellite and submarine coaxial cable transmissions. Some international broadcasts received but domestic broadcast facilities sparse; only larger populated places receive television and radio.

Government and Politics

Government: Revised constitution of February 1989, suspended by military government in January 1992, ended commitment to socialism embodied in National Charter and earlier constitutions.

Political system based on strong presidential rule; provides in theory for multiparty system, separation of religious institution and state, and military subordination to civilian authority.

Politics: Liberalizing government of President Chadli Benjedid toppled by military in January 1992. Presidency replaced by military-dominated High Council of State. Emergency rule enacted to prevent national electoral victory by Islamist (fundamentalist) movement, spearheaded by Islamic Salvation Front. In January 1994, military named General Lamine Zeroual president; High Council of State abolished. Zeroual to rule in coordination with High Security Council. Political violence and terrorism endemic, including killings of numerous foreigners since 1992. Some legislative functions exercised by National Transitional Council, created in May 1994; 200-member body provided for political party, trade union, professional, and civil service representation.

Judicial System: Legal system derived from French and Arabic legal traditions and influenced by socialism. Supreme Court of four chambers reviews application of law by forty-eight provincial courts and lower tribunals. Civilian judicial system effectively replaced by military tribunals in January 1992.

Administrative Divisions: Forty-eight provinces administered by centrally appointed governors. In 1994 no elected assemblies existed at national, provincial, or communal level.

Foreign Relations: Policy founded on nonalignment, national self-determination, and support for Palestine Liberation Organization in Arab-Israeli dispute. Membership in League of Arab States and Organization of African Unity. Relations with West improved during 1980s and early 1990s, primarily as result of expanding trade and increasing economic cooperation.

National Security

Armed Forces: In late 1993, consisted of 121,700 total active forces; included army of 105,000; navy of 6,700, with 10,000-member air force; and coast guard of 630. Reserve force of 150,000 at unknown level of readiness. Internal security forces include Gendarmerie Nationale of 24,000, Sûreté Nationale force of 16,000, and 1,200-member Republican Guard Brigade.

Major Tactical Units: Army organized into six geographically defined military regions. Bulk of army stationed in populated areas of north and in and near major cities as well as near borders with Morocco and Western Sahara. Major army units in 1993: two armored divisions (each with three tank regiments and one mechanized regiment); two mechanized divisions (each with three mechanized regiments and one tank regiment); number of independent brigades and regiments unclear; five motorized infantry brigades, one airborne division, seven independent artillery battalions, five air defense battalions, and four engineer battalions. Air force in 1993 had 193 combat aircraft, fifty-eight armed helicopters configured in three fighter-ground attack squadrons, eight fighter squadrons, one reconnaissance squadron, one maritime reconnaissance squadron, two transport squadrons, five helicopter squadrons of which three attack squadrons, two transport squadrons, of which one heavy and one medium. Separate air defense force with three brigades for air defense and three regiments with SAM missiles. Navy bases at Mers el Kebir, Algiers, Annaba, and Jijel. Major naval equipment in 1993 consisted of two submarines, three frigates, three corvettes, eleven missile craft, eight patrol craft, one minesweeper, and three amphibious landing ships.

Defense Expenditures: 1992 defense budget DA23.0 billion (US$1.05 billion); 1993 defense budget DA29.8 billion (US$1.19 billion); military expenditures per capita in 1989 US$94.

Internal Security: Sûreté Nationale, under the Ministry of Interior, Local Communities, Environment, and Administrative Reform, performs most urban police duties. Gendarmerie Nationale, under the Ministry of Interior but considered paramilitary adjunct of armed forces, responsible for rural police matters. Military Security responsible for domestic and foreign intelligence operations.

Introduction

ALGERIA IN OCTOBER 1994 was in a state bordering on civil war. The military in late January 1994 had named General Lamine Zeroual, previously minister of defense, as president. He was to rule in coordination with the High Security Council (Haut Conseil de Sûreté) because the High Council of State (Haut Conseil d'État—HCÉ), created two years previously, had been abolished. In April armed forces leaders removed Prime Minister Redha Malek from his post after an incumbency of only eight months, replacing him with Mokdad Sifi, an engineer technocrat who had served as minister of equipment. Efforts to achieve a workable compromise with the major Islamic activist group, the Islamic Salvation Front (Front Islamique du Salut—FIS), appeared unsuccessful. Martial law, imposed in February 1992, continued.

To understand the forces behind recent events, one must look at the factors that have shaped Algeria's history. The indigenous peoples of the region of North Africa that today constitutes Algeria comprise an ethnic group known as the Berbers. In the mid-1990s, the Berbers represented only about 20 percent of Algeria's population. In A.D. 642, following conquests by the Romans, the Vandals, and the Byzantines, the region came under the influence of Islam and the Arabs. Hence, the vast majority of the population, about 80 percent, are Arabs. Islam and arabization, therefore, have profoundly influenced the area.

The Arab rulers of Algeria have come from various groups. In chronological order, they have included the Umayyads, the Abbasids, the Fatimids, the Almoravids, the Almohads, and the Zayanids. The latter group was followed in the sixteenth century and early seventeenth century by a series of privateer merchant captains. One of the early sixteenth-century Muslim privateers, Khair ad Din, ruled present-day Algeria on behalf of the Ottoman Turks, who gave him the title of provincial governor. The Ottoman sultan nominally controlled the area into the nineteenth century but in reality exerted minimal influence.

From their base in Algeria, the privateers preyed on French vessels and those of other Western nations. Because France was occupied with the Napoleonic wars and their aftermath in the first part of the nineteenth century, it was not in a position to act against the Algerian privateers. In 1827, however, as a result of an alleged slight to the French consul by the local ruler, or dey, France undertook what became a three-year blockade of Algiers. The incident led to a full-scale French invasion of Algeria in 1830 and the imposition of French rule, which lasted until Algeria obtained its independence in 1962.

In the course of French colonization of Algeria, discontent on the part of the inhabitants led to several uprisings. The most prominent of these was a revolt that originated in the Kabylie region in eastern Algeria in 1871 and spread through much of the country. Serious disturbances also broke out on V-E (Victory in Europe) Day, 1945. In response to the latter uprisings, the French military killed more than 1,500 Algerians and arrested more than 5,400 persons. French actions and growing Algerian nationalism led in 1954 to the creation by Ahmed Ben Bella and his colleagues of the National Liberation Front (Front de Libération Nationale—FLN) and a military network throughout Algeria, the National Liberation Army (Armée de Libération Nationale—ALN).

The FLN launched the War of Independence on November 1, 1954, and called on all Algerian Muslims to support it. A bloody war ensued. The conflict ended on July 1, 1962, with Algeria obtaining independence at the cost of as many as 300,000 Algerian dead. The major reason for the prolongation of the war was France's determination to maintain direct control of Algeria because of its strategic location. Seeking to integrate Algeria into the Third French Republic, France had made Algeria a part of France proper, whereas under similar circumstances it had given Morocco and Tunisia the status of protectorates. France granted independence to Morocco and Tunisia in March 1956, although their institutions were less developed than those of Algeria, believing that it could continue to exercise control over the other two states through Algeria.

In the thirty-two years since independence, the Algerian republic has seen a number of regimes and several forceful overthrows of governments in which the military has played a major rôle. From 1963 to 1989, Algeria was technically a socialist state. In February 1979, following the death of Houari Boumediene in December 1978, Chadli Benjedid became president. Beginning in 1980, Benjedid began to liberalize Algeria's economy, shifting from investment in heavy industry to concentration on agriculture and light industry. In addition, the regime disbanded a number of large government enterprises and state farms. The drop of world oil prices in 1986, however, together with poor domestic economic management, aggravated the already depressed economic situation. Despite some attempts at diversification, the oil industry and especially natural gas remained major sources of national income. The economy was characterized by high unemployment, particularly among younger males in the cities. (About 70 percent of Algerians are under thirty years old, and 44 percent of the total population are under age fifteen.) The resulting social unrest stemmed from the discontent of those youths who were either unemployed or in dead-end jobs and from food and housing shortages. The unrest culminated in a series of strikes in late September and early October 1988 in major industrial areas and cities, including Algiers. The strikes were repressed by the military with considerable force and a loss of life estimated in the hundreds.

To counter this unrest and the rising appeal of the Islamists (Muslim activists, sometimes seen as fundamentalists), Benjedid expanded the reforms designed to encourage private agriculture and small businesses. In 1989 he also instituted political reforms, including a new constitution that eliminated the term *socialist*, separated the FLN from the state, and granted freedom of expression, association, and meeting. However, because Boumediene's socialist policies had been exacted at such a high cost to the economy, Benjedid's reforms came too late, in the opinion of many observers. Furthermore, the control of one party, the FLN, between 1962 and 1980 had led to an authoritarianism that was difficult to overcome and that had resulted in the rise of Islamists, particularly in the form of the FIS.

In response to the newly gained right to form political organizations, parties proliferated, of which the FIS constituted the leading opposition party. The FIS demonstrated its appeal, or perhaps the extent of popular disillusionment with the FLN, by defeating the FLN in June 1990 local and provincial elections, winning in such major cities as Algiers, Constantine, and Oran. The Berber party, Front of Socialist Forces (Front des Forces Socialistes—FFS), and Ben Bella's Movement for Democracy in Algeria (Mouvement pour la Démocratie en Algérie—MDA) and several other small opposition parties did not participate.

Again in the December 1991 national elections, the FIS surprised many by its large-scale victories despite the presence in jail of the party's leadership, including Abbassi Madani and Ahmed Belhadj. To prevent the holding of second-stage, run-off elections in mid-January 1992, which the FIS presumably would have won decisively, the army staged a coup led by Minister of Defense General Khaled Nezzar. Martial law was reimposed, and Benjedid resigned. The military named Sid Ahmed Ghozali president and head of a short-lived, six-person High Security Council, which was replaced by the five-person HCÉ. Both bodies were dominated by the military. Army leaders recalled Mohamed Boudiaf from his self-imposed exile in Morocco to serve on the HCÉ and be head of state.

In response to the popular demonstrations that occurred in February 1992, the authorities banned the FIS in early March and dissolved the communal and municipal assemblies. The court banned the FIS on the ground that it violated the constitution, which prohibited political parties based on religion, race, or regional identity. After an initial period of calm, many Islamists were arrested and tried by military courts, receiving severe sentences; in 1992 about 10,000 Algerians were sent to prison camps in the Sahara. The military government's repression of the FIS brought sharp responses from other political parties; the FLN and the FFS sought an alliance with the FIS to preserve the democratic process. Furthermore, the repression caused some elements in the FIS and in the military to become more radical. Rapidly, a violent environment was created, leading to the assassination of Boudiaf in June 1992 and to terrorist attacks on civilians as well as military personnel. Ali Kafi of the HCÉ succeeded Boudiaf as head of state, but he was unsuccessful in resolving the country's political and economic problems.

The military named Redha Malek prime minister in August 1993. Recognizing the need for some compromise, Malek sought to initiate talks with the opposition, despite his firm stance against terrorism. However, because the banned FIS was not included in the proposed dialogue scheduled for mid-December 1993 when the authorization for the HCÉ was due to end, other parties boycotted the talks. The HCÉ's mandate was extended into January 1994, but because most parties had lost confidence in the government only smaller parties participated in the dialogue. By September 1994, in the fourth round of the national dialogue, five parties were taking part.

In naming General Zeroual as new president, the army took direct responsibility for governing. Despite opposition criticism of the renewed military rule, Zeroual committed himself to working with the opposition, including the FIS. This stance has caused divisions within the military over political strategy and prompted the removal of Malek as prime minister in April. In a conciliatory gesture toward the FIS, in mid-September 1994 the government released five senior leaders from prison. Included among those released were Abbassi Madani and Ali Belhadj, who were placed under house arrest and asked by the government to assist it in reaching a reconciliation with the FIS. In pursuit of some sort of accommodation with the FIS, in late September three generals were holding negotiations on behalf of the government separately with Madani and Belhadj in their homes.

Meanwhile, violence has increased, and more than 10,000 (some estimates range as high as 30,000) Algerians are reliably reported to have been killed between January 1992 and October 1994. Between February 22, 1993, and May 15, 1994, death sentences were passed on 489 persons, of which twenty-six sentences have been carried out. In addition, some sixty-eight foreigners—the number is variously reported—had been killed by October 1994. As a result of the violence, numerous West European countries and the United States in 1993 urged their nationals to leave Algeria. French citizens were particularly affected by such warnings because in late 1993 the French government estimated that approximately 76,000 French nationals, including those holding dual nationality, resided in Algeria.

The main body of the FIS was willing to consider reconciliation with the authorities under certain conditions, such as the freeing of FIS members who had been imprisoned and the legalization of the party. The most radical group, however, the Armed Islamic Group (Groupe Islamique Armé—GIA), had split from the FIS, which it considered too conciliatory, and rejected any compromise. Instead, the GIA, an urban terrorist group, began military action in November 1991. It claimed responsibility for killing the majority of the sixty-eight foreigners and also targeted oil installation personnel. Particularly embarrassing to the government was the GIA's kidnapping of the Omani and Yemeni ambassadors in July 1994. (They were subsequently released.) Another Muslim activist group, the FIS-sponsored Armed Islamic Movement (Mouvement Islamique Armé—MIA), later renamed the Islamic Salvation Army

(Armée Islamique du Salut—AIS), engaged in traditional guerrilla warfare. The AIS consisted in late 1994 of about 10,000 men and attacks military bases; it denies any involvement in attacks on civilians and foreigners.

While working on the one hand to promote dialogue, the government on the other hand instituted sharp repressive measures on Islamists. Curfews designed to counter terrorism, instituted in December 1992, were not lifted until 1994, and martial law continued to apply. The government undertook a counteroffensive against radical Islamist groups beginning in 1992, and had succeeded in killing several leaders of the GIA, including the group's head, Mourad Sid Ahmed (known as Djafar al Afghani), in February 1994 and Cherif Gousmi, Djafar al Afghani's successor, in September 1994. The government's apparent inability to stop the killing of unveiled women led to the formation of at least two anti-Islamic groups: the Organization of Free Young Algerians, which announced in March 1994 that it would resort to counterkillings of veiled women at the rate of twenty to one, and the Secret Organization for Safeguarding the Algerian Republic. Also in March, thousands of Algerians, particularly women, took to the streets to protest against the killing of unveiled women and to demonstrate their disillusionment with both the government and the FIS. Furthermore, the regime seemed unable or unwilling to prevent Islamist attacks on Berbers. In consequence, in 1993 Berbers began arming themselves in self-defense. Also indicative of the questionable effectiveness of government security measures was the successful escape of about 1,000 prisoners from the Tazoult high-security prison near Batna in March 1994.

Given the absence of basic government bodies such as elected assemblies, contemporary Algeria is being governed by the military. In late 1994, the only body that theoretically exercised some legislative functions was the National Transitional Council (Conseil National de Transition—CNT), created in May 1994. Zeroual installed the CNT, which in principle was to consist of 200 members: eighty-five from political parties; eighty-five representing unions and professional and social organizations; and thirty-five civil service members. In actuality, the twenty-two seats for the five legal political parties (the FIS was not included) were unoccupied because the parties refused to participate.

Leaders of the armed forces became the main force rejecting Islamists. Elements of the army, however, recognized that a compromise with moderate Islamists appeared to be necessary if the country were to move ahead. Furthermore, military leaders seemed aware that the FIS had made inroads within the lower ranks of the armed forces. Zeroual undertook a large-scale reorganization of the top echelons of military leadership after coming to power, introducing younger officers more willing to consider compromise with Islamists. In addition to military service staff appointments, he named new commanders to five out of the six military regions in May 1994. In June Zeroual appointed new governors to thirty-nine of the forty-eight *wilayat*, or governorates.

Public frustration has led to some growth in the number of Islamists, but accurate figures as to their strength are lacking. The overall Algerian attraction to Islamist groups appears to stem from increasing skepticism as to the likelihood of democratic government being restored.

The position of Islamists in general and the FIS in particular in contemporary Algerian society reflects the role of Islam in Algeria. Historically, the marabouts, or Muslim holy men, played a prominent role among the beduin tribes that constituted the major element of the culture of the area. A number of marabouts were also associated with mystical Sufi Islamic brotherhoods that existed primarily in rural and mountainous areas of North Africa. When the French came to dominate Algeria from 1830 onward, they endeavored to undermine Muslim culture and to substitute Western ways. Therefore, the contemporary efforts of the FIS to restore the Islamic heritage of Algerians can be seen not only as a religious and cultural phenomenon but also as part of a nationalist resurgence to revive a way of life that was discouraged by a colonial power.

Since independence in 1962, Algeria has experienced ambivalence about the role of Islam in society. The 1962 constitution made Islam the state religion because the founders saw Islam as a force for bringing cohesion to the new country. The government assumed control of mosques and religious schools and administered religious endowments. In the late 1960s and the 1970s, Boumediene's development policies, which led to the redistribution of oil revenues, were often considered to be instances of Islamic activism. However, many French-educated Algerians in the upper and upper-middle classes were secularly oriented and wished to minimize the role of Islam in Algerian society.

A number of Western observers believe that Islamist movements grew as a result of political underrepresentation and economic hardships experienced by the average Algerian. The FIS in particular saw itself as the heir of the FLN. It promised to continue the redistribution of wealth that the FLN had promoted in the 1960s and the 1970s, using oil revenues. For example, the FIS capitalized on its well-organized party structure after the 1989 earthquake by distributing food and medical supplies in affected areas and providing such services as garbage collection and school tutoring. Such social service programs, when added to the FIS's role of providing religious instruction, met with popular response and constituted a threat in the eyes of many of those in positions of government power.

Because of economic constraints, the government found it very difficult in the late 1980s and early 1990s to counter any Islamist activities relating to the economy and social services. Despite its deteriorating economy, Algeria for years had avoided rescheduling its debt payments for fear of losing its political and economic independence. Thus, in 1993 the country devoted 96 percent of its hydrocarbon export revenues to debt repayment. When the economic situation became critical in 1994, partly because of a severe drought that resulted in Algeria's being able to meet only about 10 percent of its grain needs and the consequent death by starvation of about 1,000 persons monthly, the regime was obliged to act. In addition, most industries were operating only at 50 percent of capacity because of lack of funds for raw materials and other inputs; inflation officially was estimated at 25 percent but actually was considerably higher (for example, in September 1991 it had reached 227 percent); the 1993 gross domestic product (GDP—see Glossary) growth rate was –1.7 percent; land erosion was causing the loss of about 40,000 hectares of cultivated land annually; and water distribution losses were as high as 40 percent, according to the World Bank (see Glossary).

To qualify for an International Monetary Fund (IMF—see Glossary) structural adjustment loan, the government needed to take preliminary reform measures. These steps included instituting 20 percent to 100 percent price increases in late March 1994 on nine basic commodities—among which were bread, flour, and milk—and devaluing the Algerian dinar (for value of the dinar—see Glossary) by 40 percent in early April. Following the IMF's approval in May of a US$1.1 billion standby economic stabilization loan extending to April 1995, Algeria was able to ask the Paris Club (see Glossary) of official creditors for rescheduling of other government debt (total indebtedness, including loans from private banks, was estimated at US$26 billion). In July Algeria received economic aid in the amount of US$1.1 billion from France as well as a loan from the European Union. In October 1994, Algeria had not yet completed its plans for rescheduling its commercial loan repayments with the London Club (see Glossary).

In order to gain popular support for the structural adjustment program, the IMF specifically asked that other donors make loans that would facilitate housing construction. Algeria faces a severe housing crisis because between 1962 and 1989 the country built only about 48,000 housing units annually. This figure is in contrast to the 107,000 needed to prevent further deterioration of the situation and the 234,000 units needed per year to provide each household with a unit. With regard to other services, to maintain its existing health level, the country requires an additional 24,000 hospital beds and 5,000 more paramedics. To meet the needs of the number of new students resulting from Algeria's high population growth rate (variously estimated at 2.7 percent to 2.9 percent per year), it needs 24,000 additional classrooms and 8,000 more teachers by 2005.

Because of the serious economic situation, when Islamists made such a good showing in the June 1990 elections, and again in the December 1991 elections, some Western observers considered the results primarily a vote against the FLN rather than an endorsement of Islamism. The military, whose leadership was secularly oriented, felt threatened, however, and determined to take decisive action.

The repressive measures adopted demonstrated that democracy constituted a thin veneer. Algeria's military leaders were apparently unwilling to accept the risks connected with political pluralism and liberalization. Furthermore, the country lacked a solid commitment to the electoral process. In the December 1991 elections, of the 13.2 million Algerians eligible to vote, only 7.8 million, or 59 percent, voted. Moreover, the continued influence of the military on the processes of government represents a further obstacle to true democracy.

While undergoing these domestic difficulties, the Algerian government has sought to obtain not only economic assistance from abroad but also political support. Traditionally, Algeria's closest economic relations have been with France, to which it ships most of its exports and to which thousands of Algerian workers continue to migrate, often illegally in contravention of immigration restrictions. However, given Algeria's colonial heritage, a love-hate relationship exists between it and France. Many older Algerians, particularly military officers, are proud of their French culture and training but also resent past dependence; many younger people are ardent nationalists or Islamists and tend to reject France's role and the influence of the West in general. Furthermore, France, concerned at the unrest so close to it as well as the potential for subversion of thousands of Algerians in France, seems to have been pressuring Algeria to take harsh measures against Islamists. The United States has been more conciliatory, stressing the need for the Algerian government to compromise with Islamists in order to move toward greater democracy. Democracy appears to be a more acceptable course than socialism, in view of developments in Eastern Europe in recent years and the questionable success of Boumediene's socialist policies.

On the regional level, Algeria historically has tended to view itself as the leading state of the Arab Maghrib. In recent years, however, the country's economic plight has limited its regional influence, and the role of Morocco appears to be growing. Algeria is a founding member of the Union of the Arab Maghrib (Union du Maghreb Arabe—UMA), which came into existence in 1989, designed to create a common market among Algeria, Libya, Mauritania, Morocco, and Tunisia. Benjedid saw the UMA as a factor for peace and stability in the region as well as for social and economic progress. Formed at the time of the Soviet Union's disintegration and the prospect of serious economic competition from the European Community, the UMA was intended not only to promote economic cooperation but also to promote common policies in the broader political and social fields. For example, at its November 1992 meeting, the UMA ministers of foreign affairs agreed to take common action to counter the rise of Islamism in the Maghrib. However, at their February 1993 meeting the ministers decided on a "pause" in the UMA's work. In actuality, because of economic differences among the members, none of the fifteen conventions adopted since 1989 has been implemented.

Thus, in late 1994 the Algerian government was challenged on a number of fronts. Its greatest problems lay in the domestic field: the strength of Islamism, which threatened to topple the regime, and the economy. The IMF loan, supplemented by Paris Club, London Club, and other foreign financial assistance, gave some hope of relieving economic hardships in the long run. In all likelihood, however, the austerity measures nonetheless would create in the immediate future further unemployment and cost-of-living increases that would have a serious impact on less affluent members of society. Therefore, the government needs to make progress in the social and infrastructure fields, particularly in housing and to a lesser extent in health care and education, if it is to offer a domestic program to counteract the popular appeal of Islamists. Wise use for such purposes of funds obtained from abroad, while simultaneously seeking to negotiate a compromise with moderate Islamist groups like the FIS, may represent the government's best hope of remaining in power.

October 27, 1994   Helen Chapin Metz

Chapter 1. Historical Setting

Roman arch dedicated to Emperor Caracalla (r. A.D. 212–17) at Djemila in northern Algeria

MODERN-DAY ALGERIA is a leading state of the Arab Maghrib (see Glossary), the term applied to the western part of Arab North Africa. Algeria is inhabited predominantly by Muslim Arabs, but it has a large Berber minority. The most significant forces in the country's history have been the spread of Islam, arabization, colonization, and the struggle for independence.

North Africa served as a transit region for peoples moving toward Europe or the Middle East. Thus, the region's inhabitants have been influenced by populations from other areas. Out of this mix developed the Berber people, whose language and culture, although pushed from coastal areas by conquering and colonizing Carthaginians, Romans, and Byzantines, dominated most of the land until the spread of Islam and the coming of the Arabs.

The introduction of Islam and Arabic had a profound impact on the Maghrib beginning in the seventh century. The new religion and language introduced changes in social and economic relations, established links with a rich culture, and provided a powerful idiom of political discourse and organization. From the great Berber dynasties of the Almoravids and Almohads to the militants seeking an Islamic state in the early 1990s, the call to return to true Islamic values and practices has had social resonance and political power. For 300 years, beginning in the early sixteenth century, Algeria was a province of the Ottoman Empire under a regency that had Algiers as its capital. During this period, the modern Algerian state began to emerge as a distinct territory between Tunisia and Morocco.

The French occupation of Algeria, beginning in 1830, had great influence. In addition to enduring the affront of being ruled by a foreign, non-Muslim power, many Algerians lost their lands to the new government or to colonists. Traditional leaders were eliminated, coopted, or made irrelevant; social structures were stressed to the breaking point. Viewed by the Europeans with condescension at best and contempt at worst—never as equals—the Algerians endured 132 years of colonial subjugation. Nonetheless, this period saw the formation of new social classes, which, after exposure to ideas of equality and political liberty, would help propel the country to independence. During the years of French domination, the struggles to

Neolithic cave paintings found in Tassili-n-Ajjer (Plateau of the Chasms) region of the Sahara
Courtesy LaVerle Berry

survive, to co-exist, to gain equality, and to achieve independence shaped a large part of the Algerian national identity.

The War of Independence (1954–62), brutal and long, was the most recent major turning point in the country's history. Although often fratricidal, it ultimately united Algerians and seared the value of independence and the philosophy of anticolonialism into the national consciousness. Since independence in 1962, Algeria has sought to create political structures that reflect the unique character of the country and that can cope with the daunting challenges of rebuilding a society and an economy that had been subject to years of trauma and painful transformation.

Prehistory of Central North Africa

The cave paintings found at Tassili-n-Ajjer, north of Tamanrasset, and at other locations depict vibrant and vivid scenes of everyday life in the central Maghrib between about 8000 B.C. and 4000 B.C. They were executed by a hunting people in the Capsian period of the Neolithic age who lived in a savanna region teeming with giant buffalo, elephant, rhinoceros, and hippopotamus, animals that no longer exist in the now-desert area. The pictures provide the most complete record of a prehistoric African culture.

Earlier inhabitants of the central Maghrib have left behind equally significant remains. Early remnants of hominid occupation in North Africa, for example, were found in Ain el Hanech, near Saïda (ca. 200,000 B.C.). Later, Neanderthal tool makers produced hand axes in the Levalloisian and Mousterian styles (ca. 43,000 B.C.) similar to those in the Levant. According to some sources, North Africa was the site of the highest state of development of Middle Paleolithic flake-tool techniques. Tools of this era, starting about 30,000 B.C., are called Aterian (after the site Bir el Ater, south of Annaba) and are marked by a high standard of workmanship, great variety, and specialization.

The earliest blade industries in North Africa are called Ibero-Maurusian or Oranian (after a site near Oran). The industry appears to have spread throughout the coastal regions of the Maghrib between 15,000 and 10,000 B.C. Between about 9000 and 5000 B.C., the Capsian culture began influencing the Ibero-Maurusian, and after about 3000 B.C. the remains of just one human type can be found throughout the region. Neolithic civilization (marked by animal domestication and subsistence agriculture) developed in the Saharan and Mediterranean Maghrib between 6000 and 2000 B.C. This type of economy, so richly depicted in the Tassili-n-Ajjer cave paintings, predominated in the Maghrib until the classical period.

The amalgam of peoples of North Africa coalesced eventually into a distinct native population that came to be called Berbers. Distinguished primarily by cultural and linguistic attributes, the Berbers lacked a written language and hence tended to be overlooked or marginalized in historical accounts. Roman, Greek, Byzantine, and Arab Muslim chroniclers typically depicted the Berbers as "barbaric" enemies, troublesome nomads, or ignorant peasants. They were, however, to play a major role in the area's history.

Algeria: A Country Study

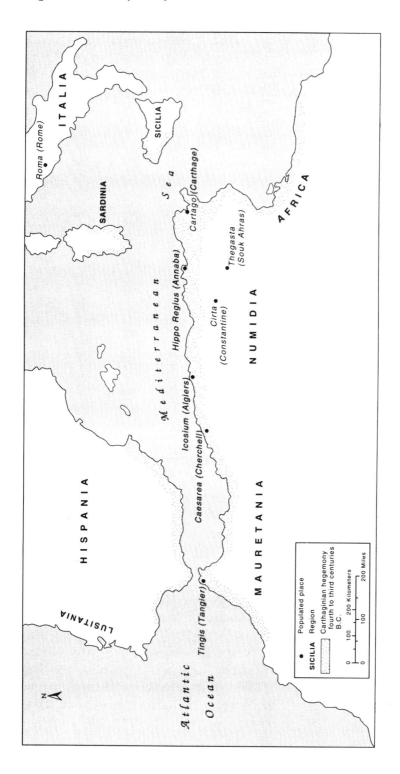

Figure 2. *Roman North Africa, Fourth Century B.C. to Third Century A.D.*

North Africa During the Classical Period

Carthage and the Berbers

Phoenician traders arrived on the North African coast around 900 B.C. and established Carthage (in present-day Tunisia) around 800 B.C. By the sixth century B.C., a Phoenician presence existed at Tipasa (east of Cherchell in Algeria). From their principal center of power at Carthage, the Carthaginians expanded and established small settlements (called *emporia* in Greek) along the North African coast; these settlements eventually served as market towns as well as anchorages. Hippo Regius (modern Annaba) and Rusicade (modern Skikda) are among the towns of Carthaginian origin on the coast of present-day Algeria.

As Carthaginian power grew, its impact on the indigenous population increased dramatically. Berber civilization was already at a stage in which agriculture, manufacturing, trade, and political organization supported several states. Trade links between Carthage and the Berbers in the interior grew, but territorial expansion also resulted in the enslavement or military recruitment of some Berbers and in the extraction of tribute from others. By the early fourth century B.C., Berbers formed the single largest element of the Carthaginian army. In the Revolt of the Mercenaries, Berber soldiers rebelled from 241 to 238 B.C. after being unpaid following the defeat of Carthage in the First Punic War. They succeeded in obtaining control of much of Carthage's North African territory, and they minted coins bearing the name *Libyan*, used in Greek to describe natives of North Africa. The Carthaginian state declined because of successive defeats by the Romans in the Punic Wars; in 146 B.C. the city of Carthage was destroyed.

As Carthaginian power waned, the influence of Berber leaders in the hinterland grew. By the second century B.C., several large but loosely administered Berber kingdoms had emerged. Two of them were established in Numidia, behind the coastal areas controlled by Carthage (see fig. 2). West of Numidia lay Mauretania, which extended across the Moulouya River in Morocco to the Atlantic Ocean. The high point of Berber civilization, unequaled until the coming of the Almohads and Almoravids more than a millennium later, was reached during the reign of Masinissa in the second century B.C. After Masinissa's death in 148 B.C., the Berber kingdoms were divided and reunited several times. Masinissa's line survived until A.D.

24, when the remaining Berber territory was annexed to the Roman Empire.

The Roman Era

Increases in urbanization and in the area under cultivation during Roman rule caused wholesale dislocations of Berber society. Nomadic tribes were forced to settle or move from traditional rangelands. Sedentary tribes lost their autonomy and connection with the land. Berber opposition to the Roman presence was nearly constant. The Roman emperor Trajan (r. A.D. 98-117) established a frontier in the south by encircling the Aurès and Nemencha mountains and building a line of forts from Vescera (modern Biskra) to Ad Majores (Hennchir Besseriani, southeast of Biskra). The defensive line extended at least as far as Castellum Dimmidi (modern Messaad, southwest of Biskra), Roman Algeria's southernmost fort. Romans settled and developed the area around Sitifis (modern Sétif) in the second century, but farther west the influence of Rome did not extend beyond the coast and principal military roads until much later.

The Roman military presence in North Africa was relatively small, consisting of about 28,000 troops and auxiliaries in Numidia and the two Mauretanian provinces. Starting in the second century A.D., these garrisons were manned mostly by local inhabitants.

Aside from Carthage, urbanization in North Africa came in part with the establishment of settlements of veterans under the Roman emperors Claudius (r. A.D. 41-54), Nerva (r. A.D. 96-98), and Trajan. In Algeria such settlements included Tipasa, Cuicul (modern Djemila, northeast of Sétif), Thamugadi (modern Timgad, southeast of Sétif), and Sitifis. The prosperity of most towns depended on agriculture. Called the "granary of the empire," North Africa, according to one estimate, produced 1 million tons of cereals each year, one-quarter of which was exported. Other crops included fruit, figs, grapes, and beans. By the second century A.D., olive oil rivaled cereals as an export item.

The beginnings of the decline of the Roman Empire were less serious in North Africa than elsewhere. There were uprisings, however. In A.D. 238, landowners rebelled unsuccessfully against the emperor's fiscal policies. Sporadic tribal revolts in the Mauretanian mountains followed from 253 to 288. The

Roman ruins at Djemila, west of Constantine
Courtesy Bechtel Corporation
Arch to Emperor Trajan (r. A.D. 98–117) at Timgad,
southwest of Annaba
Courtesy ANEP

towns also suffered economic difficulties, and building activity almost ceased.

The towns of Roman North Africa had a substantial Jewish population. Some Jews were deported from Palestine in the first and second centuries A.D. for rebelling against Roman rule; others had come earlier with Punic settlers. In addition, a number of Berber tribes had converted to Judaism.

Christianity arrived in the second century and soon gained converts in the towns and among slaves. More than eighty bishops, some from distant frontier regions of Numidia, attended the Council of Carthage in 256. By the end of the fourth century, the settled areas had become Christianized, and some Berber tribes had converted en masse.

A division in the church that came to be known as the Donatist controversy began in 313 among Christians in North Africa. The Donatists stressed the holiness of the church and refused to accept the authority to administer the sacraments of those who had surrendered the scriptures when they were forbidden under the Emperor Diocletian (r. 284-305). The Donatists also opposed the involvement of Emperor Constantine (r. 306-37) in church affairs in contrast to the majority of Christians who welcomed official imperial recognition.

The occasionally violent controversy has been characterized as a struggle between opponents and supporters of the Roman system. The most articulate North African critic of the Donatist position, which came to be called a heresy, was Augustine, bishop of Hippo Regius. Augustine (354-430) maintained that the unworthiness of a minister did not affect the validity of the sacraments because their true minister was Christ. In his sermons and books, Augustine, who is considered a leading exponent of Christian truths, evolved a theory of the right of orthodox Christian rulers to use force against schismatics and heretics. Although the dispute was resolved by a decision of an imperial commission in Carthage in 411, Donatist communities continued to exist through the sixth century.

Vandals and Byzantines

Led by their king, Gaiseric, some 80,000 Vandals, a Germanic tribe, crossed into Africa from Spain in 429. In the following year, the invaders advanced without much opposition to Hippo Regius, which they took after a siege in which Augustine died. After further advances, the Vandals in 435 made an agreement with Rome to limit their control to Numidia and Mauretania. But in 439 Gaiseric conquered and pillaged Carthage and the rest of the province of Africa.

The resulting decline in trade weakened Roman control. Independent kingdoms emerged in mountainous and desert areas, towns were overrun, and Berbers, who had previously been pushed to the edges of the Roman Empire, returned.

Belisarius, general of the Byzantine emperor Justinian based in Constantinople, landed in North Africa in 533 with 16,000 men and within a year destroyed the Vandal kingdom. Local opposition delayed full Byzantine control of the region for twelve years, however, and imperial control, when it came, was but a shadow of the control exercised by Rome. Although an impressive series of fortifications were built, Byzantine rule was compromised by official corruption, incompetence, military weakness, and lack of concern in Constantinople for African affairs. As a result, many rural areas reverted to Berber rule.

Islam and the Arabs, 642-1830

Unlike the invasions of previous religions and cultures, the coming of Islam, which was spread by Arabs, was to have pervasive and long-lasting effects on the Maghrib. The new faith, in its various forms, would penetrate nearly all segments of society, bringing with it armies, learned men, and fervent mystics, and in large part replacing tribal practices and loyalties with new social norms and political idioms.

Nonetheless, the Islamization and arabization of the region were complicated and lengthy processes. Whereas nomadic Berbers were quick to convert and assist the Arab invaders, not until the twelfth century under the Almohad Dynasty did the Christian and Jewish communities become totally marginalized.

The first Arab military expeditions into the Maghrib, between 642 and 669, resulted in the spread of Islam. These early forays from a base in Egypt occurred under local initiative rather than under orders from the central caliphate. When the seat of the caliphate moved from Medina to Damascus, however, the Umayyads (a Muslim dynasty ruling from 661 to 750) recognized that the strategic necessity of dominating the Mediterranean dictated a concerted military effort on the North African front. In 670, therefore, an Arab army under Uqba ibn Nafi established the town of Al Qayrawan about 160 kilometers south of present-day Tunis and used it as a base for further operations.

Abu al Muhajir Dina, Uqba's successor, pushed westward into Algeria and eventually worked out a modus vivendi with Kusayla, the ruler of an extensive confederation of Christian Berbers. Kusayla, who had been based in Tilimsan (modern Tlemcen), became a Muslim and moved his headquarters to Takirwan, near Al Qayrawan.

This harmony was short-lived, however. Arab and Berber forces controlled the region in turn until 697. By 711 Umayyad forces helped by Berber converts to Islam had conquered all of North Africa. Governors appointed by the Umayyad caliphs ruled from Al Qayrawan, the new *wilaya* (province) of Ifriqiya, which covered Tripolitania (the western part of present-day Libya), Tunisia, and eastern Algeria.

Paradoxically, the spread of Islam among the Berbers did not guarantee their support for the Arab-dominated caliphate. The ruling Arabs alienated the Berbers by taxing them heavily; treating converts as second-class Muslims; and, at worst, by enslaving them. As a result, widespread opposition took the form of open revolt in 739–40 under the banner of Kharijite Islam. The Kharijites objected to Ali, the fourth caliph, making peace with the Umayyads in 657 and left Ali's camp (*khariji* means "those who leave"). The Kharijites had been fighting Umayyad rule in the East, and many Berbers were attracted by the sect's egalitarian precepts. For example, according to Kharijism, any suitable Muslim candidate could be elected caliph without regard to race, station, or descent from the Prophet Muhammad.

After the revolt, Kharijites established a number of theocratic tribal kingdoms, most of which had short and troubled histories. Others, however, like Sijilmasa and Tilimsan, which straddled the principal trade routes, proved more viable and prospered. In 750 the Abbasids, who succeeded the Umayyads as Muslim rulers, moved the caliphate to Baghdad and reestablished caliphal authority in Ifriqiya, appointing Ibrahim ibn Al Aghlab as governor in Al Qayrawan. Although nominally serving at the caliph's pleasure, Al Aghlab and his successors ruled independently until 909, presiding over a court that became a center for learning and culture.

Just to the west of Aghlabid lands, Abd ar Rahman ibn Rustum ruled most of the central Maghrib from Tahirt, southwest of Algiers. The rulers of the Rustumid imamate, which lasted from 761 to 909, each an Ibadi (see Glossary) Kharijite imam (see Glossary), were elected by leading citizens. The imams gained a reputation for honesty, piety, and justice. The court at Tahirt was noted for its support of scholarship in mathematics, astronomy, and astrology, as well as theology and law. The Rustumid imams, however, failed, by choice or by neglect, to organize a reliable standing army. This important factor, accompanied by the dynasty's eventual collapse into decadence, opened the way for Tahirt's demise under the assault of the Fatimids.

Fatimids

In the closing decades of the ninth century, missionaries of the Ismaili sect of Shia (see Glossary) Islam converted the Kutama Berbers of what was later known as the Petite Kabylie region and led them in battle against the Sunni (see Glossary) rulers of Ifriqiya. Al Qayrawan fell to them in 909. The Ismaili imam, Ubaydallah, declared himself caliph and established Mahdia as his capital. Ubaydallah initiated the Fatimid Dynasty, named after Fatima, daughter of Muhammad and wife of Ali, from whom the caliph claimed descent.

The Fatimids turned westward in 911, destroying the imamate of Tahirt and conquering Sijilmasa in Morocco. Ibadi Kharijite refugees from Tahirt fled south to the oasis at Ouargla beyond the Atlas Mountains, whence in the eleventh century they moved southwest to Oued Mzab. Maintaining their cohesion and beliefs over the centuries, Ibadi religious leaders have dominated public life in the region to this day.

For many years, the Fatimids posed a threat to Morocco, but their deepest ambition was to rule the East, the Mashriq, which included Egypt and Muslim lands beyond. By 969 they had conquered Egypt. In 972 the Fatimid ruler Al Muizz established the new city of Cairo as his capital. The Fatimids left the rule of Ifriqiya and most of Algeria to the Zirids (972–1148). This Berber dynasty, which had founded the towns of Miliana, Médéa, and Algiers and centered significant local power in Algeria for the first time, turned over its domain west of Ifriqiya to the Banu Hammad branch of its family. The Hammadids ruled from 1011 to 1151, during which time Bejaïa became the most important port in the Maghrib.

This period was marked by constant conflict, political instability, and economic decline. The Hammadids, by rejecting the Ismaili doctrine for Sunni orthodoxy and renouncing submission to the Fatimids, initiated chronic conflict with the Zirids. Two great Berber confederations—the Sanhaja and the

Zenata—engaged in an epic struggle. The fiercely brave, camel-borne nomads of the western desert and steppe as well as the sedentary farmers of the Kabylie region to the east swore allegiance to the Sanhaja. Their traditional enemies, the Zenata, were tough, resourceful horsemen from the cold plateau of the northern interior of Morocco and the western Tell in Algeria.

In addition, raiders from Genoa, Pisa, and Norman Sicily attacked ports and disrupted coastal trade. Trans-Saharan trade shifted to Fatimid Egypt and to routes in the west leading to Spanish markets. The countryside was being overtaxed by growing cities.

Contributing to these political and economic dislocations was a large incursion of Arab beduin from Egypt starting in the first half of the eleventh century. Part of this movement was an invasion by the Banu Hilal and Banu Sulaym tribes, apparently sent by the Fatimids to weaken the Zirids. These Arab beduin overcame the Zirids and Hammadids and in 1057 sacked Al Qayrawan. They sent farmers fleeing from the fertile plains to the mountains and left cities and towns in ruin. For the first time, the extensive use of Arabic spread to the countryside. Sedentary Berbers who sought protection from the Hilalians were gradually arabized.

Almoravids

The Almoravid movement developed early in the eleventh century among the Sanhaja of the western Sahara, whose control of trans-Saharan trade routes was under pressure from the Zenata Berbers in the north and the state of Ghana in the south. Yahya ibn Ibrahim al Jaddali, a leader of the Lamtuna tribe of the Sanhaja confederation, decided to raise the level of Islamic knowledge and practice among his people. To accomplish this, on his return from the hajj (Muslim pilgrimage to Mecca) in 1048-49, he brought with him Abd Allah ibn Yasin al Juzuli, a Moroccan scholar. In the early years of the movement, the scholar was concerned only with imposing moral discipline and a strict adherence to Islamic principles among his followers. Abd Allah ibn Yasin also became known as one of the marabouts, or holy persons (from *al murabitun*, "those who have made a religious retreat." *Almoravids* is the Spanish transliteration of *al murabitun*—see Marabouts, this ch.).

The Almoravid movement shifted from promoting religious reform to engaging in military conquest after 1054 and was led by Lamtuna leaders: first Yahya, then his brother Abu Bakr, and then his cousin Yusuf ibn Tashfin. With Marrakech as their capital, the Almoravids had conquered Morocco, the Maghrib as far east as Algiers, and Spain up to the Ebro River by 1106. Under the Almoravids, the Maghrib and Spain acknowledged the spiritual authority of the Abbasid caliphate in Baghdad, reuniting them temporarily with the Islamic community in the Mashriq.

Although it was not an entirely peaceful time, North Africa benefited economically and culturally during the Almoravid period, which lasted until 1147. Muslim Spain (Andalus in Arabic) was a great source of artistic and intellectual inspiration. The most famous writers of Andalus worked in the Almoravid court, and the builders of the Grand Mosque of Tilimsan, completed in 1136, used as a model the Grand Mosque of Córdoba.

Almohads

Like the Almoravids, the Almohads found their initial inspiration in Islamic reform. Their spiritual leader, the Moroccan Muhammad ibn Abdallah ibn Tumart, sought to reform Almoravid decadence. Rejected in Marrakech and other cities, he turned to his Masmuda tribe in the Atlas Mountains for support. Because of their emphasis on the unity of God, his followers were known as Al Muwahhidun (unitarians, or Almohads).

Although declaring himself mahdi, imam, and *masum* (infallible leader sent by God), Muhammad ibn Abdallah ibn Tumart consulted with a council of ten of his oldest disciples. Influenced by the Berber tradition of representative government, he later added an assembly composed of fifty leaders from various tribes. The Almohad rebellion began in 1125 with attacks on Moroccan cities, including Sus and Marrakech.

Upon Muhammad ibn Abdallah ibn Tumart's death in 1130, his successor Abd al Mumin took the title of caliph and placed members of his own family in power, converting the system into a traditional monarchy. The Almohads entered Spain at the invitation of the Andalusian amirs, who had risen against the Almoravids there. Abd al Mumin forced the submission of the amirs and reestablished the caliphate of Córdoba, giving the Almohad sultan supreme religious as well as political authority within his domains. The Almohads took control of Morocco in 1146, captured Algiers around 1151, and by 1160 had completed the conquest of the central Maghrib and advanced to Tripolitania. Nonetheless, pockets of Almoravid

Algeria: A Country Study

resistance continued to hold out in the Kabylie region for at least fifty years.

After Abd al Mumin's death in 1163, his son Abu Yaqub Yusuf (r. 1163-84) and grandson Yaqub al Mansur (r. 1184-99) presided over the zenith of Almohad power. For the first time, the Maghrib was united under a local regime, and although the empire was troubled by conflict on its fringes, handcrafts and agriculture flourished at its center and an efficient bureaucracy filled the tax coffers. In 1229 the Almohad court renounced the teachings of Muhammad ibn Tumart, opting instead for greater tolerance and a return to the Maliki (see Glossary) school of law. As evidence of this change, the Almohads hosted two of the greatest thinkers of Andalus: Abu Bakr ibn Tufayl and Ibn Rushd (Averroes).

The Almohads shared the crusading instincts of their Christian adversaries, but the continuing wars in Spain over-taxed their resources. In the Maghrib, the Almohad position was compromised by factional strife and was challenged by a renewal of tribal warfare. The Bani Merin (Zenata Berbers) took advantage of declining Almohad power to establish a tribal state in Morocco, initiating nearly sixty years of warfare there that concluded with their capture of Marrakech, the last Almohad stronghold, in 1271. Despite repeated efforts to subjugate the central Maghrib, however, the Merinids were never able to restore the frontiers of the Almohad Empire.

Zayanids

From its capital at Tunis, the Hafsid Dynasty made good its claim to be the legitimate successor of the Almohads in Ifriqiya, while, in the central Maghrib, the Zayanids founded a dynasty at Tlemcen. Based on a Zenata tribe, the Bani Abd el Wad, which had been settled in the region by Abd al Mumin, the Zayanids also emphasized their links with the Almohads.

For more than 300 years, until the region came under Ottoman suzerainty in the sixteenth century, the Zayanids kept a tenuous hold in the central Maghrib. The regime, which depended on the administrative skills of Andalusians, was plagued by frequent rebellions but learned to survive as the vassal of the Merinids or Hafsids or later as an ally of Spain.

Many coastal cities defied the ruling dynasties and asserted their autonomy as municipal republics. They were governed by their merchant oligarchies, by tribal chieftains from the surrounding countryside, or by the privateers who operated out of their ports.

Nonetheless, Tlemcen prospered as a commercial center and was called the "pearl of the Maghrib." Situated at the head of the Imperial Road through the strategic Taza Gap to Marrakech, the city controlled the caravan route to Sijilmasa, gateway for the gold and slave trade with the western Sudan. Aragon came to control commerce between Tlemcen's port, Oran, and Europe beginning about 1250. An outbreak of privateering out of Aragon, however, severely disrupted this trade after about 1420.

Marabouts

The successor dynasties in the Maghrib—Merinids, Zayanids, and Hasfids—did not base their power on a program of religious reform as their predecessors had done. Of necessity they compromised with rural cults that had survived the triumph of puritanical orthodoxy in the twelfth century despite the efforts of the Almoravids and Almohads to stamp them out.

The aridity of official Islam had little appeal outside the mosques and schools of the cities. In the countryside, wandering marabouts, or holy people, drew a large and devoted following. These men and women were believed to possess divine grace (*baraka*) or to be able to channel it to others. In life, the marabouts offered spiritual guidance, arbitrated disputes, and often wielded political power. After death, their cults—some local, others widespread—erected domed tombs that became sites of pilgrimage.

Many tribes claimed descent from marabouts. In addition, small, autonomous republics led by holy men became a common form of government in the Maghrib. In Algeria, the influence of the marabouts continued through much of the Ottoman period, when the authorities would grant political and financial favors to these leaders to prevent tribal uprisings.

European Offensive

The final triumph of the 700-year Christian reconquest of Spain, marked by the fall of Granada in 1492, was accompanied by the forced conversion of Spanish Muslims (Moriscos). As a result of the Inquisition, thousands of Jews fled or were deported to the Maghrib, where many gained influence in government and commerce.

Without much difficulty, Christian Spain imposed its influence on the Maghrib coast by constructing fortified outposts (presidios) and collecting tribute during the fifteenth and early sixteenth centuries. On or near the Algerian coast, Spain took control of Mers el Kebir in 1505, Oran in 1509, and Tlemcen, Mostaganem, and Ténès, all west of Algiers, in 1510. In the same year, the merchants of Algiers handed over one of the rocky islets in their harbor, where the Spaniards built a fort. The presidios in North Africa turned out to be a costly and largely ineffective military endeavor that did not guarantee access for Spain's merchant fleet. Indeed, most trade seemed to be transacted in the numerous free ports. Moreover, from the sixteenth to the eighteenth century, sailing superior ships and hammering out shrewd concessions, merchants from England, Portugal, Holland, France, and Italy, as well as Spain, dominated Mediterranean trade.

Why Spain did not extend its North African conquests much beyond a few modest enclaves has puzzled historians. Some suggest that Spain held back because it was preoccupied with maintaining its territory in Italy; others that Spain's energies were absorbed in obtaining the riches of the New World. Still another possibility is that Spain was more intent on projecting its force on the high seas than on risking defeat in the forbidding interior of Africa.

Privateers

Privateering was an age-old practice in the Mediterranean. North African rulers engaged in it increasingly in the late sixteenth and early seventeenth century because it was so lucrative, and because their merchant vessels, formerly a major source of income, were not permitted to enter European ports. Although the methods varied, privateering generally involved private vessels raiding the ships of an enemy in peacetime under the authority of a ruler. Its purposes were to disrupt an opponent's trade and to reap rewards from the captives and cargo.

Privateering was a highly disciplined affair conducted under the command of the *rais* (captain) of the fleets. Several captains became heros in Algerian lore for their bravery and skill. The captains of the corsairs banded together in a self-regulating *taifa* (community) to protect and further the corporate interests of their trade. The *taifa* came to be ethnically mixed, incorporating those captured Europeans who agreed to convert to Islam and supply information useful for future raids. The *taifa* also gained prestige and political influence because of its role in fighting the infidel and providing the merchants and rulers of Algiers with a major source of income. Algiers became the privateering city-state par excellence, especially between 1560 and 1620. And it was two privateer brothers who were instrumental in extending Ottoman influence in Algeria.

Ottoman Rule

At about the time Spain was establishing its presidios in the Maghrib, the Muslim privateer brothers Aruj and Khair ad Din—the latter known to Europeans as Barbarossa, or Red Beard—were operating successfully off Tunisia under the Hafsids. In 1516 Aruj moved his base of operations to Algiers, but was killed in 1518 during his invasion of Tlemcen. Khair ad Din succeeded him as military commander of Algiers. The Ottoman sultan gave him the title of *beylerbey* (provincial governor) and a contingent of some 2,000 janissaries, well-armed Ottoman soldiers. With the aid of this force, Khair ad Din subdued the coastal region between Constantine and Oran (although the city of Oran remained in Spanish hands until 1791). Under Khair ad Din's regency, Algiers became the center of Ottoman authority in the Maghrib, from which Tunis, Tripoli, and Tlemcen would be overcome and Morocco's independence would be threatened.

So successful was Khair ad Din at Algiers that he was recalled to Constantinople in 1533 by the sultan, Süleyman I (r. 1520–66), known in Europe as Süleyman the Magnificent, and appointed admiral of the Ottoman fleet. The next year, he mounted a successful seaborne assault on Tunis.

The next *beylerbey* was Khair ad Din's son Hassan, who assumed the position in 1544. Until 1587 the area was governed by officers who served terms with no fixed limits. Subsequently, with the institution of a regular Ottoman administration, governors with the title of *pasha* ruled for three-year terms. Turkish was the official language, and Arabs and Berbers were excluded from government posts.

The pasha was assisted by janissaries, known in Algeria as the *ojaq* and led by an *agha*. Recruited from Anatolian peasants, they were committed to a lifetime of service. Although isolated from the rest of society and subject to their own laws and courts, they depended on the ruler and the *taifa* for income. In the seventeenth century, the force numbered about 15,000, but it was to shrink to only 3,700 by 1830. Discontent among the *ojaq* rose in the mid-1600s because they were not paid regularly, and they repeatedly revolted against the pasha. As a result, the *agha* charged the pasha with corruption and incompetence and seized power in 1659.

The *taifa* had the last word, however, when in 1671 it rebelled, killed the *agha*, and placed one of its own in power. The new leader received the title of *dey*, which originated in Tunisia. After 1689 the right to select the dey passed to the divan, a council of some sixty notables. The divan at first was dominated by the *ojaq*, but by the eighteenth century it became the dey's instrument. In 1710 the dey persuaded the sultan to recognize him and his successors as regent, replacing the pasha in that role. Although Algiers remained a part of the Ottoman Empire, the Sublime Porte, or Ottoman government, ceased to have effective influence there.

The dey was in effect a constitutional autocrat, but his authority was restricted by the divan and the *taifa*, as well as by local political conditions. The dey was elected for a life term, but in the 159 years (1671-1830) that the system survived, fourteen of the twenty-nine deys were removed from office by assassination. Despite usurpation, military coups, and occasional mob rule, the day-to-day operation of government was remarkably orderly. In accordance with the millet system applied throughout the Ottoman Empire, each ethnic group—Turks, Arabs, Kabyles, Berbers, Jews, Europeans—was represented by a guild that exercised legal jurisdiction over its constituents.

The dey had direct administrative control only in the regent's enclave, the Dar as Sultan (Domain of the Sultan), which included the city of Algiers and its environs and the fertile Mitidja Plain. The rest of the territory under the regency was divided into three provinces (*beyliks*): Constantine in the east; Titteri in the central region, with its capital at Médéa; and a western province that after 1791 had its seat at Oran, abandoned that year by Spain when the city was destroyed in an earthquake. Each province was governed by a bey appointed by the dey, usually from the same circle of families.

A contingent of the *ojaq* was assigned to each bey, who also had at his disposal the provincial auxiliaries provided by the privileged *makhzen* tribes, traditionally exempted from paying taxes on condition that they collect them from other tribes. Tax revenues were conveyed from the provinces to Algiers twice yearly, but the beys were otherwise left to their own

Painting of Khair ad Din, founder of modern Algeria
Courtesy ANEP

devices. Although the regency patronized the tribal chieftains, it never had the unanimous allegiance of the countryside, where heavy taxation frequently provoked unrest. Autonomous tribal states were tolerated, and the regency's authority was seldom applied in the Kabylie region.

Relations with the United States

European maritime powers paid the tribute demanded by the rulers of the privateering states of North Africa (Algiers, Tunis, Tripoli, and Morocco) to prevent attacks on their shipping by corsairs. No longer covered by British tribute payments after the American Revolution, United States merchant ships were seized and sailors enslaved in the years that followed independence. In 1794 the United States Congress appropriated funds for the construction of warships to counter the privateering threat in the Mediterranean. Despite the naval preparations, the United States concluded a treaty with the dey of Algiers in 1797, guaranteeing payment of tribute amounting to US$10 million over a twelve-year period in return for a promise that Algerian corsairs would not molest United States shipping. Payments in ransom and tribute to the privateering states amounted to 20 percent of United States government annual revenues in 1800.

The Napoleonic wars of the early nineteenth century diverted the attention of the maritime powers from suppressing what they derogatorily called piracy. But when peace was restored to Europe in 1815, Algiers found itself at war with Spain, the Netherlands, Prussia, Denmark, Russia, and Naples. In March of that year, the United States Congress authorized naval action against the Barbary States, the then-independent Muslim states of Morocco, Algiers, Tunis, and Tripoli. Commodore Stephen Decatur was dispatched with a squadron of ten warships to ensure the safety of United States shipping in the Mediterranean and to force an end to the payment of tribute. After capturing several corsairs and their crews, Decatur sailed into the harbor of Algiers, threatened the city with his guns, and concluded a favorable treaty in which the dey agreed to discontinue demands for tribute, pay reparations for damage to United States property, release United States prisoners without ransom, and prohibit further interference with United States trade by Algerian corsairs. No sooner had Decatur set off for Tunis to enforce a similar agreement than the dey repudiated the treaty. The next year, an Anglo-Dutch fleet, commanded by British admiral Viscount Exmouth, delivered a punishing, nine-hour bombardment of Algiers. The attack immobilized many of the dey's corsairs and obtained from him a second treaty that reaffirmed the conditions imposed by Decatur. In addition, the dey agreed to end the practice of enslaving Christians.

France in Algeria, 1830-1962

Most of France's actions in Algeria, not least the invasion of Algiers, were propelled by contradictory impulses. In the period between Napoleon's downfall in 1815 and the revolution of 1830, the restored French monarchy was in crisis, and the dey was weak politically, economically, and militarily. The French monarch sought to reverse his domestic unpopularity. As a result of what the French considered an insult to the French consul in Algiers by the dey in 1827, France blockaded Algiers for three years. France used the failure of the blockade as a reason for a military expedition against Algiers in 1830.

Invasion of Algiers

Using Napoleon's 1808 contingency plan for the invasion of Algeria, 34,000 French soldiers landed twenty-seven kilometers west of Algiers, at Sidi Ferruch, on June 12, 1830. To face the

French, the dey sent 7,000 janissaries, 19,000 troops from the beys of Constantine and Oran, and about 17,000 Kabyles. The French established a strong beachhead and pushed toward Algiers, thanks in part to superior artillery and better organization. Algiers was captured after a three-week campaign, and Hussein Dey fled into exile. French troops raped, looted (taking 50 million francs from the treasury in the Casbah), desecrated mosques, and destroyed cemeteries. It was an inauspicious beginning to France's self-described "civilizing mission," whose character on the whole was cynical, arrogant, and cruel.

Hardly had the news of the capture of Algiers reached Paris than Charles X was deposed, and his cousin Louis Philippe, the "citizen king," was named to preside over a constitutional monarchy. The new government, composed of liberal opponents of the Algiers expedition, was reluctant to pursue the conquest ordered by the old regime, but withdrawing from Algeria proved more difficult than conquering it. A parliamentary commission that examined the Algerian situation concluded that although French policy, behavior, and organization were failures, the occupation should continue for the sake of national prestige. In 1834 France annexed the occupied areas, which had an estimated Muslim population of about 3 million, as a colony. Colonial administration in the occupied areas—the so-called *régime du sabre* (government of the sword)—was placed under a governor general, a high-ranking army officer invested with civil and military jurisdiction, who was responsible to the minister of war.

The Land and Colonizers

Even before the decision was made to annex Algeria, major changes had taken place. In a bargain-hunting frenzy to take over or buy at low prices all manner of property—homes, shops, farms, and factories—Europeans poured into Algiers after it fell. French authorities took possession of the *beylik* lands, from which Ottoman officials had derived income. Over time, as pressures increased to obtain more land for settlement by Europeans, the state seized more categories of land, particularly that used by tribes, religious foundations, and villages.

Soon after the conquest of Algiers, the soldier-politician Bertrand Clauzel and others formed a company to acquire agricultural land and, despite official discouragement, to subsidize its settlement by European farmers, triggering a land rush.

Clauzel recognized the farming potential of the Mitidja Plain and envisioned the production there of cotton on a large scale. As governor general (1835–36), he used his office to make private investments in land and encouraged army officers and bureaucrats in his administration to do the same. This development created a vested interest among government officials in greater French involvement in Algeria. Commercial interests with influence in the government also began to recognize the prospects for profitable land speculation in expanding the French zone of occupation. They created large agricultural tracts, built factories and businesses, and exploited cheap local labor.

Called *colons* (colonists) or, more popularly, *pieds noirs* (literally, black feet), the European settlers were largely of peasant farmer or working-class origin from the poor southern areas of Italy, Spain, and France. Others were criminal and political deportees from France, transported under sentence in large numbers to Algeria. In the 1840s and 1850s, to encourage settlement in rural areas official policy was to offer grants of land for a fee and a promise that improvements would be made. A distinction soon developed between the *grands colons* (great colonists) at one end of the scale, often self-made men who had accumulated large estates or built successful businesses, and the *petits blancs* (little whites), smallholders and workers at the other end, whose lot was often not much better than that of their Muslim counterparts. According to historian John Ruedy, although by 1848 only 15,000 of the 109,000 European settlers were in rural areas, "by systematically expropriating both pastoralists and farmers, rural colonization was the most important single factor in the destructuring of traditional society."

Opposition to the Occupation

Whatever initial misgivings Louis Philippe's government may have had about occupying Algeria, the geopolitical realities of the situation created by the 1830 intervention argued strongly for reinforcing the French presence there. France had reason for concern that Britain, which was pledged to maintain the territorial integrity of the Ottoman Empire, would move to fill the vacuum left by a French pullout. The French devised elaborate plans for settling the hinterland left by Ottoman provincial authorities in 1830, but their efforts at state building were unsuccessful on account of lengthy armed resistance.

The most successful local opposition immediately after the fall of Algiers was led by Ahmad ibn Muhammad, bey of Constantine. He initiated a radical overhaul of the Ottoman administration in his *beylik* by replacing Turkish officials with local leaders, making Arabic the official language, and attempting to reform finances according to the precepts of Islam. After the French failed in several attempts to gain some of the bey's territories through negotiation, an ill-fated invasion force led by Bertrand Clauzel had to retreat from Constantine in 1836 in humiliation and defeat. Nonetheless, the French captured Constantine the following year.

Abd al Qadir

The French faced other opposition as well in the area. The superior of a religious brotherhood, Muhyi ad Din, who had spent time in Ottoman jails for opposing the dey's rule, launched attacks against the French and their *makhzen* allies at Oran in 1832. In the same year, tribal elders chose Muhyi ad Din's son, twenty-five-year-old Abd al Qadir, to take his place leading the jihad. Abd al Qadir, who was recognized as *amir al muminin* (commander of the faithful), quickly gained the support of tribes throughout Algeria. A devout and austere marabout, he was also a cunning political leader and a resourceful warrior. From his capital in Tlemcen, Abd al Qadir set about building a territorial Muslim state based on the communities of the interior but drawing its strength from the tribes and religious brotherhoods. By 1839 he controlled more than two-thirds of Algeria. His government maintained an army and a bureaucracy, collected taxes, supported education, undertook public works, and established agricultural and manufacturing cooperatives to stimulate economic activity.

The French in Algiers viewed with concern the success of a Muslim government and the rapid growth of a viable territorial state that barred the extension of European settlement. Abd al Qadir fought running battles across Algeria with French forces, which included units of the Foreign Legion, organized in 1831 for Algerian service. Although his forces were defeated by the French under General Thomas Bugeaud in 1836, Abd al Qadir negotiated a favorable peace treaty the next year. The treaty gained conditional recognition for Abd al Qadir's regime by defining the territory under its control and salvaged his prestige among the tribes just as the shaykhs were about to desert him. To provoke new hostilities, the French deliberately broke the treaty in 1839 by occupying Constantine. Abd al Qadir took up the holy war again, destroyed the French settlements on the Mitidja Plain, and at one point advanced to the outskirts of Algiers itself. He struck where the French were weakest and retreated when they advanced against him in greater strength. The government moved from camp to camp with the amir and his army. Gradually, however, superior French resources and manpower and the defection of tribal chieftains took their toll. Reinforcements poured into Algeria after 1840 until Bugeaud had at his disposal 108,000 men, one-third of the French army. Bugeaud's strategy was to destroy Abd al Qadir's bases, then to starve the population by destroying its means of subsistence—crops, orchards, and herds. On several occasions, French troops burned or asphyxiated noncombatants hiding from the terror in caves. One by one, the amir's strongholds fell to the French, and many of his ablest commanders were killed or captured so that by 1843 the Muslim state had collapsed. Abd al Qadir took refuge with his ally, the sultan of Morocco, Abd ar Rahman II, and launched raids into Algeria. However, Abd al Qadir was obliged to surrender to the commander of Oran Province, General Louis de Lamoricière, at the end of 1847.

Abd al Qadir was promised safe conduct to Egypt or Palestine if his followers laid down their arms and kept the peace. He accepted these conditions, but the minister of war—who years earlier as general in Algeria had been badly defeated by Abd al Qadir—had him consigned to prison in France. In 1852 Louis Napoleon, the president of the Second Republic who would soon establish the Second Empire as Napoleon III, freed Abd al Qadir and gave him a pension of 150,000 francs. In 1855 Abd al Qadir moved from the Byrsa, the citadel area of Carthage, to Damascus. There in 1860 Abd al Qadir intervened to save the lives of an estimated 12,000 Christians, including the French consul and staff, during a massacre instigated by local Ottoman officials. The French government, in appreciation, conferred on him the Grand Cordon of the Legion of Honor, and additional honors followed from a number of other European governments. Declining all invitations to return to public life, he devoted himself to scholarly pursuits and charity until his death in Damascus in 1883.

Abd al Qadir is recognized and venerated as the first hero of Algerian independence. Not without cause, his green and white standard was adopted by the Algerian liberation movement during the War of Independence and became the national flag of independent Algeria. The Algerian government brought his remains back to Algeria to be interred with much ceremony on July 5, 1966, the fourth anniversary of independence and the 136th anniversary of the French conquest. A mosque bearing his name has been constructed as a national shrine in Constantine.

Colonization and Military Control

A royal ordinance in 1845 called for three types of administration in Algeria. In areas where Europeans were a substantial part of the population, colons elected mayors and councils for self-governing "full exercise" communes (*communes de plein exercice*). In the "mixed" communes, where Muslims were a large majority, government was in the hands of appointed and some elected officials, including representatives of the *grands chefs* (great chieftains) and a French administrator. The indigenous communes (*communes indigènes*), remote areas not adequately pacified, remained under the *régime du sabre*.

By 1848 nearly all of northern Algeria was under French control. Important tools of the colonial administration, from this time until their elimination in the 1870s, were the *bureaux arabes* (Arab offices), staffed by Arabists whose function was to collect information on the indigenous people and to carry out administrative functions, nominally in cooperation with the army. The *bureaux arabes* on occasion acted with sympathy toward the local population and formed a buffer between Muslims and rapacious colons.

Under the *régime du sabre*, the colons had been permitted limited self-government in areas where European settlement was most intense, but there was constant friction between them and the army. The colons charged that the *bureaux arabes* hindered the progress of colonization. They agitated against military rule, complaining that their legal rights were denied under the arbitrary controls imposed on the colony and insisting on a civil administration for Algeria fully integrated with metropolitan France. The army warned that the introduction of civilian government would invite Muslim retaliation and threaten the security of Algeria. The French government vacillated in its policy, yielding small concessions to the colon demands on the one hand while maintaining the *régime du sabre* to protect the interests of the Muslim majority on the other.

Shortly after Louis Philippe's constitutional monarchy was overthrown in the revolution of 1848, the new government of

Algeria: A Country Study

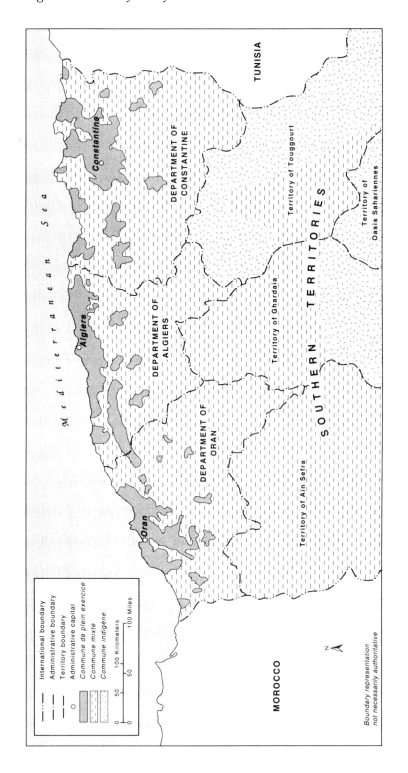

Figure 3. *French Algeria, 1845–1962*

the Second Republic ended Algeria's status as a colony and declared the occupied lands an integral part of France. Three "civil territories"—Algiers, Oran, and Constantine—were organized as French *départements* (local administrative units) under a civilian government (see fig. 3). For the first time, French citizens in the civil territories elected their own councils and mayors; Muslims had to be appointed, could not hold more than one-third of council seats, and could not serve as mayors or assistant mayors. The administration of territories outside the zones settled by colons remained under a *régime du sabre*. Local Muslim administration was allowed to continue under the supervision of French military commanders, charged with maintaining order in newly pacified regions, and the *bureaux arabes*. Theoretically, these areas were closed to European colonization.

European migration, encouraged during the Second Republic, stimulated the civilian administration to open new land for settlement against the advice of the army. With the advent of the Second Empire in 1852, Napoleon III returned Algeria to military control. In 1858 a separate Ministry of Algerian Affairs was created to supervise administration of the country through a military governor general assisted by a civil minister.

Napoleon III visited Algeria twice in the early 1860s. He was profoundly impressed with the nobility and virtue of the tribal chieftains, who appealed to the emperor's romantic nature, and was shocked by the self-serving attitude of the colon leaders. He determined to halt the expansion of European settlement beyond the coastal zone and to restrict contact between Muslims and the colons, whom he considered to have a corrupting influence on the indigenous population. He envisioned a grand design for preserving most of Algeria for the Muslims by founding a *royaume arabe* (Arab kingdom) with himself as the *roi des Arabes* (king of the Arabs). He instituted the so-called politics of the *grands chefs* to deal with the Muslims directly through their traditional leaders.

To further his plans for the *royaume arabe*, Napoleon III issued two decrees affecting tribal structure, land tenure, and the legal status of Muslims in French Algeria. The first, promulgated in 1863, was intended to renounce the state's claims to tribal lands and eventually provide private plots to individuals in the tribes, thus dismantling "feudal" structures and protecting the lands from the colons. Tribal areas were to be identified, delimited into *douars* (administrative units), and given over to councils. Arable land was to be divided among members of the *douar* over a period of one to three generations, after which it could be bought and sold by the individual owners. Unfortunately for the tribes, however, the plans of Napoleon III quickly unraveled. French officials sympathetic to the colons took much of the tribal land they surveyed into the public domain. In addition, some tribal leaders immediately sold communal lands for quick gains. The process of converting arable land to individual ownership was accelerated to only a few years when laws were enacted in the 1870s stipulating that no sale of land by an individual Muslim could be invalidated by the claim that it was collectively owned. The *cudah* and other tribal officials, appointed by the French on the basis of their loyalty to France rather than the allegiance owed them by the tribe, lost their credibility as they were drawn into the European orbit, becoming known derisively as *beni-oui-ouis* (yesmen).

Napoleon III visualized three distinct Algerias: a French colony, an Arab country, and a military camp, each with a distinct form of local government. The second decree, issued in 1865, was designed to recognize the differences in cultural background of the French and the Muslims. As French nationals, Muslims could serve on equal terms in the French armed forces and civil service and could migrate to metropolitan France. They were also granted the protection of French law while retaining the right to adhere to Islamic law in litigation concerning their personal status. But if Muslims wished to become full citizens, they had to accept the full jurisdiction of the French legal code, including laws affecting marriage and inheritance, and reject the competence of the religious courts. In effect, this meant that a Muslim had to renounce his religion in order to become a French citizen. This condition was bitterly resented by Muslims, for whom the only road to political equality became apostasy. Over the next century, fewer than 3,000 Muslims chose to cross the barrier and become French citizens.

When the Prussians captured Napoleon III at the Battle of Sedan (1870), ending the Second Empire, the colons in Algiers toppled the military government and installed a civilian administration. Meanwhile, in France the government directed one of its ministers, Adolphe Crémieux, "to destroy the military regime ... [and] to completely assimilate Algeria into France."

In October 1870, Crémieux, whose concern with Algerian affairs dated from the time of the Second Republic, issued a series of decrees providing for representation of the Algerian *départements* in the National Assembly of France and confirming colon control over local administration. A civilian governor general was made responsible to the Ministry of Interior. The Crémieux Decrees also granted blanket French citizenship to Algerian Jews, who then numbered about 40,000. This act set them apart from Muslims, in whose eyes they were identified thereafter with the colons. The measure had to be enforced, however, over the objections of the colons, who made little distinction between Muslims and Jews. (Automatic citizenship was subsequently extended in 1889 to children of non-French Europeans born in Algeria unless they specifically rejected it.)

The loss of Alsace-Lorraine to Germany in 1871 led to pressure on the French government to make new land available in Algeria for about 5,000 Alsatian and Lorrainer refugees who were resettled there. During the 1870s, both the amount of European-owned land and the number of settlers were doubled, and tens of thousands of unskilled Muslims, who had been uprooted from their land, wandered into the cities or to colon farming areas in search of work.

The most serious native insurrection since the time of Abd al Qadir broke out in 1871 in the Kabylie region and spread through much of Algeria. The revolt was triggered by Crémieux's extension of civil (that is, colon) authority to previously self-governing tribal reserves and the abrogation of commitments made by the military government, but it clearly had its basis in more long-standing grievances. Since the Crimean War (1854–56), the demand for grain had pushed up the price of Algerian wheat to European levels. Silos were emptied when the world market's impact was felt in Algeria, and Muslim farmers sold their grain reserves—including seed grain—to speculators. But the community-owned silos were the fundamental adaptation of a subsistence economy to an unpredictable climate, and a good year's surplus was stored away against a bad year's dearth. When serious drought struck Algeria and grain crops failed in 1866 and for several years following, Muslim areas faced starvation, and with famine came pestilence. It was estimated that 20 percent of the Muslim population of Constantine died over a three-year period. In 1871 the civil authorities repudiated guarantees made to tribal chieftains by the previous military government for loans to replenish their seed supply. This act alienated even pro-French Muslim leaders, while it undercut their ability to control their people. It was against this background of misery and hopelessness that the stricken Kabyles rose in revolt.

In the aftermath of the 1871 uprising, French authorities imposed stern measures to punish and control the whole Muslim population. France confiscated more than 500,000 hectares of tribal land and placed the Kabylie region under a *régime d'exception* (extraordinary rule), which denied the due process guaranteed French nationals. A special *indigénat* (native code) listed as offenses acts such as insolence and unauthorized assembly not punishable by French law, and the normal jurisdiction of the *cudah* was sharply restricted. The governor general was empowered to jail suspects for up to five years without trial. The argument was made in defense of these exceptional measures that the French penal code as applied to Frenchmen was too permissive to control Muslims.

Hegemony of the Colons

A commission of inquiry set up by the French Senate in 1892 and headed by former Premier Jules Ferry, an advocate of colonial expansion, recommended that the government abandon a policy that assumed French law, without major modifications, could fit the needs of an area inhabited by close to 2 million Europeans and 4 million Muslims. Muslims had no representation in Algeria's National Assembly and were grossly underrepresented on local councils. Because of the many restrictions imposed by the authorities, by 1915 only 50,000 Muslims were eligible to vote in elections in the civil communes. Attempts to implement even the most modest reforms were blocked or delayed by the local administration in Algeria, dominated by colons, and by colon representatives in the National Assembly, to which each of the three *départements* sent six deputies and three senators.

Once elected to the National Assembly, colons became permanent fixtures. Because of their seniority, they exercised disproportionate influence, and their support was important to any government's survival. The leader of the colon delegation, Auguste Warnier, succeeded during the 1870s and 1880s in modifying or introducing legislation to facilitate the private transfer of land to settlers and continue the Algerian state's appropriation of land from the local population and distribution to settlers. Consistent proponents of reform, like Georges

Clemenceau and socialist Jean Jaurès, were rare in the National Assembly.

The bulk of Algeria's wealth in manufacturing, mining, agriculture, and trade was controlled by the *grands colons*. The modern European-owned and -managed sector of the economy centered around small industry and a highly developed export trade, designed to provide food and raw materials to France in return for capital and consumer goods. Europeans held about 30 percent of the total arable land, including the bulk of the most fertile land and most of the areas under irrigation. By 1900 Europeans produced more than two-thirds of the value of output in agriculture and practically all agricultural exports. The modern, or European, sector was run on a commercial basis and meshed with the French market system that it supplied with wine, citrus, olives, and vegetables. Nearly half of the value of European-owned real property was in vineyards by 1914. By contrast, subsistence cereal production—supplemented by olive, fig, and date growing and stock raising—formed the basis of the traditional sector, but the land available for cropping was submarginal even for cereals under prevailing traditional cultivation practices.

The colonial regime imposed more and higher taxes on Muslims than on Europeans. Muslims, in addition to paying traditional taxes dating from before the French conquest, also paid new taxes, from which the colons were often exempted. In 1909, for instance, Muslims, who made up almost 90 percent of the population but produced 20 percent of Algeria's income, paid 70 percent of direct taxes and 45 percent of the total taxes collected. And colons controlled how these revenues would be spent. As a result, colon towns had handsome municipal buildings, paved streets lined with trees, fountains, and statues, while Algerian villages and rural areas benefited little if at all from tax revenues.

The colonial regime proved severely detrimental to overall education for Algerian Muslims, who had previously relied on religious schools to learn reading, writing, and engage in religious studies (see Education, ch. 2). Not only did the state appropriate the *habus* lands (the religious foundations that constituted the main source of income for religious institutions, including schools) in 1843, but colon officials refused to allocate enough money to maintain schools and mosques properly and to provide for an adequate number of teachers and religious leaders for the growing population. In 1892 more than five times as much was spent for the education of Europeans as for Muslims, who had five times as many children of school age. Because few Muslim teachers were trained, Muslim schools were largely staffed by French teachers. Even a stateoperated *madrasah* (school) often had French faculty members. Attempts to institute bilingual, bicultural schools, intended to bring Muslim and European children together in the classroom, were a conspicuous failure, rejected by both communities and phased out after 1870. According to one estimate, fewer than 5 percent of Algerian children attended any kind of school in 1870.

Efforts were begun by 1890 to educate a small number of Muslims along with European students in the French school system as part of France's "civilizing mission" in Algeria. The curriculum was entirely French and allowed no place for Arabic studies, which were deliberately downgraded even in Muslim schools. Within a generation, a class of well-educated, gallicized Muslims—the *évolués* (literally, the evolved ones)— had been created. Almost all of the handful of Muslims who accepted French citizenship were *évolués*; more significantly, it was in this privileged group of Muslims, strongly influenced by French culture and political attitudes, that a new Algerian self-consciousness developed.

Reporting to the French Senate in 1894, Governor General Jules Cambon wrote that Algeria had "only a dust of people left her." He referred to the destruction of the traditional ruling class that had left Muslims without leaders and had deprived France of *interlocuteurs valables* (literally, valid go-betweens), through whom to reach the masses of the people. He lamented that no genuine communication was possible between the two communities.

The colons who ran Algeria maintained a condescending dialogue only with the *beni-oui-ouis*. Later they deliberately thwarted contact between the *évolués* and Muslim traditionalists on the one hand and between *évolués* and official circles in France on the other. They feared and mistrusted the francophone *évolués*, who were classified either as assimilationists, insisting on being accepted as Frenchmen but on their own terms, or as integrationists, eager to work as members of a distinct Muslim elite on equal terms with the French.

Algerian Nationalism

A new generation of Muslim leadership emerged in Algeria

at the time of World War I and grew to maturity during the 1920s and 1930s. It consisted of a small but influential class of *évolués*, other Algerians whose perception of themselves and their country had been shaped by wartime experiences, and a body of religious reformers and teachers. Some of these people were members of the few wealthy Muslim families that had managed to insinuate themselves into the colonial system in the 1890s and had with difficulty succeeded in obtaining for their sons the French education so coveted by progressive Algerians. Others were among the about 173,000 Algerians who had served in the French army during World War I or the several hundred thousand more who had assisted the French war effort by working in factories. In France they became aware of a standard of living higher than any they had known at home and of democratic political concepts, taken for granted by Frenchmen in France, which colons, soldiers, and bureaucrats had refused to apply to the Muslim majority in Algeria. Some Algerians also became acquainted with the pan-Arab nationalism growing in the Middle East.

Political Movements

One of the earliest movements for political reform was an integrationist group, the Young Algerians (Jeunesse Algérienne). Its members were drawn from the small, liberal elite of well-educated, middle-class *évolués* who demanded an opportunity to prove that they were French as well as Muslim. In 1908 they delivered to France's Prime Minister Georges Clemenceau a petition that expressed opposition under the status quo to a proposed policy to conscript Muslim Algerians into the French army. If, however, the state granted the Muslims full citizenship, the petition went on, opposition to conscription would be dropped. In 1911, in addition to demanding preferential treatment for "the intellectual elements of the country," the group called for an end to unequal taxation, broadening of the franchise, more schools, and protection of indigenous property. The Young Algerians added a significant voice to the reformist movement against French colonial policy that began in 1892 and continued until the outbreak of World War I. In part to reward Muslims who fought and died for France, Clemenceau appointed reform-minded Charles Jonnart as governor general. Reforms promulgated in 1919 and known as the Jonnart Law expanded the number of Muslims permitted to vote to about 425,000. The legislation also removed all voters from the jurisdiction of the humiliating *indigénat*.

The most popular Muslim leader in Algeria after the war was Khalid ibn Hashim, grandson of Abd al Qadir and a member of the Young Algerians, although he differed with some members of the group over acceptance of the Jonnart Law. Some Young Algerians were willing to work within the framework set out by the reforms, but Emir Khalid, as he was known, continued to press for the complete Young Algerian program. He was able to win electoral victories in Algiers and to enliven political discourse with his calls for reform and full assimilation, but by 1923 he tired of the struggle and left Algeria, eventually retiring to Damascus.

Some of the Young Algerians in 1926 formed the Federation of Elected Natives (Fédération des Élus Indigènes—FÉI) because many of the former group's members had joined the circle of Muslims eligible to hold public office. The federation's objectives were the assimilation of the *évolués* into the French community, with full citizenship but without surrendering their personal status as Muslims, and the eventual integration of Algeria as a full province of France. Other objectives included equal pay for equal work for government employees, abolition of travel restrictions to and from France, abolition of the *indigénat* (which had been reinstituted earlier), and electoral reform.

The first group to call for Algerian independence was the Star of North Africa (Étoile Nord-Africain, known as Star). The group was originally a solidarity group formed in 1926 in Paris to coordinate political activity among North African workers in France and to defend "the material, moral, and social interests of North African Muslims." The leaders included members of the French Communist Party and its labor confederation, and in the early years of the struggle for independence the party provided material and moral support. Ahmed Messali Hadj, the Star's secretary general, enunciated the groups demands in 1927. In addition to independence from France, the Star called for freedom of press and association, a parliament chosen through universal suffrage, confiscation of large estates, and the institution of Arabic schools. The Star was banned in 1929 and operated underground until 1934, when its newspaper reached a circulation of 43,500. Influenced by the Arab nationalist ideas of Lebanese Druze Shakib Arslan, Messali Hadj turned away from communist ideology to a more nationalist outlook, for which the French Communist Party attacked the Star. He returned to Algeria to organize urban workers and peasant farmers and in 1937 founded the Party of the Algerian People (Parti du Peuple Algérien—PPA) to mobilize the Algerian working class at home and in France to improve its situation through political action. For Messali Hadj, who ruled the PPA with an iron hand, these aims were inseparable from the struggle for an independent Algeria in which socialist and Islamic values would be fused.

Algeria's Islamic reform movement took inspiration from Egyptian reformers Muhammad Abduh and Muhammad Rashid Rida and stressed the Arab and Islamic roots of the country. Starting in the 1920s, the reform ulama, religious scholars, promoted a purification of Islam in Algeria and a return to the Quran and the sunna, or tradition of the Prophet (see Islam and the Algerian State, ch. 2). The reformers favored the adoption of modern methods of inquiry and rejected the superstitions and folk practices of the countryside, actions that brought them into confrontation with the marabouts. The reformers published their own periodicals and books, and established free modern Islamic schools that stressed Arabic language and culture as an alternative to the schools for Muslims operated for many years by the French. Under the dynamic leadership of Shaykh Abd al Hamid Ben Badis, the reformist ulama organized the Association of Algerian Muslim Ulama (Association des Uléma Musulmans Algériens—AUMA) in 1931. Although their support was concentrated in the Constantine area, the AUMA struck a responsive chord among the Muslim masses, with whom it had closer ties than did the other nationalist organizations. As the Islamic reformers gained popularity and influence, the colonial authorities responded in 1933 by refusing them permission to preach in official mosques. This move and similar ones sparked several years of sporadic religious unrest.

European influences had some impact on indigenous Muslim political movements because Ferhat Abbas and Messali Hadj essentially looked to France for their ideological models. Ben Badis, however, believed that "Islam is our religion, Arabic our language, Algeria our fatherland." Abbas summed up the philosophy of the liberal integrationists in opposition to the claims of the nationalists when he denied in 1936 that Algeria had a separate identity. Ben Badis responded that he, too, had looked to the past and found "that this Algerian nation is not

France, cannot be France, and does not want to be France . . . [but] has its culture, its traditions and its characteristics, good or bad, like every other nation of the earth."

The colons, for their part, rejected any movement toward reform, whether instigated by integrationist or nationalist organizations. Reaction in Paris to the nationalists was divided. In the 1930s, French liberals saw only the *évolués* as a possible channel for diffusing political power in Algeria, denigrating Messali Hadj for demagoguery and the AUMA for religious obscurantism. At all times, however, the French government was confronted by the monolithic intransigence of the leaders of the European community in Algeria in opposing any devolution of power to Muslims, even to basically pro-French *évolués*. The colons also had powerful allies in the National Assembly, the bureaucracy, the armed forces, and the business community, and were strengthened in their resistance by their almost total control of the Algerian administration and police.

Viollette Plan

The mounting social, political, and economic crises in Algeria for the first time induced older and newly emerged classes of indigenous society to engage from 1933 to 1936 in numerous acts of political protest. The government responded with more restrictive laws governing public order and security. In 1936 French socialist Léon Blum became premier in a Popular Front government and appointed Maurice Viollette his minister of state. The ulama, sensing a new attitude in Paris that would favor their agenda, cautiously joined forces with the FÉI.

Representatives of these groups and members of the Algerian Communist Party (Parti Communiste Algérien—PCA) met in Algiers in 1936 at the first Algerian Muslim Congress. (Messali Hadj and the Star were left out owing to misgivings about their more radical program.) The congress drew up an extensive Charter of Demands, which called for the abolition of laws permitting imposition of the *régime d'exception*, political integration of Algeria and France, maintenance of personal legal status by Muslims acquiring French citizenship, fusion of European and Muslim education systems in Algeria, freedom to use Arabic in education and the press, equal wages for equal work, land reform, establishment of a single electoral college, and universal suffrage.

Blum and Viollette gave a warm reception to a congress delegation in Paris and indicated that many of their demands could be met. Meanwhile, Viollette drew up for the Blum government a proposal to extend French citizenship with full political equality to certain classes of the Muslim "elite," including university graduates, elected officials, army officers, and professionals. Messali Hadj saw in the Viollette Plan a new "instrument of colonialism . . . to split the Algerian people by separating the elite from the masses." The components of the congress—the ulama, the FÉI, and communists—were heartened by the proposal and gave it varying measures of support. Mohamed Bendjelloul and Abbas, as spokesmen for the *évolués*, who would have the most to gain from the measure, considered this plan a major step toward achieving their aims and redoubled their efforts through the liberal FÉI to gain broad support for the policy of Algerian integration with France. Not unexpectedly, however, the colons had taken uncompromising exception to the Viollette Plan. Although the project would have granted immediate French citizenship and voting rights to only about 21,000 Muslims, with provision for adding a few thousand more each year, spokesmen for the colons raised the specter of the European electorate's being submerged by a Muslim majority. Colon administrators and their supporters threw procedural obstacles in the path of the legislation, and the government gave it only lukewarm support, resulting in its ultimate failure.

While the Viollette Plan was still a live issue, however, Messali Hadj made a dramatic comeback to Algeria and had significant local success in attracting people to the Star. A mark of his success was the fact that in 1937 the government dissolved the Star. The same year Messali Hadj formed the PPA, which had a more moderate program, but he and other PPA leaders were arrested following a large demonstration in Algiers. Although Messali Hadj spent many years in jail, his party had the most widespread support of all opposition groups until it was banned in 1939.

Disillusioned by the failure of the Viollette Plan to win acceptance in Paris, Abbas shifted from a position of favoring assimilation of the *évolués* and full integration with France to calling for the development of a Muslim Algeria in close association with France but retaining "her own physiognomy, her language, her customs, her traditions." His more immediate goal was greater political, social, and economic equality for Muslims with the colons. By 1938 the cooperation among the parties that made up the congress began to break up.

Polarization and Politicization

Algerian Muslims rallied to the French side at the start of World War II as they had done in World War I. Nazi Germany's quick defeat of France, however, and the establishment of the collaborationist Vichy regime, to which the colons were generally sympathetic, not only increased the difficulties of Muslims but also posed an ominous threat to Jews in Algeria. The Algerian administration vigorously enforced the anti-Semitic laws imposed by Vichy, which stripped Algerian Jews of their French citizenship. Potential opposition leaders in both the European and the Muslim communities were arrested.

Allied landings were made at Algiers and Oran by 70,000 British and United States troops on November 8, 1942, in coordination with landings in Morocco. As part of Operation Torch under the overall command of Lieutenant General Dwight D. Eisenhower, Algiers and Oran were secured two days later after a determined resistance by French defenders. On November 11, Admiral Jean Louis Darlan, commander in chief of Vichy French forces, ordered a cease-fire in North Africa. Algeria provided a base for the subsequent Allied campaign in Tunisia.

After the fall of the Vichy regime in Algeria, General Henri Giraud, Free French commander in chief in North Africa, slowly rescinded repressive Vichy laws despite opposition by colon extremists. He also called on the Muslim population to supply troops for the Allied war effort. Ferhat Abbas and twenty-four other Muslim leaders replied that Algerians were ready to fight with the Allies in freeing their homeland but demanded the right to call a conference of Muslim representatives to develop political, economic, and social institutions for the indigenous population "within an essentially French framework." Giraud, who succeeded in raising an army of 250,000 men to fight in the Italian campaign, refused to consider this proposal, explaining that "politics" must wait until the end of the war.

In March 1943, Abbas, who had abandoned assimilation as a viable alternative to self-determination, presented the French administration with the Manifesto of the Algerian People, signed by fifty-six Algerian nationalist and international leaders. Outlining the past evils of colonial rule and denouncing continued suppression, the manifesto demanded specifically an Algerian constitution that would guarantee immediate and effective political participation and legal equality for Muslims. It called for agrarian reform, recognition of Arabic as an official language on equal terms with French, recognition of a full range of civil liberties, and the liberation of political prisoners of all parties.

The French governor general created a commission composed of prominent Muslims and Europeans to study the manifesto. This commission produced a supplementary reform program, which was forwarded to General Charles de Gaulle, leader of the Free French movement. De Gaulle and his newly appointed governor general in Algeria, General Georges Catroux, a recognized liberal, viewed the manifesto as evidence of a need to develop a mutually advantageous relationship between the European and Muslim communities. Catroux was reportedly shocked by the "blinded spirit of social conservatism" of the colons, but he did not regard the manifesto as a satisfactory basis for cooperation because he felt it would submerge the European minority in a Muslim state. Instead, the French administration in 1944 instituted a reform package, based on the 1936 Viollette Plan, that granted full French citizenship to certain categories of "meritorious" Algerian Muslims—military officers and decorated veterans, university graduates, government officials, and members of the Legion of Honor—who numbered about 60,000.

A new factor influencing Muslim reaction to the reintroduction of the Viollette Plan—which by that date even many moderates had rejected as inadequate—was the shift in Abbas's position from support for integration to the demand for an independent Algerian state federated with France. Abbas gained the support of the AUMA and of Messali Hadj, who joined him in forming the Friends of the Manifesto and Liberty (Amis du Manifeste et de la Liberté—AML) to work for Algerian independence. Within a short time, the AML's newspaper, *Égalité*, claimed 500,000 subscribers, indicating unprecedented interest in independence.

During this time, the outlawed PPA was creating secret political cells throughout the country and paramilitary groups in the Kabylie region and the Constantine region. In addition, PPA supporters joined the AML in large numbers and attempted to promote Messali Hadj's independence concept in contrast to the more moderate autonomy advocates. Social unrest grew in the winter of 1944-45, fueled in part by a poor wheat harvest, shortages of manufactured goods, and severe unemployment. On May Day, the AML organized demonstrations in twenty-one towns across the country, with marchers demanding freedom for Messali Hadj and independence for Algeria. Violence erupted in some locations, including Algiers and Oran, leaving many wounded and three dead.

Nationalist leaders were resolving to mark the approaching liberation of Europe with demonstrations calling for their own liberation, and it was clear that a clash with the authorities was imminent. The tensions between the Muslim and colon communities exploded on May 8, 1945, V-E Day, in an outburst of such violence as to make their polarization complete, if not irreparable. Police had told AML organizers they could march in Sétif only if they did not display nationalist flags or placards. They ignored the warnings, the march began, and gunfire resulted in which a number of police and demonstrators were killed. Marchers rampaged, leading to the killing of 103 Europeans. Word spread to the countryside, and villagers attacked colon settlements and government buildings.

The army and police responded by conducting a prolonged and systematic *ratissage* (literally, raking over) of suspected centers of dissidence. In addition, military airplanes and ships attacked Muslim population centers. According to official French figures, 1,500 Muslims died as a result of these countermeasures. Other estimates vary from 6,000 to as high as 45,000 killed.

In the aftermath of the Sétif violence, the AML was outlawed, and 5,460 Muslims, including Abbas, were arrested. Abbas deplored the uprising but charged that its repression had taken Algeria "back to the days of the Crusades." In April 1946, Abbas once again asserted the demands of the manifesto and founded the Democratic Union of the Algerian Manifesto (Union Démocratique du Manifeste Algérien—UDMA), abandoning the alliance that the AML had made with Messali Hadj's PPA and the AUMA. Abbas called for a free, secular, and republican Algeria loosely federated with France. Upon his release from a five-year house arrest, Messali Hadj returned to Algeria and formed the Movement for the Triumph of Democratic Liberties (Mouvement pour le Triomphe des Libertés Démocratiques—MTLD), which quickly drew supporters from a broad cross-section of society. Committed to unequivocal independence, the MTLD firmly opposed Abbas's proposal for federation. The PPA continued to operate, but clandestinely, always striving for an independent, Arab, and Islamic Algeria. The clandestine Special Organization (Organisation Spéciale—OS) was created within the MTLD by Hocine Ait Ahmed in 1947 to conduct terrorist operations when political protest through legal channels was suppressed by authorities. Ait Ahmed was later succeeded as chief of the OS by Ahmed Ben Bella, one of the early Algerian nationalist leaders.

The National Assembly approved the government-proposed Organic Statute of Algeria in August 1947. This law called for the creation of an Algerian Assembly with one house representing Europeans and "meritorious" Muslims, and the other representing the more than 8 million remaining Muslims. The statute also replaced mixed communes with elected local councils, abolished military government in the Algerian Sahara, recognized Arabic as an official language with French, and proposed enfranchising Muslim women. Muslim and colon deputies alike abstained or voted against the statute but for diametrically opposed reasons: the Muslims because it fell short of their expectations and the colons because it went too far.

The sweeping victory of Messali Hadj's MTLD in the 1947 municipal elections frightened the colons, whose political leaders, through fraud and intimidation, attempted to obtain a result more favorable to them in the following year's first Algerian Assembly voting. The term *élection algérienne* became a synonym for rigged election. The MTLD was allowed nine seats, Abbas's UDMA was given eight, and government-approved "independents" were awarded fifty-five seats. These results may have reassured some of the colons that the nationalists had been rejected by the Muslim community, but the elections suggested to many Muslims that a peaceful solution to Algeria's problems was not possible.

At the first session of the colon-controlled Algerian Assembly, a MTLD delegate was arrested at the door, prompting other Muslim representatives to walk out in protest. A request by Abbas to gain the floor was refused. Frustrated by these events, the nationalist parties, joined by the PCA, formed a common political front that undertook to have the results of the election voided. French socialists and moderates tried to initiate a formal inquiry into the reports of vote fraud but were prevented from doing so by the assembly's European delegates, who persuaded the governor general that an investigation would disturb the peace. New elections in 1951 were subject to the same sort of rigging that had characterized the 1948 voting.

In 1952 anti-French demonstrations precipitated by the OS led to Messali Hadj's arrest and deportation to France. Internal divisions and attacks by the authorities severely weakened the

MTLD, draining its energies. Colon extremists took every opportunity to persuade the French government of the need for draconian measures against the emergent independence movement.

Ben Bella created a new underground action committee to replace the OS, which had been broken up by the French police in 1950. The new group, the Revolutionary Committee of Unity and Action (Comité Révolutionnaire d'Unité et d'Action—CRUA), was based in Cairo, where Ben Bella had fled in 1952. Known as the *chefs historiques* (historical chiefs), the group's nine original leaders—Ait Ahmed, Mohamed Boudiaf, Belkacem Krim, Rabah Bitat, Larbi Ben M'Hidi, Mourad Didouch, Moustafa Ben Boulaid, Mohamed Khider, and Ben Bella—were considered the leaders of the Algerian War of Independence.

Between March and October 1954, the CRUA organized a military network in Algeria comprising six military regions (referred to at the time as *wilayat*; sing., *wilaya*). The leaders of these regions and their followers became known as the "internals." Ben Bella, Khider, and Ait Ahmed formed the External Delegation in Cairo. Encouraged by Egypt's President Gamal Abdul Nasser (president, 1954–71), their role was to gain foreign support for the rebellion and to acquire arms, supplies, and funds for the *wilaya* commanders. In October the CRUA renamed itself the National Liberation Front (Front de Libération Nationale—FLN), which assumed responsibility for the political direction of the revolution. The National Liberation Army (Armée de Libération Nationale—ALN), the FLN's military arm, was to conduct the War of Independence within Algeria.

War of Independence

In the early morning hours of All Saints' Day, November 1, 1954, FLN *maquisards* (guerrillas) launched attacks in various parts of Algeria against military installations, police posts, warehouses, communications facilities, and public utilities. From Cairo, the FLN broadcast a proclamation calling on Muslims in Algeria to join in a national struggle for the "restoration of the Algerian state, sovereign, democratic, and social, within the framework of the principles of Islam." The French minister of interior, socialist François Mitterrand, responded sharply that "the only possible negotiation is war." It was the reaction of Premier Pierre Mendès-France, who only a few months before had

Historical Setting

completed the liquidation of France's empire in Indochina, that set the tone of French policy for the next five years. On November 12, he declared in the National Assembly: "One does not compromise when it comes to defending the internal peace of the nation, the unity and integrity of the Republic. The Algerian departments are part of the French Republic. They have been French for a long time, and they are irrevocably French . . . . Between them and metropolitan France there can be no conceivable secession."

FLN

The FLN uprising presented nationalist groups with the question of whether to adopt armed revolt as the main mode of action. During the first year of the war, Abbas's UDMA, the ulama, and the PCA maintained a friendly neutrality toward the FLN. The communists, who had made no move to cooperate in the uprising at the start, later tried to infiltrate the FLN, but FLN leaders publicly repudiated the support of the party. In April 1956, Abbas flew to Cairo, where he formally joined the FLN. This action brought in many *évolués* who had supported the UDMA in the past. The AUMA also threw the full weight of its prestige behind the FLN. Bendjelloul and the prointegrationist moderates had already abandoned their efforts to mediate between the French and the rebels.

After the collapse of the MTLD, Messali Hadj formed the leftist National Algerian Movement (Mouvement National Algérien—MNA), which advocated a policy of violent revolution and total independence similar to that of the FLN. The ALN subsequently wiped out the MNA guerrilla operation, and Messali Hadj's movement lost what little influence it had had in Algeria. However, the MNA gained the support of a majority of Algerian workers in France through the Union of Algerian Workers (Union Syndicale des Travailleurs Algériens). The FLN also established a strong organization in France to oppose the MNA. Merciless "café wars," resulting in nearly 5,000 deaths, were waged in France between the two rebel groups throughout the years of the War of Independence.

On the political front, the FLN worked to persuade—and to coerce—the Algerian masses to support the aims of the independence movement. FLN-oriented labor unions, professional associations, and students' and women's organizations were organized to rally diverse segments of the population. Frantz Fanon, a psychiatrist from Martinique who became the FLN's

Algeria: A Country Study

leading political theorist, provided a sophisticated intellectual justification for the use of violence in achieving national liberation. From Cairo, Ben Bella ordered the liquidation of potential *interlocuteurs valables*, those independent representatives of the Muslim community acceptable to the French through whom a compromise or reforms within the system might be achieved.

As the FLN campaign spread through the countryside, many European farmers in the interior sold their holdings and sought refuge in Algiers, where their cry for sterner countermeasures swelled. Colon vigilante units, whose unauthorized activities were conducted with the passive cooperation of police authorities, carried out *ratonnades* (literally, rat-hunts; synonymous with Arab-killings) against suspected FLN members of the Muslim community. The colons demanded the proclamation of a state of emergency, the proscription of all groups advocating separation from France, and the imposition of capital punishment for politically motivated crimes.

By 1955 effective political action groups within the colon community succeeded in intimidating the governors general sent by Paris to resolve the conflict. A major success was the conversion of Jacques Soustelle, who went to Algeria as governor general in January 1955 determined to restore peace. Soustelle, a one-time leftist and by 1955 an ardent Gaullist, began an ambitious reform program (the Soustelle Plan) aimed at improving economic conditions among the Muslim population.

Philippeville

An important watershed in the War of Independence was the massacre of civilians by the FLN near the town of Philippeville in August 1955. Before this operation, FLN policy was to attack only military and government-related targets. The *wilaya* commander for the Constantine region, however, decided a drastic escalation was needed. The killing by the FLN and its supporters of 123 people, including old women and babies, shocked Soustelle into calling for more repressive measures against the rebels. The government claimed it killed 1,273 guerrillas in retaliation; according to the FLN, 12,000 Muslims perished in an orgy of bloodletting by the armed forces and police, as well as colon gangs. After Philippeville, all-out war began in Algeria.

*Martyrs' monument, Algiers, dedicated to the dead in the War of Independence, 1954–62
Courtesy Anthony Toth and Middle East Report*

Soustelle's successor, Governor General Robert Lacoste, a socialist, abolished the Algerian Assembly. Lacoste saw the assembly, which was dominated by colons, as hindering the work of his administration, and he undertook to rule Algeria by decree-law. He favored stepping up French military operations and granted the army exceptional police powers—a concession of dubious legality under French law—to deal with the mounting terrorism. At the same time, Lacoste proposed a new administrative structure that would give Algeria a degree of autonomy and a decentralized government. Although remaining an integral part of France, Algeria was to be divided into five districts, each of which would have a territorial assembly elected from a single slate of candidates. Colon deputies were able to delay until 1958 passage of the measure by the National Assembly.

In August-September 1956, the internal leadership of the FLN met to organize a formal policy-making body to synchronize the movement's political and military activities. The highest authority of the FLN was vested in the thirty-four-member National Council of the Algerian Revolution (Conseil National de la Révolution Algérienne—CNRA), within which the five-man Committee of Coordination and Enforcement (Comité de Coordination et d'Exécution—CCE) formed the executive. The externals, including Ben Bella, knew the conference was taking place but by chance or design on the part of the internals were unable to attend.

Meanwhile, in October 1956 Lacoste had the FLN external political leaders who were in Algeria at the time arrested and imprisoned for the duration of the war. This action caused the remaining rebel leaders to harden their stance.

France took a more openly hostile view of President Nasser's material and political assistance to the FLN, which some French analysts believed was the most important element in sustaining continued rebel activity in Algeria. This attitude was a factor in persuading France to participate in the November 1956 Anglo-Suez Campaign, meant to topple Nasser from power.

During 1957 support for the FLN weakened as the breach between the internals and externals widened. To halt the drift, the FLN expanded its executive committee to include Abbas, as well as imprisoned political leaders such as Ben Bella. It also convinced communist and Arab members of the United Nations (UN) to apply diplomatic pressure on the French government to negotiate a cease-fire.

Conduct of the War

From its origins in 1954 as ragtag *maquisards* numbering in the hundreds and armed with a motley assortment of hunting rifles and discarded French, German, and United States light weapons, the ALN had evolved by 1957 into a disciplined fighting force of nearly 40,000. More than 30,000 were organized along conventional lines in external units that were stationed in Moroccan and Tunisian sanctuaries near the Algerian border, where they served primarily to divert some French manpower from the main theaters of guerrilla activity to guard against infiltration. The brunt of the fighting was borne by the internals in the *wilayat*; estimates of the numbers of internals range from 6,000 to more than 25,000, with thousands of part-time irregulars.

During 1956 and 1957, the ALN successfully applied hit-and-run tactics according to the classic canons of guerrilla warfare. Specializing in ambushes and night raids and avoiding direct contact with superior French firepower, the internal forces targeted army patrols, military encampments, police posts, and colon farms, mines, and factories, as well as transportation and communications facilities. Once an engagement was broken off, the guerrillas merged with the population in

Historical Setting

the countryside. Kidnapping was commonplace, as were the ritual murder and mutilation of captured French military, colons of both genders and every age, suspected collaborators, and traitors. At first, the revolutionary forces targeted only Muslim officials of the colonial regime; later, they coerced or killed even those civilians who simply refused to support them. Moreover, during the first two years of the conflict, the guerrillas killed about 6,000 Muslims and 1,000 Europeans.

Although successful in engendering an atmosphere of fear and uncertainty within both communities in Algeria, the revolutionaries' coercive tactics suggested that they had not as yet inspired the bulk of the Muslim people to revolt against French colonial rule. Gradually, however, the FLN/ALN gained control in certain sectors of the Aurès region, the Kabylie region and other mountainous areas around Constantine and south of Algiers and Oran. In these places, the ALN established a simple but effective—although frequently temporary—military administration that was able to collect taxes and food and to recruit manpower. But it was never able to hold large fixed positions. Muslims all over the country also initiated underground social, judicial, and civil organizations, gradually building their own state.

The loss of competent field commanders both on the battlefield and through defections and political purges created difficulties for the FLN. Moreover, power struggles in the early years of the war split leadership in the *wilayat*, particularly in the Aurès region. Some officers created their own fiefdoms, using units under their command to settle old scores and engage in private wars against military rivals within the ALN. Although identified and exploited by French intelligence, factionalism did not materially impair the overall effectiveness of ALN military operations.

To increase international and domestic French attention to their struggle, the FLN decided to bring the conflict to the cities and to call a nationwide general strike. The most notable manifestation of the new urban campaign was the Battle of Algiers, which began on September 30, 1956, when three women placed bombs at three sites including the downtown office of Air France. The ALN carried out an average of 800 shootings and bombings per month through the spring of 1957, resulting in many civilian casualties and inviting a crushing response from the authorities. The 1957 general strike, timed to coincide with the UN debate on Algeria, was imposed on Muslim

Algeria: A Country Study

workers and businesses. General Jacques Massu, who was instructed to use whatever methods were necessary to restore order in the city, frequently fought terrorism with acts of terrorism. Using paratroopers, he broke the strike and systematically destroyed the FLN infrastructure there. But the FLN had succeeded in showing its ability to strike at the heart of French Algeria and in rallying a mass response to its appeals among urban Muslims. Moreover, the publicity given the brutal methods used by the army to win the Battle of Algiers, including the widespread use of torture, cast doubt in France about its role in Algeria.

Despite complaints from the military command in Algiers, the French government was reluctant for many months to admit that the Algerian situation was out of control and that what was viewed officially as a pacification operation had developed into a major colonial war. By 1956 France had committed more than 400,000 troops to Algeria. Although the elite airborne units and the Foreign Legion received particular notoriety, approximately 170,000 of the regular French army troops in Algeria were Muslim Algerians, most of them volunteers. France also sent air force and naval units to the Algerian theater.

The French army resumed an important role in local Algerian administration through the Special Administration Section (Section Administrative Spécialisée—SAS), created in 1955. The SAS's mission was to establish contact with the Muslim population and weaken nationalist influence in the rural areas by asserting the "French presence" there. SAS officers—called *képis bleus* (blue caps)—also recruited and trained bands of loyal Muslim irregulars, known as *harkis*. Armed with shotguns and using guerrilla tactics similar to those of the ALN, the *harkis*, who eventually numbered about 150,000 volunteers, were an ideal instrument of counterinsurgency warfare.

Late in 1957, General Raoul Salan, commanding the French army in Algeria, instituted a system of *quadrillage*, dividing the country into sectors, each permanently garrisoned by troops responsible for suppressing rebel operations in their assigned territory. Salan's methods sharply reduced the instances of FLN terrorism but tied down a large number of troops in static defense. Salan also constructed a heavily patrolled system of barriers to limit infiltration from Tunisia and Morocco. The best known of these was the Morice Line (named for the French defense minister, André Morice), which consisted of an electrified fence, barbed wire, and mines over a 320-kilometer stretch of the Tunisian border.

The French military command ruthlessly applied the principle of collective responsibility to villages suspected of sheltering, supplying, or in any way cooperating with the guerrillas. Villages that could not be reached by mobile units were subject to aerial bombardment. The French also initiated a program of concentrating large segments of the rural population, including whole villages, in camps under military supervision to prevent them from aiding the rebels—or, according to the official explanation, to protect them from FLN extortion. In the three years (1957–60) during which the *regroupement* program was followed, more than 2 million Algerians were removed from their villages, mostly in the mountainous areas, and resettled in the plains, where many found it impossible to reestablish their accustomed economic or social situations. Living conditions in the camps were poor. Hundreds of empty villages were devastated, and in hundreds of others orchards and croplands were destroyed. These population transfers apparently had little strategic effect on the outcome of the war, but the disruptive social and economic effects of this massive program continued to be felt a generation later.

The French army shifted its tactics at the end of 1958 from dependence on *quadrillage* to the use of mobile forces deployed on massive search-and-destroy missions against ALN strongholds. Within the next year, Salan's successor, General Maurice Challe, appeared to have suppressed major rebel resistance. But political developments had already overtaken the French army's successes.

Committee of Public Safety

Recurrent cabinet crises focused attention on the inherent instability of the Fourth Republic and increased the misgivings of the army and of the colons that the security of Algeria was being undermined by party politics. Army commanders chafed at what they took to be inadequate and incompetent government support of military efforts to end the rebellion. The feeling was widespread that another debacle like that of Indochina in 1954 was in the offing and that the government would order another precipitate pullout and sacrifice French honor to political expediency. Many saw in de Gaulle, who had not held office since 1946, the only public figure capable of rallying the nation and giving direction to the French government.

After his tour as governor general, Soustelle had returned to France to organize support for de Gaulle's return to power, while retaining close ties to the army and the colons. By early 1958, he had organized a coup d'état, bringing together dissident army officers and colons with sympathetic Gaullists. An army junta under General Massu seized power in Algiers on the night of May 13. General Salan assumed leadership of a Committee of Public Safety formed to replace the civil authority and pressed the junta's demands that de Gaulle be named by French president René Coty to head a government of national union invested with extraordinary powers to prevent the "abandonment of Algeria." De Gaulle became premier in June and was given carte blanche to deal with Algeria.

De Gaulle

Europeans as well as many Muslims greeted de Gaulle's return to power as the breakthrough needed to end the hostilities. On his June 4 trip to Algeria, de Gaulle calculatedly made an ambiguous and broad emotional appeal to all the inhabitants, declaring "Je vous ai compris" (I have understood you). De Gaulle raised the hopes of colons and the professional military, disaffected by the indecisiveness of previous governments, with his exclamation of "Vive Algérie française" (long live French Algeria) to cheering crowds in Mostaganem. At the same time, he proposed economic, social, and political reforms to ameliorate the situation of Muslims. Nonetheless, de Gaulle later admitted to having harbored deep pessimism about the outcome of the Algerian situation even then. Meanwhile, he looked for a "third force" among Muslims and Europeans, uncontaminated by the FLN or the "ultras"—colon extremists—through whom a solution might be found.

De Gaulle immediately appointed a committee to draft a new constitution for France's Fifth Republic, which would be declared early the next year, with which Algeria would be associated but of which it would not form an integral part. Muslims, including women, were registered for the first time with Europeans on a common electoral roll to participate in a referendum to be held on the new constitution in September 1958.

De Gaulle's initiative threatened the FLN with the prospect of losing the support of the growing numbers of Muslims who were tired of the war and had never been more than lukewarm in their commitment to a totally independent Algeria. In reaction, the FLN set up the Provisional Government of the Algerian Republic (Gouvernement Provisionel de la République Algérienne—GPRA), a government-in-exile headed by Abbas and based in Tunis. Before the referendum, Abbas lobbied for international support for the GPRA, which was quickly recognized by Morocco, Tunisia, and several other Arab countries, by a number of Asian and African states, and by the Soviet Union and other East European states.

ALN commandos committed numerous acts of sabotage in France in August, and the FLN mounted a desperate campaign of terror in Algeria to intimidate Muslims into boycotting the referendum. Despite threats of reprisal, however, 80 percent of the Muslim electorate turned out to vote in September, and of these 96 percent approved the constitution. In February 1959, de Gaulle was elected president of the new Fifth Republic. He visited Constantine in October to announce a program to end the war and create an Algeria closely linked to France in which Europeans and Muslims would join as partners. De Gaulle's call on the rebel leaders to end hostilities and to participate in elections was met with adamant refusal. "The problem of a cease-fire in Algeria is not simply a military problem," said the GPRA's Abbas. "It is essentially political, and negotiation must cover the whole question of Algeria." Secret discussions that had been underway were broken off.

In 1958-59 the French army had won military control in Algeria and was the closest it would be to victory. During that period in France, however, opposition to the conflict was growing among many segments of the population. Thousands of relatives of conscripts and reserve soldiers suffered loss and pain; revelations of torture and the indiscriminate brutality the army visited on the Muslim population prompted widespread revulsion; and a significant constituency supported the principle of national liberation. International pressure was also building on France to grant Algeria independence. Annually since 1955, the UN General Assembly had considered the Algerian question, and the FLN position was gaining support. France's seeming intransigence in settling a colonial war that tied down half the manpower of its armed forces was also a source of concern to its North American Treaty Organization (NATO) allies. In a September 1959 statement, de Gaulle dramatically reversed his stand and uttered the words "self-determination," which he envisioned as leading to majority rule in an Algeria formally associated with France. In Tunis, Abbas acknowledged that de Gaulle's statement might be accepted as a basis for settlement, but the French government refused to recognize the GPRA as the representative of Algeria's Muslim community.

Claiming that de Gaulle had betrayed them, the colons, backed by units of the army, staged an insurrection in Algiers in January 1960 that won rapid support in France. As the police and army stood by, rioting colons threw up barricades in the streets and seized government buildings. In Paris, de Gaulle called on the army to remain loyal and rallied popular support for his Algeria policy in a televised address. Most of the army heeded his call, and in Algiers General Challe quickly defused the insurrection. The failure of the colon uprising and the loss of many ultra leaders who were imprisoned or transferred to other areas did not deter the militant colons. Highly organized and well-armed vigilante groups stepped up their terrorist activities, which were directed against both Muslims and progovernment Europeans, as the move toward negotiated settlement of the war and self-determination gained momentum. To the FLN rebellion against France were added civil wars between extremists in the two communities and between the ultras and the French government in Algeria.

The Generals' Putsch

Important elements of the French army and the ultras joined in another insurrection in April 1961. The leaders of this "generals' putsch" intended to seize control of Algeria as well as topple the de Gaulle regime. Units of the Foreign Legion offered prominent support, and the well-armed Secret Army Organization (Organisation de l'Armée Secrète—OAS) coordinated the participation of colon vigilantes. Although a brief fear of invasion swept Paris, the revolt collapsed in four days largely because of cooperation from the air force and army.

The "generals' putsch" marked the turning point in the official attitude toward the Algerian war. De Gaulle was now prepared to abandon the colons, the group that no previous French government could have written off. The army had been discredited by the putsch and kept a low profile politically throughout the rest of France's involvement with Algeria. Talks with the FLN reopened at Évian in May 1961; after several false starts, the French government decreed that a cease-fire would take effect on March 19, 1962. In their final form, the Évian Accords allowed the colons equal legal protection with Algerians over a three-year period. These rights included respect for property, participation in public affairs, and a full range of civil and cultural rights. At the end of that period, however, Europeans would be obliged to become Algerian citizens or be classified as aliens with the attendant loss of rights. The French electorate approved the Évian Accords by an overwhelming 91 percent vote in a referendum held in June 1962.

During the three months between the cease-fire and the French referendum on Algeria, the OAS unleashed a new terrorist campaign. The OAS sought to provoke a major breach in the cease-fire by the FLN but the terrorism now was aimed also against the French army and police enforcing the accords as well as against Muslims. It was the most wanton carnage that Algeria had witnessed in eight years of savage warfare. OAS operatives set off an average of 120 bombs per day in March, with targets including hospitals and schools. Ultimately, the terrorism failed in its objectives, and the OAS and the FLN concluded a truce on June 17, 1962. In the same month, more than 350,000 colons left Algeria. Within a year, 1.4 million refugees, including almost the entire Jewish community and some pro-French Muslims, had joined the exodus to France. Fewer than 30,000 Europeans chose to remain.

On July 1, 1962, some 6 million of a total Algerian electorate of 6.5 million cast their ballots in the referendum on independence. The vote was nearly unanimous. De Gaulle pronounced Algeria an independent country on July 3. The Provisional Executive, however, proclaimed July 5, the 132d anniversary of the French entry into Algeria, as the day of national independence.

The FLN estimated in 1962 that nearly eight years of revolution had cost 300,000 dead from war-related causes. Algerian sources later put the figure at approximately 1.5 million dead, while French officials estimated it at 350,000. French military authorities listed their losses at nearly 18,000 dead (6,000 from noncombat-related causes) and 65,000 wounded. European civilian casualties exceeded 10,000 (including 3,000 dead) in 42,000 recorded terrorist incidents. According to French figures, security forces killed 141,000 rebel combatants, and more than 12,000 Algerians died in internal FLN purges during the war. An additional 5,000 died in the "café wars" in France between the FLN and rival Algerian groups. French sources also estimated that 70,000 Muslim civilians were killed, or abducted and presumed killed, by the FLN.

Historian Alistair Horne considers that the actual figure of war dead is far higher than the original FLN and official French estimates, even if it does not reach the 1 million adopted by the Algerian government. Uncounted thousands of Muslim civilians lost their lives in French army *ratissages*, bombing raids, and vigilante reprisals. The war uprooted more than 2 million Algerians, who were forced to relocate in French concentration camps or to flee to Morocco, Tunisia, and into the Algerian hinterland, where many thousands died of starvation, disease, and exposure. Additional pro-French Muslims were killed when the FLN settled accounts after independence.

Independent Algeria, 1962-92

In preparation for independence, the CNRA had met in Tripoli in May 1962 to work out a plan for the FLN's transition from a liberation movement to a political party. The Tripoli Program called for land reform, the large-scale nationalization of industry and services, and a strong commitment to nonalignment and anticolonialism in foreign relations. The platform also envisioned the FLN as a mass organization broad enough to encompass all nationalist groups. Adoption of the Tripoli Program notwithstanding, deep personal and ideological divisions surfaced within the FLN as the war drew to a close and the date for independence approached. Competition and confrontation among various factions not only deprived the FLN of a leadership that spoke with a single voice, but also almost resulted in full-scale civil war. According to historian John Ruedy, these factions, or "clans" did not embody "family or regional loyalties, as in the Arab East, because the generations-long detribalization of Algeria had been too thorough. Rather, they represented relationships based on school, wartime or other networking."

The ALN commanders and the GPRA struggled for power, including an unsuccessful attempt to dismiss Colonel Houari Boumediene, chief of staff of the ALN in Morocco. Boumediene formed an alliance with Ben Bella, who together with Khider and Bitat, announced the formation of the Political Bureau (Bureau Politique) as a rival government to the GPRA, which had installed itself in Algiers as the Provisional Executive. Boumediene's forces entered Algiers in September, where he was joined by Ben Bella, who quickly consolidated his power. Ben Bella purged his political opponents from the single slate of candidates for the forthcoming National Assembly elections. However, underlying opposition to the Political Bureau and to the absence of alternative candidates was manifested in an 18 percent abstention rate nationwide that rose to 36 percent of the electorate in Algiers.

The creation of the Democratic and Popular Republic of Algeria was formally proclaimed at the opening session of the National Assembly on September 25, 1962. Abbas, a moderate unconnected with the Political Bureau, was elected president of the assembly by the delegates. On the following day, after being named premier, Ben Bella formed a cabinet that was representative of the Political Bureau but that also included Boumediene as defense minister as well as other members of the so-called Oujda Group, who had served under him with the external forces in Morocco. Ben Bella, Boumediene, and Khider initially formed a triumvirate linking the leadership of the three power bases—the army, the party, and the government, respectively. However, Ben Bella's ambitions and authoritarian tendencies were to lead the triumvirate to unravel and provoke increasing discontent among Algerians.

Aftermath of the War

The war of national liberation and its aftermath severely disrupted Algeria's society and economy. In addition to the physical destruction, the exodus of the colons deprived the country of most of its managers, civil servants, engineers, teachers, physicians, and skilled workers—all occupations from which the Muslim population had been excluded or discouraged from pursuing by colonial policy. The homeless and displaced numbered in the hundreds of thousands, many suffering from illness, and some 70 percent of the work force was unemployed. Distribution of goods was at a standstill. Departing colons destroyed or carried off public records and utility plans, leaving public services in a shambles.

The months immediately following independence had witnessed the pell-mell rush of Algerians, their government, and its officials to claim the lands, houses, businesses, automobiles, bank accounts, and jobs left behind by the Europeans. By the 1963 March Decrees, Ben Bella declared that all agricultural, industrial, and commercial properties previously operated and occupied by Europeans were vacant, thereby legalizing their confiscation by the state. The term *nationalization* was not used in the decrees, presumably to avoid indemnity claims.

The FLN called its policy of widespread state involvement in the economy "Algerian socialism." Public-sector enterprises were gradually organized into state corporations that participated in virtually every aspect of the country's economic life. Although their activities were coordinated by central authorities, each state corporation was supposed to retain a measure of autonomy within its own sphere.

The departure of European owners and managers from factories and agricultural estates gave rise to a spontaneous, grassroots phenomenon, later termed *autogestion*, which saw workers take control of the enterprises to keep them operating. Seeking to capitalize on the popularity of the self-management movement, Ben Bella formalized *autogestion* in the March Decrees. As the process evolved, workers in state-owned farms and enterprises and in agricultural cooperatives elected boards of managers that directed production activities, financing, and marketing in conjunction with state-appointed directors. The system proved to be a failure, however. The crucial agricultural sector suffered particularly under self-management, partly as result of bureaucratic incompetence, graft, and theft.

Ben Bella and the FLN

Whereas Ben Bella could count on the support of an overwhelming majority in the National Assembly, an opposition group led by Ait Ahmed soon emerged. Opponents outside the government included the supporters of Messali Hadj, the PCA, and the left-wing Socialist Revolution Party (Parti de la Révolution Socialiste—PRS) led by Boudiaf. The communists, who were excluded from the FLN and therefore from any direct political rule, were particularly influential in the postindependence press. The activities of all these groups were subsequently banned, and Boudiaf was arrested. When opposition from the General Union of Algerian Workers (Union Générale des Travailleurs Algériens—UGTA) was perceived, the trade union organization was subsumed under FLN control.

Contrary to the intent of the Tripoli Program, Ben Bella saw the FLN as an elite vanguard party that would mobilize popular support for government policies and reinforce his increasingly personal leadership of the country. Because Khider envisioned the FLN as playing a more encompassing, advisory role, Ben Bella forced him from office in April 1963 and replaced him as party secretary general. Khider later absconded with the equivalent of US$12 million in party funds into exile in Switzerland.

In August 1963, Abbas resigned as assembly president to protest what he termed the FLN's usurpation of the legislature's authority. He was subsequently put under house arrest. A new constitution drawn up under close FLN supervision was approved by nationwide referendum in September, and Ben Bella was confirmed as the party's choice to lead the country for a five-year term. Under the new constitution, Ben Bella as president combined the functions of chief of state and head of government with that of supreme commander of the armed forces. He formed his government without needing legislative approval and was responsible for the definition and direction of its policies. There was no effective institutional check on its powers.

Ait Ahmed quit the National Assembly to protest the increasingly dictatorial tendencies of the regime, which had reduced the functions of the legislature to rubber-stamping presidential directives. The Kabyle leaders also condemned the government for its failure to carry through on reconstruction projects in the war-ravaged Kabylie region, but Ait Ahmed's aims went beyond rectifying regional complaints. He formed a clandestine resistance movement, the Front of Socialist Forces (Front des Forces Socialistes—FFS), based in the Kabylie region and dedicated to overthrowing the Ben Bella regime by force. Late summer 1963 saw sporadic incidents attributed to the FFS and required the movement of regular troops into the Kabylie region.

More serious fighting broke out a year later in the Kabylie as well as in the southern Sahara. The insurgent movement was organized by the National Committee for the Defense of the Revolution (Comité National pour la Défense de la Révolution—CNDR), which joined the remnants of Ait Ahmed's FFS and Boudiaf's PRS with the surviving regional military leaders. Khider was believed to have helped finance the operation. The army moved quickly and in force to crush the rebellion. Ait Ahmed and Colonel Mohamed Chabaani, a *wilaya* commander leading insurgents in the Sahara, were captured and sentenced to death in 1965, after a trial in which Khider and Boudiaf were similarly condemned in absentia. Chabaani was executed, but Ait Ahmed's sentence was subsequently commuted to life imprisonment. In 1966 he escaped from prison and fled to Europe where he joined the two other *chefs historiques* in exile.

As minister of defense, Boumediene had no qualms about sending the army to crush regional uprisings when he felt they posed a threat to the state. However, when Ben Bella attempted to co-opt allies from among some of the same regionalists whom the army had been called out to suppress, tensions increased between Boumediene and Ben Bella. In April 1965, Ben Bella issued orders to local police prefects to report directly to him rather than through normal channels in the Ministry of Interior. The minister, Ahmed Medeghri, one of Boumediene's closest associates in the Oujda Group, resigned his portfolio in protest and was replaced by a Political Bureau loyalist. Ben Bella next sought to remove Abdelaziz Bouteflika, another Boumediene confidant, as minister of foreign affairs and was believed to be planning a direct confrontation with Boumediene to force his ouster. On June 19, however, Boumediene deposed Ben Bella in a military coup d'état that was both swift and bloodless. The ousted president was taken into custody and held incommunicado.

Boumediene Regime

Boumediene described the military coup as a "historic rectification" of the Algerian War of Independence. Boumediene dissolved the National Assembly, suspended the 1963 constitution, disbanded the militia, and abolished the Political Bureau, which he considered an instrument of Ben Bella's personal rule.

Until a new constitution was adopted, political power resided in the Council of the Revolution, a predominantly military body intended to foster cooperation among various factions in the army and the party. The council's original twenty-six members included former internal military leaders, former Political Bureau members, and senior officers of the Armée Nationale Populaire (ANP—People's National Army) closely associated with Boumediene in the coup. They were expected to exercise collegial responsibility for overseeing the activities of the new government, which was conducted by the largely civilian Council of Ministers, or cabinet, appointed by Boumediene. The cabinet, which shared some functions with the Council of the Revolution, was also inclusive; it contained an Islamic leader, technical experts, FLN regulars, as well as others representing a broad range of Algerian political and institutional life.

Boumediene showed himself to be an ardent nationalist, deeply influenced by Islamic values, and he was reportedly one of the few prominent Algerian leaders who expressed himself better in Arabic than in French. He seized control of the country not to initiate military rule, but to protect the interests of the army, which he felt were threatened by Ben Bella. Boumediene's position as head of government and of state was not secure initially, partly because of his lack of a significant power base outside the armed forces. This situation may have accounted for his deference to collegial rule as a means of reconciling competing factions. Nonetheless, FLN radicals criticized Boumediene for neglecting the policy of *autogestion* and betraying "rigorous socialism"; in addition, some military officers were unsettled by what they saw as a drift away from collegiality. There were coup attempts and a failed assassination in 1967-68, after which opponents were exiled or imprisoned and Boumediene's power consolidated.

Agricultural production, meanwhile, still failed to meet the country's food needs. The so-called agricultural revolution that Boumediene launched in 1971 called for the seizure of additional property and the redistribution of the newly acquired public lands to cooperative farms (see Land Tenure and Reform, ch. 3).

Eleven years after he took power, in April 1976, Boumediene set out in a draft document called the National Charter the principles on which the long-promised constitution would be based. After much public debate, the constitution was promulgated in November 1976, and Boumediene was elected president with 95 percent of the votes (see Structure of the National Government, ch. 4). Boumediene's death on December 27, 1978, set off a struggle within the FLN to choose a successor. As a compromise to break a deadlock between two other candidates, Colonel Chadli Benjedid, a relative outsider, was sworn in on February 9, 1979.

Chadli Benjedid and Afterward

Benjedid, who had collaborated with Boumediene in the plot that deposed Ben Bella, was regarded as a moderate not identified with any group or faction; he did, however, command wide support within the military establishment. In June 1980, he summoned an extraordinary FLN Party Congress to examine the draft of the five-year development plan for 1980-84. The resultant First Five-Year Plan liberalized the economy and broke up unwieldy state corporations (see Development Planning, ch. 3).

The Benjedid regime was also marked by protests from Berber university students who objected to arabization measures in government and especially in education. Although Benjedid reaffirmed the government's long-term commitment to arabization, he upgraded Berber studies at the university level and granted media access to Berber-language programs. These concessions, however, provoked counterprotests from Islamists (also seen as fundamentalists).

The Islamists gained increasing influence in part because the government was unable to keep its economic promises (see The Islamist Factor, ch. 4). In the late 1970s, Muslim activists engaged in isolated and relatively small-scale assertions of their will: harassing women whom they felt were inappropriately dressed, smashing establishments that served alcohol, and evicting official imams from their mosques. The Islamists escalated their actions in 1982, when they called for the abrogation of the National Charter and the formation of an Islamic government. Amidst an increasing number of violent incidents on campuses, Islamists killed one student. After police arrested 400 Islamists, about 100,000 demonstrators thronged to Friday prayers at the university mosque. The arrests of hundreds more activists, including prominent leaders of the movement, Shaykh Abdelatif Sultani and Shaykh Ahmed Sahnoun, resulted in a lessening of Islamist actions for several years. Nonetheless, in light of the massive support the Islamists could muster, the authorities henceforth viewed them as a potentially grave threat to the state and alternately treated them with harshness and respect. In 1984, for example, the government opened in Constantine one of the largest Islamic universities in the world. In the same year, acceding to Islamist demands, the government changed family status law to deprive women of freedom to act on their own by making them wards of their families before marriage and of their husbands after marriage.

The country's economic crisis deepened in the mid-1980s, resulting in, among other things, increased unemployment, a lack of consumer goods, and shortages in cooking oil, semolina, coffee, and tea. Women waited in long lines for scarce and expensive food; young men milled in frustration on street corners unable to find work. An already bad situation was aggravated by the huge drop in world oil prices in 1986. Dismantling Algeria's state-controlled economic system seemed to Benjedid the only way to improve the economy. In 1987 he announced reforms that would return control and profits to private hands, starting with agriculture and continuing to the large state enterprises and banks.

Notwithstanding the introduction of reform measures, incidents indicating social unrest increased in Algiers and other cities as the economy foundered from 1985 to 1988. The alienation and anger of the population were fanned by the widespread perception that the government had become corrupt and aloof. The waves of discontent crested in October 1988 when a series of strikes and walkouts by students and workers in Algiers degenerated into rioting by thousands of young men, who destroyed government and FLN property. When the violence spread to Annaba, Blida, Oran, and other cities and towns, the government declared a state of emergency and began using force to quell the unrest. By October 10, the security forces had restored a semblance of order; unofficial estimates were that more than 500 people were killed and more than 3,500 arrested.

The stringent measures used to put down the riots of "Black October" engendered a ground swell of outrage. Islamists took control of some areas. Unsanctioned independent organizations of lawyers, students, journalists, and physicians sprang up to demand justice and change. In response, Benjedid conducted a house cleaning of senior officials and drew up a program of political reform. In December he was offered the chance to implement the reforms when he was reelected, albeit by a reduced margin. A new constitution, approved overwhelmingly in February 1989, dropped the word *socialist* from the official description of the country; guaranteed freedoms of expression, association, and meeting; and withdrew the guarantees of women's rights that appeared in the 1976 constitution. The FLN was not mentioned in the document at all, and the army was discussed only in the context of national defense, reflecting a significant downgrading of its political status.

Politics were reinvigorated in 1989 under the new laws. Newspapers became the liveliest and freest in the Arab world, while political parties of nearly every stripe vied for members and a voice. In February 1989, Abbassi Madani and Ali Belhadj (also seen as Benhadj) founded the Islamic Salvation Front (Front Islamique du Salut—FIS). Although the constitution prohibited religious parties, the FIS came to play a significant role in Algerian politics. It handily defeated the FLN in local and provincial elections held in June 1990, in part because most secular parties boycotted the elections. The FLN's response was to adopt a new electoral law that openly aided the FLN. The FIS, in turn, called a general strike, organized demonstrations, and occupied public places. Benjedid declared martial law on June 5, 1991, but he also asked his minister of foreign affairs, Sid Ahmed Ghozali, to form a new government of national reconciliation. Although the FIS seemed satisfied with Ghozali's appointment and his attempts to clean up the electoral law, it continued to protest, leading the army to arrest Belhadj, Madani, and hundreds of others. The state of emergency ended in September.

Algeria's leaders were stunned in December 1991 when FIS candidates won absolute majorities in 188 of 430 electoral districts, far ahead of the FLN's fifteen seats. Some members of Benjedid's cabinet, fearing a complete FIS takeover, forced the president to dissolve parliament and to resign on January 11, 1992. Leaders of the takeover included Ghozali, and generals Khaled Nezzar (minister of defense) and Larbi Belkheir (minister of interior). After they declared the elections void, the takeover leaders and Mohamed Boudiaf formed the High Council of State to rule the country. The FIS, as well as the FLN, clamored for a return of the electoral process, but police and troops countered with massive arrests. In February 1992, violent demonstrations broke out in many cities, and on February 9 the government declared a one-year state of emergency and the next month banned the FIS.

The end of FLN rule over Algeria opened a period of uncertain transition. Widespread discontent with the party stemmed from many roots. People were frustrated and angry because they had no voice in their own affairs, had few or no prospects for employment, and had a deteriorating standard of living. In addition, the poor and the middle class grew outraged over the privileges enjoyed by party members, and many Algerians became alienated by what they felt was the unwelcome encroachment of secular, or Western, values. Algeria's brief democratic interlude unleashed these pent-up feelings, and, as in earlier periods of the country's history, the language of Islam served many as the preferred medium of social and political protest.

* * *

Whereas the vast majority of the historical writings on Algeria are in French, several excellent works are available in English. John Ruedy's *Modern Algeria* provides a masterful synthesis and analysis focusing on the period from the French occupation to early 1992. *Land Policy in Colonial Algeria* by the same author is also interesting. *A History of the Maghrib in the Islamic Period* by Jamil Abu-Nasr provides a thoughtful and detailed look at the region going back to the Arab conquests. For an in-depth treatment of the struggle for independence, especially political and military affairs, see Alistair Horne's *A Savage War of Peace*. For the precolonial period, see Charles-André Julien's *Histoire de l'Afrique du nord*. Julien's *Histoire de l'Algérie contemporaine* and Charles-Robert Ageron's book by the same title cover the colonial period. Raphael Danziger's *Abd al-Qadir and the Algerians* is a serious and comprehensive study of this national hero. (For further information and complete citations, see Bibliography.)

Chapter 2. The Society and Its Environment

Modern domed houses at El Oued in eastern Algeria

ALGERIAN SOCIETY has undergone major changes since the mid-1980s. Urbanization has increased steadily, and in 1990 more than 50 percent of the population lived in urban areas, found primarily near the coast. Furthermore, dislocation caused by the steep fall of oil prices in 1986 and inefficiencies in the public sector caused the government to initiate extensive reforms encompassing the economic, social, and political sectors. The government shifted from its rigid centralized system of decision making to a greater emphasis on market forces. With the help of international organizations such as the World Bank (see Glossary), major transformations began taking place in agriculture, banking, and in price controls, thereby changing Algeria's socioeconomic structure. The government also increased public expenditures in the early 1990s to upgrade education and health care.

Despite those positive changes, the early 1990s have seen a rise in unemployment, a drop in per capita income, critical housing shortages, and other problems. In part, these problems resulted from the policies of previous governments, but they were exacerbated by the sharp downturn in oil prices in the mid-1980s. Further affecting Algeria's progress on the socioeconomic front has been the political turmoil resulting from the confrontation between government forces and Islamists (sometimes seen as fundamentalists). Islamists have sought to redefine Algerian identity to be more Arab and more Muslim and have questioned the legitimacy of the existing political system, which they perceive as too secular and too Western.

Physical Setting

Algeria comprises 2,381,741 square kilometers, more than four-fifths of which is desert. Its Arabic name, Al Jazair (the islands), is believed to derive from the rocky islands along the Mediterranean coastline. The northern portion, an area of mountains, valleys, and plateaus between the Mediterranean Sea and the Sahara Desert, forms an integral part of the section of North Africa known as the Maghrib (see Glossary). This area includes Morocco, Tunisia, and the northwestern portion of Libya known historically as Tripolitania (see fig. 4).

Algeria: A Country Study

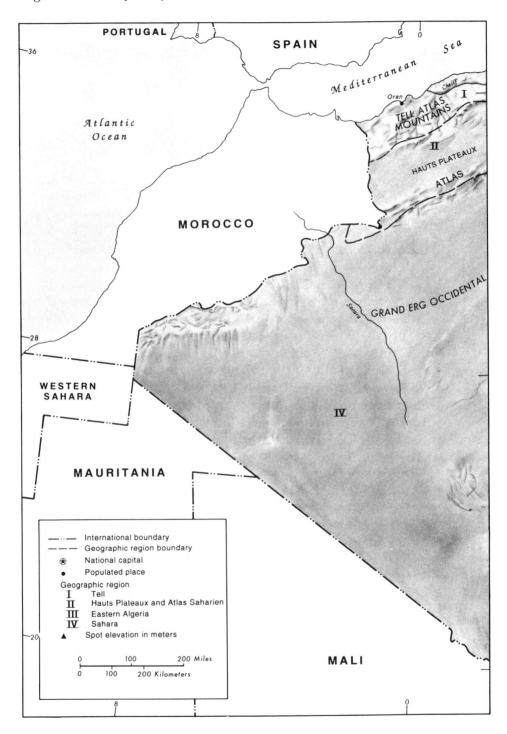

Figure 4. Topography and Drainage

The Society and Its Environment

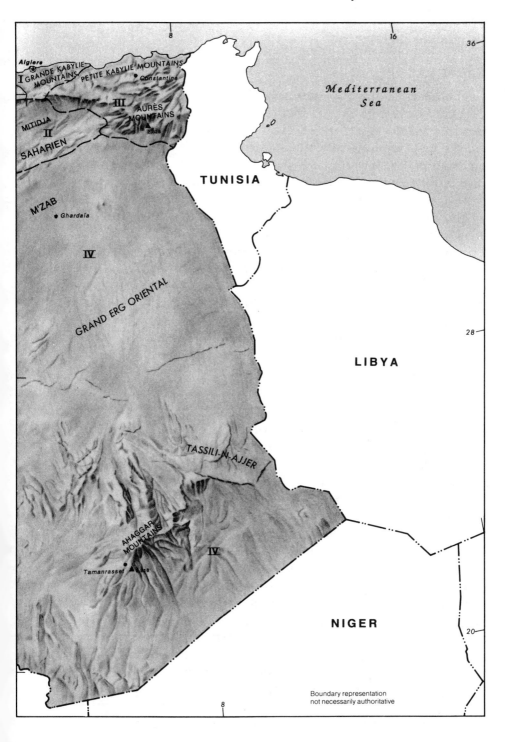

Geographic Regions

The Tell

The fertile Tell is the country's heartland, containing most of its cities and population. Made up of hills and plains of the narrow coastal region, the several Tell Atlas mountain ranges, and the intermediate valleys and basins, the Tell extends eastward from the Moroccan border to the mountains of the Grande Kabylie and the Bejaïa Plain on the east. Its eastern terminus is the Soummam River.

The best agricultural areas are the gentle hills extending 100 kilometers westward from Algiers; the Mitidja Plain, which was a malarial swamp before being cleared by the French; and the Bejaïa Plain. The alluvial soils in these areas permitted the French to establish magnificent vineyards and citrus groves. By contrast, in the great valley of the Chelif River and other interior valleys and basins, aridity and excessive summer heat have limited the development of agriculture. The Grande Kabylie is a zone of impoverished small farm villages tucked into convoluted mountains.

The High Plateaus and the Saharan Atlas

Stretching more than 600 kilometers eastward from the Moroccan border, the High Plateaus (often referred to by their French name Hauts Plateaux) consist of undulating, steppelike plains lying between the Tell and Saharan Atlas ranges. The plateaus average between 1,100 and 1,300 meters in elevation in the west, dropping to 400 meters in the east. So dry that they are sometimes thought of as part of the Sahara, the plateaus are covered by alluvial debris formed when the mountains eroded. An occasional ridge projects through the alluvial cover to interrupt the monotony of the landscape.

Higher and more continuous than the Tell Atlas, the Sahara Atlas range is formed of three massifs: the Ksour near the Moroccan border, the Amour, and the Oulad Nail south of Algiers. The mountains, which receive more rainfall than those of the High Plateaus, include some good grazing land. Watercourses on the southern slopes of these massifs disappear into the desert but supply the wells of numerous oases along the northern edge of the desert, of which Biskra, Laghouat, and Béchar are the most prominent.

Northeastern Algeria

Eastern Algeria consists of a massif area extensively dissected into mountains, plains, and basins. It differs from the western portion of the country in that its prominent topographic features do not parallel the coast. In its southern sector, the steep cliffs and long ridges of the Aurès Mountains create an almost impenetrable refuge that has played an important part in the history of the Maghrib since Roman times. Near the northern coast, the Petite Kabylie Mountains are separated from the Grande Kabylie range at the eastward limits of the Tell by the Soummam River. The coast is predominantly mountainous in the far eastern part of the country, but limited plains provide hinterlands for the port cities of Bejaïa, Skikda, and Annaba. In the interior of the region, extensive high plains mark the region around Sétif and Constantine; these plains were developed during the French colonial period as the principal centers of grain cultivation. Near Constantine, salt marshes offer seasonal grazing grounds to seminomadic sheep herders.

The Sahara

The Algerian portion of the Sahara extends south of the Saharan Atlas for 1,500 kilometers to the Niger and Mali frontiers. The desert is an otherworldly place, scarcely considered an integral part of the country. Far from being covered wholly by sweeps of sand, however, it is a region of great diversity. A characteristic is the *erg*, or desert area of shifting sand. Such areas occupy about one-quarter of the territory. The largest such region is the Grand Erg Oriental (Great Eastern Erg), where enormous dunes two to five meters high are spaced about forty meters apart. Much of the remainder of the desert is covered by rocky platforms called *humud* (sing., *hamada*), and almost the entire southeastern quarter is taken up by the high, complex mass of the Ahaggar and Tassili-n-Ajjer highlands, some parts of which reach more than 2,000 meters. Surrounding the Ahaggar are sandstone plateaus, cut into deep gorges by ancient rivers, and to the west a desert of pebbles stretches to the Mali frontier.

The desert consists of readily distinguishable northern and southern sectors, the northern sector extending southward a little less than half the distance to the Niger and Mali frontiers. The north, less arid than the south, supports most of the few persons who live in the region and contains most of the desert's oases. Sand dunes are the most prominent features of this area's topography, but between the desert areas of the Grand Erg Oriental and the Grand Erg Occidental (Great Western Erg) and extending north to the Atlas Saharien are plateaus, including a complex limestone structure called the Mzab where the Mzabite Berbers have settled. The southern zone of the Sahara is almost totally arid and is inhabited only by the Tuareg nomads and, recently, by oil camp workers. Barren rock predominates, but in some parts of Ahaggar and Tassili-n-Ajjer alluvial deposits permit garden farming.

Climate and Hydrology

Northern Algeria is in the temperate zone and enjoys a mild, Mediterranean climate. It lies within approximately the same latitudes as southern California and has somewhat similar climatic conditions. Its broken topography, however, provides sharp local contrasts in both prevailing temperatures and incidence of rainfall. Year-to-year variations in climatic conditions are also common.

In the Tell, temperatures in summer average between 21°C and 24°C and in winter drop to 10°C to 12°C. Winters are not cold, but the humidity is high and houses are seldom adequately heated. In eastern Algeria, the average temperatures are somewhat lower, and on the steppes of the High Plateaus winter temperatures hover only a few degrees above freezing. A prominent feature of the climate in this region is the sirocco, a dusty, choking south wind blowing off the desert, sometimes at gale force. This wind also occasionally reaches into the coastal Tell.

In Algeria only a relatively small corner of the Sahara lies across the Tropic of Cancer in the torrid zone, but even in winter, midday desert temperatures can be very hot. After sunset, however, the clear, dry air permits rapid loss of heat, and the nights are cool to chilly. Enormous daily ranges in temperature are recorded.

Rainfall is fairly abundant along the coastal part of the Tell, ranging from forty to sixty-seven centimeters annually, the amount of precipitation increasing from west to east. Precipitation is heaviest in the northern part of eastern Algeria, where it reaches as much as 100 centimeters in some years. Farther inland the rainfall is less plentiful. Prevailing winds that are easterly and northeasterly in summer change to westerly and northerly in winter and carry with them a general increase in

Landscape in Saharan area of Tassili-n-Ajjer contains needle-like rocks and petrified sand in shapes of castles and cathedrals.
Courtesy LaVerle Berry

precipitation from September to December, a decrease in the late winter and spring months, and a near absence of rainfall during the summer months.

Terrain

Clearing of land for agricultural use and cutting of timber over the centuries have severely reduced the once bountiful forest wealth. Forest fires have also taken their toll. In the higher and wetter portions of the Tell Atlas, cork oak and Aleppo pine grow in thick soils. At lower levels on thinner soils, drought-resistant shrubs predominate. The grapevine is indigenous to the coastal lowlands, and grasses and scrub cover the High Plateaus. On the Saharan Atlas, little survives of the once extensive forests of Atlas cedar that have been exploited for fuel and timber since antiquity.

The forest reserves in Algeria were severely reduced during the colonial period. In 1967 it was calculated that the country's forested area extended over no more than 2.4 million hectares of terrain, of which 1.8 million hectares were overgrown with brushwood and scrub. By contrast, woodlands in 1830 had covered 4 million hectares. In the mid-1970s, however, the government embarked on a vast reforestation program to help control erosion, which was estimated to affect 100,000 cubic meters of arable land annually. Among projects was one to create a *barrage vert* (green barrier) more or less following the ridge line of the Saharan Atlas and extending from Morocco to the Tunisian frontier in a zone 1,500 kilometers long and up to twenty kilometers wide.

The *barrage vert* consists principally of Aleppo pine, a species that can thrive in areas of scanty rainfall. It is designed to restore a damaged ecological balance and to halt the northern encroachment of the Sahara. By the early 1980s, the desert had already penetrated the hilly gap between the Saharan Atlas and the Aurès Mountains as far as the town of Bou Saâda, a point well within the High Plateaus region. The *barrage vert* project was ended in the late 1980s because of lack of funds.

Population

Demographic Profile

Algeria's population in January 1990 was 25.1 million, of whom 12.4 million were female and almost 12.7 were male. The figure compared with 12 million recorded in the 1966 census, 8.7 million on the eve of the War of Independence in 1954, and 4 million at the turn of the century. During the first twenty years after independence in 1962, the population doubled. The United States government estimate of Algeria's population in 1993 was 27.4 million, and projections were that there would be 32.5 million people in the country by the year 2000.

Various French censuses conducted during the colonial period were inexact surveys relying on such techniques as counting tents and multiplying by six to determine the number of nomads. The surveys were enough, however, to paint a picture of a quickening rate of population growth, the average annual rate of increase rising from 0.5 percent between 1900 and 1910 to 2.7 percent between 1950 and 1955. During the period of hostilities that extended from 1954 to 1962, the population grew at a greatly reduced rate because of the number of people killed in the war. The exact number of deaths is not known; French officials estimated it at 350,000, but Algerians placed it at 1.5 million.

Population growth resumed at the end of hostilities, and in 1966 the annual growth rate was estimated at 3.3 percent. Subsequently, the rate rose to 3.4 percent before subsiding to 3.2

The Society and Its Environment

percent in the late 1970s, 3.1 in the early 1980s, and 2.8 percent for the 1990s, according to World Bank projections.

The crude birth rate per 1,000 inhabitants fell in 1989 to 34.3 from 45 in 1985, 48.8 for the 1970 to 1975 period, and 50.4 for the 1960 to 1965 period, as estimated by the Population Division of the Department of Economic and Social Affairs of the United Nations (UN) and by the World Bank. Under progressively improving conditions of health and sanitation, the crude death rate declined from twenty-four deaths per 1,000 in the period from 1950 to 1955 to eighteen per 1,000 in 1965, three years after independence. By 1990 it had fallen to eight per 1,000. Life expectancy at birth rose from forty-two years for males and forty-four for females in the 1950 to 1955 period, to forty-nine years for males and fifty-one years for females in 1965, to sixty-five years for males and sixty-six for females in 1990, a marked improvement reflecting the major transformations in the health sector.

From the mid-1960s to the mid-1970s, the average Algerian woman produced seven to eight children. The figure rose to slightly more than nine for women who married before the age of eighteen, but fell to nearly seven in the case of females who married after the age of twenty-one. The birth rate was only slightly lower in urban than in rural areas. In 1990 it was estimated that the total fertility rate had fallen to 5.1 children per woman, a considerable decline.

The 1966 census showed that the population was very young; some 48.2 percent of Algerians were under the age of fifteen. The 1977 census confirmed this pattern, although the age-group under fifteen declined slightly to 47.9 percent of the population. By 1990, only 40.6 percent of the population (10.6 million Algerians) were under the age of fifteen. The proportion of the population under nineteen also showed signs of decline. In the mid-1980s, official sources reported that about 57 percent of the population was under age nineteen, but by 1990 that age-group constituted just over one-half the population, or 51.2 percent, a drop of almost 6 percentage points in five years.

In terms of age structure, detailed data showed that in 1990 males were slightly more numerous than females at birth and through the forty- to forty-four age-group. Thereafter, women predominated in all age categories because of the somewhat higher death rates for men than for women in the higher age-groups (see fig. 5).

Migration

Two major external migratory movements have reshaped the settlement pattern since World War II: the abrupt departure of most of the European colonists in 1962 and 1963 and the flow of Algerian workers to the European continent—chiefly to France. In 1945 Algerian workers and their families in France numbered about 350,000, and in 1964 they numbered an estimated 500,000. By the early 1980s, they totaled 800,000, according to official French figures. About 350,000 were male workers, the remainder being women and children under seventeen years of age. Many were from the Kabylie, a poor agricultural region that suffered severely during the War of Independence. In addition to these migrants, 400,000 *harkis* (Algerians who served with the French army in the War of Independence) resided permanently in France, mostly in the south.

In 1968 the Algerian and French governments set a quota on migrants of 35,000 per year, which was reduced to 25,000 in 1971. Although Algeria suspended all migration to France in 1973, an estimated 7,000 Algerians nonetheless continued to migrate illegally each year at the end of the 1970s. In the mid-1970s, both France and Algeria offered incentives to migrants to return home, one of them being guaranteed housing. Although figures were hard to obtain, it appeared that few responded to these gestures.

The economic crisis in Europe in the aftermath of the Arab oil embargo of 1973 led to a recession that affected Algerians as well as other North Africans working in Europe, primarily in France. Because of rising unemployment, French trade unions began to agitate against migrant workers, claiming that they took jobs from French men and women. Governments in France and other European countries instituted new policies to control migration from North Africa and other parts of the developing world.

The impact of those new policies had a paradoxical effect on Algerian and other North African migrants in France. They had been quite content until then to move back and forth between France and their homeland, never quite settling in France, and generally keeping their families in Algeria, Tunisia, or Morocco. After the new policies were instituted, migrants feared that they might never be able to return to France if they went home to visit their families. Rather than risk losing their residence abroad, many migrants opted to bring their families to Europe and set up more permanent forms of residence there.

French trade unions reacted by formulating policies that restricted the rights of migrant workers even more than before. By 1980 Algerians and other North African workers had lost their union rights and benefits, and by 1984 the unions that had sprung up to represent the migrants were no longer insisting that they have the same economic and social rights as the indigenous work force. Whereas in 1974 French trade union resolutions stated that migration had to be contained, a decade later they had taken the position that migration had to be stopped.

To make matters worse, Algerians and other migrants from the Maghrib were always perceived as migrant workers and so were rarely naturalized in France. The majority, therefore, in the early 1990s had no voice in the French political system and did not represent a political force or even an interest group that could exert pressure to defend its rights. Their visibility and vulnerability, however, made them an easy target for those who wished to find scapegoats for the problems ailing European economies.

Urbanization and Density

Data from the World Bank's *World Development Report, 1992* indicated that in 1990 about 52 percent of the Algerian population lived in urban regions. By comparison, in 1981 the UN estimated the urbanized segment of the population at 44 percent, up from 41 percent in 1977 and 30 percent in 1960. Urbanization has occurred in part through population growth, which has converted villages into towns and towns into cities, but urban migration has played at least as important a role. During the decade of the 1970s, unofficial estimates held that 1.7 million peasants settled in Algiers, Oran, Constantine, and Annaba, a continuation of the enormous shift in population from the countryside to the cities that began at independence. The largest cities attracted many of these migrants, but the 1977 census showed that many smaller towns and cities grew even faster, probably because of economic and administrative decentralization efforts during the 1970s. Algiers remained the largest urbanized area. A city of fewer than 500,000 people with a predominantly European population in 1954, it increased to nearly 1 million inhabitants by 1966 despite the loss of most of its European inhabitants. In 1987 census figures showed that

Algeria: A Country Study

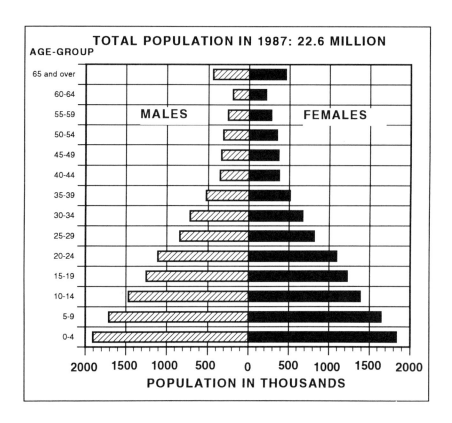

Figure 5. *Population by Age and Gender, 1987*

Source: Based on information from United Nations, *Demographic Yearbook, 1991,* New York, 1992, 152–53.

Algiers proper contained 1,483,000 inhabitants and was still growing. Algeria's other major cities also grew between 1977 and 1987: Oran's population increased from 490,000 to 590,000; Constantine from 344,000 to 438,000; Annaba from 240,000 to 310,000; Batna from 102,000 to 182,000; Sétif from 129,000 to 168,000; and Blida from 138,000 to 165,000.

In the mid-1980s the pace of urbanization, estimated unofficially at 5.6 percent per year, was causing concern to planning authorities, who were endeavoring to slow its tempo if not stop it altogether. Government-sponsored agrarian reform programs and investment in rural housing were initiated to improve the quality of farm life and thus to stabilize the rural population. It was hoped that these same measures would relieve the acute pressure on urban housing, a by-product of massive urbanization.

According to Algerian government figures, 87 percent of the population resided on 17 percent of the nation's land. The population density, averaging 10.5 inhabitants per square kilometer in mid-1990, varied enormously from 2,500 per square kilometer in Algiers to less than one per square kilometer in the mid-Sahara. All major cities and most of the rural population occupied a quadrilateral that extended about 100 kilometers from the coast and stretched from Morocco to Tunisia. Within this area, there was a difference in the way the land was used. In the west, formerly the area of French vineyards and citrus groves, was a region of socialized *autogestion* (see Glossary) farms. A short distance east of Algiers, the land rises toward the Kabylie and Aurès mountain zones of eastern Algeria. In an area only about two hours distant by highway from Algiers, a densely packed rural population continues to live in remote mountain areas, sheltered from outside influences and maintaining Berber languages and customs in their purest forms.

In the heavily populated northern part of the country, the average population density does not change substantially from west to east. Farther inland the population density declines progressively southward through the High Plateaus and the Saharan Atlas mountains, averaging from forty-nine persons down to ten people per square kilometer. Within the Sahara, the same trend of diminishing population from north to south is evident. In the northern half of the Sahara, road distances between populated oases seldom exceed 170 kilometers. The southern half of the Algerian Sahara, however, is peopled by only a few thousand Tuareg. The only town of any importance is Tamanrasset, deep in the Ahaggar highlands.

Ethnic Groups and Languages

The Peoples

The origins of the Berbers are unclear; a number of waves of people, some from Western Europe, some from sub-Saharan Africa, and others from Northeast Africa, eventually settled in North Africa and made up its indigenous population. Because present-day Berbers and the overwhelming majority of the Arabs largely descend from the same indigenous stock, physical distinctions carry little or no social connotation and are in most instances impossible to make. The term *Berber* is derived from the Greeks, who used it to refer to the people of North Africa. The term was retained by the Romans, Arabs, and other groups who occupied the region, but is not used by the people themselves. Identification with the Berber or Arab community is largely a matter of personal choice rather than of membership in discrete and bounded social entities. In addition to their own language, many adult Berbers also speak Arabic and French; for centuries Berbers have entered the general society and merged, within a generation or two, into the Arab group.

This permeable boundary between the two major ethnic groups permits a good deal of movement and, along with other factors, prevents the development of rigid and exclusive ethnic blocs. It appears that whole groups slipped across the ethnic "boundary" in the past—and others may do so in the future. In areas of linguistic contiguity, bilingualism is common, and in most cases Arabic eventually comes to predominate.

Algerian Arabs, or native speakers of Arabic, include descendants of Arab invaders and of indigenous Berbers. Since 1966, however, the Algerian census no longer has had a category for Berbers; thus, it is only an estimate that Algerian Arabs, the major ethnic group of the country, constitute 80 percent of Algeria's people and are culturally and politically dominant. The mode of life of Arabs varies from region to region. Nomadic herders are found in the desert, settled cultivators and gardeners in the Tell, and urban dwellers on the coast. Linguistically, the various Arab groups differ little from each other, except that dialects spoken by nomadic and seminomadic peoples are thought to be derived from beduin dialects; the dialects spoken by the sedentary population of the north are thought to stem from those of early seventh-century invaders. Urban Arabs are more apt to identify with the Algerian nation, whereas ethnic loyalties of more remote rural Arabs are likely to be limited to the tribe.

The major Berber groups are the Kabyles of the Kabylie Mountains east of Algiers and the Chaouia of the Aurès range south of Constantine. Smaller groups include the Mzab of the northern Sahara region and the Tuareg of the southern Ahaggar highlands, both of which have clearly definable characteristics. The Berber peasantry can also be found in the Atlas Mountains close to Blida, and on the massifs of Dahra and Ouarsenis on either side of the Chelif River valley. Altogether, the Berbers constitute about 20 percent of the population.

In the hills north of the Chelif River and in some other parts of the Tell, Berbers live in villages among the sedentary Arabs, not sharply distinguished in their way of life from the Arabic speakers but maintaining their own language and a sense of ethnic identity. In addition, in some oasis towns of the Algerian Sahara, small Berber groups remain unassimilated to Arab culture and retain their own language and some of their cultural differences.

By far the largest of the Berber-speaking groups, the Kabyles, do not refer to themselves as Berbers but as Imazighen or, in the singular, as Amazigh, which means noble or free men. Some traces of the original blue-eyed and blond-haired Berbers survive to contrast the people from this region with the darker-skinned Arabic speakers of the plains. The land is poor, and the pressure of a dense and rapidly growing population has forced many to migrate to France or to the coastal cities. Kabyles can be found in every part of the country, but in their new environments they tend to gather and to retain some of their clan solidarity and sense of ethnic identity.

Kabyle villages, built on the crests of hills, are close-knit, independent, social and political units composed of a number of extended patrilineal kin groups. Traditionally, local government consisted of a *jamaa* (village council), which included all adult males and legislated according to local custom and law. Efforts to modify this democratic system were only partially successful, and the *jamaa* has continued to function alongside the civil administration. The majority of Berber mountain peasants hold their land as *mulk*, or private property, in contrast to those of the valleys and oases where the tribe retains certain rights over land controlled by its members.

Set apart by their habitat, language, and well-organized village and social life, Kabyles have a highly developed sense of independence and group solidarity. They have generally opposed incursions of Arabs and Europeans into their region, and much of the resistance activity during the War of Independence was concentrated in the Kabylie region. Major Kabyle uprisings took place against the French in 1871, 1876, and 1882; the Chaouia rebelled in 1879.

Perhaps half as numerous as the Kabyles and less densely settled, the Chaouia have occupied the rugged Aurès Mountains of eastern Algeria since their retreat to that region from Tunisia during the Arab invasions of the Middle Ages. In the north they are settled agriculturalists, growing grain in the uplands and fruit trees in the valleys. In the arid south, with its date-palm oases, they are seminomadic, shepherding flocks to the high plains during the summer. The distinction between the two groups is limited, however, because the farmers of the north are also drovers, and the seminomads of the south maintain plots of land.

In the past, the Chaouia lived in isolation broken only by visits of Kabyle peddlers and Saharan camel raisers, and relatively few learned to speak either French or Arabic. Like their society, their economy was self-sufficient and closed. Emigration was limited, but during the War of Independence the region was a stronghold of anti-French sentiment, and more than one-half of the population was removed to concentration camps. During the postindependence era, the ancient Chaouia isolation has lessened.

Far less numerous than their northern Berber kin are the Mzab, whose number was estimated at 100,000 in the mid-1980s. They live beside the Oued Mzab, from which comes their name. Ghardaïa is their largest and most important oasis community. The Mzab are Ibadi (see Glossary) Muslims who practice a puritanical form of Islam that emphasizes asceticism, literacy for men and women, and social egalitarianism.

The Mzab used to be important in trans-Saharan trade but now have moved into other occupations. Some of their members have moved to the cities, where in Algiers, for example, they dominate the grocery and butchery business. They have also extended their commerce south to sub-Saharan Africa, where they and other tribal people trade with cash and letters of exchange, make loans on the harvest, and sell on credit.

Of all Berber subgroups, the Tuareg until recently have been the least affected by the outside world. Known as "the blue men" because of their indigo-dyed cotton robes and as "people of the veil" because the men—but not the women—always veil, the Tuareg inhabit the Sahara from southwest Libya to Mali. In southern Algeria, they are concentrated in the highlands of Tassili-n-Ajjer and Ahaggar and in the 1970s were estimated to number perhaps 5,000 to 10,000. They are organized into tribes and, at least among the Ahaggar Tuareg, into a three-tiered class system of nobles, vassals, and slaves and servants, the last group often being of negroid origin. Tuareg women enjoy high status and many privileges. They do not live in seclusion, and their social responsibilities equal those of men.

Tuareg tribesmen dancing
Courtesy ANEP

A Kabyle woman
Courtesy Nadia Benchallal and
Middle East Report

In the past, the Tuareg were famed as camel and cattle herdsmen and as guides and protectors of caravans that plied between West Africa and North Africa. Both occupations have greatly declined during the twentieth century under the impact of colonial and independent government policies, technology, and consumerism associated with the hydrocarbon industry and, most recently, drought. The result has been the breakup of the old social hierarchy and gradual sedentarization around such oases as Djanet and Tamanrasset.

Although of considerable importance before independence, the non-Muslim minorities have shrunk to a mere fraction of their former size. Immediately after independence, approximately 1 million Europeans, including 140,000 Jews, left the country. Most of the Europeans who left had French citizenship, and all identified with French rather than Arab culture and society. During colonial times, the Algerian and European groups had effectively formed two separate subsocieties having little social interaction or intermarriage except among highly Europeanized Algerians.

In the early 1980s, the total foreign population was estimated at roughly 117,000. Of this number, about 75,000 were Europeans, including about 45,000 French. Many foreigners worked as technicians and teachers.

Languages: Arabic and Berber

Except for Europeans, ethnic communities in Algeria were distinguished primarily by language. Before the arrival of Arabic-speaking invaders, Berber was the language of the indigenous population. Arabic encroached gradually, spreading through the areas most accessible to migrants and conquerors. Berber remained the mother tongue in many rural areas.

Arabic, the language of the majority and the official language of the country, is a Semitic tongue related to Hebrew, Aramaic, and Amharic. The dominant language throughout North Africa and the Middle East, Arabic was introduced to the coastal regions by the Arab conquerors of the seventh and eighth centuries A.D. (see Islam and the Arabs, 642–1830, ch. 1). Arabic language and culture had an even greater impact under the influence of the beduin Arabs, who arrived in greater numbers from the eleventh century onward.

Written Arabic is psychologically and sociologically important as the vehicle of Islam and Arab culture and as the link with other Arab countries. Two forms are used: the classical

Arabic of the Quran and Algerian dialectical Arabic. Classical Arabic is the essential base of written Arabic and formal speech throughout the Arab world. It is the vehicle of a vast religious, scientific, historical, and literary heritage. Arabic scholars or individuals with a good classical education from any country can converse with one another.

In classical Arabic as in other Semitic scripts, only the consonants are written; vowel signs and other diacritical marks to aid in pronunciation are employed occasionally in printed texts. The script is cursive, lending itself to use as decoration.

There has been considerable borrowing of words between Berber and Arabic. In some Arabic-speaking areas, the words for various flora and fauna are still in Berber, and Berber place-names are numerous throughout the country, some of them borrowed. Examples of Berber place-names are Illizi, Skikda, Tamanrasset, Tipasa, and Tizi Ouzou.

Berber is primarily a spoken language, although an ancient Berber script called *tifinagh* survives among the Tuareg of the Algerian Sahara, where the characters are used more for special purposes than for communication. Several Berber dialect groups are recognized in modern Algeria, but only Kabyle and Chaouia are spoken by any considerable number. The Chaouia dialect, which is distinguishable from but related to Kabyle, bears the mark and influence of Arabic. Separate dialects, however, are spoken by the Tuareg and by the Mzab.

Arabization

Of all Arab countries subject to European rule, Algeria absorbed the heaviest colonial impact. The French controlled education, government, business, and most intellectual life for 132 years and through a policy of cultural imperialism attempted to suppress Algerian cultural identity and to remold the society along French lines. The effects of this policy, which continued to reverberate throughout Algeria after 1962, have perhaps been most evident in the legacy of a dual language system.

French colonial policy was explicitly designed to "civilize" the country by imposing French language and culture on it. A French report written on the eve of the French conquest noted that in 1830 the literacy rate in Algeria was 40 percent, a remarkable rate even by modern standards. Quranic schools were primarily responsible for literacy in Algeria, as reading meant being able to learn the Quran. Twenty years later, only half the schools continued to operate as a result of the French colonial policy of dismantling the existing education system and replacing it with a French system.

As a result, education was oriented toward French, and advanced education in literary Arabic declined drastically. Dialectical Arabic remained the language of everyday discourse among the vast majority of the population, but it was cut off from contemporary intellectual and technological developments and consequently failed to develop the flexibility and vocabulary needed for modern bureaucratic, financial, and intellectual affairs.

The better schools and the University of Algiers aimed at comparability with French institutions and prepared students for French examinations. Gradually, a small but influential French-speaking indigenous elite was formed, who competed with European colonists for jobs in the modern sector. Berbers, or more specifically, Kabyles, were represented in disproportionately large numbers in this elite because the French, as part of their "divide and rule" policy, deliberately favored Kabyles in education and employment in the colonial system. As a result, in the years after independence Kabyles moved into all levels of state administration across Algeria, where they remained a large and influential group.

In reaction to French cultural and linguistic imperialism, the leaders of the War of Independence (1954–62) and successive governments committed themselves to reviving indigenous Arabic and Islamic cultural values and to establishing Arabic as the national language. The aim was to recover the precolonial past and to use it, together with Arabic, to restore—if not create—a national identity and personality for the new state and population. Translated into an official policy called arabization, it was consistently supported by arabists, who were ascendant in the Algerian government following independence. Their goal was a country where the language (Arabic), religion (Islam), and national identity (Algerian) were free, as far as practical, of French language and influence.

Culturally, the emphasis was on developing the various forms of public communication and on cultivating Algerian themes that could then be popularized through these media. The major effort, however, centered on language, and it was the quest for a "national" language that became the hallmark of arabization and that has aroused the most controversy and outright opposition.

Beginning in the late 1960s, the government of President Houari Boumediene decided upon complete arabization as a national goal and began the first steps to promote Arabic in the bureaucracy and in the schools. Arabization was introduced slowly in schools, starting with the primary schools and in social science and humanities subjects; only in the 1980s did Arabic begin to be introduced as the language of instruction in some grades and some subjects at the secondary level (see Education, this ch.).

The problems inherent in the process of language promotion immediately came to the fore. One of the most obvious involved literary Arabic, a language in which many Algerians were not conversant. Qualified Arabic teachers were almost totally lacking. Other obstacles included the widespread use of French in the state-run media and the continued preference for French as the working language of government and of urban society. It soon became obvious to students who obtained an education in Arabic that their prospects for gainful employment were bleak without facility in French, a fact that contributed to general public skepticism about the program.

Important as these problems were, the real opposition came from two main quarters: the "modernizers" among bureaucrats and technocrats and the Berbers, or, more specifically, the Kabyles. For the urban elite, French constituted the medium of modernization and technology. French facilitated their access to Western commerce and to economic development theory and culture, and their command of the language guaranteed their continued social and political prominence.

The Kabyles identified with these arguments. Young Kabyle students were particularly vocal in expressing their opposition to arabization. In the early 1980s, their movement and demands formed the basis of the "Berber question" or the Kabyle "cultural movement."

Militant Kabyles complained about "cultural imperialism" and "domination" by the Arabic-speaking majority. They vigorously opposed arabization of the education system and the government bureaucracy. They also demanded recognition of the Kabyle dialect as a primary national language, respect for Berber culture, and greater attention to the economic development of Kabylie and other Berber homelands.

The Kabyle "cultural movement" was more than a reaction against arabization. Rather, it challenged the centralizing policies the national government had pursued since 1962 and sought wider scope for regional development free of bureaucratic controls. Essentially, the issue was the integration of Kabylie into the Algerian body politic. To the extent that the Kabyle position reflected parochial Kabyle interests and regionalism, it did not find favor with other Berber groups or with Algerians at large.

Long-simmering passions about arabization boiled over in late 1979 and early 1980. In response to demands of Arabic-language university students for increased arabization, Kabyle students in Algiers and Tizi Ouzou, the provincial capital of Kabylie, went on strike in the spring of 1980. At Tizi Ouzou, the students were forcibly cleared from the university, an action that precipitated tension and a general strike throughout Kabylie. A year later, there were renewed Kabyle demonstrations.

The government's response to the Kabyle outburst was firm yet cautious. Arabization was reaffirmed as official state policy, but it proceeded at a moderate pace. The government quickly reestablished a chair of Berber studies at the University of Algiers that had been abolished in 1973 and promised a similar chair for the University of Tizi Ouzou, as well as language departments for Berber and dialectical Arabic at four other universities. At the same time, levels of development funding for Kabylie were increased significantly.

By the mid-1980s, arabization had begun to produce some measurable results. In the primary schools, instruction was in literary Arabic; French was taught as a second language, beginning in the third year. On the secondary level, arabization was proceeding on a grade-by-grade basis. French remained the main language of instruction in the universities, despite the demands of arabists.

A 1968 law requiring officials in government ministries to acquire at least minimal facility in literary Arabic has produced spotty results. The Ministry of Justice came closest to the goal by arabizing internal functions and all court proceedings during the 1970s. Other ministries, however, were slower to follow suit, and French remained in general use. An effort was also made to use radio and television to popularize literary Arabic. By the mid-1980s, programming in dialectical Arabic and Berber had increased, whereas broadcasts in French had declined sharply.

The arabization issue developed political aspects as well. For example, in 1991 when political parties were allowed to form and run in national elections, the Front of Socialist Forces, headed by Hocine Ait Ahmed, representing the Kabyle people, ran on a secular and culturally pluralist platform. Another party, also representing the Kabyle, was the Rally for Culture and Democracy, which ran on a platform defending Kabyle culture and opposing the exclusive use of Arabic at the official level and all programs of arabization.

Structure of Society

As is true of other peoples of the Maghrib, Algerian society has considerable historical depth and has been subjected to a number of external influences and migrations. Fundamentally Berber in cultural and racial terms, the society was organized around extended family, clan, and tribe and was adapted to a rural rather than an urban setting before the arrival of the Arabs and, later, the French. An identifiable modern class structure began to materialize during the colonial period. This structure has undergone further differentiation in the period since independence, despite the country's commitment to egalitarian ideals.

Preindependence Society

During the Ottoman period, before the coming of the French in 1830, the people were divided among a few ancient cities and a sparsely settled countryside where subsistence farmers and nomadic herdsmen lived in small, ethnically homogeneous groups. Rural patterns of social organization had many common features, although some differences existed between Arabs and Berbers and between nomads and settled cultivators. The groups did not form a cohesive social class because individual behavior and action were circumscribed by the framework of tribe or clan.

In this period, 5 to 6 percent of the population lived in cities. The cities were the location of the principal mosques and the major sharia (Islamic law) courts and institutions of higher Islamic learning. Various Islamic legal schools, such as the Hanafi (see Glossary) and Maliki (see Glossary) as well as the Ibadi schools, also had their mosques in the cities. In addition, cities had public baths and markets, where goods coming from various parts of the world were traded. Local military forces were housed in citadels that towered over urban centers, and the houses and administrative offices of the Ottoman ruling elite were also located in some of the principal cities, such as Algiers.

The cities were divided into quarters that were self-contained and self-sufficient. For security they could be closed off at night and during times of crises, and their own leading citizens managed the internal affairs of the quarters.

The heterogeneous population of the cities included men of mixed Turkish and Algerian descent called Kouloughli Moors, a term coined by the French to refer to descendants of Andalusian refugees; Christian slaves from around the Mediterranean captured by Barbary Coast pirates; and African slaves who worked as laborers and domestics. The cities also had small Jewish communities that would become more important under the French colonial system. Many cities had small groups of Mzab who owned grocery and butcher shops and operated the public baths, and Kabyles who came briefly to the cities before returning to their areas of origin.

In the rural areas, social organization depended primarily on kinship ties. The basic kinship unit was the *ayla*, a small lineage whose members claimed descent through males from a common grandfather or great-grandfather. The male members of such a group maintained mutual economic obligations and recognized a form of collective ownership of pastoral or agricultural lands. More than one *ayla* formed the larger lineage, whose members traced their origin to a more remote male ancestor. Beyond these lineages were the patrilineal clans called *adhrum* by the Kabyles and *firq* by the Arabs, in which kinship was assumed and the links between individuals and families were close. The largest units consisted of tribes that were aggregations of clans claiming common or related ancestors or of clans brought together by the force of circumstance. Sharing a common territory, name, and way of life, member units of a tribe, particularly among the Berbers, had little political cohesion and tended to accept the authority of a chief only when faced with the danger of alien conquest or subjugation. Tribal confederations were rare in the modern era but were more common before the nineteenth century.

Among settled and nomadic Arab groups, tribes and their components were arranged along a gradient of social prestige. The standing of an individual depended on membership in a ranked group; tribal rank depended on the standing of the highest-ranking lineage of each tribe. The *shurfa* (nobles allegedly descended from the Prophet Muhammad) and marabouts, venerated for their spiritual power, held the highest ranks. Affairs of mutual interest to all clans were administered by the clan heads under the leadership of a *qaid* (tribal chief), who exercised nearly absolute authority.

Settled Berber groups were democratic and egalitarian. The community, an aggregation of localized clans consisting of a cluster of hamlets or a village inhabited by a single clan, was governed by a *jamaa* composed of all adult males. Social stratification of the kind found in Arab groups did not exist in Berber villages.

The typical Kabyle villages in the Aurès Mountains and the Atlas Mountains around Blida were always built above cultivated lands, on or close to mountain tops. They were enclosed by walls with doors that opened inward. The slopes were often terraced to allow the Kabyles to cultivate olive and fruit orchards and to grow wheat and barley. The animals kept by the Kabyles grazed on the vegetation that grew on rocky slopes unsuitable for agriculture.

French rule and European settlement brought far-reaching social changes. Europeans took over the economic and political life of the country, monopolizing professional, large-scale commercial, and administrative activities, exploiting agricultural and other resources of the land, and remaining socially aloof. The small Algerian middle stratum of urban merchants and city artisans was squeezed out, and landowners of the countryside were dispossessed.

The European population increased rapidly in the nineteenth century, more than quadrupling from 26,987 in the early 1840s to 125,963 a decade later, and reaching almost 2 million by the turn of the century. This population growth, coupled with the appropriation of cultivated and pastoral lands by colonials, which increased sharply in the early twentieth century, created tremendous pressures on the cultivable land. Displaced villagers and tribesmen flocked to towns and cities, where they formed an unskilled labor mass, ill-adapted to industrial work, scorned by Europeans, and isolated from the kinship units that had formerly given them security and a sense of solidarity. This urban movement increased after World War I and after World War II. At the same time, large numbers of Algerians migrated to France in search of work. The Kabyles were the principal migrants; during the 1950s, as many as 10 percent of the people of the Kabylie region were working in

France at any one time; even larger numbers were working in cities of the Tell.

Europeans constituted a separate sector of society, and the European-Algerian dichotomy was the country's basic social division. The settlers who came to Algeria in the nineteenth century included not only French but also large numbers of Italians and Spaniards who could not find work in their home countries and came in search of new opportunities. The expression *pieds noirs* (black feet), used to refer to settlers, was allegedly based on the barefoot condition of many of the impoverished European settlers.

The top echelon of the country included a few Algerians who had amassed land and wealth, as well as some respected Arabic scholars and a few successful professionals. An indigenous landowning aristocracy of any importance had never existed, however, and French colonials did not want an Algerian middle class competing with them for jobs and status. Moreover, the Algerians lived in quarters of the cities separate from the Europeans and seldom intermarried with them.

In the early twentieth century, a new Algerian merchant group began to intermarry with the old upper-stratum families. Their children were educated in French schools, at home or in France, to become a new Western-oriented elite composed of lawyers, physicians, pharmacists, teachers, administrators, and a small scattering of political leaders. The opportunity for social mobility for these Westernized Algerians, or *évolués*, however, remained extremely limited; on the eve of the revolution, only a scattering of jobs requiring professional or technical skills were held by Algerians.

The peasant migrants to the cities tended to gather in separate quarters according to their ethnic origin, and certain peoples became associated with specific occupations. But overcrowding and housing shortages often forced persons of a given tribe or village to scatter throughout a city, and the solidarity of migrant groups decreased. Nevertheless, many migrants retained contact with family members.

Nomadic clans no longer holding sufficient flocks or territory were obliged to accept the humiliation of sedentary existence. The process of sedentarization usually started with the settling of a few nomadic families on the outskirts of a town with which they had maintained trading relations. Accepted eventually as part of the community by the original clan inhabitants, the former nomads often assumed as their own one of the traditional ancestors or marabouts of the community. Residential propinquity usually did not, however, overcome the social distance between traditional cultivators and former herders because each looked down on the way of life of the other.

The Revolution and Social Change

After generations of gradual change under the French, the War of Independence struck Algerian society with cataclysmic force, and victory introduced other major social changes. The influence of the war permeated the society in both country and city and at the personal, familial, and local levels.

In response to the conflict, individuals developed new perceptions of themselves, their abilities, and their roles through wartime activities. Women, accustomed to a sheltered and segregated life, found themselves suddenly thrust into revolutionary militancy. For many, the war offered the first opportunity for independent activity in the world beyond the home. Many young people struck out independently of their families and their elders, and new leaders emerged, chosen more for personal traits than for social position.

The often brutal fighting, stretching across much of the country for nearly eight years, disrupted or emptied many rural villages. The deliberate French policy of resettlement of rural populations gathered more than 2 million villagers in French-built fortified settlements under a *regroupement* program. The total number of Algerians displaced by the war cannot be accurately known, but Algerian authorities place the figure at more than 3 million permanently or temporarily moved. In 1965 about 2 million people remained in the centers. By 1972 their numbers had decreased markedly and some of the centers closed; several centers, however, became permanent settlements.

As a result of these displacements, a sizable portion of the population lost its ties with the land on which ancestors had lived for generations and consequently with the social groups the land had supported. Families found themselves separated from fellow clan members and extended family members. The housing supplied by the French was suitable for the nuclear family rather than the traditional extended household, and persons who had formerly lived by subsistence farming became accustomed to functioning in a cash economy.

The disappearance of small communities of kin eliminated the social control by reputation and gossip that had formerly existed. Instead, residents of the French relocation centers began to develop feelings of solidarity with strangers who had shared a common fate. The destruction of the old communities particularly affected the lives of women, sometimes in contradictory ways. Despite being released from the restraints imposed by family scrutiny, women from rural villages, where wearing the veil was rare, adopted the veil voluntarily as a means of public concealment.

Traditional relations between generations also were overturned, and class differences were submerged. The young could adapt to the new ways, but the old were ill-equipped for change and so relinquished much of their former prestige and authority. In addition, rural people became more interested in comfort and consumption, which began to replace the frugality that had characterized traditional village life.

Toward a Modern Society

At independence Algerian society differed greatly from its condition at the beginning of the struggle for liberation. The exodus of Europeans in 1962–63, left a society composed primarily of illiterate peasants and sizable numbers of urban laborers. It was estimated that less than 1 percent of the 1964 population had belonged to the middle and upper classes during the 1950s. Educated persons remaining in the country were insufficient to staff all the positions in government and industry vacated by the Europeans. A criteria of prestige stemming from the war had also entered the social reckoning; those who had participated actively in the fighting or suffered loss because of it became eligible for special benefits or consideration.

During the colonial period, the country's most significant social distinctions had been those that separated Europeans from Algerians. Europeans had ranged from great industrialists through middle-class businesspeople, professionals, and farmers to unskilled workers. The Algerian population had also covered a range from well-to-do business and professional families to landless rural laborers. Distinctions, however, were blurred by the disabilities and discrimination suffered during the war by all Algerians and by the ideological emphasis on the unity of the Algerian people.

The removal of the European community permitted the appearance of the rudiments of a modern class system in which probably the most influential group consisted of French-

The Society and Its Environment

trained technocrats, civil servants, army officers, and senior functionaries of the National Liberation Front (Front de Libération Nationale—FLN). The few indigenous industrialists lacked great influence, but the bureaucrats and technocrats who managed the government and its expanding enterprises began to form a conspicuous and highly influential group that was to contribute upper-echelon personnel for public administration and state enterprises. Education, more than any other single factor, became the criterion for membership in the new elite.

Houari Boumediene, who was president from 1967 to 1978, headed a government that was dedicated to furthering Islamic socialism and held that, because early Islam in Algeria had its own egalitarian tendencies, no contradiction was involved. The pursuit of socialism since the 1960s, however, has produced its own rich assortment of social contradictions and tensions.

The Boumediene government at times has been criticized for its state capitalist tendencies because of its single-minded pursuit of industrialization, which led to the emergence of a prosperous and reasonably competent elite. After 1968 Boumediene gradually brought more and more educated young bureaucrats and technocrats into government service; by the late 1970s, they formed part of an administrative and managerial elite who staffed the government ministries and planned and operated the state industrial sector. Largely in control of the country, the new social group nonetheless shared status and influence with the army and functioned under the supervision of senior political officials. Although the explicit ideology of the government discouraged the formation of social classes, this relatively wealthy and powerful elite seemed to represent an important barrier on the road to an egalitarian society.

The technocrats and bureaucrats tended to be modernizers influenced by Western ideas. In general, they subscribed to the modernist view of Algerian society and believed that all members of society, including women, should participate actively to change the environment to suit the needs of society and its members. In socialist-oriented Algeria, the concepts of the nation-state, self-determination, and state planning came to the fore among members of the elite; local loyalties and family ties declined in importance as the society became more modern, urban, and educated.

Aside from the bureaucratic and technocratic elite, the middle class consisted of employees of state industrial and service enterprises; small businesspeople and shopkeepers; professionals, such as teachers, physicians, and lawyers; and artisans. Except for businesspeople, this stratum increased greatly after independence, moving to help fill the void created by the departure of the French and by the demand for services and skilled labor in the postindependence economy. Residing mostly in the cities and larger towns, the middle class was by Algerian standards relatively well-off.

An urbanized working class had similarly come into being over the previous few decades, finding employment, for example, in state and private industries, construction, public works, and transportation. As with the urban middle class, this group grew steadily in size after 1962 as a consequence of economic expansion. Another sizable group also found in the cities consisted of the unemployed. A substantial number of the unemployed were young males, many of them migrants from rural areas, who were often forced to settle in squalid housing. Usually monolingual in Arabic, lacking job skills, and possessing only a primary education, the migrants and the unemployed survived on the largesse of the state welfare system. Finally, there were the rural agricultural workers, including small and medium-sized landowners, landowning and landless peasants, and those who worked on large state farms. Some members of this class benefited from land distribution in the 1970s and early 1980s. Others, such as medium-sized landowners who survived land redistribution and the formation of large agricultural enterprises, reportedly were enjoying a measure of prosperity and favored government investment in roads and services in rural areas.

As the nation continued to modernize in the 1980s and early 1990s, millions of Algerians were torn between a tradition that no longer commanded their total loyalty and a modernism that did not satisfy their psychological and spiritual needs. This dilemma especially affected the nation's youth. Educated young women were torn between the lure of study and a career and the demands of their husbands and fathers. Young men faced conflicting models of cultural behavior and achievement, conflict between demands for fluency in modern Arabic and fluency in French, and conflict between devotion to Islam and the secularism of modernization. Above all loomed the reality of youth unemployment, which reached a staggeringly high 41 percent in the early 1990s (compared to 30 percent for the overall working-age population). With no solution in sight, unemployment was a prime factor accounting for the boredom, frustration, and disillusionment that characterized the younger generation. Many young people became major supporters of the Islamic Salvation Front(Front Islamique du Salut—FIS) whose groups were located on campuses and in major cities throughout the country. Young people contributed to the clashes with government forces ongoing since the late 1980s and to the general political instability.

To strengthen a sense of national pride in the country's culture, in 1970 an officially sponsored "cultural revolution" was launched to restore historic monuments and to develop the means to communicate cultural themes via radio, television, the press, libraries, and museums. In realms such as economics and politics where the past offered no guidance, new structures were to be devised in keeping with the theory of the 1962 Tripoli Program. This program rejected capitalism, which it associated with Western colonial powers, and disavowed an economic system that would make it dependent on the West. Instead, it favored a socialist system that allowed for state control both of the means of production and of the plan for national development. The program opted for a one-party political system that would represent the aspirations of the rural and urban masses. Other aspects of the cultural revolution included substituting Arabic for French and eliminating foreign teachers and foreign influence from the educational establishment—all part of a policy of constructing an Algeria distinctive in personality and proud of its heritage and achievements.

The cultural revolution was fifteen years old in 1985; beyond language and education development, however, its achievements were hard to measure. The program had suffered from neglect and lack of funds for projects involving monuments and archeological sites, museums, the arts, and the publishing industry. A national seminar on the history of the Algerian Revolution was successfully organized in 1981, however, and in late 1983 Chadli Benjedid (president, 1979–92) issued a renewed call for serious attention to cultural affairs and to the study of Algerian national history.

The Individual, the Family, and the Sexes

In the early 1990s, the tradition of strong family life still dominated most areas of the country. A basic social principle affecting both the individual and the family was a kind of division between the sexes that made gender one of the most important determinants of social status. Seclusion of women was not universally practiced, but men and women constituted largely separate societies in public life. In private they were bound by the same culture, values, traditions, and beliefs and the same closeness between generations found in other parts of the Middle East.

The War of Independence and the impetus given to education by the socialist governments of Ahmed Ben Bella (1962–65), Boumediene, and Benjedid led to a change in the position of women in Algerian society. Girls were sent to school in large numbers; later, many continued their studies in university and then pursued professional lives, especially in urban centers.

Family and Household

Before independence the basic Algerian family unit, particularly in the countryside, was the extended family consisting of grandparents, their married sons and families, unmarried sons, daughters if unmarried or if divorced or widowed with their children, and occasionally other related adults. The structure of the family was patriarchal and patrilineal, with the senior male member making all major decisions affecting family welfare, dividing land and work assignments, and representing it in dealings with outsiders. Each married couple usually had a separate room opening onto the family courtyard and prepared meals separately. Women spent their lives under male authority—first that of their fathers, then of their husbands—and were expected to devote themselves entirely to the activities of the home. Children were raised by all members of the group, who passed on to them the concept and value of family solidarity.

Members of a single patrilineage lived in one compound and shared the work on the family's common land. The lineage expressed solidarity by adhering to a code of honor that obligated members to provide aid to relatives in need and even in the clinging together of members who had gone to the city to find work. Among Berber groups, the honor and wealth of the lineage were so important that blood revenge was justified in their defense.

Since independence there has been a trend toward smaller family units consisting only of a husband and wife and their unmarried children. Upon marriage a young man who can afford to do so sets up a household for himself and his bride, and on the death of the head of an extended family, male members and their dependents break off into separate households.

The trend toward the smaller nuclear family has affected the extended family structure in both urban and rural areas, although it is more pronounced in the former. The nuclear family is fast becoming the prevalent family structure. This change has occurred gradually in response to many factors, including increased urbanization and the development of wage labor.

In the early 1990s, younger and better educated Algerians tended to favor smaller families than did previous generations. They preferred to live in separate quarters, have fewer children, and run their lives independently. Familial ties of loyalty and respect were not in question, although they tended to loosen. Rather, family relationships were rearranged with respect to living space and decision making.

Marriage is traditionally a family rather than a personal affair and is intended to strengthen already existing families. An Islamic marriage is a civil contract rather than a sacrament, and consequently, representatives of the bride's interests negotiate a marriage agreement with representatives of the bridegroom. Although the future spouses must, by law, consent to the match, they usually take no part in the arrangements. The contract establishes the terms of the union and outlines appropriate recourse if they are broken. In the early 1990s, Algeria continued to have one of the most conservative legal codes concerning marriage in the Middle East, strictly observing Islamic marriage requirements.

Men and Women

In Algeria, as in the rest of the Middle East, women are traditionally regarded as weaker than men in mind, body, and spirit. The honor of the family depends largely on the conduct of its women; consequently, women are expected to be decorous, modest, and discreet. The slightest implication of impropriety, especially if publicly acknowledged, can damage the family's honor. Female virginity before marriage and fidelity afterward are considered essential to the maintenance of family honor. If they discover a transgression, men are traditionally bound to punish the offending woman. Girls are brought up to believe that they are inferior to men and must cater to them, and boys are taught to believe that they are entitled to the care and solicitude of women.

The legal age for marriage is twenty-one for men, eighteen for women. Upon marriage the bride usually goes to the household, village, or neighborhood of the bridegroom's family, where she lives under the critical surveillance of her mother-in-law. Much marital friction centers on the difficult relationship between mother-in-law and daughter-in-law.

Because a woman begins to gain status in her husband's home when she produces sons, mothers love and favor their boys, often nursing them longer than they do the girls. The relation between mother and son remains warm and intimate, whereas the father is a more distant figure.

Traditionally, concern for the purity of women led to a marked restriction of their activities. Women spent most of their adult lives behind their courtyard walls or visiting other women in similar courtyards. It was considered improper for a woman to be seen by men to whom she was not related, and in many areas women were veiled in public.

French colonizers actively opposed veiling because they viewed it as a symbol of national and religious values and beliefs that they sought systematically to undermine. In reaction to French pressure, Algerians stubbornly clung to the practice and after independence actually increased its use. Paradoxically, however, this development also resulted from the increased freedom enjoyed by women. The veil provides mobile seclusion, and the more frequent entry of women into public situations called for an increased incidence of veiling.

Within the confines of the traditional system, there was considerable variation in the treatment of women. In Arab tribes, women could inherit property; in Berber tribes, they could not. In Berber society, Kabyle women seem to have been the most restricted. A husband could not only divorce his wife by repudiation, but he could also forbid her remarriage. Chaouia women fared much better because they were allowed to choose their own husbands.

During the War of Independence, women fought alongside men or, at the least, maintained the household in their absence. They thus achieved a new sense of their own identity and a measure of acceptance from men that they had not enjoyed before. In the aftermath of the war, some women maintained their new-found emancipation and became more

Men sharing snuff in downtown Algiers
Courtesy Anthony Toth and
Middle East Report

Women in traditional garb on the street
Courtesy Nadia Benchallal and
Middle East Report

actively involved in the development of the new state, whereas others returned to their traditional roles at home.

After 1962 the status of women began improving, primarily because of the increased education of family members, broader economic and social development, and the willingness or necessity for ever-larger numbers of women to seek gainful employment. In the mid-1950s, about 7,000 women were registered as wage earners; by 1977 a total of 138,234 women, or 6 percent of the active work force, were engaged in full-time employment. Corresponding figures for the mid-1980s were about 250,000, or 7 percent of the labor force. Many women were employed in the state sector as teachers, nurses, physicians, and technicians.

Although by 1989 the number of women in the work force had increased to 316,626, women still constituted only a little over 7 percent of the total work force. The number of women in the work force, however, may be much higher than official statistics suggested. Women in the rural work force were not counted; only 140 were listed in official statistics. Among the reasons for their omission was their position as unpaid family members; culturally, heads of households in a patriarchal society did not acknowledge publicly or to census workers that the women of their household were workers. In fact, the majority of rural women work full time and should be considered part of the Algerian work force.

Family Code

The real battleground over the status and rights of women has been the family code, a set of legal provisions regulating marriage and the family. Debated between those who wanted family life organized along Western secularist lines and those who favored a family structure conforming to Islamic principles and ethics, the code was proposed, discussed, and shelved at least three times over a period of two decades before being adopted into law in 1984. In one instance, in 1981, the code's provisions provoked vehement opposition from female members of the National People's Assembly and street demonstrations by women in Algiers, both almost unprecedented events in Algeria.

Although some of the 1984 code's provisions are more liberal than those of the 1981 version, the code essentially reflects the influence of Islamic conservatives. The family unit is "the basic unit of society"; the head of the family is the husband, to whom the wife owes obedience. According to the sharia, a Muslim woman may not marry a non-Muslim; polygyny is permitted under certain conditions (although it is rarely practiced); and women do not inherit property equally with men. A woman cannot be married without her consent, and she may sue for divorce in specified circumstances, including desertion and nonsupport. Custody of children under age seven in divorce cases passes to the wife but reverts to the husband when the children are older. Divorce rates have risen steadily since independence, but divorce remains much easier for men than for women.

Family Planning

Before 1980 Algeria lacked an official birth control program, in contrast to other Arab countries, nearly all of which had some kind of family planning program or a policy of limiting population. To a large extent, this situation reflected the conviction that Algeria was not overpopulated, given the vast empty expanse of the Sahara and the High Plateaus and the scattered population clusters even in the Tell. There was also a desire to make up the alleged 1.5 million population loss in the War of Independence and the conviction of many parents that their well-being lay in producing as many children as possible, a common view held by peasants. Despite an employment problem arising from overpopulation, Boumediene favored economic growth over birth control as the solution to overpopulation and unemployment. His policy received the blessing of the Islamic religious establishment.

At 1980 growth rates, Algeria's population would have risen from 18.3 million to more than 35 million by the year 2000. Faced with a demographic explosion that threatened to inhibit further social and economic development, if not obliterate what had been achieved, the Benjedid government reversed directions and devised a cautious family planning policy that took into account Islamic sensitivities. The new program referred to "birth spacing" rather than "birth control" and emphasized the improvement in the health of the mother and children and the well-being of the family that would occur if births were spaced and families were smaller. The goal was voluntary participation on the part of women of childbearing age. The program also aimed at creating the infrastructure within the Ministry of Public Health that would enable it to provide birth control services, educate the population about family planning, and conduct research on the relationship between population growth and economic development.

To implement the program, Maternal and Infant Protection Centers (PMICS) were established to dispense advice and contraceptives. In 1980 there were about 260 centers. An educational campaign was also launched, using television, billboards, and handbills to point out the consequences of unrestrained demographic growth and to advertise the services of the PMICS. A major effort was made to reconcile family planning with the dictates of religion. Religious scholars found birth spacing and the use of contraceptives compatible with Islam as long as participation was voluntary and practices such as abortion and sterilization were proscribed.

By the mid-1980s, family planning had begun to meet with some success. The number of PMICS had risen to 300, and the demand for information about the program reportedly outstripped supply in some areas. It was estimated that about 10 percent of the population of childbearing age was using some form of contraception, and the government was increasing its publicity to encourage still greater participation.

In 1986 the government created the National Committee on Population. Its charter promoted a balance between social and economic development needs on the one hand, and population growth on the other. Three years later, in 1989, the United Nations Fund for Population Activities (UNFPA) launched a US$8 million program to support maternal and child health care, help create a center for the production of oral contraceptives, and develop an effective education system to inform the general population on the use of contraceptives. The UNFPA program also supported demographic research and advised the government on population strategies and policies. In 1989 it was estimated that 35 percent of Algerian women of childbearing age used some form of contraception. This percentage would account in part for the sharp drop in population growth from 3.1 percent in the mid-1980s to 2.8 percent in 1990.

Islam

Islam, the religion of almost all of the Algerian people, pervades most aspects of life. It provides the society with its central social and cultural identity and gives most individuals their basic ethical and attitudinal orientation. Orthodox observance

Celebration of the circumcision of a young boy
Courtesy ANEP

of the faith is much less widespread and steadfast than is identification with Islam.

Since the revolution, regimes have sought to develop an Islamic Arab socialist state, and a cabinet-level ministry acts for the government in religious affairs. Although the Boumediene regime consistently sought, to a far greater extent than its predecessor, to increase Islamic awareness and to reduce Western influence, the rights of non-Muslims continued to be respected. The Benjedid government pursued a similar policy.

Early History

During the seventh century, Muslim conquerors reached North Africa, and by the beginning of the eighth century the Berbers had been for the most part converted to Islam. Orthodox Sunni (see Glossary) Islam, the larger of the two great branches of the faith, is the form practiced by the overwhelming majority of Muslims in Algeria. Shia (see Glossary) Islam is not represented apart from a few members of the Ibadi sect, a Shia offshoot.

Before the Arab incursions, most of the Berber inhabitants of the area's mountainous interior were pagan. Some had adopted Judaism, and in the coastal plains many had accepted Christianity under the Romans. A wave of Arab incursions into the Maghrib in the latter half of the seventh century and the early eighth century introduced Islam to parts of the area.

One of the dominant characteristics of Islam in North Africa was the cult of holy men, or maraboutism. Marabouts were believed to have *baraka*, or divine grace, as reflected in their ability to perform miracles. Recognized as just and spiritual men, marabouts often had extensive followings locally and regionally. Muslims believed that *baraka* could be inherited, or that a marabout could confer it on a follower.

The *turuq* (sing., *tariqa*, way or path), or brotherhoods, were another feature of Islam in the Maghrib from the Middle Ages onward. Each brotherhood had its own prescribed path to salvation, its own rituals, signs, symbols, and mysteries. The brotherhoods were prevalent in the rural and mountainous areas of Algeria and other parts of North Africa. Their leaders were often marabouts or shaykhs. The more orthodox Sunni Muslims dominated the urban centers, where traditionally trained men of religion, the ulama, conducted the religious and legal affairs of the Muslim community.

Tenets of Islam

The *shahada* (testimony) states the central belief of Islam: "There is no god but God (Allah), and Muhammad is his Prophet." This simple profession of faith is repeated on many ritual occasions, and recital in full and unquestioning sincerity designates one a Muslim. The God preached by Muhammad was not one previously unknown to his countrymen because Allah, rather than a particular name, is the Arabic for God. Muhammad denied the existence of the many minor gods and spirits worshiped before his ministry and declared the omnipotence of the unique creator, God. "Islam" means submission, and the one who submits to God is a Muslim. Muhammad is the "seal of the Prophets"; his revelation is said to complete for all time the series of biblical revelations received by Jews and Christians. God is believed to have remained one and the same throughout time, but humans strayed from God's true teachings until set right by Muhammad. Muslims recognize the prophets and sages of the biblical tradition, such as Abraham and Moses, and consider Jesus to be another prophet. Islam accepts the concepts of guardian angels, the Day of Judgment, general resurrection, heaven and hell, and an eternal life for the soul.

The duties of the Muslim form the "five pillars" of faith. These are *shahada*, testimony and recitation of the creed; *salat*, daily prayer; *zakat*, almsgiving; *sawm*, fasting; and hajj, pilgrimage. The believer is to pray in a prescribed manner after purification through ritual ablutions at dawn, midday, midafternoon, sunset, and nightfall. Prescribed genuflections and prostrations are to accompany the prayers, which the worshiper recites while facing Mecca.

Whenever possible, men pray in congregation at the mosque under an imam, or prayer leader, and on Friday they are obliged to do so. Women may also attend public worship at the mosque, where they are segregated from the men, although most frequently those who pray do so in seclusion at home. A special functionary, the muezzin, intones a call to prayer to the entire community at the appropriate hours; people out of earshot determine the proper hour by other means.

In the early days of Islam, the authorities imposed a tax on personal property proportionate to the individual's wealth, which was distributed to the mosques and to the needy. In the modern era, *zakat*, or almsgiving, while still a duty of the believer, has become a more private matter. Properties contributed to support religious activities have usually been administered as religious foundations, or *habus* in North Africa.

The ninth month of the Muslim calendar is Ramadan, a period of obligatory fasting in commemoration of Muhammad's receipt of God's revelation, the Quran. During this month, all but the sick and certain others are enjoined from eating, drinking, smoking, or sexual intercourse during the daylight hours.

Finally, all Muslims at least once in their lifetime should, if possible, make the hajj to the holy city of Mecca. There they participate in special rites held at several locations during the twelfth month of the Islamic calendar.

Islam and the Algerian State

The Prophet enjoined his followers to convert nonbelievers

to the true faith. Jews and Christians, whose religions he recognized as the precursors of Islam and who were called "people of the book" because of their holy scriptures, were permitted to continue their own communal and religious life as long as they recognized the temporal domain of Muslim authorities, paid their taxes, and did not proselytize or otherwise interfere with the practice of Islam.

Soon after arriving in Algeria, the French colonial regime set about undermining traditional Muslim Algerian culture. According to Islam, however, a Muslim society permanently subject to non-Muslim rulers is unacceptable. Muslims believe that non-Muslim rule must be ended as quickly as possible and Muslim rulers restored to power. For this reason, Islam was a strong element of the resistance movement to the French.

After independence the Algerian government asserted state control over religious activities for purposes of national consolidation and political control. Islam became the religion of the state in the new constitution and the religion of its leaders. No laws could be enacted that would be contrary to Islamic tenets or that would in any way undermine Islamic beliefs and principles. The state monopolized the building of mosques, and the Ministry of Religious Affairs controlled an estimated 5,000 public mosques by the mid-1980s. Imams were trained, appointed, and paid by the state, and the Friday *khutba*, or sermon, was issued to them by the Ministry of Religious Affairs. That ministry also administered religious property (the *habus*), provided for religious education and training in schools, and created special institutes for Islamic learning.

Those measures, however, did not satisfy everyone. As early as 1964 a militant Islamic movement, called Al Qiyam (values), emerged and became the precursor of the Islamic Salvation Front of the 1990s. Al Qiyam called for a more dominant role for Islam in Algeria's legal and political systems and opposed what it saw as Western practices in the social and cultural life of Algerians.

Although militant Islamism was suppressed, it reappeared in the 1970s under a different name and with a new organization. The movement began spreading to university campuses, where it was encouraged by the state as a counterbalance to left-wing student movements. By the 1980s, the movement had become even stronger, and bloody clashes erupted at the Ben Aknoun campus of the University of Algiers in November 1982. The violence resulted in the state's cracking down on the movement, a confrontation that would intensify throughout the 1980s and early 1990s (see The Islamist Factor, ch. 4).

The rise of Islamism had a significant impact on Algerian society. More women began wearing the veil, some because they had become more conservative religiously and others because the veil kept them from being harassed on the streets, on campuses, or at work. Islamists also prevented the enactment of a more liberal family code despite pressure from feminist groups and associations.

Religious Minorities

Christianity came to North Africa in the Roman era. Its influence declined during the chaotic period of the Vandal invasions but was strengthened in the succeeding Byzantine period, only to disappear gradually after the Arab invasions of the seventh century.

The Roman Catholic Church was reintroduced after the French conquest, when the diocese of Algiers was established in 1838. Proselytization of the Muslim population was at first strictly prohibited; later the prohibition was less vigorously enforced, but few conversions took place. The several Roman Catholic missions established in Algeria were concerned with charitable and relief work; the establishment of schools, workshops, and infirmaries; and the training of staff for the new establishments. Some of the missionaries of these organizations remained in the country after independence, working among the poorer segments of the population. In the early 1980s, the Roman Catholic population numbered about 45,000, most of whom were foreigners or Algerians who had married French or Italians. In addition, there was a small Protestant community. Because the government adopted a policy of not inquiring about religious affiliation in censuses or surveys to avoid provoking religious tensions, the number of Christians in the early 1990s was not known.

The Jewish community is of considerable antiquity, some members claiming descent from immigrants from Palestine at the time of the Romans. The majority are descendants of refugees from Spanish persecution early in the fifteenth century. They numbered about 140,000 before the Algerian revolutionary period, but at independence in 1962 nearly all of them left the country. Because the 1870 Crémieux Decrees, which aimed at assimilating the colons of Algeria to France, gave Jews full citizenship, most members of the Jewish community emigrated to France.

The government of independent Algeria discouraged anti-Semitism, and the small remaining Jewish population appeared to have stabilized at roughly 1,000. It was thought to be close to this number in the early 1990s. Although no untoward incidents occurred during the Arab-Israeli wars of 1967 and 1973, a group of youths sacked the only remaining synagogue in Algiers in early 1977.

Education

The French colonial education imposed on Algeria was designed primarily to meet the needs of the European population and to perpetuate the European cultural pattern. A large majority of the students were children of the colonists. French was the language of instruction, and Arabic, when taught, was offered as an optional foreign language.

Segregated schooling of French and Algerian children was abolished in 1949, and increases in Muslim enrollments were scheduled in the comprehensive 1954 Constantine Plan to improve Muslim living conditions. On the eve of independence, however, the European-oriented curricula were still taught exclusively in French, and less than one-third of school-age Muslim children were enrolled in schools at the primary level. At the secondary and university levels, only 30 percent and 10 percent of the students, respectively, were Algerians.

At the beginning of the 1963 school year, the education system was in complete disarray, and enrollments in schools at all levels totaled only 850,000. In the years immediately following, teachers were trained hastily or recruited abroad; classrooms were improvised, many in the vacated homes of former French residents. Attendance climbed to 1.5 million in 1967, to nearly 3 million by 1975, and to 6.5 million in 1991–92 (see table 2, Appendix).

At the time of independence in 1962, the Algerian government inherited the remnants of an education system focused on European content and conducted in a foreign language by foreign teachers. Algerian authorities set out to redesign the system to make it more suited to the needs of a developing nation. The hallmarks of their program were indigenization, arabization, and an emphasis on scientific and technical studies. They sought to increase literacy, provide free education, make primary school enrollment compulsory, remove foreign

Mosque in Blida, south of Algiers
Courtesy ANEP

teachers and curricula, and replace French with Arabic as the medium of instruction. They also planned to channel students into scientific and technical fields, reflecting the needs of Algerian industrial and managerial sectors. The approach to education has been gradual, incremental, and marked by a willingness to experiment—unusual characteristics in a developing country.

The high priority assigned by the government to national education was reflected in the amount of money spent on it and on the existence of free schooling at all levels. Between 1967 and 1979, a total of DA171 billion (for value of the dinar—see Glossary) was allocated for operating expenditures in this sector. In 1985 approximately 16.5 percent of the government's investment budget was devoted to education; in 1990 the education sector received 29.7 percent of the national budget.

Algeria received substantial assistance from the World Bank. Between 1973 and 1980, Algeria contracted five education loan agreements for sums totaling US$276 million. The World Bank has continued to provide funds and technical assistance in connection with a fundamental reform of education, the latest phase of which occurred in 1993. The structure of the existing basic and secondary systems was being revised, and much heavier emphasis was being given to technical and vocational schooling.

In the mid-1970s, the primary and middle education levels were reorganized into a nine-year system of compulsory basic education. Thereafter, on the secondary level, pupils followed one of three tracks—general, technical, or vocational—and then sat for the baccalaureate examination before proceeding to one of the universities, state technical institutes, or vocational training centers, or directly to employment. The process of reorganization was completed only in 1989, although in practice the basic system of schooling remained divided between the elementary level, including grades one to six, and the middle school level of grades seven to nine. Despite government support for the technical training programs meant to produce middle- and higher-level technicians for the industrial sector, a critical shortage remained of workers in fields requiring those technical skills.

The reforms of the mid-1970s included abolishing all private education. Formerly, private education was primarily the realm of foreign institutions and schools often run by Roman Catholic missions. Legislation passed in 1975 stipulated that education was compulsory for nine years between the ages of six and fifteen, and that it would be free at all levels. The Ministry of National Education and the Ministry of Higher Education were assigned sole responsibility for providing and regulating the education system.

In 1982 about 4 million pupils were enrolled in the nine-year basic education track at a time when the government claimed 81 percent of all six-year-olds were attending school. Attendance approached 90 percent in urban centers and 67 percent in rural areas. Teachers were nearly all Algerian, and instruction was entirely in Arabic, French being introduced only in the third year.

In the 1991–92 school year, about 5.8 million pupils were enrolled in grades one through nine; and the gross enrollment ratios reached 93 percent for the first six years of school and 75 percent for the next three years. Algerian society in the early 1990s was still not fully accustomed to women assuming roles outside the home, and female enrollments remained slightly lower than might have been expected from the percentage of girls in the age-group.

Secondary enrollments totaled 280,000 in 1982, compared with 51,000 in 1962–63. The number of secondary schools increased from thirty-nine to 319 over the decade, while the percentage of Algerian teachers increased from 41 in 1975 to 71 in 1982. French continued as the favored language of instruction in general, particularly in mathematics and science. Despite these impressive gains, enrollments still fell short of planned targets, especially in scientific and technical fields. The same was true of female education. Nationwide, in 1982 girls accounted for 38.8 percent of total enrollments in secondary and technical schools. A great variation also existed between the number of girls attending school in Algiers, where the percentage nearly equaled that of boys, and Tamanrasset in the south, where the percentage dropped to as low as 7. In 1984 national primary and secondary enrollments totaled 5 million.

In 1990-91, secondary school enrollments represented a total of 752,000 students, of whom 20 percent had entered a *technicum*, or technical high school. The proportion of girls in that cycle of education was 31 percent and constituted 47 percent of total enrollment at the secondary level. Teachers were more than 90 percent Algerian at all levels. Arabization of the education system was considered an important objective of the 1990s.

Vocational education at the secondary level received attention as part of the reorganization of the mid-1970s. The program was designed with the requirements of industry and agriculture in mind; students were to be trained as apprentices for up to five years. As of 1990, a total of 325 vocational training schools were in operation, and about 200,000 apprentices were in training. Vocational skills were also taught as part of the national service program, which provided employment and work experience for large numbers of young men (see Labor and Employment, ch. 3).

The major universities in 1993 were the University of Oran, the University of Science and Technology at Oran, the University of Algiers, and universities at Tlemcen, Sidi Bel Abbes, Constantine, and Annaba and the Houari Boumediene University of Science and Technology. There were also universities at Batna, Blida, Sétif, and Tizi Ouzou and university centers at Bejaïa, Mostaganem, Chelif, and Tiaret. Total higher education enrollment for the academic year 1989–90 was 177,560 students as compared with 103,000 in 1983–84 and close to 8,000 in 1967. Only the Algiers campus predated independence, having been founded in 1909.

The higher education system first adopted by the University of Algiers was based on the French model. As such, it stressed autonomy of the university faculties not only in administration but also in designing curricula and organizing courses of study aimed at particular degrees. The system resulted in unwieldiness, duplication of academic offerings, and complete loss of credits by students changing programs. In addition, it led to a very high attrition rate. Some reforms designed to modernize the university system were introduced in 1971, and major reforms were introduced in 1988. Nevertheless, the universities still loosely resemble the French model, and French remains widely used for instructional purposes. The number of French instructors has declined, however, as the number of Algerian teachers has increased after 1980. In 1981–82, for instance, 64.6 percent of the teachers at all levels of education were Algerian. By the academic year 1990–91, the percentage had increased to 93.4 percent. Arabic was widely taught at the tertiary level, and Zouaouah, the dialect of the Kabyle Berbers, was taught at the University of Tizi Ouzou.

In addition to the universities, a number of state institutes provide specialized technical, agricultural, vocational, and teacher training. Some function under the direct jurisdiction of appropriate ministries and provide one to five years of technical training and job experience for trainees. The Ministry of Energy and Petrochemical Industries and the Ministry of Agriculture and Fishing each has a number of institutes. Algeria in the early 1990s had more than thirty institutes of higher learning, including technical studies, teacher-training colleges, and Islamic institutes.

Many Algerian students also study abroad. Most go to France or other West European countries, various countries of Eastern Europe, and the United States.

A variety of literacy programs for adults was initiated after 1962, when the national literacy rate was below 10 percent. The Conquest of Literacy program was mounted to help people attain literacy in Arabic or French or both languages. Volunteer

Great Mosque and University of Islamic Studies, Constantine
Courtesy Embassy of Algeria, Washington
School children, Algiers
Courtesy Anthony Toth and Middle East Report

teachers held classes on the job, in homes, and in abandoned buildings; old French or Arabic grammars, copies of the Quran, and political tracts were pressed into service as texts. Wide-ranging approaches, including correspondence courses and use of the public media, were introduced during the Second Four-Year Plan, 1974–77. Major responsibility for out-of-school education was assigned to two specialized government agencies. These agencies benefited from technical assistance under the second of the three World Bank education loans, but the main emphasis of the government's education program has been on the rapid development of the formal school system.

Progress in literacy has been noteworthy. About 42 percent of the population was literate in 1977. By 1990 adult literacy had reached 57.4 percent, according to estimates by the United Nations Educational, Scientific, and Cultural Organization (UNESCO); 69.8 percent of Algerian men and 45.5 percent of Algerian women were literate. Because, however, priority has been given to the education of youth, adult illiteracy has not yet received the attention it needs.

Health and Welfare

Health

At independence the Algerian health care system was skeletal, consisting of one physician per 33,000 people (or an estimated 300 doctors in all) and one trained paramedic per 40,000. The approach at the time was primarily curative rather than preventive.

Since then the country has made tremendous progress in health care. From 1975 onward, a new system of almost free national health care was introduced. Hospitalization, medicines, and outpatient care were free to all. In 1984 the government formally adopted a plan to transform the health sector from a curative system to a preventive one more suited to the needs of a young population. Rather than investing in expensive hospitals, the government emphasized health centers and clinics, together with immunization programs. The results were impressive: whereas the infant mortality rate was 154 per 1,000 live births in 1965, it had fallen to sixty-seven per 1,000 live births by 1990.

By 1991 Algeria had about 23,000 physicians, or one for every 1,200 inhabitants, and one nurse per 330 people. About 90 percent of the population had access to medical care, and only in remote rural areas did people have difficulty reaching health care services. Algeria also had 2,720 basic health units, 1,650 health centers, thirteen university hospitals, 178 general hospitals, and eighteen specialized hospitals. Overall, there was one hospital bed for every 380 people. The average occupancy rate of hospitals was 55 percent, while the average length of stay was six days.

In 1993 most health services were provided by the public sector, although a small private sector comprising some 20 percent of Algerian physicians also existed. A network of hospitals and ambulatory facilities was organized into health districts. The districts consisted of a general hospital, one or more urban and rural maternity centers, health care centers, and dispensaries. These facilities were complemented by specialized clinics and teaching hospitals. Three regional public pharmaceutical enterprises oversaw the wholesale purchase and distribution of drugs, a public company imported and maintained medical equipment, and a number of pharmaceutical units produced a limited quantity of serums, vaccines, and other drugs.

Expenditures for this health care system increased at an annual average rate of 14 percent during the 1980s. Estimates for health services expenditures were 5.4 percent of Algeria's gross domestic product (GDP—see Glossary), compared with a 5.2 percent average for countries with similar middle income, and 7.2 percent for some of the lower-income Organisation for Economic Co-operation and Development (OECD) countries. Funding came from the state budget (20 percent), the social security system (60 percent), and individual households (20 percent).

In the early 1990s, tuberculosis, trachoma, and venereal infections were the most serious diseases; gastrointestinal complaints, pneumonia, diphtheria, scarlet fever, and mumps were relatively common, as were waterborne diseases such as typhoid fever, cholera, dysentery, and hepatitis among all age-groups. Tuberculosis was considered the most serious health hazard, and trachoma ranked next; only a small minority of the population was entirely free from this fly-borne eye infection, which was directly or indirectly responsible for most cases of blindness. Malaria and poliomyelitis, both formerly endemic, had been brought under control. Acquired immune deficiency syndrome (AIDs), does not appear to be a serious problem, but ninety-two cases had been reported as of August 1991. The incidence of disease is related to nutritional deficiencies, crowded living conditions, a general shortage of water, and insufficient knowledge of personal sanitation and modern health practices.

Medical training has been a priority for the Algerian government since independence. In 1990 the following institutions had schools of medicine, dentistry, and pharmacy: Algiers, with branches in Blida and Tizi Ouzou; Annaba; Constantine, with branches in Setif and Batna; and Oran, with branches in Sidi Bel Abbes and Tlemcen. The total number of students enrolled in those programs in the 1988-89 academic year was 27,472. In addition, the government maintained public health schools for paramedical personnel in Algiers, Constantine, and Oran that recruited from secondary schools for their programs.

Medical schools have been graduating a large number of physicians: 800 to 1,000 annually in the first half of the 1980s, and even more in the second half of that decade. Several thousand women are enrolled in medical school. It is estimated that between 1990 and 1995 some 25,000 new doctors will graduate, the majority of whom will probably be unable to find work in the public health sector. The private sector was expected to expand significantly to absorb the large number of graduating physicians.

The Algerian government has made major efforts to train women as nurses and technicians since the mid-1970s. Two-year nursing courses at the secondary level are offered in Algiers and at several regional centers. Training for midwives is available in Oran and Constantine. Problems exist, however, with the paramedical staff. Since the mid-1980s, the ratio of nursing staff to physicians has dropped from 5.7 percent to one to 2.7 percent to one, in part because of low salaries, little opportunity for advancement, difficulty in recruiting good teachers for paramedical schools, and low compensation for those teachers. Furthermore, in an effort to reform the training system for medical personnel, a number of those schools were temporarily shut down in the latter 1980s, further reducing enrollment in those programs.

Despite the threat of oversupply of medical personnel, a small percentage of foreigners has always practiced in Algeria. They come from France, Russia, Eastern Europe, and Vietnam. Their number, however, is declining rapidly. In 1986 there were 1,724 specialized physicians, 241 general practitioners, eight pharmacists, and nineteen dental surgeons who were not Algerian; by 1990 only 767 specialized physicians, sixty-seven general practitioners, one pharmacist, and ten dental surgeons who were not Algerian remained in Algeria.

Social Welfare

The social system that prevailed before the coming of the French had little need for public welfare. Extended families, clans, and tribes cared for their elderly and needy members, and granaries maintained by villages or tribal units stored grain for use in years of poor harvest. During the French colonial period, the old way of life was substantially altered, but in the early 1990s enough of the old system remained for the traditional sense of personal responsibility to rank high among accepted social values.

The fabric of the socialist system, however, was based largely on the concept of public responsibility for welfare, and during the first years after independence the government of Algeria set about extending the public welfare program. A system of family allowances for employed persons had been instituted by the French in 1943, and in 1949 a limited social security program had been initiated for urban employees and some agricultural workers. These systems remained in effect after independence. In 1971 a new social security ordinance extended to all agricultural personnel the benefits already enjoyed by industrial and service-sector workers. This program has provided sickness and disability insurance, old-age pensions, and family allowances and has been financed by contributions from employees, employers, and the government.

Housing

Unchecked population growth and a steady flow of urban migration have combined to produce a severe housing shortage. The Algerian housing problem has been less pressing than in many other developing countries, however, owing to the postindependence departure of most Europeans. Nearly all of the Europeans had been city dwellers, living in the new towns surrounding a *medina* (traditional city) housing the Algerian population. In 1961 and 1962, many Europeans simply abandoned their properties to squatters from the countryside who promptly occupied them; sometimes as many as six Algerian families lived in a residence that had formerly housed a single European family. Property abandonment was so common that *biens vacants* (empty properties) became a term in common use.

Several years were required for the government to inventory the vacant properties. In 1965, however, a government financial reform endeavored to regularize ownership and collection of rents from about 500,000 nationalized or sequestered apartments and houses in the major cities.

Rural migrants settled into *bidonvilles,* named after the flattened *bidons* (tin cans) used extensively in their ramshackle construction. After independence the *bidonville* population of Algiers alone soon exceeded 100,000. *Bidonvilles* appeared in other cities, and during the early 1970s they emerged on the fringes of the oil camps in the Algerian Sahara.

The proliferation of urban shantytowns has been a worldwide phenomenon in developing countries. Proportionately fewer have sprung up in Algeria than in neighboring Morocco, in part because of government projects to limit urban sprawl by creating industrial villages near new factories. In the early 1970s, industrial villages were started near Algiers and in the vicinity of Annaba and Oran.

During the first twenty years after independence, public investment was concentrated in the industrial sector, and little attention was paid to the housing sector. Private construction was minimal because of tight government regulation and difficult access to landownership. In Algiers in particular, the government sought to discourage the flood of migration by almost freezing the housing sector and confining itself to improving sanitation and public utility service.

The consequence of those policies was a severe housing shortage starting at the end of the 1970s. By the early 1980s, the occupancy rate per three-room housing unit stood at seven persons, and the shortfall in public housing was placed at 1 million units. In 1992 the shortage had become critical and had risen to 2 million housing units. The shortage had resulted in an average occupancy rate of 8.8 persons per unit, comparatively one of the highest in the world.

Between 1990 and August 1993, as part of a series of reforms, the government sought to eliminate the housing backlog and built about 360,000 public housing units and launched new housing programs for low-income groups. Earlier plans to produce 100,000 public housing units between 1980 and 1984 achieved only a 57 percent rate of success. In the Second Five-Year Plan (1985–89), the success rate for completed housing was even lower, convincing the government that major reforms were necessary.

Largely as a result of import restrictions that included building materials, the public housing sector in 1992 could produce only 35,000 units per year, up from 24,000 units in 1991, but down from the 1986 peak year of 88,000 units. At this rate, public housing shortages will not only continue but become worse.

In November 1990, new land legislation (Loi d'Orientation Foncière) was enacted to abolish the local government monopoly over land transactions, thus freeing urban landowners to buy and sell their land as they wish. The law was also intended to encourage private-sector investment in housing and construction. Furthermore, new standards were introduced in 1991 to simplify urban development procedures by the private sector.

To encourage the private sector to invest in housing, the government is proposing legislation that will permit private contractors to compete with public enterprises and have access to building materials that are exclusively for public housing. The private sector is also encouraged to produce locally some of the building materials needed, in order to compensate for market shortages and for the cost of importing those materials. By the early 1990s, some Algerians in the private sector had begun producing bricks, ceramic tiles, and steel rods.

Registered private construction companies remain very small and work primarily to build private family homes. Individuals also hire workers and architects to build their own houses. In 1991 alone, 85,000 building permits were issued to private households wishing to build dwellings. Between 1989 and 1992, an estimated 300,000 such housing units were built by private individuals.

The most conspicuous development in rural housing during the postindependence years has been the One Thousand Socialist Villages program undertaken in 1972 in conjunction with the agrarian revolution program. Socialist villages represented a pilot plan for improving rural housing. According to the plan, each village would have a population of as many as 1,500 people housed in 200 individual units, together with schools and clinics. Each unit was to have three rooms and would be provided with electricity, heat, and running water. By mid-1979 about 120 such villages had been completed. Although the villages had much to commend them, the program has done little to slow migration to urban areas.

In the mid-1980s, urban housing varied from the most modern apartment buildings and private dwellings of concrete and glass to crowded shantytowns. The cities had grown so rapidly that the small-windowed walls and courtyards of a *medina* occupied only a small fraction of the urban area. The most common rural dwellings are called *gourbi*, some of which are mere huts constructed of mud and branches. Others are more solidly built, having walls of stone or clay and containing several rooms. Tiled or tin roofs are usually flat; but in parts of eastern Algeria subject to heavy rainfall or winter snows, the roofs are steeply slanted.

As a consequence of the heavy urban migration of early postindependence years, entire *gourbi* settlements appeared in Annaba and other coastal cities. During this period, the Kabylie region was the only part of Algeria to enjoy a housing boom. A large majority of the immigrant laborers in France were Berbers from the Kabylie, and the funds remitted by them to their families at home made the surge of building possible in this generally impoverished region.

Significant changes have occurred in Algeria in the last decade in the sectors of health, education, and welfare. The increase in health care facilities and the general upgrading of health services have met the needs of the very young Algerian population. The education system also has undergone major reforms and has become more responsive to the economic and social needs of Algerian society. However, the housing shortage, which worsened in the 1980s, has become critical in the 1990s. Private-sector involvement may alleviate this shortage as it plays a larger role in the economy. Another major problem confronting the nation is that of unemployment, particularly among younger workers. Thus, despite Algeria's achievements in some areas, the country in 1993 was facing a number of difficult societal pressures that, combined with militant religious forces and economic difficulties, posed ongoing challenges to the government.

*   *   *

One of the best and most comprehensive recent studies on Algerian history and society is John Ruedy's *Modern Algeria: The Origins and Development of a Nation*. Of particular importance are Ruedy's descriptions of the structure of the society and how it changed as a result of the political and economic upheavals that shook the country, especially in the nineteenth and twentieth century. Two older studies, John P. Entelis's *Algeria: The Revolution Institutionalized* and the study edited by I. William

Zartman, *Man, State, and Society in the Contemporary Maghrib*, remain of critical importance to an understanding of present-day Algerian society. A number of French writers such as Jean-Claude Vatin, Rémy Leveau, and Jean Leca have written extensively on Algerian society and are essential reading.

World Bank reports contain the latest information and statistics on major development indicators in Algeria; they have contributed greatly to this chapter. Some excellent articles on Algeria also have appeared in publications such as the *Middle East Journal, Third World Quarterly, Annals of the Academy of Political and Social Sciences,* and *Annuaire de l'Afrique du Nord.* (For further information and complete citations, see Bibliography.)

Chapter 3. The Economy

Lighthouse along the Mediterranean coast with fishing boat in foreground

ALGERIA IN 1993 was in transition, moving from a centralized system toward an open market economy. In this connection, its physical resources of arable land and hydrocarbons played major roles. Algeria's close to 2.4 million square kilometers make it the second largest country in Africa, after Sudan, and one-third the size of the United States. More than 2 million square kilometers are desert or semiarid steppes extending into the southern Sahara region, but the country also contains a fertile strip of cultivable land concentrated along the coast of the Mediterranean Sea. Algeria's main physical resources are hydrocarbons: 3.2 trillion cubic meters of proven natural gas reserves and 9.2 billion barrels in recoverable reserves of crude oil. Algeria, with 4 percent of proven world reserves of natural gas, ranks fifth in the world; moreover, only 17 percent of the reserves have been exploited. Other resources include iron, zinc, phosphates, uranium, and mercury. In 1993 the country's population, predominantly Arabs and Berbers traditionally dependent on agriculture, was estimated by the United States government at 27.4 million, and the work force was thought to exceed 5.5 million.

A bloody eight-year revolution brought independence to Algeria's population, at that time numbering about 10 million, in 1962. The departure of the French colons and other foreigners, who had held a tight stranglehold on the country's administration, nearly brought the economy to a halt. The formerly productive agricultural sector was especially hard-hit, mainly because most Algerians were untrained and hence excluded from managing any aspect of agriculture or industry. The total commitment of the first independent government, headed by Ahmed Ben Bella, to a socialist system of centralized administrative management and economic self-sufficiency (because of its perceived positive correlation to political independence) also took a severe toll on the economy. Furthermore, Ben Bella's preoccupation with playing a major role in political relations with developing countries did not help matters.

Not until the late 1970s, when more pragmatic and less ideological leaders took over the reins of government under President Chadli Benjedid, did Algeria recognize the urgent need for social and economic reform. Government development plans until then had been driven by rigid central control and state ownership of most of the means of production and agriculture. The resulting inefficiencies and shortages spurred the government to devise an economic program aimed at increasing productivity and growth. But it was the widespread bread riots of "Black October" 1988 that compelled the government to institute a more serious and accelerated economic reform program. What is also referred to as the "Couscous Revolt" was attributed to an unacceptably slow pace of political and economic reform, as well as critical food shortages caused by the 1986 oil price drop and ensuing decrease in hydrocarbon export earnings.

The main goals of the accelerated reform program were to transform the national economy from a tightly controlled centralized system to a market-oriented one, create a climate more conducive to foreign investment and increased trade, and encourage domestic savings and investment. To achieve these objectives, the government gave management autonomy to two-thirds of the 450 state-owned enterprises, including banks, while instituting a profit accountability system for their managers. The government also eliminated state-controlled monopolies for import and distribution and allowed both Algerian and foreign companies to engage in these activities. Finally, the authorities encouraged continuation of the de facto privatization of the agricultural sector.

Algeria's development plans reflected the progress made toward achieving the goals of economic growth, infrastructure building, and movement from a government-dominated economy to decentralized reliance on market forces. These plans were influenced by the various leaders' personal vision and sociopolitical approach to the economic issues facing their country.

Development Planning

When the French left Algeria, they took with them most of the trained European cadre and left behind an economy in a state of chaos. The primary reason for this chaos was the lack of a trained or semiskilled Algerian labor force. Ahmed Ben Bella reacted by instituting a highly centralized socialist system that endowed the government with unlimited authority either to run the economy or to turn it over to workers' committees. These committees, which were guided by socialist principles, proved to be totally ineffective. Ben Bella then shifted his attention to seeking a role for Algeria on the international stage and finding a leadership role for himself as a voice for developing countries.

Houari Boumediene, who took over in 1965 through a military coup, was a more pragmatic president. Boumediene's First Three-Year Plan (1967–69) marked the beginning of long-term development planning in Algeria. In 1970 a newly created Secretariat of State for Planning took over economic planning from the Ministry of Finance, underscoring the regime's emphasis on social and economic development. The new secretariat developed the First Four-Year Plan (1970–73) and the Second Four-Year Plan (1974–77), which emphasized investment in capital-intensive heavy industry at the expense of more labor-intensive small industries that would generate badly needed employment. The years from 1977 to 1979 were a transitional period devoted to assessing previous development plans and devising new strategies.

The First Five-Year Plan (1980–84) and Second Five-Year Plan (1985–89) aimed at building a diversified economy and reflected the more moderate views of the less ideological Chadli Benjedid. A special congress of the National Liberation Front (Front de Libération Nationale—FLN) had selected Benjedid in January 1979 to succeed Boumediene, who had died of a rare blood disease in December 1978. The 1985–89 plan marked a significant policy shift by placing greater emphasis on agriculture. Benjedid's economic liberalization also resulted in less central planning and a decrease in government control, as evidenced by the abolition in 1987 of the Ministry of Planning, which had earlier replaced the Secretariat of State for Planning.

Further proof of this trend came when the Third Five-Year Plan (1990–94) turned out to be more of a broad policy outline than a directive plan of action. Its main objectives were to liberalize the economy, allow more business entities to break away from the state and become Public Economic Enterprises (Entreprises Publiques Économiques—EPÉs), and attract foreign investment.

Government Role

The spirit of jealously guarded independence was the driving force behind the new republic's economic plans. The government's policies, in turn, were initially dictated by the political philosophy of a group of freedom fighters with varying degrees of commitment to a socialist ideology. Such an ideology favored a self-sufficient economy that would satisfy the basic needs of the masses. But these same economic policies also evolved in response to a combination of other factors. These factors included the legacy of an untrained labor force left by the colons and an early obsession with intensive projects for national development even at the expense of imposing severe hardships on consumers. Other elements influencing economic policies were soaring prices, spiraling unemployment, runaway population explosion, and popular discontent. Ultimately, later and more pragmatic leaders realized that liberalization of the economy, political life, and social infrastructure was inevitable.

In the immediate postindependence period, the government concentrated on investment in large-scale heavy industry turnkey projects, such as steel mills and oil refineries. The early 1980s saw a reversal of this policy. Large enterprises were broken into smaller, more efficient units, and larger amounts of the investment budget were shifted to light industries, such as textiles, food processing, and housing construction. The government retained a preponderant economic role, however, in large strategic state companies, such as the National Company for Research, Production, Transportation, Processing, and Commercialization of Hydrocarbons (Société Nationale pour la Recherche, la Production, le Transport, la Transformation et la Commercialisation des Hydrocarbures—Sonatrach). Sonatrach was established in 1963 but was divided in 1980 into thirteen more autonomous and specialized units. The government's austerity program, which directed hydrocarbon revenues toward national development, and the continued aversion of the authorities to labor-intensive sectors such as agriculture and manufacturing created more acute unemployment problems and unprecedented food shortages. The 1986 oil price crash forced the government to rethink its petroleum-dependence policies and pay more attention to agriculture and other sectors.

The October 1988 bread riots, however, were probably the precipitating event that caused Benjedid to embark on a serious program of political and economic liberalization. Some of the more significant economic reforms came in the form of legislation promulgated in 1990 and 1991. The new laws defined specific regulations governing such critical issues as foreign investment and trade, joint ventures, repatriation of capital and profits, and recourse to international arbitration of

Hydrocarbons plant at Alrar, in eastern Algeria near the Libyan border, produces liquefied petroleum gas, butane, propane, and condensates.
Courtesy Embassy of Algeria, Washington
Laying pipeline for moving hydrocarbons across the Sahara
Courtesy Sonatrach

disputes. The extent of progress made in implementing these new laws in the 1990s will be a major factor in determining Algeria's economic outlook. Another important determinant is the future course of hydrocarbon prices. This factor, although beyond the government's control, has prompted it to initiate a policy of diversifying hydrocarbon earnings by increasing both natural gas and liquefied natural gas (LNG) exports, as well as condensates and petrochemicals.

The World Bank (see Glossary) *World Development Report, 1989* gave Algeria high marks for its efforts to move its economy from a directed system based on central planning to a more decentralized, market-oriented system. The results of this change included returning to individual farmers land collectivized in the 1970s, privatizing low-productivity state farms, establishing autonomous public enterprises, and giving the Central Bank of Algeria (Banque Centrale d'Algérie; hereafter, Central Bank) the authority to control credit and money supply. Since the establishment in January 1963 of the Central Bank to replace the French Colonial Bank of Algeria and act as the government's financial agent, the banking system has been under state control. New legislation on banking and credit introduced in 1986 and 1987 defined relationships between the Central Bank and commercial banks and allowed the latter to provide credit to state enterprises and private companies alike.

Public Finances

Algeria ranked in the upper range of medium-income countries in 1992, and the government had concentrated for some years on enlarging its industrial sector. The emphasis placed on manufacturing industries resulted in an average gross domestic product (GDP—see Glossary) increase of 18 percent over the decade from the mid-1970s to the mid-1980s. But accelerated industrialization was achieved at the expense of the agricultural sector, whose GDP share declined from 15 percent in 1965 to 9 percent in 1985 (see table 3, Appendix). The decline compelled the government to spend hard-earned foreign currency on food imports to meet serious food shortages facing a population that was growing at an average annual rate of about 3.2 percent in the late 1970s. Oil and gas revenues remained Algeria's largest single source of income, but the government in 1993 used up to 98 percent of its hydrocarbon export revenues to ensure its foreign-exchange needs. The government in 1993 also revised its budget to reflect the fluctuating, i.e., decreasing, percentage of hydrocarbon earnings caused by oil price changes. As a result, the government has decided to diversify the hydrocarbon industry away from crude oil toward natural gas, condensates, refined products, and petrochemicals. The success of this policy notwithstanding, and in spite of enhanced revenues from other sectors, additional taxation, and customs duties, the government has been unwilling to cut public expenditures significantly, fearing an adverse socioeconomic impact. Whereas the government has committed itself to reducing its external debt in the 1990s, it seemingly cannot afford to abandon investing in critically needed social infrastructure plans.

The government eventually instituted some reforms in public finance management by shifting the responsibility for financing economic activity from the Ministry of Finance to financial institutions and by decentralizing the decision-making process. Begun in 1986, these reforms were designed to transfer economic financing to local governments and public enterprises, including state-owned banks. Financial institutions, which had been limited to acting as cashiers for the ministry, took over the function of financing public enterprises and investment. Ministry of Finance investment financing was limited to strategic projects. The financial system also absorbed most of the ministry's role in housing finance. The Law on Money and Credit, promulgated in 1990, formally transferred the role of financial management to the Central Bank and the Money and Credit Council (see Investment, this ch.).

Budget

The government's commitment to nurturing a self-sufficient economy caused its investment expenditure to exceed 50 percent of total current expenditures in the 1970s and the first half of the 1980s. Most of the nontax revenue came from the hydrocarbons industry, which constituted the largest single source of income and provided almost 65 percent of the country's total revenues until the early 1980s. But the oil price crash of 1986 forced the government to revise the budget to bring hydrocarbon revenues down to almost 30 percent of the total. The *Journal Officiel* showed the percentage of oil and gas revenues dropping from 44 in the 1985 budget to 32 in 1986 and to 23 in the following three years. These figures continued to vary as the government introduced new forms of taxation, such as corporate, income, road, and property taxes. As of early 1993, the most recent tax to have been introduced was the value-added tax of April 1992, which established a 7 percent tax on strategic goods (e.g., electricity), 13 percent on reduced tariff products (e.g., construction materials), 21 percent on regular rate goods (e.g., automobiles), and 40 percent on luxury items.

The government continued to face the dilemma of reconciling an austerity policy designed to reduce a huge foreign debt with a commitment to sustain a socialist economy with a ferocious appetite for public expenditure. Rising tax receipts helped the government cut investment spending by 26 percent in 1986. Continuation of the austerity program reduced the fiscal deficit by 50 percent between 1987 and 1989. Fortuitously, increased hydrocarbon revenues in 1989 reduced 1988's deficit of more than US$4.4 billion to just over US$1.0 billion.

Historically, the proportion of investment expenditure received by each economic sector has varied from year to year. The variation resulted from such factors as the underlying philosophy of each development plan and the government's proclivity toward heavy industries. A clear trend has favored either basic infrastructure projects or education, health, and other social services. The government could not ignore the latter areas without exposing itself to serious public criticism or even social unrest. Education, for instance, received the lion's share of current expenditures in 1989 (26.9 percent) and in 1991 (25.8 percent), whereas defense was limited to 9 percent and 8.8 percent for those years. The construction industry exemplified a neglected sector in early development plans. The construction sector later caught the government's eye, however, because of its socially explosive impact on the severe housing shortage, about which less-advantaged Algerians had been complaining bitterly.

External Debt and Payments

Another area of financial concern relates to Algeria's external debt and debt-service payments. The country's substantial debt dates back to the 1970s, when the government borrowed heavily to finance development projects and meet rising consumer needs. When the debt mounted to US$16.9 billion in 1980, Benjedid decided to limit borrowing to DA50 million (for value of the dinar—see Glossary) a year, which reduced the debt steadily until 1984. Because payments came under pressure starting in 1985, however, the debt-service ratio more than doubled between 1985 and 1988, increasing from 35 percent to 80 percent. Amortization payments increased by 38 percent until they reached US$6.2 billion in 1990. In spite of falling oil production and prices, the government managed to avoid debt rescheduling by cleverly obtaining soft finance and trade credits.

By the end of 1990, the country's external debt slightly exceeded US$26 billion, of which almost US$2 billion was in short-term loans. To reduce the debt-servicing burden, the government subsequently concentrated on obtaining medium- and long-term loans to repay its financial obligations as soon as they became due. Also, to augment its efforts to obtain more concessional financing, such as bilateral lines of credit, the government has discouraged importers from borrowing from suppliers; such loans are usually of short duration and hence are more expensive than long-term lines of credit. Countries that have bilateral credit lines with Algeria include Belgium, France, Italy, Japan, and Spain.

Algeria has viewed debt rescheduling as a politically unacceptable step. The government was obliged, however, to make another politically unpopular move in 1991, by reaching a standby agreement with the International Monetary Fund (IMF—see Glossary). The FLN had always opposed such a move as an encroachment on sovereignty. The IMF standby agreement, however, had a positive effect on creditors and potential donors, including the World Bank, which decided to grant Algeria a US$300 million structural adjustment loan. The European Community (EC—see Glossary) also agreed in 1991 to provide a loan worth US$470 million. A year earlier, the Banque Nationale de Paris (BNP) had provided a seven-year loan of 1 billion French francs to be used in converting short-term borrowing into longer-term loans. Another positive sign was Algeria's apparent determination not to miss debt-service payments despite a debt service exceeding US$7 billion in 1991.

Currency and Exchange Rates

The Central Bank sets the daily price of the Algerian dinar, keyed to a basket of currencies most widely used in payment for exports but primarily linked to the United States dollar and the French franc. The dinar has had a long history of being overvalued, resulting in a runaway black market on which the dinar was traded at several times the official rate for many years. In a serious attempt to bring down black-market rates and thus achieve convertibility for the dinar, the government decreed a major devaluation in mid-1990 and allowed the dinar to drop about 52 percent, from DA8.5 = US$1 in July of that year to DA16.6 = US$1 in March 1991. Although this step helped the authorities meet IMF demands for reaching a new standby agreement, they were concerned about the raised price of imported consumer products and the potential social implications for the poorer majority of the population. The considerable gap between prices and economic costs for certain essential commodities, such as energy products, prompted the government to institute a policy of gradually reducing consumer subsidies while recognizing the importance of price supports in protecting the most disadvantaged people. Whereas the government tempered its policy of moving rapidly to a system in which almost all prices were to be determined by market forces, in 1991 it adjusted the prices of subsidized products, electricity, natural gas, and petroleum products. These steps resulted in reducing total 1991 subsidies by DA9.6 billion.

Foreign Aid

Until the early 1990s, foreign assistance to Algeria consisted mainly of generous loans extended by Arab countries on unusually favorable terms. Algerian businesses have also managed to obtain soft credits from trading partners, mostly in France, Italy, and Spain.

The EC's Fourth Protocol (1992–96), however, has called for more generous treatment of the Mediterranean countries that are not members of the EC, including Algeria, Morocco, and Tunisia. The Fourth Protocol increased EC spending under the Third Protocol by 28 percent and provided for financing regionally based projects undertaken by Algeria and its Union of the Arab Maghrib partners. The Fourth Protocol also allowed Algeria to obtain larger loans and draw on an EC budget allocation of 70 million European currency units (ECU), compared with ECU54 million in the Third Protocol. Algeria's risk capital provision also jumped from ECU6 million to ECU15 million.

Another important factor that should further enhance Algeria's foreign-aid prospects is the World Bank's increasing support for the government's economic reform program. The World Bank's loans to Algeria between 1990 and 1995 are expected to more than double the US$1.4 billion extended in the period 1985–89.

Investments

In another major policy shift, the government decided to seek badly needed cash and access to credit in order to ensure sustained economic growth. Despite concerns about foreign ownership of the Algerian "patrimony," economic pragmatism dictated passage of the Law on Money and Credit of April 1990. This law liberalized the country's foreign-investment code to the extent that only telecommunications, electricity production, hydrocarbon refining and distribution, and railroad transport remained closed to foreigners. As for the exchange system, the new law prohibited multiple exchange rates for the dinar and assigned the Money and Credit Council, a board composed of Central Bank and other Algerian government officials, the responsibility of setting foreign-exchange and external-debt policy. The council was also charged with approving foreign investments and joint ventures.

Another objective of the April 1990 law was to attract foreign capital by formalizing the legal framework for investment. The law permitted the repatriation of capital and accumulated profits, subject to approval by the Central Bank. Investments in the hydrocarbon sector, however, were still governed by Law 86-14 of August 1986, which limited foreign investors to joint ventures with Sonatrach. The government's investment priorities were listed as agriculture and agribusiness; agricultural machinery; mineral, hydrocarbon, and electricity production and distribution; petrochemicals; basic and primary transformed steel and metallurgical products; railroad transport; capital goods; and tourism.

The Law on Money and Credit not only created a more positive investment climate but also proved to be quite a contrast to previous foreign-investment laws of August 1982 and August 1986. These two laws had allowed only the repatriation of profits and indemnities awarded by Algerian courts to foreign investors, who were denied any recourse to international arbitration of disputes, except those covered by a special Franco-Algerian protocol, and whose commercial disputes could be resolved only under Algerian law.

The Supplementary Finance Law of August 1990 introduced the system of concessionaires and wholesalers (exclusive dealers representing foreign companies) as a major ingredient of the import liberalization process. Before this law was passed, only monopolies could import goods for resale. The same law also broadened the right to use a foreign-currency account to include any business in addition to individuals. The new accounts could be used for making any legitimate payments relating to the business of the account holder. In April 1991, the government announced a change in the import system: all imports of merchandise not prohibited were given full access to foreign exchange at the official exchange rate. All import licensing restrictions were abolished, except for imports receiving government subsidies, which continued to be subject to administrative control because of domestic trading restrictions.

Several other measures also served to attract foreign capital. In December 1987, the government joined the International Finance Corporation, a World Bank body that specializes in encouraging private enterprises. In June 1990, it signed an agreement allowing the Overseas Private Investment Corporation to operate its investment promotion, financing, and insurance program for United States investors in Algeria. In October 1990, the government established the Agency for Development and Promotion of Investment to familiarize potential foreign investors with Algeria's business climate and to facilitate their investments in its companies.

Although the authorities indicated a strong and understandable interest in enhancing employment opportunities in the eastern and southern desert areas of the country, geographic investment preferences were not made a prerequisite for foreign investment. Nor were sectoral preferences required, but it was clear that the authorities would evaluate any foreign-investment proposal for its potential contribution to increasing Algeria's productive capability, nonhydrocarbon exports, and technology transfer. The Ministry of Economy issued a supplementary regulation in September 1990, outlining its own priorities and defining the objectives of investments. These were to finance production of goods and services that generated hard currency; to reduce imports of goods and services; to improve distribution of goods and equipment; and to engage in economic activities that enhanced the profitability of public transport, telecommunications, and water and electricity distribution—subject to approval by the competent government agencies. Both foreign investors and Algerian entities were given equal access to credit from local banks, with no restrictions on reinvestment. No discriminatory or preferential export or import regulations were to be applied to foreign-owned businesses. Any firm engaged in exporting its output would, regardless of ownership, be allowed to retain 100 per-

Carpet merchant in suq at Khroub near Algiers
Courtesy United Nations
Workman decorating a table top in a small Algerian furniture factory
Courtesy Embassy of Algeria, Washington

cent of its foreign-exchange earnings for use in importing raw materials and machinery needed to sustain its production.

Services

Banking

The banking sector is a major facilitator of investment. The magnitude of the government's banking reforms can best be understood by comparing the current system with that of the French colonial era. Under the French, most of Algeria's banks were branches of French banks; after independence they sold out or were nationalized. The Central Bank of Algeria was established in January 1963, to replace the Colonial Bank of Algeria and act as the government's agent in financial transactions, currency issue, and other central bank functions. In 1971 the Central Bank assumed the role of supervising the country's three major commercial banks, the most important of which was the National Bank of Algeria (Banque Nationale d'Algérie), which served both the private and public sectors and held the bulk of total bank deposits. The other two, the Foreign Bank of Algeria (Banque Extérieure d'Algérie) and the Popular Credit of Algeria (Crédit Populaire d'Algérie) were more sector oriented, with the former handling energy and foreign trade and the latter financing smaller sectors.

The government's economic development and decentralization policies of the 1980s resulted in the establishment of more specialized financial institutions. The Agriculture and Rural Development Bank (Banque de l'Agriculture et du Développement Rural) provides loans to the farming and food processing industries. The National Fund for Provident Savings (Caisse Nationale d'Épargne et de Prévoyance) furnishes savings and housing loans. The Bank of Manufacturing and Services (Banque des Industries de Transformation et des Services) deals with the service sector and light industries. The Bank of Local Development (Banque de Développement Local) was formed in 1985 to finance communal development projects. The Algerian Development Bank (Banque Algérienne de Développement) was created in 1963 to provide long-term (ten- to twenty-year) loans.

Tourism

Algeria shares with Morocco and Tunisia a coastline with great potential as a tourist attraction. Its tourism industry, however, has always lagged behind that of its closest neighbors. Mainly because of the government's failure to promote tourism and the lack of well-run quality hotels and tourist sites, the number of foreign visitors to Algeria in the 1980s never exceeded one-fourth and one-sixth of those to Tunisia and Morocco, respectively.

Since 1989, however, the government has shown greater interest in promoting tourism because of its potential as a source of foreign exchange. As part of its efforts to liberalize the country's economy, the government has decentralized the national tourism company and granted autonomy to many state-owned hotels. The government has also allowed foreign companies to run newly constructed hotels, such as the Hilton just outside Algiers. Another large hotel (350 rooms), managed by the French chain Sofitel, opened in early 1992 in the Hamma district of the capital. The government continued to encourage local private investment and foreign participation in joint ventures, hoping to increase hotel capacity to 50,000 rooms within a decade. The government's decision to lift the DA35 million ceiling on local private investments also is expected to generate considerable hotel construction activity.

Labor and Employment

Algeria's rapidly growing labor force of about 5.5 million unskilled agricultural laborers and semiskilled workers in the early 1990s accurately reflected the high rate of population growth. More than 50 percent of the labor force was between fifteen and thirty-four years old. Almost 40 percent of the labor force either had no formal education or had not finished primary school; 20 percent of the labor force had completed secondary school or beyond. Women officially constituted only just over 7 percent of the labor force, but that figure did not take into account women working in agriculture. Unskilled laborers constituted 39 percent of the total active work force, but nonprofessional skilled workers, such as carpenters, electricians, and plumbers, were in short supply because most tended to migrate to Europe. The Benjedid government tried without much success to entice them to return to their homeland to help the domestic economy—even at the expense of losing their foreign-exchange remittances. Algerian remittances, however, have always been much lower than those of other Maghrib (see Glossary) emigrants. Although Algerian workers in France and other EC (see Glossary) countries outnumbered other

North Africans, their annual remittances were estimated at US$350 million, whereas non-Algerian transfers amounted to US$2 billion.

The labor force grew at an annual average rate of 4 percent between 1985 and 1990, but the growth in employment has lagged seriously. The result has been acute unemployment and underemployment. Official estimates put the 1990 unemployment rate at 26 percent. (Official figures tended to underestimate actual unemployment because they counted only those males actively seeking work.) In 1990 almost 65 percent of all the unemployed were fifteen to twenty-four years old, raising the unemployment rate within this age bracket to 41 percent. Recognizing that the country's demographics would make youth unemployment a thorny social problem, in 1988 the government established the Youth Employment Program (Programme d'Emploi des Jeunes) to provide jobs and training for youths between sixteen and twenty-four years of age. Because this program failed to meet its target of creating 40,000 training opportunities and 60,000 jobs each year, in 1990 the government initiated two other programs to help establish new enterprises either operated by or employing young people. One program would subsidize, by up to 30 percent of the initial investment, the establishment of new enterprises by young people. The other would guarantee bank loans extended to young entrepreneurs.

Two basic salaries, both paid by the government, set the wage scale for the formal sector and the framework for the rest of the country. The National Guaranteed Minimum Wage (Salaire National Minimum Garanti) is the amount paid by the government to people who are unemployed. The sum constitutes what the government considers a basic minimum wage, but it is not legally binding. The minimum wage was introduced in 1978 at DA1,000 per month and was not changed until 1990, when the government and the largest labor union, the General Union of Algerian Workers (Union Générale des Travailleurs Algériens—UGTA), agreed to raise the amount to DA1,800 in January 1991 and to DA2,000 in July of the same year. The second salary figure, the Minimum Activity Wage (Salaire Minimum d'Activité), is the minimum paid by the government to its employees; it is considered a minimum for the rest of the formal sector. The same agreement with the UGTA incrementally increased this minimum until it reached DA2,500 in July 1991. In a move consistent with its continuing reform policies, the government later decided to decentralize the wage negotiation process. As a result, autonomous public enterprises, which had been required to adhere to the civil service wage scale, were allowed to negotiate independently with their employees.

Algerian workers lacked the right to form multiple autonomous labor unions until the June 1990 Law on Trade Union Activity was passed by the National Assembly, thus ending the monopoly of the FLN party-linked UGTA on labor representation. Another 1990 law on industrial relations provided for collective bargaining, abolishing a previous ban on strikes and guaranteeing workers the right to press their demands. It required, however, that labor-management disputes be submitted to a conciliation procedure that was administered by the local inspection office but that also provided both parties with recourse to arbitration. If the dispute persisted, workers were allowed to strike after giving eight days' notice. The new legislation also provided managers with a more flexible framework for administering personnel policies, including hiring and firing procedures.

Natural Resources and Energy

Hydrocarbons

Algeria's economy is dominated by the hydrocarbon sector, which in 1990 represented just over 23 percent of GDP and which was the largest source of its exports (see table 3, Appendix). In 1990, for example, US$12.3 billion of the country's total export earnings of US$12.7 billion (i.e., 97 percent) came from oil, gas, and refined products exports: crude and condensates (US$6.1 billion), refined products (US$2.7 billion), natural gas (US$2.8 billion), and liquefied petroleum gas, known as LPG (US$730 million). Algeria's oil, a light variety with low sulfur content that commanded a premium in international markets, was the main natural resource on which the government depended heavily to sustain its economic development programs through the 1970s. Crude oil production, concentrated in the Hassi Messaoud field near Haoud el Hamra pumping station, south of Constantine, and in the areas of the Zarzaïtine and Edjeleh fields near the Libyan border, however, has been diminishing steadily; in the early 1990s it accounted for no more than 1 percent of world production (see fig. 6).

Algeria: A Country Study

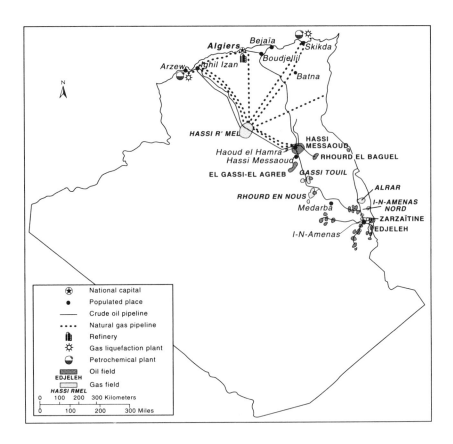

Figure 6. Oil and Gas Industry, 1993

Although about fifty oilfields have been producing since 1989, the peak production level of 1.2 million barrels per day (bpd—see Glossary) reached in 1978 was reduced to approximately 700,000 bpd in 1990. The government imposed the output restriction to prolong the life span of the oilfields and to abide by production quotas of the Organization of the Petroleum Exporting Countries (OPEC). Algeria's total refining capacity stood at 475,000 bpd in 1990.

The country's oil reserves are expected to be depleted within three decades at 1992 rates of production. This alarming assessment, coupled with slumping world oil prices and diminishing prospects of growth in crude oil sales, prompted the government to focus on involving foreign companies in its oil industry by liberalizing the application of the August 1986 exploration code. When the parliament amended this law in December 1991, Sonatrach, which has retained firm control over all oil policies despite the 1980 restructuring of the hydrocarbon industry, was obliged to allow joint ventures with international companies interested in exploring low-deposit areas that require high-technology methods to enhance production. The government also announced that international arbitration would be allowed in case of dispute.

Algeria's considerable natural gas reserves of about 3,200 billion cubic meters of proven recoverable gas are expected to last more than sixty years at 1992 production rates. Natural gas has become the country's most valuable export as a result of the decline of oil production and prices—and as an outcome of the government's diversification strategy. The Hassi R'Mel field south of Algiers is the largest and contains almost two-thirds of the country's reserves. Other large fields include, in descending order, Hassi Messaoud, Alrar (in central Algeria, near the Libyan border), Gassi Touil (southeast of Ouargla), and Rhourd en Nous (in the center of Algeria).

The four plants that liquefy natural gas are owned by Sonatrach, which in the early 1990s sought to promote pipeline sales through the existing trans-Mediterranean pipeline. It was estimated that Algeria's 1990 sales of 12.5 billion cubic meters of LNG could be doubled if plans to build a second trans-Mediterranean line to Spain were to materialize. After an ill-fated attempt by Sonatrach to raise LNG prices—at the insistence of politicians clamoring that Algeria was not getting fair compensation for its natural resources—the government decided to abandon OPEC fixed prices and switched to a more realistic market-based pricing policy. This new approach resulted in contracts extending past 2000 with such clients as Gaz de France, Enagas of Spain, Distrigaz of Belgium, and Panhandle of the United States.

Algeria's condensate reserves, which are extensively used in the petrochemicals industry and most of which are located at Hassi R'Mel, are estimated at 400 million tons. Condensate sales in the 1980s helped to make up for the downturn in oil revenues. The respite is likely to be short-lived, however, because the drop in the condensate exports is expected to be accompanied by a corresponding decrease in output from 1989 to 1995.

Enhancing LPG production has been another government priority in its diversification strategy. Fortuitously, domestic demand for LPG in individual households and public transportation has increased steadily. To meet this constantly growing demand, Sonatrach reopened its old Arzew plant, west of Algiers, in 1990. It also renovated the equipment at Hassi Messaoud and planned a construction program of extraction and processing plants, pumping stations, 1,000 kilometers of pipeline between Alrar and Hassi R'Mel, and, finally, the long-awaited massive new LPG plant at Arzew. Despite Sonatrach's successful implementation of its diversification strategy, the government was well aware of its overdependence on the revenue from oil and gas exports to finance its ambitious national development program and service its external debt.

Minerals

Algeria's nonfuel minerals are used extensively as raw materials for domestic manufacturing, but some, such as high-grade iron ore, phosphate, mercury, and zinc, have also been exported since the early 1970s. The state mining and prospecting corporation, the National Company for Mineral Research and Exploration (Société Nationale de Recherches et d'Exploitations Minières), was established in 1967. As a result of the government's decentralization policy, the company was restructured in 1983 into separate production and distribution entities. The most important of these were an iron ore and phosphate company known as Ferphos, which had three production units and a port complex at Annaba, and another company called Erem that specialized in conducting mineral research at Boumerdas on the Mediterranean Sea and Tamanrasset in the south (see fig. 7).

Iron ore is found at Beni Saf in the northwest and the Ouenza and Bou Khadra region near the eastern border. Production levels have tended to vary significantly over the years, fluctuating between 1 million and 2 million tons between the early 1970s and the early 1990s. The deposits at Ouenza represent 75 percent of total production and have been exported primarily to Italy and Britain. However, there are massive reserves of medium-grade ore at Gara Djebilet, near Tindouf in the west. These deposits of an estimated 2 billion tons of medium-grade ore have been said to be the largest in the Arab world. The most significant zinc deposits have been found at the mountain of El Abed near the Algerian-Moroccan border and at Kherzet-Youssef in the Sétif region. Lead is also mined at El Abed and Kherzet-Youssef.

The large phosphate deposits at Djebel Onk in the northeast have been mined since the early 1960s; phosphate rock output reached 1.3 million tons in 1988. The total was almost evenly divided between export (primarily to France and Spain) and local consumption or processing at the Annaba fertilizer plant, approximately 350 kilometers away. Most major mines are linked by rail to Algeria's ports. Djebel Onk phosphate mines near the Tunisian border, as well as the Ouenza iron ore mines, are linked by electric rail line to Annaba. Zinc and lead mines at El Abed near the Moroccan border in the west are linked to Oran.

Electric Power

The mounting demand for LPG use in individual households has been matched by a similar increase in the demand for electricity—a factor of the rapid rate of national development and housing construction. Overall energy consumption throughout the country quadrupled between the early 1970s and the early 1990s, largely as a result of government efforts to complete the rural electrification program and extend the domestic gas network. The National Company for Electricity and Gas (Société Nationale de l'Électricité et du Gaz—Sonelgaz) is the state utility company responsible for producing and distributing electric power and gas. Sonelgaz has estimated that the country's low- and medium-tension power network will reach almost 350,000 kilometers by 2005, compared with 102,000 kilometers in 1987 (the latest figure available in 1993).

Before independence in 1962, almost half of Algeria's electricity was generated by hydroelectric power; three decades later, only 7 percent of capacity was hydroelectric. The main sources of electricity generation are thermal plants located at Algiers, Annaba, and Oran. The Kabylie region has a group of small hydroelectric stations. Most production plants had converted from coal to gas by the early 1980s.

In its search for alternative energy sources, the government established the Commissariat for New Energy (Commissariat aux Énergies Nouvelles) in 1982 to develop nuclear energy, solar energy, and other potential sources of power. Whereas solar power was proving to have considerable potential, particularly in desert locations, nuclear power may become a casualty of international concerns and allegations that it could be used for military purposes.

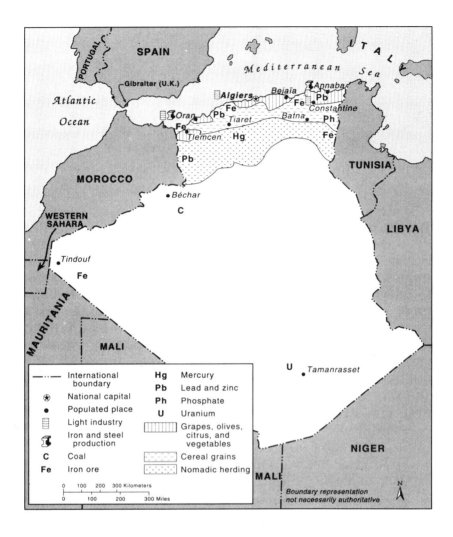

Figure 7. Economic Activity, 1993

Industry

In the early 1990s, the industrial sector represented Algeria's greatest hope in its search for economic independence. The major component of this part of the economy consists of hydrocarbon-related processing plants (see Hydrocarbons, this ch.). In addition, heavy industrial manufacturing and construction constitute significant elements of this sector.

Manufacturing

Industry is a growing factor in Algeria's economy, and in 1990 constituted 10 percent of GDP. Steel production began in El Hadjar near Annaba in the early 1970s, when the government was emphasizing heavy industry. A decade later, however, this plant was operating at 20 percent of its expanded capacity of 2 million tons per year, as a result of poor management, shortage of inputs, and heavy-handed bureaucratic procedures. Although the Benjedid government continued to invest in manufacturing, it was sensitive to consumer demands and hence amenable to allocating more funds to lighter industries that create more jobs.

Since the 1970s, smaller manufacturers of shoes and clothes and even smaller steel mills have been located in many parts of the country and have created some worthwhile opportunities for private investors. The manufacture of agricultural equipment, trucks, and machine tools, once the exclusive domain of the National Company for Mechanical Construction (Société Nationale de Constructions Mécaniques), has been decentralized and used as a model for restructuring other large national companies. The success of this experiment encouraged the World Bank in 1990 to extend Algeria a US$99.5 million loan for restructuring other industrial companies.

Construction

Algeria's chronic housing shortage, which has ranked high on the government's priority list because of its social implications, has had a consistent impact on the construction industry. The population over the years has been unevenly distributed: about 87 percent of the population lives in the coastal and subcoastal regions, which comprise 17 percent of the country's total area (see Urbanization and Density, ch. 2). The influx of Algerians moving from rural areas into urban housing left vacant by the French and other Europeans, coupled with rapid economic development and high birth rates, has dramatically accelerated the pace of urbanization.

Government attention to housing was not evident, however, until it was included in economic development plans in the 1980s. The five-year plans for 1980–84 and 1985–89 outlined a number of objectives for housing policies: reduction of construction delays, integration of housing within social services designed to raise living standards, control of expansion of housing developments to preserve agricultural land, and sale of government-owned dwellings to their occupants. In addition, the plans sought to improve the efficiency of the construction sector and the financial institutions involved in housing and to develop the construction material industry.

The seriousness with which the government viewed the housing problem was underlined in 1992 when a new minister of housing was appointed and assigned the responsibility of urban development in addition to the traditional function of overseeing housing construction. Even with governmental encouragement of manufacturers of building materials to produce more, the public sector has been unable to meet the constantly growing demand for new housing—estimated at about 250,000 units a year. In 1993 there was a shortage of 2 million housing units. A major obstacle was a chronic shortage of inputs in cement production, which was controlled by four regional Enterprises for Cement and Derivatives (Entreprises des Ciments et Dérives). Private-sector firms have been active, however, in introducing prefabricated construction techniques under the umbrella of the National Office to Promote Prefabricated Construction (Office National de la Promotion de la Construction en Préfabriqué).

Agriculture

Algerian independence and the subsequent departure of French colons and other settlers signaled the collapse of the agricultural sector. Agriculture used to be Algeria's dominant sector. From the beginning of French colonization until the early 1960s, it satisfied almost all of the country's food requirements. It was critically handicapped, however, by the sudden loss of foreign managers and skilled labor. Perhaps more important was the disruption of a profit-motivated system that was not content with self-sufficiency but that also managed to export some products. Whereas Algeria produced more than 90 percent of its grain needs in 1962, the 1989 rate stood at 25 percent. Before the advent of the oil and gas era, the agricultural sector accounted for 63 percent of export revenues. But the importance of agriculture dwindled steadily as hydrocarbons became the driving force of the economy and the government's development policy favored heavy industries over agriculture-related projects. Similarly, agricultural employment dropped from 40 percent of the total labor force in the 1960s to 24 percent in 1990. The percentage of GDP provided by agriculture in 1990 was estimated to be between 7 and 11 percent; it was clear that agriculture's impact on the economy had declined appreciably since colonial times.

Nevertheless, agriculture remains highly significant. In the early 1990s, at least 22 percent of the population lived in rural areas and depended on agriculture as a means of livelihood. But a number of natural factors beyond the government's control have had a negative impact on Algerian agriculture, among them unreliable rainfall patterns, floods, and drought. The country's arable land is limited to less than 3 percent of its total area—about 7.5 million hectares. Another 12 percent of Algeria's total area is suitable only for forestry and grazing. Because 40 to 50 percent of the cultivable land is usually left fallow in any one season, only about 1.7 percent of the total area (about 4.2 million hectares) is actually cultivated; more than half of the cultivable area, 2.7 million hectares, is used for grains alone. In addition, only one-tenth of the cultivable land receives adequate rainfall. In 1989 the government, finally recognizing that irrigation projects were essential to allow more intensive cultivation and substitution of higher-yielding vegetables for grains, provided more than 1.8 billion cubic meters of water by irrigation to increase agricultural production.

Land Tenure and Reform

The government emphasis on agriculture and the importance of irrigation in the 1990s is reminiscent of the role of agriculture in Algeria's preindependence era. European settlers then held most of the irrigated land and about one-half of the cultivated area. At independence, the newly installed government took over for its own use farms vacated by the French and other foreigners; the lands remained legally owned by the settlers, however. This arrangement lasted until October 1963, when the authorities decreed that all land abandoned by the colons would be owned by the state. By mid-1966 all remaining unoccupied properties had been nationalized and turned over to workers under a self-management system (*autogestion*—see Glossary). A small portion of farmland had been occupied by Algerians claiming to be previous owners, as well as by laborers who had worked for the colons. The authorities also gave some land as a reward to veterans of the War of Independence. Most of the expropriated 2.7 million hectares, however, were turned into state farms run by workers' committees, under a socialist sector that received almost all of the funds allocated to agricul-

Djanet, a Saharan oasis in southeastern Algeria
Courtesy LaVerle Berry

ture but that suffered from a cumbersome central government bureaucracy and lack of motivation.

Dissolution of the state farming sector was announced in 1971 by Boumediene, who introduced an agrarian reform program that called for breaking up large state-owned farms and redistributing them to landless peasants. The only condition with which these peasants had to comply was to join government-organized cooperatives, which would provide them with state loans, seed, fertilizers, and agricultural equipment. By early 1974, Boumediene's agrarian revolution (1974–78) had given ten hectares of private land to each of 60,000 peasants and had organized them into 6,000 agricultural cooperatives. Encouraged by the initial success of his agrarian reform, Boumediene inaugurated a new program to construct One Thousand Socialist Villages; in fact, its ultimate objective was to build 1,700 villages to house 140,000 farmers.

After Boumediene's death in 1978, this program ended, presumably because of the heavy financial losses it had incurred. Other contributing factors may have been the new government's concern over poor agricultural productivity, rising costly food imports, and the generally unsatisfactory performance of communal farms. Therefore the Benjedid government decided to allocate more public funds to agricultural infrastructure, especially dam construction and water projects.

Serious reforms, which eventually reversed the policy of concentrating production in state-owned farms in favor of a system of private-sector management, started with the 1980–84 five-year plan. The government assigned approximately 700,000 hectares to private farmers, increasing the total private-sector area to 5 million hectares. At the same time, it liberalized the system for marketing agricultural products and gave incentives for intensive farming. Further reforms included the government's decision in 1987 to break up 3,400 state farms (about 700 hectares each) into privately owned farms averaging eighty hectares each. Because the right of ownership was permanent and transferable—provided the farm remained undivided to ensure adequate cultivation size—and the new owners were entitled to own all their equipment, this measure proved an effective incentive for individual farmers. The new system resulted in higher production as early as 1988.

Further proof of the authorities' concern with improving agricultural production to prepare the country for "life after oil" was found in the 1985–89 plan. The plan allocated higher percentages of public funds to the agricultural sector, especially water projects. Investment in such projects rose from 10 percent of the total budget in 1985 to 14.5 percent in 1990, and the government announced its intention to add 20,000 irrigated hectares a year.

Although as of 1993 Algeria was a net agricultural importer (total agricultural imports increased 45 percent in 1989 to US$3.1 billion), the government has made a special effort to ensure an affordable food supply for a rapidly growing population. As a result, it continued to control and subsidize the price of staples—bread, cooking oil, flour, milk, and sugar. The economic necessity of lowering food import costs, however, generated enough political support to allow relatively free markets in agriculture. An important step was the liberalization of the marketing of inputs and agricultural output. A 1988 decree allowed private farmers to purchase inputs from any suppliers they chose. As of April 1991, individuals and farm cooperatives could engage in wholesale trading in agricultural inputs; they were also authorized to import agricultural inputs at the official rate of exchange. Another law promulgated in 1991 deregulated land transactions and eliminated the municipalities' monopoly ownership of property reserves, making them available for public purchase.

Crops

Wheat and barley are Algeria's major grain crops, representing 63 percent of all cultivated areas in 1987. In spite of the government's longstanding objective of boosting productivity, however, grain self-sufficiency dropped from 91 percent at independence to 18 percent in 1990. The drop resulted from such factors as the rapidly multiplying population, erratic climatic conditions, agricultural mismanagement, and rural migration to urban centers. Grain production plunged 25 percent between 1986 and 1990, but returned to a record level in 1991. The bulk of the production was in wheat and barley (see table 4, Appendix). Despite the comeback, Algeria continued to import 75 percent of its grain needs. The EC was the major supplier of barley. Corn imports also doubled between 1985 and 1990; the United States provided 75 percent of the total.

Other main crops include grapes, citrus fruits, vegetables, olives, tobacco, and dates. In the early 1990s, Algeria was the world's fifth largest producer of dates. About three-quarters of the annual average of 200,000 tons are consumed locally.

Wine production, however, although it continues to be Algeria's major agricultural export as it had been during French occupation, has shown a steady and drastic decline. The drop has occurred in part because of decreased demand in European markets but also because of the government view that dependence on wine exports is economically and politically risky as well as possibly inappropriate for a Muslim state. France's decision to stop importing Algerian wines in retaliation for the nationalization of its oil assets in 1969 has been cited as one reason for the drop. The country's annual output of wine declined from 15 million hectoliters in 1962 to 1 million hectoliters in 1988; the area under vine cultivation dropped correspondingly from 370,000 hectares to 82,000 hectares for the same period.

In 1990 olive groves covered at least 160,000 hectares, but unsatisfactory levels of olive oil production caused the government in 1990 to initiate a ten-year program to rehabilitate an additional 100,000 hectares of groves and build 200 oil-pressing plants. The authorities also sought to expand tomato cultivation in addition to other agro-industry projects. Tobacco, however, remained the main industrial crop, producing 4,000 tons a year and employing 13,000 workers.

Livestock

Although sheep and goat herds have been increasing since independence, especially when contrasted with grain production levels, the viability of the livestock sector as a whole depends heavily on such factors as improvement of breeding methods, disease control, and imported feed—feed grain imports rose sharply in the 1980s. Whereas meat production increased through the 1970s, growth tapered off during the 1980s, and the government was concerned about the failure to meet the production target of 228,000 tons in 1989. At least 60 percent of milk requirements were imported in 1990. Poultry production scored remarkable successes and reached self-sufficiency by the mid-1980s. Earlier, the agrarian revolution had tried to restructure the system of grazing on the high plateaus but failed to change the pattern of livestock ownership: 5 percent of herders in 1990 owned 50 percent of the total herds. In 1990, according to United Nations Food and Agriculture Organization estimates, Algeria had about 1.4 million head of cattle, 3.7 million goats, and 13.4 million sheep. The majority of livestock spend the winter on the open range and the spring and

Grape production has decreased, but vineyards still flourish in some areas.
Courtesy United States Department of Agriculture

Cutting hay; women in the foreground, men in the rear
Courtesy Nadia Benchallal and Middle East Report

summer in the grain-raising area grazing on what is left after the wheat and barley harvests.

Forestry

In 1991 about 4 million hectares of forest remained in Algeria according to official estimates, but most experts thought that reality fell far short of that figure. The area covered by forests had been dwindling for decades despite government efforts to increase wooded hectarage and prevent the erosion of cultivable land. The 1985–89 plan included a project to reforest 364,000 hectares. An earlier twenty-year project begun in 1975 had initiated the construction of a 1,500-kilometer-long green barrier (*barrage vert*) of forest along the northern edge of the Sahara from Morocco to Tunisia. Although the project managed in theory to increase the total forest area by 10 percent annually, the percentage being swallowed up by the desert and by sheep grazing was greater.

A state monopoly, the National Association of Cork and Wood Industries (Société Nationale des Industries des Lièges et du Bois), operates the timber industry. The industry processed more than 300,000 cubic meters of wood and cork in 1991. Algeria ranked third in world cork production, after Spain and Portugal.

Fishing

Despite Algeria's 1,000 kilometers of Mediterranean coast, the fishing industry remains underdeveloped. The government, aware of the industry's potential, established joint enterprises with Mauritania and Senegal by the 1980s to exploit the rich fishing waters of the Atlantic. In 1991 the government was also modernizing and expanding fishing ports on the Mediterranean Sea, hoping to increase the 1988 catch of 106,000 tons to an annual rate of 115,000 tons. In 1989 the catch had fallen to 99,000 tons.

Transportation and Telecommunications

Transportation

Algeria's transportation infrastructure, mostly inherited from the French, was badly neglected through the 1970s. However, the government has devoted considerable attention and funding to it since the early 1980s in order to meet the growing needs for balanced regional development and to deal with the pressure of rapid urbanization. Public funds have been allocated to expand, modernize, and upgrade the country's roads, railroads, ports, and airports to accommodate constantly rising traffic and passenger demands. But the government's insistence in the early 1990s on continuing its policy of austerity and lowering expenditure levels could lead to rehabilitating the existing infrastructure rather than investing in new systems.

Railroads

Railroads are a state monopoly run by the National Railroad Transportation Company (Société Nationale des Transports Ferroviaires—SNTF), a semi-autonomous public entity operating under the aegis of the Ministry of Transport. The approximately 4,000-kilometer railroad system, which is old and poorly designed, is further handicapped by the lack of long-distance traffic. Phosphate and iron ore traffic in the eastern region is almost the only commercially profitable freight traffic. Passenger traffic is concentrated mostly around the major urban areas, especially the capital (see fig. 8). A main railroad line connects major cities along the coast and joins the Moroccan and Tunisian systems at their respective borders. However, rail links with Morocco were closed for twelve years as a result of tension between the two countries and reopened only in September 1988.

SNTF has argued that rail transport is 75 percent cheaper than road transport and that it should be developed to carry up to 40 percent of freight, as in France. The fact that the railroads carried 53 million passengers and 13 million tons of freight in 1989 lent further credence to SNTF's ambitious US$11 billion program to double the length and freight capacity of the existing rail network. The expansion program includes a new line running east-west across the Hauts Plateaux, new track, freight centers, and stations. Although the government's austerity policy may affect the level of investment in railroad improvement, several new lines were under construction in 1993 and others were under renovation, including the Jijel-Ramdane Djamal line in the northeast and stretches of the line in western Algeria.

Funding for Algeria's railroads has come from outside sources. In 1991 the African Development Bank approved a loan to finance construction of a railroad tunnel that would cost US$130 million and take more than three years to com-

Algeria: A Country Study

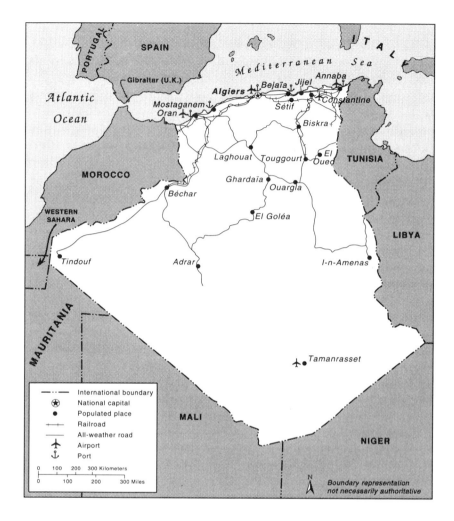

Figure 8. Transportation System, 1993

plete. Part of a US$211 million loan from the World Bank in 1989 was allotted to the reconstruction of Algeria's railroads.

An urban rail project involving work on the first twenty-six kilometers of the Algiers subway system, which had been planned for 1985, was begun in August 1989. The whole system is to total sixty-four kilometers when completed in 1994.

Ports

Shipping is also a government monopoly run by the state concern, the National Corporation for Maritime Transport and the Algerian National Navigation Company (Société Nationale de Transports Maritimes et Compagnie Nationale Algérienne de Navigation—SNTM-CNAN). SNTM-CNAN started with nine vessels in 1971; in the late 1980s, the organization owned seventy vessels and twenty tugboats. Although the Ministry of Transport is responsible for coordinating maritime functions, semiautonomous port authorities created in 1984 handle port operations. Algeria's major ports—Algiers, Annaba, Oran, Skikda, Bejaïa, and Mostaganem—handled about 84 million tons of cargo in 1990. The three largest ports handled 71 percent of total traffic in 1991; Algiers took 32 percent, Annaba 23 percent, and Oran 16 percent. Bejaïa and Skikda remain important ports for exporting hydrocarbons and minerals, Mostaganem handles general cargo, and Arzew boasts large LNG terminals. The new container port of Djendjene near Jijel, funded by Saudi Arabia and built by an Italian-Dutch consortium, is to serve the planned Bellara steelworks in eastern Algeria. The port may need a massive financial infusion to make it fully operative.

The need to develop container facilities, especially at the congested Algiers port, and to continue modernizing other ports ranked high on the government's priority list in 1992. The World Bank provided a US$63 million loan in 1989 to upgrade the port facilities of Algiers, Annaba, and Oran. In connection with port improvement programs, the government needed to clarify the division of responsibility between the Ministry of Transport, which has authority to coordinate all port operations, and the Ministry of Public Works, which oversees construction and maintenance of port infrastructures.

Roads

Algeria has more than 90,000 kilometers of national roads, including 30,000 kilometers of primary routes, or *routes nationales* (RN), and 20,000 kilometers of secondary roads, or *chemins de wilaya* (CW). The rest of the road network consists of tertiary but generally accessible roads and tracks known as *chemins communaux* (CC), mainly serving rural areas in the north and in the Sahara region. The RN and CW system of major roads is managed by the Ministry of Public Works and its regional services, known as Directorates for Basic Infrastructures (Directions des Infrastructures de Base); the Ministry of Interior, Local Communities, and Tourism and local authorities are responsible for tertiary roads. The road network is unevenly distributed among the various regions, but it accurately reflects the topography and demographic pattern of the country. Thus, the network is much more developed in the northern coastal region where economic activities and population concentrations are heaviest. The south is served by a limited number of national roads linking the few densely populated areas.

Three major east-west highways run through Algeria and link Morocco with Tunisia, and three others run from north to south. The most extensive highway project, however, is a transSaharan road, known as the Road of African Unity. It runs from El Goléa south to Tamanrasset, all the way to the southern borders, branching before it reaches into Niger and Mali.

Figures on vehicle fleets on Algeria's roads are neither readily available nor very reliable, mainly because vehicle registration data are not adjusted for vehicle scrapping. Best estimates put the number of privately owned cars and trucks at well over 1 million in the early 1990s. This number is expected to increase as the government continues to ease restrictions on imports of cars by migrant workers returning to Algeria. Stateowned trucks constitute about 80 percent of the total vehicle fleet capacity.

Airports

Civil aviation is an important ingredient of the transportation system because of the distances involved in such a large country and the dispersion of population, particularly in the south. The hydrocarbon industry is partly responsible for the mushrooming of the dozens of small airfields and airstrips needed to support oil and natural gas exploration and surveying in various areas. Civil aviation can be expected to receive special attention from the government—in spite of increasing resource constraints—because of the need for regional development on the Hauts Plateaux and for integrating the deep south desert region with the rest of the economy.

Internationally, Algeria's four major airports—Algiers, Constantine, Annaba, and Oran—dominate the scene and provide 97 percent of all services. In the late 1980s and early 1990s, airport infrastructure improvements administered by the Airport Directorate of the Ministry of Public Works included the extension of one of the two runways in Algiers, completion of improvements to airports in the south, construction of a second runway at Tamanrasset, and modernization of navigation facilities and equipment at several airports.

*Port of Algiers, the country's principal maritime
facility for general cargo and passengers
Courtesy United Nations*

Air Algérie, which was established in 1946 as a charter airline by Air France, became the national carrier in 1972 when the Algerian government purchased full ownership. It was restructured in 1984, when domestic routes were assigned to the newly formed Inter-Air Services. In 1989 Inter-Air Services carried almost 2 million passengers on its internal network and a similar number on international flights. Air Algérie planned a major expansion of its passenger fleet in the 1990s, and its ten-year renewal program is expected to cost US$1.5 billion.

Air Algérie has daily passenger and air freight service to Europe and weekly service to the Middle East and Africa. Air France flies daily into Algiers and less frequently into other major airports. Other foreign carriers also have regularly scheduled flights.

Telecommunications

Algeria's domestic telecommunications system consists of high-capacity radio-relay and coaxial-cable trunk routes that link all the major population areas along the Mediterranean. Lower-capacity routes branch off the trunk routes to the south, providing communications with towns in the interior. A domestic satellite system with fifteen ground stations is used for telephone and television links from the main station near Algiers to remote areas in the Sahara.

In 1992 Algeria had 900,000 telephones, or 3.4 telephones per 100 inhabitants. Although 95 percent of the service is automatic and capable of international direct-dial service, 5 percent of the telephones are still connected to manual exchanges, requiring an operator to complete all calls. Demand for new service far outstrips the government's ability to install new lines. To alleviate some of the pressure for new telephones, the government ordered 3,000 new public telephones in 1991 to augment the 6,000 public telephones already in service. Mobile telephone service, with an initial capacity of 3,000 lines, was also introduced in major coastal cities in 1991.

International telecommunications are considered excellent and use a mix of satellite, undersea cable, coaxial cable, and radio relay. The coaxial cable and radio-relay lines along the coast extend into Morocco in the west and Tunisia in the east. A smaller radio-relay line in southeastern Algeria links directly with the Libyan national system. Six submarine coaxial cables under the Mediterranean Sea provide 3,200 simultaneous channels to Europe; two of the cables go to Spain, three to France, and one to Italy. Telephone, television, and data communication to most of Asia and the Americas go via two satellite ground stations, one working with the International Telecommunications Satellite Corporation's (Intelsat's) Atlantic Ocean satellite and the other with Intelsat's Indian Ocean satellite. Television transmission and telephone calls to and from other countries in the Middle East are routed through a ground station linked to the Arab Organization for Space Communications (Arabsat) satellite. Arabsat not only provides telephone, data transmission, telex, and facsimile transmission but also is heavily used for live broadcasts of prayers from Mecca and Medina and for showing inter-Arab sports events.

In contrast to international communications links, in 1993 domestic broadcast facilities were sparse. Only the larger populated areas of the country are able to receive television and radio. The country has twenty-six amplitude modulation (AM) radio stations, broadcasting in Arabic, French, and Kabyle; there are no frequency modulation (FM) radio stations. A moderate-strength shortwave station with programs in Arabic, French, Spanish, and English broadcasts to remote areas of the south and to neighboring countries. Eighteen transmitters provide television service to major cities. The country had an estimated 3.5 million radios and 2 million television sets in 1993.

Trade

Algeria continued in 1992 to depend on hydrocarbons for approximately 95 percent of its export revenues. The government had hoped to reduce such dependence by augmenting exports of nonhydrocarbon goods, but rising exports of petroleum products and gas seem to have foiled Sonatrach's efforts in that direction. Another distinguishing feature of Algeria's foreign trade has been the major disruption in trade patterns resulting from the erosion of its special relationship with France. The changes are not considered to be permanently devastating to trade, however. To cite one example: France's 81 percent share of Algeria's exports and 82 percent of imports before independence dropped to 13 percent and 24 percent, respectively, in 1977. By the late 1980s, however, the Algerian oil nationalization crisis and France's earlier decision to import the bulk of its crude oil needs from Saudi Arabia were swept aside by new economic cooperation protocols between Algeria and France.

Trading Partners

As trade patterns changed, in 1989 the United States joined France and Italy to become one of Algeria's three major markets, as well as its suppliers (see table 5, Appendix). The appreciable growth in United States exports (US$948 million in 1990) resulted from a high level of Commodity Credit Corporation guarantees for United States agricultural sales and a considerable increase in sales of industrial equipment, aircraft, and spare parts. Other items that have dominated the United States share of the Algerian import market include pharmaceuticals, mining machinery, electric-power generating equipment, computers, plastics-processing equipment, medical supplies, and telecommunications gear. Algeria's economic austerity since the latter 1980s, however, has limited the demand for imported finished products.

The resumption of contracts between Sonatrach and United States gas importers in 1989 was the main cause of increased United States imports from Algeria (US$2.6 billion in 1990). Anadarko Petroleum Corporation in October 1989 signed an oil exploration/production contract for US$100 million over ten years. Occidental Petroleum Corporation in June 1991 signed a similar contract for US$32 million. Pfizer in October 1990 signed a contract establishing a joint venture with the Algerian state National Enterprise for Production of Pharmaceuticals (Entreprise Nationale de Production de Produits Pharmaceutiques), for construction of a US$27 million pharmaceutical plant near Reghaïa, east of Algiers. Air Products Company joined forces with Aire Liquide (France) in signing a contract with Sonatrach in July 1990 for construction of a US$90 million plant at Arzew to produce helium and nitrogen gases.

Despite its close relationship with France, as a socialist country committed to safeguarding its economic and political independence, Algeria has developed and maintained special links to developing countries and Eastern Europe. However, in the early 1990s it continued to rely heavily on Western industrialized countries for the bulk of its foreign trade. The European Community alone, for example, accounted in 1990 for 35 percent of exports and 40 percent of imports. By contrast, Algeria's partners in the Union of the Arab Maghrib—Morocco, Tunisia, Libya, and Mauritania—accounted for less than 2 percent of its trade. After diplomatic relations between Algeria and Morocco resumed in 1988, the five countries formed the

The Economy

union to promote "economic integration and cooperation" in February 1989. Algeria, Tunisia, and Libya have agreed since to construct a gas pipeline between Algeria and Libya across Tunisia.

Exports and Imports

As a continuation of its efforts to increase nonhydrocarbon exports, especially by the private sector, the government decreed in 1990 that privately owned companies could export surplus textiles, leather goods, agricultural produce, and phosphates. Almost half of Algeria's total hydrocarbon sales in 1990 consisted of crude oil and condensates (22 percent refined products and 30 percent natural gas). Nonhydrocarbon exports included, in order of importance, wine, metals and metal products, phosphates, fruits and vegetables, and iron ore.

Of Algeria's total imports, worth more than US$9.8 billion in 1989, foodstuffs accounted for 31.5 percent, semifinished goods 32 percent, industrial goods 25 percent, and other consumer goods 10.5 percent. After the government decreased the number of large-scale national development projects, imports of capital goods dropped correspondingly. But imports of consumer goods have been high, with foodstuffs alone costing about US$2 billion in 1989.

The government's concern over its ability to meet hard-currency payments caused it to control the level of imports, even at the expense of appearing to contradict its own policy of liberalizing the economy, including foreign trade rules. This measure, however, did not mean a return to the 1978 law that had allowed the Ministry of Commerce to monopolize trade and subjected commercial transactions to Central Bank approval. Private companies continued to import goods on their own account, to use foreign exchange generated from their exports to finance the imports they needed, and to enter into joint ventures with foreign partners. Other stringent restrictions, such as forbidding foreign firms to engage in direct sales and limiting them to opening a regional office known as a Liaison Bureau (Bureau de Liaison), were removed in 1988. Legislation passed in 1991 permitted the establishment of local marketing operations, as well as agency agreements between foreign and Algerian partners known as concessionaires. The new distribution system practically ended the government's monopoly on foreign trade. Both manufacturers and suppliers can now sell either through local wholesalers or through their own distribution networks.

Balance of Payments

The surpluses of the balance of payments in the 1970s resulted from high levels of hydrocarbon exports, considerable foreign borrowing by the government, and healthy remittances by Algerian workers abroad. The surplus slipped into deficit in the early 1980s, however, as the government decided to ease import restrictions, suspend foreign borrowing temporarily, and repay its external debt more rapidly. The 1986 drop in the world oil price decreased revenues from hydrocarbon sales, while imports of agricultural products were increasing in response to growing domestic demand; the combination of factors further worsened the balance of payments.

Algeria's balance of payments began to improve in 1988, largely because of an unexpected rise in oil prices (see table 6, Appendix). However, the price of, and demand for, imports continued to grow, and the government's interest payments on its foreign debt rose from US$1.5 billion in 1988 to nearly US$2 billion in 1989.

Trade Account

The government's measures to encourage the growth of private-sector trade, combined with fluctuating oil prices, have resulted in an erratic trade account pattern, marked mostly by a chronic deficit followed by ups and downs of surplus. The foreign trade deficit of the 1960s was not reversed until 1973–74. The world oil price boom then overturned Algeria's traditional dependence on exports of vegetables, citrus fruit, wine, tobacco, iron ore, and phosphates; instead Algeria substituted massive hydrocarbon exports. However, the authorities continued to retain control over the trade budget process, which allowed them to cut imports in 1991 to US$8.2 billion to meet the IMF's requirements for a standby agreement. The trade balance registered a healthy surplus of almost US$1.6 billion in the first half of 1991. In April 1991, the government introduced a major liberalization of the import system by eliminating the administrative allocation of hard currency for imports at the official exchange rate. Private firms were allowed to join the ranks of state-owned enterprises in purchasing foreign goods directly from overseas markets.

Trends

Algeria has made considerable progress in its transition efforts toward a market economy. A money and credit law promulgated in 1990 granted the Central Bank the authority to formulate and implement monetary and foreign-exchange policies, removed controls on foreign investment in most sectors, allowed full foreign ownership of new investment projects, and encouraged unrestricted joint ventures between foreign companies and Algerian private concerns. In a bold move designed to promote trade liberalization, the Central Bank devalued the dinar almost 100 percent between November 1990 and the end of April 1991. On the latter date, the government introduced a major liberalization of external trade to augment the already far-reaching steps taken to liberalize domestic trade.

Algeria, not unlike several other countries in North Africa and the Middle East, has had to grapple with a heavy debt burden. The country's international creditworthiness has been subjected to closer than normal scrutiny on occasion, such as when its ratio of debt to export earnings moved from 130 percent in 1980 to 280 percent in 1989 and when the debt-service ratio shot up from 25 percent in 1981 to 95 percent in 1989. However, the combination of fiscal restraint on the government's part, adamant opposition to debt restructuring (mostly for reasons of political pride), and prudent use of budget surplus and intermittent higher revenues (from fluctuating oil prices) helped repay Ministry of Finance debts to the Central Bank and retire significant portions of foreign debt.

Over the long haul, however, how much progress Algeria makes toward establishing a truly open market economy will depend on the correlation between economic liberalization efforts and the dynamics of the domestic political situation, which was continuing to evolve in the early 1990s. If, for instance, the evolving political process encourages passage of new legislation similar to the June 1990 Law on Trade Union Activity providing for the creation of autonomous labor unions and collective bargaining, other key institutional changes could accelerate the pace of social progress and generate an environment conducive to political accountability and economic reform.

* * *

Richard B. Parker's *North Africa: Regional Tensions and Strategic Concerns* provides a lucid backdrop as to why and how Algeria's various economic reforms were conceived and introduced. It has the added virtue of placing Algeria in a regional North African context, comparing its situation with that of its neighbors to the east and west. *North Africa: Contemporary Politics and Economic Development*, edited by Richard Lawless and Allan Findlay, gives a solid analysis of the Algerian economy. David B. Ottaway and Marina Ottaway's *Algeria: The Politics of a Socialist Revolution*, although published in 1970, remains an informative source. For those interested in analyzing the fast-moving developments of the Algerian scene, the *Economist* and *Middle East Economic Digest* are essential. (For further information and complete citations, see Bibliography.)

Chapter 4. Government and Politics

Mosque in traditional style in Ghardaia, in north central Algeria

ALGERIAN POLITICAL CULTURE and government reflect the impact of the country's colonial history and its cultural identification. The legacy of the revolutionary War of Independence (1954–62) and its lingering implications are still evident in recent political events and in the evolution of political processes. A strong authoritative tendency and the supremacy of the military, both remnants of the war for liberation, have resulted in a sharply divided society in which the political elite remains highly remote from, and generally unaccountable to, the masses of its impoverished, unemployed, and dissatisfied citizens. State-supported socialism, largely fed by petroleum exports, and "depoliticization" of the masses during the 1970s replaced any real source of legitimacy for the regime and left the masses almost no form of political expression short of violent confrontation.

The consequences of this political tradition materialized in January 1992 when a conservative military coup overturned four years of significant political and economic liberalization undertaken by President Chadli Benjedid in the late 1980s. Benjedid's extensive political and economic reforms, pursued to restore political legitimacy and public confidence in the government leadership, had opened the way for political opposition. The rise of the Islamic Salvation Front (Front Islamique du Salut—FIS) as the most significant opposition group threatened to challenge the secular orientation of the state. The coup took place only days before the second round of the first freely contested national elections, elections that were likely to usher in a new government dominated by Islamists (sometimes seen as fundamentalists). Since then, the virtual elimination of constitutional government and the resurrection of military authoritarianism have returned Algeria to the familiar situation of placing power in the hands of a small elite, nullifying almost all of the democratic freedoms and many of the free-market reforms of the preceding few years.

Algeria's bloody overthrow of colonial rule resulted in independence in 1962 and a legacy of an authoritarian political structure dominated by competing interests. The main actors in the national revolution continued to govern the Algerian polity after independence, struggling during the immediate postindependence period and throughout postindependence

Algerian history for political control. This tradition has evolved into a triangular system of government in which the army, party, and state apparatus share power but continually compete. Benjedid's reforms in the 1980s effectively eliminated the party (the National Liberation Front—Front de Libération Nationale—FLN) from a prominent position in the political configuration while strengthening his hand as president through constitutional reforms. The military, also having suffered a reduction of authority with the political changes implemented by the 1989 constitution, appeared to have little tolerance for the liberalization visualized by Benjedid and the more liberal faction of the FLN. Resurfacing in the early 1990s to "ensure the security of the state," the military has demonstrated once again that the army remains the dominant arm of the political triangle.

Recent political events are as much a reflection as a determinant of political culture in Algeria. The nation in late 1993 was under a state of emergency, its condition since the military coup in January 1992. Martial law ruled, essentially invalidating all political structures and institutions. The outcome of this period will be determined not only by the political leaders but also by civil society, political competition within the state, and by mass culture. If the Algerian state is to overcome its political crisis, it needs to resolve its myriad socioeconomic problems. If it is to successfully conquer its economic problems, it will need to become more democratic and decentralized. The current situation is potentially dangerous because of the explosive nature of the political tensions inherent in the repression of a discontented population.

Political Environment

Postindependence Politics and the Socialist Tradition

Algeria's current political culture is a result of the French colonial legacy, the War of Independence, the Arab and Islamic cultural traditions and the part these play in national unity and cohesion, and the integral role of the military. The consolidation of authority and the institutionalization of political structure characterized the postindependence years as the new Algerian nation struggled to overcome the instability of the revolutionary period. National integrity and national institutions were viewed as equally important as Algeria worked to consolidate its independent political structure and tradition and to overcome the administrative and economic vacuum that resulted from the departure of most Europeans who had lived in Algeria.

The Revolutionary Period and Independence

Emerging from more than 132 years of French colonial domination and nearly eight years of the War of Independence, Algeria was officially declared independent of France on July 3, 1962, but recognizes July 5 as its Independence Day. Exhausted from so many years of warfare and internally divided into fiercely competitive factions, the military/political leadership of the victorious FLN quickly deteriorated into incohesive groups vying for control of the new state.

The three major contenders for political predominance were the provisional government established by the FLN in 1958, the military officials, and the *wilaya* commands (administrative district councils established by the military in the preindependence period). The confrontation was characterized by fierce personal and ethnic loyalties as well as ideology and surfaced even before independence was officially declared. A May 1962 meeting in Tripoli of FLN leaders closed with Ahmed Ben Bella assuming control of the party and what would become the nation of Algeria under a tentative alliance with Colonel Houari Boumediene.

The "Heroic" Stage: Ben Bella's Regime, 1962–65

With the declaration of independence, Ben Bella assumed the title of national president. The first postindependence elections were held for the new National Assembly on September 20, 1962, and on September 26, the National Assembly officially elected Ben Bella premier and formally declared the Democratic and Popular Republic of Algeria. Ben Bella formed his government from the ranks of the military and close personal and political allies, indicating that the factional infighting was far from suppressed.

The first and most pressing task of the new government was to restore some normality to the war-torn economy and polity. The end of the colonial period, although not entirely eliminating the French presence in Algeria, had dramatically reduced it. The mass exodus of Europeans resulted in a severe shortage of highly skilled workers, technicians, educators, and property-owning entrepreneurs. The national government quickly assumed ownership of the abandoned industrial and agricultural properties and began a program of *autogestion* (see Glossary), or socialist workers' management. Workers were responsible for overseeing their own administration through a series of elected officials. A national system of directors and agencies was charged with ensuring that the workers conformed to a national development plan.

A new constitution was drafted that committed the country to a socialist path, established a strong presidential system, and protected the hegemonic role of the FLN as the single political party. Ben Bella assumed control of the FLN executive as general secretary. In September 1963, Ben Bella was elected president for a five-year term. As the government increasingly tended toward a dictatorship, factionalism within the leadership began to resurface.

At its first congress in April 1964, the FLN adopted a draft statement, the Algiers Charter. The charter outlined the structure of the state and government and committed Algeria to the *autogestion* program envisioned by Ben Bella. The charter also reaffirmed the significance of the Islamic tradition in Algerian political culture.

Ben Bella was never able to capture the confidence of the Algerian public or the military. He was popular among the masses more for his status as a "historic chief of the revolution" than for his leadership competency. Despite efforts to thwart the rival military faction by strengthening the leftist groups, Ben Bella was unable to overcome the political challenge of his defense minister, Colonel Houari Boumediene, whose alliance had been critical to his installation as head of government in 1962. On June 19, 1965, Algeria's first postindependence president was overthrown by Boumediene in a bloodless coup.

Boumediene and the Socialist Experiment

Council of the Revolution, 1965-75

After the coup, all political power was transferred to Boumediene and his military-dominated Council of the Revolution. The constitution and National Assembly were suspended. Boumediene was named president and prime minister, and his associates were named to the twenty other cabinet positions. No political institution other than the FLN existed for the next ten years. The objectives of the regime were to reestablish the principles of the revolution, to remedy the abuses of personal power associated with Ben Bella, to end internal divisions, and

Government and Politics

to create an "authentic" socialist society based on a sound economy. Boumediene's support came from the military and technocratic elite who believed in his gradual reformist program. Support for the new authoritarian system was not universal, and several coups were attempted in the first few years of Boumediene's regime. By the early 1970s, however, Boumediene had consolidated his regime and could focus on the pressing economic problems.

The Boumediene years were characterized by ardent socialism and state-controlled heavy industrialization, funded largely by energy exports. Dependence on France during the colonial period and the subsequent loss of capital, skill, and technology meant that Algeria's very survival in the postindependence period appeared to depend on rapid and extensive industrialization. Boumediene's industrialization program was highly centralized and involved the nationalization of almost all industrial and agricultural enterprises (see Government Role, ch. 3). By the early 1970s, almost 90 percent of the industrial sector and more than 70 percent of the industrial work force were under state control. The agricultural sector was relatively neglected at the time.

In the political realm, authority remained as concentrated as it did in the economic sphere. Aside from local and regional assemblies, administrative bodies that were essentially subordinate to the directives of the FLN, all political participation had been suspended following the coup. Boumediene had sacrificed free political exchange for regime stability and state consolidation. By 1975 the factional infighting had ceased and the internal situation had stabilized. In June 1975, the regime announced plans to resurrect public political institutions and draft a national constitution. The country was about to return to a constitutional system, Algeria's second national republic.

Formation of the Second Algerian Republic, 1976–79

The National Charter approved in June 1976 by a countrywide referendum was the subject of much public and party debate and was the product of party, trade union, and other public association negotiations. The new charter was essentially an ideological proclamation reaffirming the socialist tradition and implicitly ensuring the authoritarian nature of the regime and state. The FLN received explicit recognition as a "unique" national front representing the revolutionary heritage and ideological identification of the Algerian people.

The adoption of the National Charter was quickly followed by the drafting of a national constitution. The constitution was a long document of some 199 articles detailing a new political structure in line with the principles enunciated in the National Charter. The constitution reestablished a national legislature, the National People's Assembly (Assemblée Populaire Nationale—APN), but reasserted the preeminence of the FLN as the single legitimate party. Articles 23 through 26 of the 1976 constitution recognized the unique role of the FLN in the historical tradition and political culture of the Algerian state and confirmed its hegemonic position in the new political structure. Rather than breaking with the personalist character of the past ten years, the constitution reaffirmed the concentration of power in the executive. Boumediene was named head of state and head of government as president and prime minister, commander in chief, and minister of national security and defense, as well as secretary general of the country's single legal party.

Boumediene enjoyed the unwavering support of the military establishment. By consolidating authority and institutionalizing the Algerian political system, he instilled a degree of public confidence in his regime that Ahmed Ben Bella had been unable to achieve. Boumediene was reelected to the presidency in 1976 from a single-candidate ballot.

Elections for the APN were held in February 1977. Although all candidates were members of the FLN, they represented a variety of occupations and opinions. The diverse membership of the new assembly and the high proportion of industrial and agricultural workers and non-elites were lauded as "the final step in the construction of a socialist state" that had begun in earnest with the creation of workers' self-management assemblies at the local level in the late 1960s.

Boumediene died in December 1978. He left behind a consolidated national government, an industrializing economy, an extensive state-centered socialist program, a burgeoning energy export industry, and an apparently stable political system. He also left a political vacuum. Algeria's political development in the 1970s was heavily indebted to Boumediene's personal skills and acumen. The lack of an obvious successor left the FLN and the APN with a dilemma. The president of the APN was named interim head of state; he served until a special congress of the FLN named Colonel Chadli Benjedid secretary general of the party and candidate for president in January 1979. His selection was confirmed in a national election one week later, when 94 percent of those voting supported his nomination.

Recent Political Events

Political-Economic Liberalization under Benjedid, 1979–88

Despite his overwhelming electoral victory, Benjedid did not immediately enjoy the same respect that Boumediene had commanded. Accordingly, the new president was especially cautious in his first few years in office. His tentative and gradual reforms wandered little from the socialist course chosen by Boumediene.

Over time, however, Algeria moved slowly away from the strict socialism of the Boumediene years. After receiving a second popular mandate in 1985 with more than 95 percent of the vote in new presidential elections and after making some significant changes in government personnel, Benjedid seemed increasingly confident about instituting sweeping reforms that eventually altered radically the nature of the Algerian economy and polity.

Boumediene's socialist policy had focused almost exclusively on developing the industrial sector and relied on energy exports to finance its development at the expense of the domestic and especially the agricultural sector. Many of these industrialization projects were poorly designed and, instead of encouraging national development, eventually drained the economy. Relying on state initiative as the driving force behind economic development, large-scale industries quickly became consumed by nationalist imperatives rather than economically efficient ambitions. The fall of energy prices in the mid-1980s left Algeria, which was heavily dependent on the export of hydrocarbons, with a substantial national deficit. Agriculture, neglected in favor of heavy industry, was underdeveloped, poorly organized, and lacking in private initiative or investment. The reliance on food imports meant frequent food shortages and rapidly rising agricultural prices. Unfortunately, the crisis was not limited to the agricultural sector. The trade deficit was only one of Algeria's problems. High unemployment, one of the highest population growth rates in the world (3.1 percent per year in the early 1980s), an unbalanced industrial sector focused almost entirely on heavy industry, and rapidly declining revenues had eroded the state's welfare

Algeria: A Country Study

capacities and its ability to maintain political security and stability.

Benjedid's initial reforms concentrated on structural changes and economic liberalization. These measures included a shift in domestic investment away from heavy industry and toward agriculture, light industry, and consumer goods. State enterprises and ministries were broken up into smaller, more efficient, or at least more manageable, units, and a number of state-owned firms were divided and privatized. Benjedid opened the economy to limited foreign investment and encouraged private domestic investment. The new regime also undertook an anticorruption campaign. This campaign, aside from the obvious benefits of adding to the legitimacy of the regime, enabled Benjedid to eliminate much of the old-guard opposition loyal to Boumediene's legacy, thus strengthening his political control.

With his regime consolidated, Benjedid could intensify economic and political reform without the threat of opposition. His early reforms had been limited to the economic sector and had ensured that Benjedid remained in control of the reform process. By 1987 and 1988, however, he added political liberalization to the agenda and espoused free-market principles. He legitimized independent associations, even extending the new freedom to organize to the Algerian League of Human Rights, which had consistently criticized the regime for suppressing public political activity and demonstrations. In the economic sector, Benjedid gave state enterprises increased managerial autonomy. Central planning by the state ended, and firms became subject to the laws of supply and demand. In addition, the regime reduced subsidies, lifted price controls, and accelerated the privatization of state-owned lands and enterprises. Finally, Benjedid tackled the heavy fiscal deficit by increasing taxes and cutting spending at the central government level, as well as reducing state-purchased imports.

Despite all these measures, or perhaps because of them, Algeria found itself in a critical position politically and economically in 1988. Benjedid's reforms had exacerbated an already dismal economic situation. The dismantling and privatization of state enterprises had resulted in rising unemployment and a drop in industrial output. Trade liberalization, including import reduction and currency devaluation, and the removal of price controls and reductions in agricultural subsi-

*Former President Chadli
Benjedid (1979–92)
Courtesy Embassy of Algeria,
Washington*

dies resulted in a drastic increase in prices and an unprecedented drop in purchasing power.

The negative effects of the economic reforms were felt primarily by the disadvantaged. In contrast, the bourgeoisie and upper classes benefited greatly from economic liberalization. Economic measures legalized the private accumulation of wealth, ensured privileged access to foreign exchange and goods, and provided many with relative security as heads of recently privatized state enterprises. The result was widespread economic frustration and a lack of public confidence in the political leadership.

In October 1988, this economic and political crisis erupted in the most violent and extensive public demonstrations since independence. Following weeks of strikes and work stoppages, the riots raged for six day—from October 5 to 11. Throughout the country, thousands of Algerians attacked city halls, police stations, post offices—anything that was seen to represent the regime or the FLN. The disorder and violence were a protest against a corrupt and inefficient government and a discredited party. The riots were a product of declining living standards, rapidly increasing unemployment, and frequent food shortages. Furthermore, the riots represented a revolt against persistent inequality and the privileged status of the elite.

The poor economic situation was not unique to the Benjedid regime. Even the austere socialism of Boumediene, at least as tainted by corruption as its successor regime, had not guaranteed the economic well-being of the masses. The high oil prices in the 1970s had allowed Boumediene to fund an extensive state-supported welfare system, however, freeing him somewhat from popular political accountability. The crash of energy prices in the mid-1980s undermined this political tradeoff for a minimum standard of living and eventually undid Boumediene's successor, who had never managed to achieve quite the same level of stability. On the contrary, the political and economic liberalization under Benjedid polarized society by helping to expose the corruption and excesses of the elites while simultaneously opening up the political realm to the masses.

The government initially responded to the "Black October" riots by declaring a state of emergency and calling in the military, but the demonstrations spread. Hundreds were killed, including numerous young people, who made up the bulk of rioters in Algiers. The brutal military suppression of the riots would have far-reaching consequences, consequences that would ultimately lead to a redefinition of the military's role in the political configuration of the state. On October 10, Benjedid addressed the nation, accepting blame for the suppression and offering promises of economic and political reform. His hand had been forced. In an effort to regain the political initiative and contain the damage to his regime, Benjedid lifted the state of emergency, recalled the tanks, and announced a national referendum on constitutional reform.

Democratization, October 1988–January 11, 1992

Benjedid is given credit for responding to the country's most extensive and destructive riots since independence with political liberalization rather than suppression. For the next two years, dramatic upheavals of the political system marked the opening up of the political arena to public participation. The reasons for Benjedid's response are variously seen as a means of furthering his own political ambitions by altering the political configuration in his favor, a sincere commitment to political reform and democratic ideals, or a desperate effort to regain the political initiative. Most likely, the impetus for reform was a combination of all three factors.

In the weeks following the strikes, Benjedid tried to distance himself from the party and the old guard. He dismissed Prime

Abbassi Madani, leader of the Islamic Salvation Front (FIS)
Courtesy Middle East Report

Minister Mohamed Cherif Messadia, as well as the head of military security and a number of other officials associated with the most conservative factions of the FLN and the military. The noticeable absence of FLN party cadres in the new technocratic government presaged the president's own departure from the FLN leadership. On November 3, 1988, a number of earlier proposed reforms were approved in a national referendum, and plans for revisions of the national constitution were announced. The reforms included separation of party and state, free representation in local and national elections, and some redefinition of the executive powers.

The new constitution, accepted by national referendum in February 1989, marked the most significant changes in the ideological and political framework of the country since independence. The ideological commitment to socialism embodied in earlier constitutions was missing, and the new document formalized the political separation of the FLN and the state apparatus. The 1989 constitution allowed for the creation and participation of competitive political associations, further strengthened executive powers, diminished the role of the military in the political triangle, and only briefly alluded to the historical role of the FLN.

Subsequent legislation formally legalized political parties and established a system of proportional representation in preparation for the country's first multiparty elections. Proportional representation was intended to benefit the FLN, but the new electoral code did the exact opposite, magnifying the plurality of the Islamic Salvation Front (Front Islamique du Salut—FIS) in the local and regional elections of June 12, 1990. The FIS, competing with more than twelve political parties and numerous independent candidates in the country's first multiparty elections, captured the greatest share of the anti-FLN/antiregime protest vote. The elections were officially boycotted by the Berber Front of Socialist Forces (Front des Forces Socialistes—FFS) and Ben Bella's Movement for Democracy in Algeria (Mouvement pour la Démocratie en Algérie—MDA), along with a number of smaller opposition parties. About 65 percent of the eligible voters participated in the elections. The high turnout undoubtedly benefited the FIS, which as the largest, and possibly the only, plausible challenge to the FLN received a good percentage of its mandate as antiregime backlash. It has been argued, however, that the 35 percent abstention rate resulted largely from a deliberate political choice. Ethnic enclaves, especially in the Berber region where voters might have been expected to support such boycotting parties as the FFS, had some of the lowest turnouts in the country, at around 20 percent.

Despite the devastating defeat dealt to the ruling party, the June 1990 results went undisputed by the government, and the new council members assumed their positions. The date for national legislative elections was advanced to the following June, and the country appeared well on its way toward achieving the region's first multiparty system to transfer power peacefully to an opposition party. Then on June 5, 1991, as campaigning opened for the country's first national multiparty elections, the process came to a rapid halt as public demonstrations erupted against the government's March electoral reforms favoring the ruling party. The president called in the army to restore order, declared martial law, dismissed the government, and indefinitely postponed parliamentary elections.

Three months earlier, in March 1991, the government had presented and passed a bill reminiscent of crude gerrymandering. The bill increased the number of parliamentary seats while altering their distribution to achieve over-representation in rural areas, where the FLN's base of support rested. The bill also created a two-round voting system—if no party received an absolute majority in the first round, only the top two candidates would participate in a second-round runoff. The likely candidates in such a runoff would be the FIS and the FLN. The FLN anticipated that the general public, faced with only two choices, would favor the FLN's more traditional and secular platform over a party that represented Islamism. The remaining parties, it was thought, would win seats in parliament in their regional strongholds but would be marginalized, each expected to win no more than 10 percent of the vote.

Nearly every political party responded to this distortion of the electoral process. The FIS decried the targeting of the Islamist party by laws prohibiting the use of mosques and schools for political purposes and laws severely restricting proxy voting by husbands for their wives. The FFS and many other secular opposition parties denounced the electoral changes as leaving only "a choice between a police state and a fundamentalist state."

On May 25, the FIS called for a general strike. Tensions escalated, and by early June the military was called in for the first time since October 1988 to suppress mass protests and enforce martial law. Specifically targeting Islamists, the military arrested thousands of protesters, among them FIS leaders Abbassi Madani and Ali Belhadj (also seen as Benhadj), who were later tried and sentenced to twelve years in prison. The military also took advantage of the situation to reassert its influence in politics, calling for the resignation of Prime Minister Mouloud Hamrouche and his cabinet. The new caretaker government consisted largely of technocrats, a conservative elite drawn from the top ranks of the civil service and former state-owned enterprises. Sid Ahmed Ghozali, until then minister of foreign affairs and a former head of the state-owned gas and oil company, was named prime minister.

The Ghozali government distanced itself from the FLN party cadres while remaining subservient to the military. The FLN, meanwhile, broke into several factions. Benjedid resigned from the party leadership in July, alienating any remaining factions in the party that supported his regime. In September 1991, the state of emergency was lifted and new elections were set for December 1991 and January 1992.

Two months before the start of the elections, in October 1991, the government issued a new electoral law whose bias was hardly better disguised than that of the March reforms that had provoked the initial demonstrations in June. The law increased the number of seats in the assembly, redistributed them to favor FLN strongholds, and omitted earlier provisions facilitating the participation of independent candidates. Moreover, most of the FIS political leadership was in prison (Madani and Benhadj had been joined by the remaining six members of the *majlis ash shura*, the FIS ruling council) and all newspapers were banned. Once again, the government sought to ensure that the results of the elections would be to its, and the military's, liking.

Nearly fifty political parties participated in the first round of the elections on December 26, 1991. The result was another clear victory for the FIS and an equally clear humiliation for the FLN, which once again performed poorly. The FIS appeared certain of achieving the two-thirds parliamentary majority necessary for constitutional reform. Its next closest competitor was the FFS, followed by the FLN as a distant third. With nearly 200 seats to be decided in runoff elections set for January 16, 1992, it appeared certain that a transfer of parliamentary power to the opposition was imminent.

The military, however, quickly affirmed its unwillingness to see power transferred to a political party it regarded as a threat to the security and stability of the state. Calling the government's position toward the Islamists "accommodating," the army called for the president's resignation and the suspension of the scheduled second round of elections.

Return to Authoritarianism, January 11, 1992

The coup, led by the minister of defense, Major General Khaled Nezzar, soon returned Algeria to an extremely tense state. Military troops were put on alert throughout the country, tanks and armored cars were deployed throughout Algiers, and military checkpoints were set up. President Benjedid resigned on January 11, citing "widespread election irregularities" and a risk of "grave civil instability." The military then reappointed Sid Ahmed Ghozali as prime minister. Ghozali was also named to head the new High Security Council (Haut Conseil de Sécurité—HCS), a six-member advisory body dominated by such senior military officials as Major General Nezzar and Major General Larbi Belkheir. This new collective executive body immediately assumed full political authority, suspending all other political institutions, voiding the December 1991 election results, and postponing future elections.

Government and Politics

The HCS was soon replaced by the High Council of State (Haut Conseil d'État—HCÉ), designed as a transitional government that would have more political legitimacy than the HCS. In fact, the HCÉ differed little from the HCS. The new HCÉ was a five-member collective presidency dominated by military officials who had almost unlimited political powers. Former independence leader Mohamed Boudiaf was recalled from self-imposed exile in Morocco to lead the new HCÉ and serve as head of state.

The coup initially went almost unchallenged because even the FIS leadership discouraged its followers from provoking clashes with the military. Relative tranquility prevailed, and the military withdrew its tanks and troops in the following days.

Some Algerians even expressed support for the coup, citing fears of an Islamist government. Some 200,000 demonstrators marched in Algiers protesting the Islamists, and the main workers' union, the General Union of Algerian Workers (Union Générale des Travailleurs Algériens—UGTA), in early January threatened to resist any Islamist government.

The period of relative calm, however, was as deceptive as it was brief. Within a month, near civil war occurred as Islamists struck back against the military crackdown. The new government reimposed a state of emergency, banned the FIS in March, and dissolved the communal and municipal assemblies, most of which had been controlled by FIS members since the June 1990 elections. The government also banned all political activity in and around mosques and arrested Islamist activists on charges ranging from possession of firearms to promoting terrorism and conspiracy against the state. Military courts tried and sentenced the activists to lengthy imprisonment or death, without right of appeal and/or full awareness of the charges brought against them. Thousands of demonstrators were taken to makeshift prison camps in the Sahara while hundreds of others were detained for questioning and often tortured. Most of the remaining top FIS leadership was arrested, and thousands of rank-and-file party members were forced underground. Other reversals of the democratization process quickly followed. The press, which had slowly gained freedom, was quickly reined in, the National People's Assembly was indefinitely suspended, and the omnipresent and ubiquitous *mukhabarat* (state security apparatus) resurfaced.

Despite the military's obvious targeting of the Islamists, the latter's political suppression drew heavy criticism even from FIS rivals. The FLN and the FFS soon proposed a tactical alliance with the FIS to counter the military government in an effort to preclude the complete abandonment of the democratic process.

The repressive military actions of the government against the Islamists were reminiscent of the military force used by the French colonial authorities against the nationalists during the War of Independence. Thousands of troops were mobilized and assigned to cities and all major urban centers. Curfews were imposed, removed, and reimposed. Entire neighborhoods were sealed off because of police sweeps and other searches for accused "terrorists." Islamists retaliated by killing military personnel, government officials, and police officers by the hundreds. Some 600 members of the security forces, and hundreds more civilians and Islamist demonstrators, were killed in the first twelve months following the coup. The majority of Algerians, meanwhile, were caught in the middle, distrusting the army as much as the Islamists.

The government, citing a need to "focus its full attention" on Algeria's economic problems, warned that it would not tolerate opposition. In reply, FIS leaders warned that the popular anger aroused by the political suppression was beyond their control. Hard-liners in FIS split from the more moderate pragmatists, criticizing the FIS leadership for cooperating with the government. As a result, radical factions replaced the relatively moderate FIS leadership, now long imprisoned. Meanwhile, other independent and radical armed Islamist groups arose, impatient not only with the government but also with the FIS itself. The new radicals, FIS officials acknowledged, were beyond FIS control.

On June 29, 1992, head of state Mohamed Boudiaf was assassinated during a public speech at the opening of a cultural center in Annaba. The death of Boudiaf at the hands of a military officer illustrated the extent to which Algeria's political crisis transcended a simple contest for power between Islamists and military leaders or between religious and secular forces.

Twenty months after the coup, the country was still being torn apart by constant fighting between Islamists and the military. Following Boudiaf's assassination, HCÉ member Ali Kafi was appointed head of state. On July 8, only a week later, Prime Minister Ghozali resigned, and Belaid Abdessalam was named to replace him. Both Boudiaf and Ghozali had begun to move toward a rapprochement with the Islamists, no doubt recognizing their desperate need for popular support in the absence of any sort of constitutional legitimacy.

The months following Boudiaf's assassination and Ghozali's resignation were marked by intensified efforts to suppress "terrorism." Emergency tribunals, headed by unidentified judges who levied "exemplary" sentences with no means of appeal, were established to try Islamist "terrorists." An antiterrorism squad was headed in 1993 by General Mohamed Lamari, a former government official under Ghozali who was removed from office to facilitate talks with the opposition. Islamist activity intensified as Islamists also targeted civilians—teachers, doctors, professors, and other professionals—whose sympathies might lie with the military.

Cooperation in 1993 among various opposition groups and the predominance of professionals, including doctors and teachers, in such radical groups as the Armed Islamic Movement, was considered by a well-informed observer to imply a "considerable level of antiregime collaboration among apparently respectable middle-class Algerians." Moreover, it appeared that the radicalization of the opposition, far from receding, has spread into traditionally more moderate sectors of society.

Since independence the government has relied on veterans of the revolutionary period as leaders, although they represent little more than vague historical figures to most Algerians. The government has also ignored numerous opportunities for dialogue with the opposition, opting for rule by decree without any constitutional mandate. Moreover, divisions within the government have greatly hindered the development of an effective economic policy, undoubtedly the key to Algeria's political turmoil in the early 1990s.

Prime Minister Abdessalam was greatly hampered in his economic efforts by his connection with Boumediene's failed heavy industrialization program from 1965 to 1977. On August 23, 1993, Abdessalem was dismissed and replaced by Redha Malek, formerly a distinguished diplomat but also a traditional nationalist vehemently opposed to the FIS and an advocate of a hard-line approach to combating "terrorism."

The legacy of the past has played heavily into the current political situation. For years the government had ruled without any accountability. Until the mid-1980s, corruption and inefficiency were often masked by high oil revenues that sustained an acceptable standard of living for most Algerians. Unfortunately, this legacy has greatly undermined the country's ability to rise to the current political challenge by inhibiting the development of an effective economic sector and by provoking widespread dissatisfaction among the majority of Algerians.

Political Structure and Processes

The political triangle of army-party-state that has governed Algeria since independence underwent significant changes under the liberal reforms of Benjedid: a new constitution was adopted, the constitutionally protected role of the FLN eliminated, and the authoritarian lock on society loosened. Events since January 1992, however, have not only reversed those reforms but also reasserted the central and preeminent role of the military in the government. Algeria has been under a "state of emergency" almost since the coup through late 1993, allowing the state to suspend almost all rule of law. Although the civil institutions remained in existence, Algeria in late 1993 was essentially a military autocracy whose only functioning authority was the HCÉ and an advisory body called the National Consultative Council (Conseil Consultatif National—CCN). Created in February 1992 by presidential decree following the dissolution of the APN, the CCN was intended, in the absence of a working parliament, to function as an institutional framework for enacting legislation. In practice, it was little more than a rubber stamp for the HCÉ's proposals.

Structure of the National Government

Constitution

Since independence in 1962, Algeria has had three constitutions. The first of these was approved by a constitutional referendum in August 1963, only after prior approval and modifications by the FLN. Intended as a means of legitimizing Ben Bella's new regime, the constitution also established Algeria as a republic committed to socialism and to the preservation of Algeria's Arab and Islamic culture. The constitution lasted only two years, however, and was suspended upon Colonel Boumediene's military coup in June 1965. For the next ten years, Algeria was ruled without a constitution, although representative local and provincial institutions were created in the late 1960s in Boumediene's attempt to decentralize political authority. In 1976 the National Charter and a new constitution were drafted, debated, and eventually passed by national referenda. Together, these documents formed the national constitution and ushered in the Second Algerian Republic. The new constitution reasserted the commitment to socialism and the revolutionary tradition of the nation, and established new government institutions, including the APN. The 1986 revisions continued the conservative nature of the previous constitutions but increased the role of the private sector and diminished the socialist commitment.

The revised constitution of February 1989 altered the configuration of the state and allowed political parties to compete, opening the way for liberal democracy. The new constitution removed the commitment to socialism embodied in both the National Charter and the constitution of 1976 and its 1986 revision. The references to the unique and historic character of the FLN and the military's role as "guardian of the revolution" were eliminated. The provisions for a unicameral legislature remained.

In what was considered a sweeping mandate of support for the liberalization efforts of Benjedid, a referendum on the 1989 constitution passed February 23, 1989, with a 75 percent approval and a 78 percent participation rate. The changes embodied in the constitution were not universally accepted, however. Within a month after the ratification of the new constitution, a number of prominent senior military officers resigned from the FLN Central Committee to protest the revisions. The most divisive issues included the separation of the religious institution and the state; the abandonment of the commitment to socialism; and the liberalization of political life, allowing independent political parties.

The 1989 constitution established a "state of law," accentuating the role of the executive and, specifically, the president, at the expense of the FLN. The president, having the power to appoint and dismiss the prime minister at will, and maintaining singular authority over military affairs, emerged as the dominant force. The FLN became but one of many political parties. The responsibilities of the army were limited to defense and external security. Moreover, the army was obliged to become less visible because of its role in suppressing the October 1988 revolts.

Executive: Presidential System

Constitutional provisions have historically concentrated almost all major powers of the state in the hands of the executive. The original constitution specified more than twenty powers over which the president had sole authority. Leadership qualities of the individual presidents have augmented these constitutional prerogatives and facilitated the development of an essentially authoritarian system. In 1989 the new constitution created a "state of law," relying on a strong executive capable of implementing the political liberalization necessary to democratize Algeria.

The greatest beneficiary of the constitutional revisions was the office of president. The 1989 constitution further strengthened the presidential system at the expense of both the party and the army. As head of state, head of the High Judicial Council, commander in chief of the armed forces, and chairman of all legislative meetings, the president has effective control over all state institutions. The president appoints and dismisses the prime minister and all other nonelected civilian and military officials. The APN votes on the president's choice, but if the president's nominations are rejected twice, the assembly is dissolved. The actions of the prime minister become the responsibility of the APN although they may not have been validated by it. Only the president can initiate constitutional amendments. The president may bypass the APN by submitting legislation of "national importance" directly to a national referendum. In fact, Benjedid's third term in office consisted largely of legislation issued through his Council of Ministers, essentially rule by decree.

Legislative: National People's Assembly

Algeria's first national legislature was formed in September 1962 under the constitution drafted by the Ben Bella regime but was suspended in 1965. For the next ten years, the Council of the Revolution ruled Algeria; there was no independent parliament. By 1976, with power consolidated in his hands, Boumediene commenced a series of reforms to establish formal political institutions. One of the first measures was the recreation of a national parliament.

The 1976 constitution described the APN as a unicameral, elected, representative legislative body. Under the 1989 law, deputies are elected for five-year terms, and all Algerians "enjoying full civil and political rights" and over the age of twenty-five are eligible. Elections occur by secret, direct, and universal ballot. Until the country's first multiparty elections in December 1991, all candidates were drawn from a single party list, approved by the FLN, although multiple candidates could compete for a single constituency.

Role of Political Parties

FLN Role

The FLN had traditionally served as the only legal political party in the legislature and the only source of political identification. It controlled all aspects of political participation, including the trade unions and other civil organizations. In the prerevolutionary years, the party served as a source of national unity and mobilized the fight against French colonial domination. Having played such a dominant role in the War of Independence assured the FLN a privileged position in the emerging political configuration, a position preserved in the early constitutions.

The first Algerian constitution in 1963 established a single-party structure for the new nation and recognized the FLN as the single party. The constitution declared the party superior to the state—the party was to design national policy, the state to execute it. Political hegemony did not last long, however. Factional infighting within the party and Boumediene's heavily military-oriented presidency greatly undermined party authority. During most of the 1970s, with the Council of the Revolution as almost the sole political institution and Boumediene's cabinet primarily composed of military officers, the party's political functions were nearly eliminated. The president and his cabinet assumed the party's policy-making initiative; the elimination of the APN basically annulled mobilization responsibilities. The 1976 National Charter and constitution reasserted the party's symbolic and national role but bestowed little additional responsibility. In the late 1970s, with the reemergence of political institutions and elections, the party became again an important political actor. The creation in 1981 of a Political Bureau (or executive arm of the FLN in a communist sense), legislation requiring that all union and mass association leaders be FLN party members, and the extension of party authority resulted in the growth and increased strength of the party until the late 1980s, when its heavily bureaucratic structure came under serious scrutiny.

By the 1980s, the FLN had become discredited by corruption, inefficiency, and a broad generation gap that distanced the wealthy party elite from the realities of daily life for the masses of impoverished young Algerians. The FLN had ceased to be the national "front" its name suggests. Algeria's economic polarization was such that only 5 percent of the population was earning 45 percent of the national income, whereas another 50 percent was earning less than 22 percent of national income. Members of the party elite enjoyed privileged access to foreign capital and goods, were ensured positions at the head of state-owned enterprises, and benefited from corrupt management of state-controlled goods and services. The masses, however, suffered from the increasing unemployment and inflation resulting from government reforms and economic austerity in the mid- to late 1980s. The riots of October 1988 indicated that the FLN had lost legitimacy in the eyes of the masses.

Increasing economic polarization was but one facet of the broadening generation gap. Thirty years after independence, the FLN continued to rely on its links to Algeria's revolutionary past as its primary source of legitimacy, ignoring the fact that for most voters what mattered was not the martyrs of the past but the destitution of contemporary life. Indeed, 70 percent of the population was born after the revolution.

Benjedid's call for constitutional reform began the collapse of the FLN. The 1989 constitution not only eliminated the FLN's monopoly but also abolished all references to the FLN's unique position as party of the avant-garde. The new constitution recognized the FLN's historical role, but the FLN was obliged to compete as any other political party. By mid-1989 the military had recognized the imminent divestiture of the FLN and had begun to distance itself from the party. The resignation of several senior military officers from party membership in March 1989, generally interpreted as a protest against the constitutional revisions, also reflected a strategic maneuver to preserve the military establishment's integrity as guardian of the revolution. Finally, in July 1991 Benjedid himself resigned from the party leadership.

The legalization of political parties in 1989 caused a number of prominent party officials to defect from the FLN in the months that followed, as ministers left to form their own political parties or to join others. A break between the old guard and the reform-minded technocrats dealt the final blow to any FLN aspirations to remain a national front and foreshadowed the party's devastating defeat in the 1990 and 1991 elections. By the time of the coup in January 1992, some factions had even defected to join or lead Islamist parties, including a group that acted in alliance with the FIS.

Legalization of Political Parties and Beginnings of a Pluralist System

The legalization of political parties, further enunciated in the Law Relative to Political Associations of July 1989, was one of the major achievements of the revised constitution. More than thirty political parties emerged as a result of these reforms by the time of the first multiparty local and regional elections in June 1990; nearly sixty existed by the time of the first national multiparty elections in December 1991.

Granting the right to form "associations of a political character," the constitution recognized the existence of opposition parties. Earlier, such parties were precluded because the FLN had a national mandate as a front, eliminating the political necessity of competitive political parties. Other political associations had also been limited because trade unions and other civil associations fell under FLN direction and had little autonomy. The new constitution recognized all political associations and mandated only a commitment to national unity and sovereignty. The July law further clarified the guidelines for the establishment and participation of political parties.

The law prohibited associations formed exclusively on regional, ethnic, or religious grounds. Ironically, however, the two parties that profited most in the 1990 and 1991 elections were the FIS and the FFS from the Kabylie region. That these parties were among the first legalized in 1989 has given credence to those who maintain that Benjedid's liberalization was based more on tactical personal considerations than genuine democratic ambitions. They argue that these parties had the means and appeal to challenge the monopoly of the FLN. The FLN became the main antagonist to the liberalization program of Benjedid and his then prime minister, Hamrouche. By the time of the military coup, the FLN had completely broken with the government.

The December 1991 elections and the scheduled second-round runoffs in January 1992 provided the first national test for the new multiparty system. The elections were open to all registered parties—parties had to register before the campaign period began—and were contested by almost fifty parties. Voting was by universal and secret ballot, and assembly seats were awarded based on a proportional representation system. Only 231 of the 430 seats were decided in the first round of elections in which 59 percent of eligible voters participated, but an Islamist victory seemed assured by the Islamist command of 80 percent of the contested seats. The second round of elections was canceled by the military coup of January 11, 1992.

Electoral System

The pre-1989 electoral system allowed for multiple candidates for local and national elections, although all candidates were drawn from an FLN list. Districts were divided based on a proportional representation system. The legalization of competitive political parties in 1989 challenged the FLN with candidates drawn from other party lists. To preserve the FLN's political domination, the National People's Assembly, in which the FLN dominated, made modifications to the electoral districts. These redistributions involved heavy overrepresentation of the rural and less populated regions, traditional strongholds of the FLN, and drew heavy criticism from all political parties.

In the new system of proportional representation, all seats in the local and national assemblies are awarded to the party winning a majority of the popular vote. In the absence of an absolute majority, the party with a plurality of votes receives 51 percent of the seats, and the remaining seats are proportionally divided among all other parties receiving at least 7 percent of the total popular vote. This new electoral system actually served to undermine the FLN when the FIS emerged as the most popular party in the June 1990 local elections and again in the first round of national elections in December 1991. In May 1991 and again in October 1991, the National People's Assembly approved new electoral codes adding extra seats, so that the total number of seats came to 430, up from 261 in 1976.

Judicial System

The judicial system, in common with other aspects of Algeria's culture, shares features of its French and Arab traditions. Throughout the French colonial period, secular courts prevailed as the final judicial authority, although Islamic sharia courts had jurisdiction over lower-level cases, including civil cases, criminal offenses, family law, and other personal matters. Secular courts in Algeria owed their existence to the earlier Turkish administrative control, however, not French imposition. The French courts replaced the Turkish courts and, in so doing, modified them to reflect French principles of justice. The secular courts were authorized to review sharia court deci-

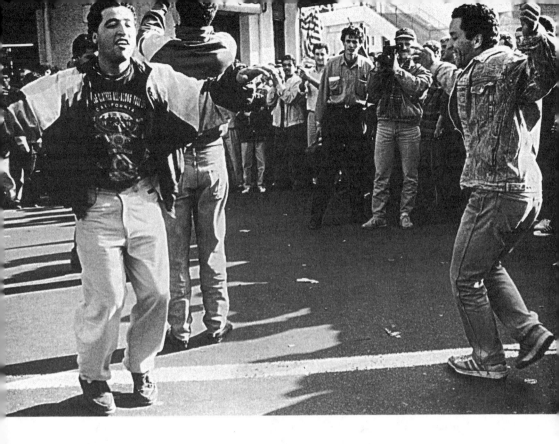

Berber men, members of the Front of Socialist Forces of Hocine Ait Ahmed, dancing on the street, 1991 Courtesy Susan Slymovics and Middle East Report

sions, although for the majority of Algerians, the sharia court was the final source of judicial authority. Following independence in 1962, the government promised to create a new judicial system that would eliminate the French colonial legacy and reflect more accurately the ideological orientation of the new state, which was committed to both socialism and the Arab and Islamic tradition. The revised legal system was not created until 1975, under Boumediene, when new civil and criminal codes were announced.

These codes reflected the divergent nature of socialist and traditional Islamic notions of justice. Family law, personal status (especially regarding the rights of women), and certain criminal penalties were divisive issues, and many were simply omitted from the new judicial codes. In the 1980s, Benjedid proposed a family code, which drew extensive public criticism but was ultimately passed in 1984.

Judges are appointed by the executive branch, and their appointment may be challenged only by the High Judicial Council. Judges are not tenured, although they remain relatively free from political pressure. The 1976 constitution asserted a judicial responsibility to uphold the principles of the revolution; this commitment has lessened in importance, however, as Algeria has moved away from its socialist origins.

The judicial tradition has stipulated that defendants be fully aware of the charges against them, that they have free access to legal counsel, and that they be able to contest a judicial outcome in a court of appeal. The constitution upholds basic principles of personal liberty and justice and prohibits the unnecessary holding of individuals for questioning for longer than forty-eight hours. Under Benjedid's political liberalization, constitutional respect for individual freedoms expanded. A number of political prisoners were released, and the elimination of exit visas and the legalization of political associations facilitated the exercise of free speech, movement, and expression.

Individual freedoms were, however, subordinate to military concerns and issues of national security and have been regularly suspended under periods of martial law. The military leadership in the early 1990s suspended almost all institutions of state, including those of the judicial branch. Islamist leaders and other criminal offenders have been tried by military tribunals and have received heavy sentences of imprisonment or death. The HCÉ, as the military presidency, is an authoritarian government responsible only to itself. Even at the best of times, the executive is not subordinate to the judicial branch, the president serving as head of the High Judicial Council. In the early 1990s, however, cases arising out of the state of emergency as opposed to ordinary civil or criminal cases have been assigned to the military tribunals.

Supreme Court

The Supreme Court resides in Algiers. Its main directive is to ensure the equal and just application of law in all parts of the country. The Supreme Court has four major divisions: a Private Law chamber for civil and commercial cases, a Social Division that presides over issues of social security and labor, a Criminal Court, and an Administrative Division. The court has appellate authority over lower court decisions through the power of abrogation. This appellate power is more limited than United States notions of judicial review. The Supreme Court can review lower court decisions only on questions of procedure, not questions of legal dispute. When overruled, lower court decisions are returned to the lower courts for retrial. The Supreme Court issues no legal decisions and lacks jurisdiction over government actions and/or the constitutionality of government decrees. Traditionally, the Supreme Court has ruled in favor of sharia law over contemporary secular law.

Provincial Courts

The forty-eight provincial courts have four divisions similar to those of the Supreme Court: civil law, criminal law, administrative, and accusation—or grand jury—courts. Civil cases may be referred to the provincial courts by appeal from the tribunals. Criminal cases can be of original or appellate review. Provincial courts have original jurisdiction for serious crimes. The Chamber of Accusation, serving as a grand jury, hears and charges a criminal suspect. The defendant must then go before a criminal tribunal, where a panel of three judges and four lay jurors hears the case.

Tribunals

Each *dairah* (pl., *dawair*; administrative district) has at least one tribunal. The tribunals are courts of first instance and cover civil and less serious criminal cases. They are intended to be easily accessible to the general public and are relatively informal in judicial practice. All of these courts are governed predominantly by Islamic law.

Military Tribunals

Military courts try matters relating to espionage, state security, and other offenses committed by military personnel. These courts are also activated under periods of martial law and have been used to try numerous Islamists, the most notable being Abbassi Madani and Ali Belhadj, leaders of the FIS, which was banned in 1992. The courts consist of three civil judges and two military judges. One of the civil judges presides.

High Judicial Council

The 1976 constitution provided for the establishment of a

High Judicial Council responsible for presiding over issues of judicial discipline and implementation and the appointment of judicial officials. The president of the nation serves as president of the council, and the minister of justice serves as vice president. The council is also charged with advising the president on the exercise of his power to pardon.

Local and Regional Government

The system of local government existing in the early 1990s was established under Boumediene in the late 1960s. The decentralization of local government during the latter period provided an alternative focus to the concentration of power in the highly centralized single-party apparatus and in Boumediene's own personalist rule. An extensive system of administration restricted the autonomy and independent action of provincial and local assemblies. Communal and provincial councils were generally confined to purely administrative and/or distributive functions, rubber stamping national government initiatives. Political campaigning was the responsibility of the FLN, not the individual candidates; this system eliminated electoral competition and resulted in a lethargic and apathetic administrative government at the local and regional levels despite the FLN's initial mandate to "politicize the masses." Voter turnout at local elections has generally been low. In contrast, in Algeria's first multiparty elections in June 1990, almost two-thirds of the population participated.

Wilayat

Algeria is divided into forty-eight *wilayat* (sing., *wilaya*), which are, in effect, provinces (see fig. 1). The *wilayat* owe their origins to the colonial system, where they served as bureaucratic units of colonial administration. The system was reformed and expanded (from fifteen provinces to forty-eight) by the Wilaya Charter of 1969, which enumerated a specific legal code for the government of the provinces. The system was reformed again in 1976 by the national constitution.

Each *wilaya* is governed by a Popular Wilaya Assembly (Assemblée Populaire de Wilaya—APW). This deliberative body consists of thirty deputies and holds elections every five years. The first APW elections were held in May 1969. Each *wilaya* is also governed by a *wali*, or governor, who is appointed by the president and is the latter's direct political representative at the regional level. Both the Executive Council of the

APW and the APW itself report directly to the *wali*. *Wilaya* government is responsible for the distribution of state services; the regulation of small and medium-sized industry, agriculture, tourism, road transport, and education institutions; and the creation of new state-owned enterprises. Efforts, most notably in the reforms of the early 1980s, to strengthen the financial and political autonomy of these regional governments have achieved only mixed success. The APWs and other popularly elected bodies were in abeyance in late 1993.

Dawair

Algeria has 227 administrative districts, or *dawair* (sing., *dairah*), units between the *wilayat* and the communes. Certain licenses and permits must be obtained from the *dawair*, although most are distributed by the local communal authorities.

Communes

The local rural governing authority is the Communal Popular Assembly (Assemblée Populaire Communale—APC). The APCs are responsible for local administration, economy and finance, social and cultural affairs, and planning. Having no economic and little political autonomy, however, the communes administer central government programs rather than initiate independent projects. Each communal assembly has ten to eighty members, who are elected for five-year terms. The first APC elections were held in February 1967. The assembly elects a communal executive from its membership. The communal executive generally consists of a president, two or more vice presidents, and several councillors. The APCs and the communal executives are directly responsible to the national Ministry of Interior, Local Communities, and Tourism and receive much assistance, direction, and supervision from various ministries.

Municipal Government

The number of seats in each Municipal Council is determined by proportional representation. Constituencies with a population of fewer than 10,000 residents have a minimum of seven council members. Council members are proportionally designated up to a maximum of thirty-three for residential districts with more than 200,000 inhabitants.

Effective Institutions

Political Configuration: The Army-Party-State Triangle

All national power and decision-making authority rest in the hands of a select elite and a select group of institutions. This elite structure has been characterized by its triangular configuration of army, party, and state. This configuration persists despite its fluidity—vacillating between peaceful coexistence and vehement competition for dominance. Events of the early 1990s and the subsequent realignment of this political configuration in favor of the military pose substantial challenges for Algeria's future development and stability because the administrative elite and top party functionaries have been relegated to a subordinate position.

In the years immediately following independence, no one faction of the political elite could control the entire political system. National preoccupation with state stability and political consolidation ensured a relatively stable balance among the competing elite factions. Under Boumediene, the party was reduced to a minor role while a civil-military autocracy in the form of the Council of the Revolution emerged as the predominant political force—consistent with Boumediene's vision of the development of a stable and secure, heavily centralized government. The party and other national institutions were allowed to disintegrate to preclude the emergence of any significant opposition to his highly concentrated government.

Renewed political institutionalization and mass politicization in the late 1970s countered this diminution of the party's role. The 1976 National Charter and constitution acknowledged the party's historical role while enhancing its position as the single legal party affiliation under which candidates could run in the newly created local, regional, and national assemblies. The elimination of the Council of the Revolution and the subsequent absorption of its remaining members into the Party Congress of the FLN after Boumediene's death further enhanced the party's national status.

Benjedid's regime, despite a reduction of formal executive powers immediately preceding his assumption of office, was marked by "power consolidation," which strengthened his personal control at the expense of state, military, and especially party elites. The deemphasis on personal politics (at least at the highest levels of government) and the increased importance of institutional life, however, eventually opened the way for the army's return as the dominant political force by greatly undermining the other sides of the political triangle.

The Elite

Historically, the elite enjoyed its greatest preeminence under the socialist Boumediene regime, with its emphasis on heavy industrialization. The elite includes civil service employees, the technocratic top personnel in the state's major nationalized industries and enterprises (e.g., the National Company for Research, Production, Transportation, Processing, and Commercialization of Hydrocarbons—Sonatrach—and the National Company for Electricity and Gas), and economic and financial planners responsible for the national development program. Together these elite groups are responsible for planning, developing, focusing, and administering Algeria's economic and industrial sector. Having expanded significantly under Boumediene, this sector contracted substantially with the economic liberalization under Benjedid, although it remained a vital force and, historically, the most efficient and productive sector of the national elite. Because personal contacts and privileged access to capital account for personal status and class in Algeria, the administrative elite and its networks represent a major factor in the political environment. The administrative elite, although generally less politically visible than the party and military elites, can directly influence development by managing programs linked to economic growth and political stability.

Since the late 1980s, the administrative elite has provided a pool of technocrats for the staff of both the civilian government and the military presidency, which rely heavily on them in modernizing Algeria's economy. At the same time, the administrative elite has increasingly been plagued by factionalism.

The other major elements of the elite consist of the FLN and the military. Within the FLN, the Party Congress is the highest political organ. It consists of national delegates, representatives from the various mass associations and professional unions, local and regional elected officials, APN deputies, and military leaders. The congress determines general party policy, adopts and revises party statutes, and elects both the secretary general of the party and its Central Committee. The Central Committee, which is divided into various commissions, is an elected assembly that serves only during recesses of the Party Congress.

The military, consisting primarily of the People's National Army (Armée Nationale Populaire—ANP), has remained a constant force in Algerian politics, at times quite visible, at times more subtle. The military's most potent source of power emanates from its monopoly of the coercive instruments of force. Equally significant, however, is the military's symbolic role as "guardian of the revolution" and guarantor of state stability. Its technical and administrative skills have been critical to Algeria's political and economic development. A certain domestic prestige stems from the military's influential role in regional and international affairs. The military is also very active in local and provincial affairs. Army officials are represented on all major political institutions and frequently have more influence in regional administration than do the civilian provincial governors.

Historically, the army has interfered only when conditions "necessitated" military intervention to ensure the security of the state. In January 1992, only days away from national legislative elections that were likely to return a sweeping Islamist victory, the military resurfaced politically in a highly visible manner. Anticipating what the armed forces interpreted to be a "grave threat" to the secular interests and political stability of the state and defying the apparent government and national volition, the military demonstrated that it alone would determine the course of Algerian politics.

Military Dictatorship

The system of power in 1993, like that between 1965 and 1978, was a military dictatorship with few legal institutions defining it. Following the coup of January 1992 that ousted Benjedid and eliminated constitutional rule, a collective presidency was established, responsible for implementing political authority. The national constitution has been suspended (a referendum on a new constitution and political structure was expected to be held in late 1993), so all political powers have been assumed on a de facto basis with almost no limitations.

High Council of State

The High Council of State (Haut Conseil d'État—HCÉ) is the official name for the collective presidency that governed Algeria in late 1993. A five-member council, it was presided

Government and Politics

over by Ali Kafi, a former War of Independence veteran and founding member of the FLN, serving as head of state. The prime minister was Redha Malek, a distinguished figure of the preindependence and postindependence periods, who served his country in several diplomatic posts including that of ambassador to the United States (1979–82); in the latter capacity he was instrumental in negotiating the release of United States hostages in Iran in 1981. The HCÉ replaced the High Security Council, the transitional government that assumed power immediately following the coup, and was dominated by military officials, although it has been marked by frequent changes of personnel. Its mandate was due to expire at the end of 1993, when it was scheduled to hand over power to a new transition government that would be entrusted with resuming the democratic process.

National Consultative Council

The National Consultative Council (Conseil Consultatif National—CCN) was conceived by head of state Mohamed Boudiaf in February 1992 as an ex-officio institution to fill the legislative vacuum and to validate HCÉ legislation. The APN, Algeria's national legislature, was suspended one week before the military coup in January 1992. The CCN is an advisory board of sixty members whose principal function is to "provide studies, analysis, and examination of policy," and in the absence of a working parliament, "to provide an institutional framework for passing legislation." The council was originally headed by Redha Malek, whose official title was president of the council. The council has no members from the FLN or from the FIS, which in 1993 was banned. It consists of business leaders, journalists, and academics. Several council members have been assassinated, allegedly by Muslim extremists intent on punishing "collaborators" of the military junta.

The Islamist Factor

Islam in Algeria is part of the political tradition dating back before independence, when the revolutionary rhetoric of the FLN drew upon the unifying force of Islam to strengthen national cohesion and opposition to colonial rule. In the postindependence period, the government, recognizing the mobilizing potential of Islam as a political force, tried to bring activist Islamist groups under its control. Despite these efforts, an independent Islamist movement eventually emerged that would form the basis for the most significant opposition party to the government in the late 1980s and early 1990s.

Whereas more than fifty independent parties and more than one Islamist organization emerged in the months following the legalization of parties, the FIS emerged as the only national contender to the hegemony of the FLN. Although not the only Islamist party, the FIS could attract a large percentage of the electorate. The FIS presented the only viable and comprehensive alternative program to that of the existing regime and offered a social and religious focus as well.

The Islamist Movement since the Late 1980s

Until the late 1980s, the government required that imams be named by the Ministry of Religious Affairs and prohibited the formation of any Islamist political or public association. Sermons and religious speeches were monitored, and worship services could be held only in officially designated mosques. But, with the urban growth that occurred during the 1970s and 1980s, the government could not keep up with the proliferation of mosques and neighborhood associations. This "imam shortage" opened the way for the independent Islamist movement, which quickly moved in to fill the public arena. These "unofficial imams" preached wherever they could find space and occupied official mosques in defiance of government legislation. The Islamists who occupied these urban mosques offered comprehensive social programs that included schooling, business development and neighborhood beautification, garbage pickup, tutoring sessions, and economic assistance for needy families. In a time of severe economic crisis and apparent government ineptitude, the Islamists did not seem to be limited by the reductions in municipal budgets and appeared committed to social welfare programs and improving the material condition of the general populace.

This social commitment would later benefit the political aspirations of the movement by creating a mass base from which to draw public support, even from those sectors unlikely to support an Islamist party. In fact, the commercial bourgeoisie—entrepreneurs driven by profit motives—were among the most important financial contributors to the Islamist movement. These businessmen were attracted to the FIS program by promises of tax cuts, deregulation, and economic incentives for business development. The Islamist movement has a national as well as a religious appeal. It has attacked the widespread corruption in the government and suggested solutions for the housing and unemployment crises. All of these efforts provide attractive campaign points for any opposition party, religious or secular, and allow the Islamist movement to transcend the traditional bases of Islamist support.

Role of the FIS

The Benjedid government in the early 1980s relaxed the restrictions on Islam and its political expression, hoping to preclude the development of a more politically active Islamist movement. Islamist political opposition to the regime was tolerated, more mosques were constructed, religious education in the schools was encouraged, and in 1984 a new family code closely following Islamic tenets was enacted. A number of prominent Islamic leaders were released from prison, including Abbassi Madani, a university professor who would be one of the founders of Algeria's first Islamic political party.

The FIS emerged as a political party on September 16, 1989. One of the first parties to apply for legal recognition in Algeria's new multiparty system, the FIS had begun to take shape in the months before the constitutional revision that legalized political parties. Islamist leaders met between February and August 1989 while the APN was debating the new legislation that would enact the constitutional provision allowing for the creation of "associations of a political character." The FIS named Shaykh Abbassi Madani, a moderate Western-educated professor of comparative literature at the University of Algiers, as its leader. His second in command was Ali Belhadj, a high school teacher known for his fiery and militant rhetoric and radical notions of the role of political Islam. This dual leadership and the lack of a clear doctrine allowed for the variable interpretation and pluralistic nature of the FIS as a political party. The more moderate Madani represented a conservative faction within the party intent on using the democratic system to implement its Islamist code. Belhadj, with wider grass-roots support, drew the younger population intent on the immediate imposition of Islamic law.

In line with the nationalist appeal of the Islamic movement, FIS as a political party has transcended religious affiliation. In the economic sphere, the FIS advocates a free-market approach with lower taxes and incentives for developing the private sector. The party also calls for cuts in military spending. Its program is largely driven by domestic interests and is not linked to an international Islamist movement. In fact, the party platform in late 1992 called for international cooperation with the West to explore and expand Algeria's natural resources and export potential.

Many people have minimized the strength of the FIS by maintaining that its greatest appeal has been in the impoverished urban centers filled with unemployed and discontented youth. To this view one must add a few qualifiers. First, in the early 1990s more than 70 percent of Algeria's total population was under the age of thirty (more than 50 percent was under the age of nineteen). To the extent that the party appeals to disgruntled youth, it appeals to a huge percentage of the population. Second, whereas large numbers of unemployed fill the ranks of the FIS, they are without work primarily as a result of poor economic policy and limited opportunity. These factors constitute an inevitable and legitimate precipitate for a backlash vote against the incumbent regime. Finally, the June 1990 local elections demonstrated that the appeal of the FIS was not limited to the poorer districts. FIS candidates won in many affluent districts in the capital and in such provinces as El Tarf, home of Benjedid.

At the time of the June 1990 elections, the FIS was a pluralist and generally moderate party. Under the leadership of Abbassi Madani, in contrast to Ali Belhadj, the FIS resembled a moderate social democratic party more than a radical Islamist party. The radicalization of the Islamists and the violent uprisings that dominated political life in 1992 and 1993 resulted from the revived political authoritarianism led by the army and were not necessarily an attribute of the party itself. In fact, the party, untested in a national capacity, can be measured only by its actions. In those local districts controlled by the FIS since the 1990 elections, few of the radical changes feared by many outsiders and the old guard in the ruling elite have transpired. In part the retention of the status quo has been caused by substantial cuts in municipal budgets and in part by the lack of time and flexibility to alter drastically existing legislation. However, disagreements within the leadership itself, especially over the timetable for implementation of Islamic principles, have been perhaps the strongest factor in the lack of change.

Civil Society

Politicized Algerian civil society owes its origins to the prerevolutionary period when it absorbed many of the French notions of associational life and state-society relations. From the 1920s until the War of Independence, Algerians were allowed to participate in French professional and trade unions and other mass organizations. Through most of Algeria's independent history, civil society and mass organizations have been subordinate to the state-party apparatus and relegated to roles of recruitment and propaganda. From 1968 until 1989, all mass associations were incorporated under the direct administration of the FLN. From the party's perspective, integrating the independent organizations enabled the party to become a true "front," a unique body representing the populace, while simultaneously inhibiting the development of any independent political opposition. Subordinate to the party administration, the associations quickly became engrossed in mobilizing mass support for the party and government and less occupied with pursuing the interests of the groups they represented.

The political crisis of the late 1980s radically altered the dynamic in which the people accepted central control in return for economic security by shifting some of the initiative away from the state and toward civil society. "Associations of a political character" were legalized and allowed to organize, recruit, and demonstrate. In 1989 the legalization of political parties resulted in a large number of independent interest groups emerging as political parties, attesting to the pervasive nature of associational life in Algerian political culture despite government efforts at "depoliticization" and heavy government supervision. Party proliferation was facilitated by a loosening of government regulations. Government authorization became necessary only for those organizations having a "national character," and legalization was extended to any party that did not pose a direct threat to national sovereignty. Hundreds of independent institutions emerged in the following years.

Algerian General Workers' Union and the Workers' Movement

If any one element of civil society has consistently presented a cohesive and substantive constituency, it is the workers' unions. The explosion of union activity following political liberalization in the late 1980s indicates that the affiliational role of the unions has persisted despite years of subordination to party directives.

The Algerian General Workers' Union (Union Générale des Travailleurs Algériens—UGTA) was created in 1956 after Algerian participation in French trade unions was banned. Despite the union's efforts to remain independent, it was taken over by the FLN leadership in 1963. Under the party structure and the socialist tenets of the National Charter, the UGTA became more of an administrative apparatus than an independent interest group. The UGTA consistently opposed mass strikes and public demonstrations that threatened productive economic activity and supported government legislation to prohibit strikes in certain industrial sectors. Until the mid-1980s, all member unions were integrated federations spanning several industries. After 1984 and in response to increasing independent activity on behalf of the workers, these large federations were broken down into smaller workers' assemblies, greatly reducing the political force of the large unions and strengthening the managerial control of the UGTA authorities. The number of strikes sharply declined in the following years.

From 1989 until January 1992, union activity increased to an intensity not previously witnessed. Splits within the UGTA, the creation of a number of new, smaller, and more active unions—including the formation of an Islamic labor union—and a rapid rise in the number of strikes and demonstrations have quickly politicized a previously dormant workers' movement. The frequency and size of labor strikes jumped; Ministry of Labor figures placed the number of strikes for 1989 at 250 per month, four times that of the previous year.

The growth of the workers' movement illustrates the genuineness of democratization in the period up to the January 1992 coup. Labor has generally not supported economic liberalization, and strikes have hampered a number of the government's free-market reforms. The government's response to and tolerance for increased mass politicization and especially union activity will undoubtedly provide clear evidence of the likelihood for successful democracy in the 1990s.

Youth and Student Unions

The FLN formed the National Union of Algerian Students (Union Nationale des Étudiants Algériens—UNÉA), but party directives had less impact on the UNÉA than on other FLN-influenced bodies such as the UGTA. The student union was quite active throughout the 1960s despite government attempts to quell the movement. Strikes, boycotts, and other violent clashes between student groups and government officials continued to upset numerous university campuses until the union was suppressed and dissolved in 1971. The student movement was subsequently absorbed into the more docile National Union of Algerian Youth (Union Nationale de la Jeunesse Algérienne—UNJA), a national conglomerate of youth organizations controlled by the FLN. The UNJA was the only youth group to be recognized officially in the list of national associations enumerated in the National Charter of 1976.

Despite a brief surge of student demonstrations in the late 1970s, the UNJA leadership has increasingly met with apathy and a lack of interest on the part of both high-school and university students—in part because of the existence of a number of local organizations that parallel UNJA activities. Most of the UNJA's roster in 1993 did not consist of students.

As has been true for most other elements of civil society, FLN dominance has translated into a greater emphasis on party propaganda and mobilization than on the association's own objectives. Implementing these objectives posed a challenge to the student union leadership. Union leaders face a disillusioned constituency—students who upon completing years of education cannot find jobs, masses of impoverished and unemployed youth with little confidence in distant authorities, and youth without nostalgia for the War of Independence they are too young to remember. When the population exploded onto the streets in October 1988, it was the students who were the first to organize and who made up the bulk of demonstrators in the six days of rioting.

The National Union of Algerian Farmers

The National Union of Algerian Farmers (Union Nationale des Paysans Algériens—UNPA) was created in 1973 and officially incorporated by the FLN. The UNPA has great organizational complexity, having a number of affiliated and administrative bodies at the local and regional levels. The UNPA has less autonomy than other national associations because the Ministry of Agriculture has assumed many of its ostensible functions. Most agricultural lands were nationalized under Boumediene, and the union thus consists of farmers having few or no noncollectivized lands. Lacking an independent history as a union before its creation as part of the party apparatus, the UNPA has been less politically active, less cohesive, and less influential than some of its counterparts. Reciprocal efforts by the government to revive the agricultural sector and by the union to educate the government regarding the inherent limitations of small cultivators have improved the number of services and general production conditions of agricultural workers. Government reforms under Benjedid decentralized and broke up ownership of most of the nationalized lands, although demands persisted for the restitution of all nationalized lands. These demands were loudest from factions that have broken off from the UNPA to form their own independent agricultural unions since 1988.

The Entrepreneurial Class

One of the most recent sectors of civil society to emerge as an independent movement is that of the entrepreneurs. For most of Algeria's political history, the socialist orientation of the state precluded the development of a class of small business owners and resulted in strong public anticapitalist sentiment. Economic liberalization under Benjedid transformed many state-owned enterprises into private entities and fostered the growth of an active and cohesive group of professional associations of small business owners, or *patronat*. The *patronat* has maintained almost continuous dialogue with the government, has strongly supported government reforms, and has persisted in its lobbying efforts. The *patronat* consists of well over 10,000 members and is steadily expanding. Some of its member associations include the Algerian Confederation of Employers, the General Confederation of Algerian Economic Operators, and the General Union of Algerian Merchants and Artisans.

Socialist Vanguard Party

The Socialist Vanguard Party (Parti de l'Avant-Garde Socialiste—PAGS), although not legally recognized, has persisted as a political opposition party throughout the single-party period. As an outgrowth of the Algerian Communist Party (Parti Communiste Algérien—PCA), which disappeared soon after Algerian independence, the PAGS has consistently opposed the government, offering sharp criticism of all political leaders and most of their programs. Its members, referred to as "Pagsistes," have infiltrated almost every legally recognized mass association despite their unofficial status. The Pagsistes have been especially prominent in such organizations as the UNJA and UGTA, encouraging leftist tendencies. The legalization and proliferation of political parties in 1989 in practice annulled the necessity of the PAGS's continued existence; the Pagsistes essentially disappeared into the plethora of nationally recognized opposition groups. No communist party or political association has been legally recognized.

The Women's Movement

The Algerian women's movement has made few gains since independence, and women in Algeria remain relegated to a subordinate position that compares unfavorably with the position of women in such neighboring countries as Tunisia and Morocco. Once the war was over, women who had played a significant part in the War of Independence were expected, by the government and society in general, to return to the home and their traditional roles. Despite this emphasis on women's customary roles, in 1962, as part of its program to mobilize various sectors of society in support of socialism, the government created the National Union of Algerian Women (Union Nationale des Femmes Algériennes—UNFA). On March 8, 1965, the union held its first march to celebrate International Women's Day; nearly 6,000 women participated.

The union never captured the interest of feminists, nor could it attract membership among rural workers who were probably most vulnerable to the patriarchal tradition. In 1964 the creation of Al Qiyam (values), a mass organization that promoted traditional Islamic values, delivered another blow to the women's movement. The resurgence of the Islamic tradition was largely a backlash against the role of French colonists in the preindependence period. During the colonial period, the French tried to "liberate" Algerian women by pushing for better education and eliminating the veil. After the revolution, many Algerians looked back on these French efforts as an attempt by the colonists to "divide and conquer" the Algerians. Islam and Arabic tradition became powerful mobilizing forces and signs of national unity.

Women's access to higher education has improved, however, even if their rights to employment, political power, and autonomy are limited. For the most part, women seem content to return to the home after schooling. Overall enrollment at all levels of schooling, from primary education through university or technical training, has risen sharply, and women represent more than 40 percent of students (see Education, ch. 2).

Another major gain of the women's movement was the Khemisti Law. Drafted by Fatima Khemisti, wife of a former foreign minister, and presented to the APN in 1963, the resolution that later came to be known as the Khemisti Law raised the minimum age of marriage. Whereas girls were still expected to marry earlier than boys, the minimum age was raised to sixteen for girls and eighteen for boys. This change greatly facilitated women's pursuit of further education, although it fell short of the nineteen-year minimum specified in the original proposal.

The APN provided one of the few public forums available to women. In 1965, following the military coup, this access was taken away when Boumediene suspended the APN. No female members were elected to the APN under Ben Bella, but women were allowed to propose resolutions before the assembly (e.g., the Khemisti Law). In the early postindependence years, no women sat on any of the key decision-making bodies, but nine women were elected to the APN when it was reinstated in 1976. At the local and regional level, however, women's public participation rose significantly. As early as 1967, ninety-nine female candidates were elected to communal assemblies (out of 10,852 positions nationwide). By the late 1980s, the number of women in provincial and local assemblies had risen to almost 300.

The 1976 National Charter went far toward guaranteeing legal equality between men and women. The charter recognizes women's right to education and refers to their role in the social, cultural, and economic facets of Algerian life. However, as of late 1993, the number of women employed outside the home remained well below that of Tunisia and Morocco.

A new family code backed by conservative Islamists and proposed in 1981 threatened to encroach on these gains and drew the protest of several hundred women. The demonstrations, held in Algiers, were not officially organized by the UNFA although many of the demonstrators were members. The women's objections to the family code were that the code did not contain sufficient reforms. The debate over the family code forced the government to withdraw its proposal, but a conservative revision was presented in 1984 and quickly passed by the APN before much debate resurfaced. The 1981 proposal had offered six grounds for divorce on the part of the wife, allowed a woman to work outside the home after marriage if specified in the marriage contract or at the consent of her husband, and imposed some restrictions on polygyny and the conditions in which the wives of a polygynous husband were kept. In the revised code, provisions for divorce initiated by women were sharply curtailed, as were the restrictions on polygyny, but the minimum marriage age was increased for both women and

*Women demonstrating in Algiers and Oran in January 1992 against the FIS election victory
Courtesy Susan Slymovics and* Middle East Report

men (to eighteen and twenty-one, respectively). In effect, however, although the legalities were altered, little changed for most women. Further, it was argued that the enunciation of specific conditions regarding the rights of the wife and the absence of such specifications for the husband, and the fact that women achieve legal independence only upon marriage whereas men become independent at age eighteen regardless of marital status, implicitly underline women's inferior status. Protest demonstrations were once again organized, but, occurring after the fact (the code had been passed on June 9), they had little impact.

A number of new women's groups emerged in the early 1980s, including the Committee for the Legal Equality of Men and Women and the Algerian Association for the Emancipation of Women, but the number of women actively participating in such movements remained limited. Fear of government retaliation and public scorn kept many women away from the women's groups. At the same time, the government had become increasingly receptive to the role of women in the public realm. In 1984 the first woman cabinet minister was appointed. Since then, the government has promised the creation of several hundred thousand new jobs for women, although the difficult economic crisis made achievement of this goal unlikely. When the APN was dissolved in January 1992, few female deputies sat in it, and no women, in any capacity, were affiliated with the HCÉ that ruled Algeria in 1993, although seven sat on the sixty-member CCN. The popular disillusionment with the secular regime and the resurgence of traditional Islamist groups threaten to further hamper the women's movement, but perhaps no more so than the patriarchal tradition of the Algerian sociopolitical culture and the military establishment that heads it.

The Press

From national independence and until the late 1980s, Algeria had almost no independent news media. Colonial legislation banned all nationalist publications during Algeria's fight for independence, and, although a few underground papers were circulated, independent Algeria emerged with no significant national news source. Ben Bella did not inhibit the freedom of the press in the immediate aftermath of the war, but self-imposed limitations kept the press rather prudently progovernment.

In 1964 government control tightened, and most Algerian news publications were nationalized. All news media became subject to heavy censorship by the government and the FLN. A union of journalists was formed under FLN auspices but was largely insignificant as an independent association until the late 1980s.

The primary function of the news media was not to inform or educate but to indoctrinate—affirming and propagating the socialist tenets of the national government, rallying mass support behind government programs, and confirming national achievements. No substantive and little surface-level criticism was levied against the regime, although evaluations of the various economic and social problems confronting the nation were available. Article 55 of the 1976 constitution provided that freedom of expression was a protected liberty but that it could not jeopardize the socialist objectives or national policy of the regime. The Ministry of Information worked to facilitate government supervision and to inhibit circulation of unauthorized periodicals. Almost all foreign newspapers and periodicals were likewise prohibited. Television and radio news programs escaped some of the more heavy censorship although they, too, were expected to affirm government policies and programs. Most news broadcasts were limited to international events and offered little domestic news other than accounts of visiting foreign delegations and outlines of the government's general agenda.

In the late 1980s, the situation changed under Benjedid. Independent national news sources were encouraged and supported. The new constitution reaffirmed the commitment to free expression, this time with no qualifying restrictions. New laws facilitated and even financially assisted emerging independent papers. Limitations on the international press were lifted, resulting in a mass proliferation of news periodicals and television programs presenting an independent position to a nation accustomed to getting only one side of the picture.

The liberalization facilitated the creation and circulation of a number of independent national French- and Arabic-language newspapers and news programs. A 1990 law legislated a guaranteed salary for the first three years to any journalists in the public sector establishing independent papers. As a result of the explosion of local papers, journals, radio and television programs as well as the relaxation of laws inhibiting the international press, the Algerian public has been educated and politicized. Journalists have become an important and influential sector of civil society. One program in particular, "Face the Press" (*Face à la Presse*), appearing weekly and pitting national leaders against a panel of journalists, has drawn immense popular enthusiasm. Among the major newspapers are *Al Moudjahid* (The Fighter), the organ of the FLN, published in Arabic and French; the Arabic dailies *Ach Chaab* (The People, also an FLN organ), *Al Badil* (The Alternate), *Al Joumhouria* (The Republic), and *An Nasr* (The Victory); and the French dailies *Horizons* and *Le Soir d'Algérie* (Algerian Evening). As part of the military crackdown following the January 1992 coup, the news media have been restricted once again. A limited number of newspapers and broadcasts continue to operate, but journalists have been brought in by the hundreds and detained for interrogating. Tens more have been arrested or have simply disappeared, or have been killed by Islamists.

The Arabization Movement

The arabization of society was largely a reaction to elite culture and colonial domination and dates back to the revolutionary period when it served as a unifying factor against French colonial forces. The Arabic and Islamic tradition of the Algerian nation has been preserved through constitutional provisions recognizing its fundamental role in developing Algerian political character and national legislation encoding its existence in Algerian daily life—in courts and in schools, on street signs, and in workplaces. Arabization is seen as a means of national unity and has been used by the national government as a tool for ensuring national sovereignty.

Under Boumediene, arabization took the form of a national language requirement on street signs and shop signs, despite the fact that 60 percent of the population could not read Arabic. Calls have been made to substitute English for French as the second national language, eliminate coeducational schooling, and effect the arabization of medical and technological schools. Algeria remains caught between strident demands to eliminate any legacy from its colonial past and more pragmatic concerns about the costs of rapid arabization.

Emotional loyalties and practical realities have made arabization a controversial issue that has consistently posed a challenge to the government. In December 1990, a law was passed that would effect complete arabization of secondary school and higher education by 1997. In early July 1993, the most recent legislation proposing a national timetable for imposing Arabic as the only legal language in government and politics was again delayed as a result of official concerns about the existence of the necessary preconditions for sensible arabization. The law was to require that Arabic be the language of official communication—including with foreign nations, on television, and in any other official capacities—and would impose substantial fines for violations.

Meanwhile the pressure for arabization has brought resistance from Berber elements in the population. Different Berber groups, such as the Kabyles, the Chaouia, the Tuareg, and the Mzab, each speak a different dialect. The Kabyles, who are the most numerous, have succeeded, for example, in instituting the study of Kabyle, or Zouaouah, their Berber language, at the University of Tizi Ouzou, in the center of the Kabylie region. Arabization of education and the government bureaucracy has been an emotional and dominant issue in Berber political participation. Young Kabyle students were particularly vocal in the 1980s about the advantages of French over Arabic.

The arabization of Algerian society would expedite the inevitable break with France. The French government has consistently maintained a tolerant position, arguing that arabization is an Algerian "internal affair"; yet it seems certain that such sweeping changes could endanger cultural, financial, and political cooperation between the two countries. Despite both Algerian and French statements concerning the wish to break free of the legacy of the colonial past, both nations have benefited from the preferential relationship they have shared, and both have hesitated to sever those ties. The language question will undoubtedly remain a persistent and emotional issue far into the future.

Foreign Policy

General Trends

Algeria's own revolutionary tradition and its commitment to self-determination and nationalism have historically influenced its foreign policy. Pledged to upholding and furthering the revolution against imperialism, Algeria has been a prominent leader in both the region and the developing world. As time has passed, the ideological ambitions of the immediate postindependence years have been subordinated to more pressing economic and strategic interests. Even during the austere socialist years of Boumediene, economic factors played a significant role in determining the course of foreign policy toward both East and West.

By the late 1980s, Algeria's own economic and political problems and the changed global situation and international economy had restricted Algerian foreign policy. The new domestic regime altered Algeria's ideological commitments, moving the country away from its socialist orientation and closer to the West. Algeria's strategic economic and political initiatives in regional affairs began to take precedence over a greater ideological commitment to the developing world and Africa. The 1976 National Charter redefined Algeria's foreign policy objectives, revoking the commitment to socialist revolution and shifting toward nonalignment in the world arena. The domestic situation—the growing popular unrest and decreasing government revenues and standard of living—limited the freedom of the government to commit itself externally. Focusing on issues of direct relevance to the domestic economy became the greatest priority. Concurrently, the surge in popular movements and opposition parties increased the political constraints on foreign policy actors, as evidenced by the dramatic reversal of the government's position on the Iraqi invasion of Kuwait in 1990.

Africa

The Maghrib

The Maghrib (see Glossary) remains a politically, economically, and strategically important area for Algerian foreign policy objectives. Sharing economic, cultural, linguistic, and religious characteristics, as well as national borders, the Maghrib nations have historically maintained highly integrated diplomatic interests. Before Algerian independence, the other Maghrib nations, former colonies themselves, supported the revolutionaries in their fight against the French, providing supplies, technical training, and political assistance. After independence, relations became strained, especially between Algeria and Morocco, whose conservative ideological orientation conflicted with Algeria's socialist direction, and tensions existed over boundary issues between the two. Accusations of harboring political insurrectionists from each other's countries damaged relations between Algeria and both Morocco and Tunisia throughout the 1970s. In the 1980s, however, political and economic liberalization in Algeria drew the countries closer together, and relations improved dramatically. As Algeria's foreign policy orientation has shifted toward regional concerns and away from unsustainable ideological commitments, efforts toward forging a Greater Maghrib have dominated Algerian foreign policy.

The notion of a Greater Maghrib has historical allusions to a more glorious and precolonial past and has provided a unifying objective to which all Maghrib leaders have subscribed. Achieving more concrete steps toward political and economic cooperation, however, has proved much more difficult because political and economic rivalries and strategic regional interests have frequently inhibited amicable relations. In 1964 a Maghrib Permanent Consultative Committee was established to achieve a Maghrib economic community. This committee was plagued with differences, however, and could not reach an agreement on economic union. In the late 1980s, following the historic diplomatic reconciliation between Algeria and Morocco, an accord finally established an economic and political Union of the Arab Maghrib (Union du Maghreb Arabe— UMA).

Morocco in June 1988 acceded to the formation of an intra-Maghrib commission responsible for developing a framework for an Arab Maghrib union. This action broadened the scope of the Treaty of Fraternity and Concord that had originated in 1983 as a bilateral agreement between Tunisia and Algeria. The treaty pledged each nation to respect the other's territorial sovereignty, to refrain from supporting insurrectionist movements in the other country, and to abstain from using force for resolving diplomatic controversies. Prompted by Tunisian diplomatic concerns about Libyan ambitions and Algeria's hope to solidify its regionally predominant position through a solid political confederation, Tunisia and Algeria opened the agreement to all other Maghrib nations, and Mauritania joined later the same year. (Mauritania's accession to the treaty precipitated a bilateral agreement between Libya and Morocco, the Treaty of Oujda, signed in August 1984, declaring political union and establishing a regional dichotomy.)

The UMA treaty—signed in February 1989 in Marrakech, Morocco, by Algeria, Libya, Mauritania, Morocco, and Tunisia—provided a loose framework for regional cooperation. It established a presidential council composed of the heads of state of each member country; the countries jointly shared a rotating presidency, a consultative council, and a judicial body. Aside from Libya, political inclinations for turning the UMA into a more substantial confederation have been weak. Plans for a common economic market will not come into effect until the year 2000, and bilateral agreements have dominated political negotiations. The greatest significance of the UMA is its symbolism. The North African economic union presents a potential counterpart to the European Community (EC—see Glossary), whose cooperation threatens to undermine the position of Maghrib exports and migrant workers. Political cooperation has presented a means of countering the rise of Islamist radicals, who in the early 1990s were challenging the political regimes in most if not all of the North African nations. Finally, the UMA provides a regional forum for resolving conflicts, the most notable of which has been the Algerian-Moroccan dispute over the Western Sahara.

Algeria's relations with Morocco, its neighbor to the west and most significant Maghrib rival, have been dominated by the issue of self-determination for the Western Sahara. The national integrity of this former colonial territory has caused a deep-seated antagonism and general mistrust between the two nations that has permeated all aspects of Moroccan-Algerian relations. Algeria's interest in the region dates back to the 1960s and 1970s when it joined Morocco in efforts to remove Spain from the territory. After Spain announced its intention to abandon the territory in 1975, the united front presented by the two nations quickly disintegrated, as a result of Morocco, and subsequently Mauritania, staking claims to the territory. Algeria, although not asserting any territorial ambitions of its own, was averse to the absorption of the territory by any of its neighbors and called for self-determination for the Saharan people. Before the Spanish evacuation, Spain, Morocco, and Mauritania agreed to divide the territory and transfer the major part to Morocco and the remaining southern portion to Mauritania. This agreement violated a United Nations (UN) resolution that declared all historical claims on the part of Mauritania or Morocco to be insufficient to justify territorial absorption and drew heavy Algerian criticism.

Guerrilla movements inside the Saharan territory, most especially the Popular Front for the Liberation of Saguia el Hamra and Río de Oro (Frente Popular para la Liberación de Saguia el Hamra y Río de Oro—Polisario), having fought for

Saharan independence since 1973, immediately proclaimed the creation of the Saharan Arab Democratic Republic (SADR). Algeria recognized this new self-proclaimed state in 1976, and has since pursued a determined diplomatic effort for international recognition of the territory; it has also supplied food, matériel, and training to the guerrillas. In 1979, after many years of extensive and fierce guerrilla warfare, Mauritania ceded its territorial claims and withdrew. Morocco quickly absorbed the vacated territory. Once the SADR gained diplomatic recognition from the Organization of African Unity (OAU) and many other independent states, Morocco came under international pressure. As a result, the Moroccan government finally proposed a national referendum to determine the Saharan territory's sovereignty in 1981. The referendum was to be overseen by the OAU, but the proposal was quickly retracted by the Moroccan king when the OAU could not reach agreement over referendum procedures. In 1987 the Moroccan government again agreed to recognize the Polisario and to meet to "discuss their grievances." Algeria stipulated a solitary precondition for restoration of diplomatic relations—recognition of the Polisario and talks toward a definitive solution to the Western Saharan quagmire. Without a firm commitment from the Moroccan king, Algeria conceded and resumed diplomatic relations with Morocco in 1988. The political stalemate and the guerrilla fighting have continued almost uninterrupted since 1987. As of late 1993, UN efforts to mediate the conflict as a prelude to a referendum on the territory seemed to be making modest headway.

Far less troublesome have been Algeria's relations with Tunisia. Smaller and in a more precarious position vis-à-vis Libya, Tunisia has consistently made efforts to align with Algeria. In the 1970s, Tunisia reversed its position on the Western Sahara so as not to antagonize Algerian authorities. Tunisia was the first nation to sign the Treaty of Fraternity and Concord with Algeria, in 1983. Throughout Algeria's independent history, it has joined in a number of economic ventures with Tunisia, including the transnational pipeline running from Algeria through Tunisia to Italy. In 1987 the departure from power in Tunisia of President Habib Bourguiba and his replacement by the more diplomatic Zine el Abidine Ben Ali brought the two nations closer again.

Similarly, relations with Libya have generally been amicable. Libyan support for the Polisario in the Western Sahara facilitated early postindependence Algerian relations with Libya. Libyan inclinations for full-scale political union, however, have obstructed formal political collaboration because Algeria has consistently backed away from such cooperation with its unpredictable neighbor. (A vote by the CCN on June 30, 1987, actually supported union between Libya and Algeria, but the proposal was tabled and later retracted by the FLN Central Committee after the heads of state failed to agree.) The Treaty of Oujda between Libya and Morocco, which represented a response to Algeria's Treaty of Fraternity and Concord with Tunisia, temporarily aggravated Algerian-Libyan relations by establishing a political divide in the region—Libya and Morocco on one side; Algeria, Tunisia, and Mauritania on the other. Finally, in 1988 Libya was invited to participate in the intra-Maghrib commission that was responsible for developing the North African union. The establishment of the UMA in February 1989 marked the first formal political or economic collaboration between the two neighbors.

Sub-Saharan Africa

Despite its membership and founding role in the OAU, Algeria remains a society much more closely affiliated with its Arab neighbors and counterparts than with the African countries to the south. In many countries, economic crisis and dependency on foreign aid have diminished the prospects of liberation movements and hence also reduced the relevance of Algeria's liberation experience for those nations. Algeria has, however, resolved its remaining border conflicts with Mali, Niger, and Mauritania and generally maintains harmonious relations with its southern counterparts. Economic linkages remain fairly limited in the 1990s, constituting less than 1 percent of Algeria's total trade balance, although a new transnational highway running across the Sahara is expected to increase trade with sub-Saharan Africa.

In the early postindependence years, Algeria committed itself to the fight against colonialism and national suppression in sub-Saharan Africa. Its commitment was reflected in its support for the revolutionary movements in Zimbabwe, Guinea-Bissau, Angola, Mozambique, and Namibia and in its condemnation of South Africa. Algeria has not officially retreated from its earlier ideological affinity for the revolutionary movements in Africa, but its role has become that of mentor rather than revolutionary front-runner. As Algeria has found its influence in the rest of Africa greatly reduced, its economic interests, ideological affiliation, and identification have fallen more in line with the Maghrib, the Mediterranean, and the Middle East.

Algeria has consistently reaffirmed its commitment to the OAU, although its interests in this regional organization have frequently been motivated more by tactical considerations than ideological affinity. Algeria has worked toward strengthening the structure and mediating capacities of the OAU, largely hoping to use the organization to further its own views on the issue of self-determination for the Western Sahara.

Arab and Middle East Affairs

Algeria's national commitment to pan-Arabism and Arab causes throughout the Middle East and North Africa has resulted in an active role in the region. It joined the League of Arab States (Arab League) immediately following national independence in 1962. Since that time, Algeria's historical and ideological commitment to national revolution and self-determination has resulted in a strong affinity for the Palestinians in Israel, one of the Arab League's most compelling causes. Algeria has consistently supported the Palestinians and the Palestine Liberation Organization (PLO) and spurned the idea of diplomatic resolution with Israel. The Algerian government has steadily backed the mainstream faction of the PLO under the leadership of Yasir Arafat—hosting sessions of the PLO's National Council, intervening on its behalf in diplomatic negotiations with Syria and Lebanon, condemning internal divisions, and working toward the reconciliation of competing factions within the organization. Algeria supported Arafat's decision, denounced by Palestinian hard-liners, to sign a peace treaty with Israel in September 1993.

Algeria's energetic efforts on behalf of the PLO and the Palestinian cause have from time to time jeopardized its relations with other Arab nations (Jordan, Lebanon, Syria, and Egypt), many of which host significant Palestinian populations of their own. Despite Algerian indebtedness to Egypt for assistance during the revolutionary period, the Algerian government severed all relations with Egypt in the late 1970s over Egypt's peace treaty with Israel; relations gradually improved only with a change of leadership in both countries. More recently, Egypt's President Husni Mubarak and Algeria's President Chadli Benjedid found each other's moderate policies more palatable than those of their predecessors and jointly worked toward a resolution of the Arab-Israeli conflict. Similarly, Algeria incurred difficulties with Iraq over its involvement in the peace talks concluding the eight-year war between Iran and Iraq. Persistent calls by Algeria for an end to the conflict that it considered so damaging to the pan-Islamic movement led to a peace proposal that Iraq viewed as overly favorable to Iran. The proposal was alleged to have provoked Iraqi fighters to shoot down an Algerian aircraft carrying prominent Algerian officials involved in the peace talks, including the country's foreign minister.

Algeria shares a cultural identity with the Arab-Islamic nations but is separated by its distance from the rest of the Middle East. The closed nature of the authoritarian regime that governed Algeria for most of its independent history has precluded the development of mass enthusiasm for, or awareness of, external causes and conflicts.

The period of the Iraqi invasion of Kuwait in August 1990 and the subsequent retaliation by the largely Western coalition forces was the first time a significant portion of the Algerian public became mobilized over a foreign policy issue. Arab identification with Iraq drew support from the masses in unprecedented numbers. The overt support for Iraq on the part of the FIS and Ben Bella's Movement for Democracy in Algeria (Mouvement pour la Démocratie en Algérie) and a mass rally in support of Iraq's Saddam Husayn resulted in a fast reversal by the government from its original position condemning the Iraqi aggression. Changing state-society relations—a more active civil society and a more informed public—have meant new foreign policy directions characteristic of a government more responsive to its public. In late 1993, Algeria's foreign policy toward nations of the Middle East, however, had not changed significantly. Its relations with the West, especially its former colonizer, had changed markedly since the immediate postindependence period.

The West

Early Algerian foreign policy caused it direct conflict with the Western powers as it struggled against colonialism. Since the latter 1970s, however, Algeria has determinedly pursued a policy of nonalignment that has facilitated relations with the West. Economic and political liberalization have likewise reduced the barriers inhibiting diplomatic relations with

Europe and the United States. As Algeria moved toward a free-market economy and liberal democratic polity, its diplomatic objectives shifted away from the Soviet Union and toward the West. In a rather surprising turn of events, the military coup that upset the Algerian democratic experiment was tolerated, even approved of, by the West.

The United States

Historically, the United States and Algeria have had competing foreign policy objectives that have come closer only gradually. Algeria's commitment to strict socialism and to a global revolution against Western capitalism and imperialism antagonized relations with the United States, seen, in Algerian eyes, to embody all that the revolution scorned. United States maintenance of good relations with France precluded close ties with Algeria in the years during and following the War of Independence, although the United States sent an ambassador to Algeria in 1962. Algeria broke diplomatic relations with the United States in 1967, following the June 1967 war between Israel and most of its neighbors, and United States relations remained hostile throughout the next decade. United States intervention in Vietnam and other developing countries, Algerian sponsorship of guerrilla and radical revolutionary groups, United States sympathies for Morocco in the Western Sahara, and United States support for Israel all aggravated a fundamental ideological and political antagonism. Official relations resumed in the mid-1970s, although it was not until the late 1970s that relations normalized. By then Algerian leniency and passive tolerance for terrorist hijackers drew enough international criticism that the government modified its policy of allowing aid and landing clearance at Algerian airports for hijackers.

In the 1980s, increased United States demands for energy and a growing Algerian need for capital and technical assistance lessened tensions and resulted in increased interaction with the United States after the relative isolation from the West during the Boumediene years. Liberalization measures undertaken by Benjedid greatly facilitated the improved relations. In fact, an economic rapport with the West had been growing throughout the previous decade despite tense political relations. Algeria was becoming an important source of petroleum and natural gas for the United States. In 1980 the United States imported more than US$2.8 billion worth of oil from Algeria and was Algeria's largest export market.

Algeria's role as intermediary in the release of the fifty-two United States hostages from Iran in January 1981 and its retreat from a militant role in the developing world as its domestic situation worsened opened the path to peaceful relations with the United States. Algeria's domestic situation was becoming increasingly critical because its traditional source of economic assistance, the Soviet Union, was threatened by internal problems. In search of alternative sources of aid, in 1990 Algeria received US$25.8 million in financial assistance and bought US$1.0 billion in imports from the United States, indicating that the United States had become an important international partner.

On January 13, 1992, following the military coup that upset Algeria's burgeoning democratic system, the United States issued a formal but low-key statement condemning the military takeover. Twenty-four hours later, Department of State spokesmen retracted the statement, calling for a peaceful resolution but offering no condemnation of the coup. Since then, the United States, like many of its Western counterparts, has appeared resigned to accepting a military dictatorship in Algeria. The military government has reaffirmed its commitment to liberalizing its domestic economy and opening the country to foreign trade, undoubtedly accounting for some of the Western support for the new Algerian regime.

France and the Mediterranean Countries

Despite ambiguous sentiment in Algeria concerning its former colonial power, France has maintained a historically favored position in Algerian foreign relations. Algeria experienced a high level of dependency on France in the first years after the revolution and a conflicting desire to be free of that dependency. The preestablished trade links, the lack of experienced Algerian government officials, and the military presence provided for in the Evian Accords ending the War of Independence ensured the continuance of French influence. France supplied much-needed financial assistance, a steady supply of essential imports, and technical personnel.

This benevolent relationship was altered in the early Boumediene years when the Algerian government assumed control of French-owned petroleum extraction and pipeline interests and nationalized industrial and energy enterprises. French military units were almost immediately pulled out. France, although apparently willing to maintain cooperative relations, was overlooked as Algeria, eager to exploit its new independence, looked to other trade partners. Shortly afterward, Algerian interest in resuming French-Algerian relations resurfaced. Talks between Boumediene and the French government confirmed both countries' interest in restoring diplomatic relations. France wanted to preserve its privileged position in the strategically and economically important Algerian nation, and Algeria hoped to receive needed technical and financial assistance. French intervention in the Western Sahara against the Polisario and its lack of Algerian oil purchases, leading to a trade imbalance in the late 1970s strained relations and defeated efforts toward bilateral rapprochement. In 1983 Benjedid was the first Algerian leader to be invited to France on an official tour, but relations did not greatly improve.

Despite strained political relations, economic ties with France, particularly those related to oil and gas, have persisted throughout independent Algerian history. Nationalized Algerian gas companies, in attempting to equalize natural gas export prices with those of its neighbors, alienated French buyers in the late 1970s and early 1980s, however. Later gas agreements resulted in a vast growth of bilateral trade into the billions of dollars. Further disputes over natural gas pricing in the late 1980s led to a drastic drop in French-Algerian imports and exports. The former fell more than 10 billion French francs, the latter 12 billion French francs between 1985 and 1987. A new price accord in 1989 resurrected cooperative ties. The new agreement provided substantial French financial assistance to correct trade imbalances and guaranteed French purchasing commitments and Algerian oil and gas prices. French support for Benjedid's government throughout the difficult period in 1988 when the government appeared especially precarious and subsequent support for economic and political liberalization in Algeria expedited improved French-Algerian relations. Finally, rapprochement with Morocco, a number of joint economic ventures between France and Algeria, and the establishment of the UMA relaxed some of the remaining tensions.

One source of steady agitation has been the issue of Algerian emigration to France. French policies toward Algerian immigrants have been inconsistent, and French popular sentiment has generally been unfavorable toward its Arab population. The French government has vacillated between sweeping commitments to "codevelopment," involving extensive social networks for immigrant Algerian laborers, and support of strict regulations concerning work and study permits, random searches for legal papers, and expeditious deportation without appeal in the event of irregularities. North African communities in France remain relatively isolated, and chronic problems persist for Algerians trying to obtain housing, education, and employment. A number of racially motivated incidents occur each year between North African immigrants and French police and citizens.

Equally problematic has been Algeria's handling of the emigrant issue. The government has provided substantial educational, economic, and cultural assistance to the emigrant community but has been less consistent in defending emigrant workers' rights in France, frequently subordinating its own workers' interests to strategic diplomatic concerns in maintaining favorable relations with France. The rise of Islamism in Algeria and the subsequent crackdown on the Islamists by the government have had serious implications for both countries: record numbers of Algerian Islamists have fled to France, where their cultural dissimilarity as Arab Islamists is alien to the country.

In the early 1990s, nearly 20 percent of all Algerian exports and imports were destined for or originated from France. More than 1 million Algerians resided in France and there were numerous francophones in Algeria, creating a tremendous cultural overlap. French remained the language of instruction in most schools and the language used in more than two-thirds of all newspapers and periodicals and on numerous television programs. Algeria and France share a cultural background that transcends diplomatic maneuvers and has persisted throughout periods of "disenchantment" and strained relations. Over time, however, the arabization of Algeria and the increasing polarization of society between the francophone elite and the Arab masses have mobilized anti-French sentiment. Support for the arabization of Algerian society—including the elimination of French as the second national language and emphasis on an arabized education curriculum—and the recent success of the FIS indicate a growing fervor in Algeria for asserting an independent national identity. Such an identity emphasizes its Arab and Islamic cultural tradition rather than its French colonial past. However, France's support for the military regime that assumed power in early 1992 indicates that the cooperative relations between the two countries remain strong.

For obvious geographic reasons, Italy, Spain, Greece, and Turkey share a privileged position in Algerian foreign relations. The economic and strategic significance of Algeria as a geographically adjacent and continentally prominent nation is relevant to the foreign policies of the Mediterranean nations. Whereas Algeria's relations with France have been complicated by confusing emotional and cultural complexities, its relations with the other Mediterranean countries have been primarily driven by economic factors. Both Spain and Italy have become substantial importers of Algerian gas—1989 figures indicated that Italy was Algeria's largest customer for natural gas. A transnational pipeline with three undersea pipes runs from Algeria through Tunisia to Italy, and work has begun on another. Greece and Turkey have both signed import agreements with Algeria's national hydrocarbons company, known as Sonatrach. Spain and Italy have extended sizable credit lines for Algerian imports of Spanish and Italian goods. Since the latter 1980s, Algeria has devoted increased attention toward regional concerns, making the geographical proximity of the Mediterranean nations of growing importance to Algeria's diplomatic and economic relations.

*   *   *

For the immediate preindependence and postindependence periods, the best political analysis is found in William B. Quandt's *Revolution and Political Leadership: Algeria, 1954–1968* and David B. Ottaway and Marina Ottaway's, *Algeria: The Politics of a Socialist Revolution.* The Boumediene and Benjedid periods are covered from contrasting conceptual perspectives in John P. Entelis's *Algeria: The Revolution Institutionalized,* Mahfoud Bennoune's *The Making of Contemporary Algeria, 1830–1987,* and Rachid Tlemcani's *State and Revolution in Algeria.* The most recent analysis incorporating political, economic, and social events through the military coup d'état of January 1992 is the work edited by John P. Entelis and Philip C. Naylor, *State and Society in Algeria.* (For further information and complete citations, see Bibliography.)

Chapter 5. National Security

Tipasa, showing Mount Chenoua in the background; Tipasa marks the terminus of the Sahel region.

BORN IN A BLOODY REVOLUTION from French colonial rule, Algeria became independent in 1962. The new nation was governed for more than twenty-five years by two military figures—Houari Boumediene from 1965 until 1978 and Chadli Benjedid from 1979 until early 1992. Although both presidents relied upon the armed forces for support, their regimes were by no means military dictatorships. The military, however, was heavily represented in the National Liberation Front (Front de Libération Nationale—FLN), the single party that controlled Algeria's socialist state until 1989. Nonetheless, under Boumediene and Benjedid civilian government institutions developed, and a multiparty parliamentary system emerged in 1989.

To avert a likely election victory by the Islamic party, the Islamic Salvation Front (Front Islamique du Salut—FIS), the minister of defense led a coup in January 1992 that brought down the civilian government, which was soon replaced by a High Council of State dominated by the military. In the course of 1992 and 1993, the army and the police were called upon to deal with armed uprisings by those groups who saw the military takeover as cheating the Islamic movement of its popular mandate. A crackdown against officials and organs of the FIS failed to bring an end to the violence, which resulted in 600 deaths among the security forces in the twelve months after the coup. Hundreds of civilians, including Islamic demonstrators and some foreigners, were also killed. The normal processes of government were paralyzed by the tense internal situation, and the army struggled to contain the uprising.

Security problems beyond the national borders, which had in the past motivated the government, aided by the Soviet Union, to build up the military, had become less pressing by the early 1990s. Algeria's support for a nationalist insurgency in the Western Sahara had collided with Morocco's ambition to absorb the territory, but by 1993 the conflict seemed to be winding down. A cooperation treaty in 1989 among the Maghrib (see Glossary) states, incorporating security clauses intended to prevent future military confrontation, reflected the more pacific climate prevailing in the region.

Algeria has a large and reasonably well-equipped military to counter foreign and domestic threats. The People's National Army (Armée Nationale Populaire—ANP) includes ground forces, an air force, a navy, and an air defense command. The National Gendarmerie (Gendarmerie Nationale), a paramilitary body, is used mainly as a police force in rural areas. The army, in the process of being reorganized into four divisions in 1993, also has numerous independent brigades and battalions. Its antecedents were the conventional military units formed in Morocco and Tunisia during the War of Independence from France. In 1993 the air force was equipped with about 193 combat aircraft and fifty-eight armed helicopters. The navy consisted of a small fleet of frigates, corvettes, and missile craft, together with two modern submarines. Except for brief clashes with Morocco in 1976, the armed forces have not been involved in hostilities against a foreign power. Their combat capabilities in defense of the country have thus remained untested.

The arms and equipment initially supplied by the Soviet Union were of good quality, but some of the matériel had been in inventory for up to two decades. Earlier shipments were later supplemented by more modern tanks, armored vehicles, and missile launchers. Because of economic dislocation and a scarcity of foreign exchange, Algeria in the early 1990s postponed the acquisition of more modern equipment. Instead, it assigned priority to training and effective maintenance of existing weapons. More than half the army's personnel strength consisted of conscripts, some of whom were detailed to economic infrastructure projects after basic training. However, since Chadli Benjedid's introduction of market-oriented economic reforms in the late 1980s, the army has curtailed its involvement in construction, agricultural, and manufacturing activities.

External Security Problems and Policies

The Algerian leadership's perceptions of the outside world—including its views on what constitutes a threat to national security—have historically been strongly influenced by ideology. The War of Independence contributed to a set of beliefs that emphasized Algeria's identification with the newly independent, less-developed countries. Dividing the globe into the rich industrial nations of the North and the poor, former colonies of the South, Algerian leaders asserted their strong opposition to what they saw as a world infected by imperialism, Zionism, colonialism, and economic domination by the former colonial powers. By definition, these attitudes implied a measure of suspicion and hostility toward the capitalist states of Europe and North America, and sympathy for liberation movements whose struggles mirrored Algeria's own.

By the early 1990s, ideology was no longer the guiding principle of Algeria's national security outlook. The views shaped by the War of Independence were tempered by more than two decades of experience as a sovereign state as well as by President Benjedid's more cautious, pragmatic style. Under him Algeria adopted an active posture as a mediator of disputes between Western nations and the more radical states of the Arab world. At the same time, Algerian external security objectives narrowed. The goals of reducing differences with its neighbors, the Maghrib countries of North Africa, and especially of settling political and economic disputes with the bordering states of Morocco and Libya, predominated.

Security Interests Outside the Maghrib

Under Ahmed Ben Bella, independent Algeria's first president, the government actively supported a host of anticolonial struggles throughout Africa. Algeria became a leading contributor to the African Liberation Committee of the Organization of African Unity (OAU), which was designed to coordinate and aid African liberation movements. In 1963 the government provided training to 1,000 guerrillas from Mozambique, South Africa, and Angola. More controversially, Ben Bella's government also sponsored efforts to overthrow independent African governments that were considered to be reactionary or too closely linked to former colonial powers. Notably, during this time the Algerians supported insurgencies against the governments of newly independent Congo (former Belgian Congo, present-day Zaire), Niger, and Morocco. Ben Bella's activism, however, was ineffective in weakening the opponents at which it was aimed. Critics charged that his stance was merely symbolic, designed to enhance the president's prestige among the "radical" bloc of African and Asian states and, by extension, to bolster his political position within Algeria.

After Ben Bella's overthrow in 1965, the Boumediene government turned its attention to domestic development issues and limited its direct involvement in destabilizing foreign governments. As a matter of principle, however, the new regime soon started assisting a number of revolutionary groups and liberation movements and allowed their representatives to operate in Algiers. These groups included liberation movements opposed to the regimes in Portuguese Africa, Southern Rhodesia (present-day Zimbabwe), South Africa, the Republic of Vietnam (South Vietnam), Israel, and others. International terrorists associated with Italy's Red Brigades, the Federal Republic of Germany's (West Germany) Baader-Meinhof Gang, and the Black Panthers, composed of radical American blacks, were granted sanctuary and support. Aircraft hijackers were allowed to land in Algeria and were often granted asylum until, under international pressure, Boumediene abandoned the practice in 1978.

An important element of Algerian security policy has been the leadership's attitudes toward Israel and the Palestinian nationalists—attitudes that were underscored by Algeria's military contributions during the June 1967 and October 1973 Arab-Israeli wars. Immediately after the 1967 conflict, the Algerians sent more than fifty aircraft to Egypt to replace some of those lost in the war. Algeria also reportedly sent small contingents of infantry and artillery to reinforce the Egyptians. Algeria's contribution to the October 1973 War consisted of a number of air force units that joined Egyptian forces on the Suez front and two medical teams that were dispatched to the Syrian front. Although the direct involvement of Algerian forces in these conflicts was minimal, Algeria apparently drew important lessons from Arab shortcomings against Israeli military power. Soon after the Arab defeat in 1967, Boumediene inaugurated conscription. Later, the Arabs' initial successes in the 1973 war using modern Soviet-supplied antiaircraft and antitank missiles were believed to have influenced Boumediene's decision to upgrade his armed forces with large purchases of sophisticated Soviet weaponry (see Foreign Military Assistance, this ch.).

Although several liberation movements were still permitted to maintain offices in Algeria after Benjedid came to power in 1979, the government was no longer a major sanctuary for terrorist groups operating abroad. It drew a distinction between terrorism, which it condemned, and violence on the part of national liberation movements, which it considered possibly legitimate. Algeria, however, has refused to sign international agreements intended to counter acts of terrorism. In addition, a representative of the Palestinian terrorist Abu Nidal Organization was allowed to remain in Algiers despite a number of attacks against Arab and Western targets and against its Palestinian opponents in Algeria. Representatives of two other terrorist groups—the Palestinian Islamic Jihad and the Palestine Liberation Front—appeared on national television to rally popular support for Iraq after the Iraqi invasion of Kuwait in 1990.

Algeria continued to back the Palestine Liberation Organization (PLO), whose efforts against Israel had long been viewed by Algerians as similar to the struggle against the French by their own revolutionaries. Although Algeria, like other Arab countries, was unable (or unwilling) to help the PLO resist the Israeli invasion of Lebanon in 1982, Benjedid's government allowed between 1,000 and 2,000 of the guerrillas evacuated from Beirut to establish themselves in military camps in Algeria. Algeria focused its main efforts on mediating among various Palestinian factions rather than supporting a resumption of PLO military activity.

Security Problems with Neighboring States

In his efforts to shape a more pragmatic foreign policy, Benjedid succeeded in moderating the stresses in the country's relationships with the West. Concurrently, Algeria's concerns shifted to improving regional stability, which had been disturbed by festering disputes with Morocco and Libya. Reflective of improving relationships was the formation in February 1989 of the Union of the Arab Maghrib (Union du Maghreb Arabe—UMA), with Algeria, Libya, Mauritania, Morocco, and Tunisia as members. The primary goal of the UMA was improved economic cohesion, but the treaty also contained important security clauses. The signatories affirmed that any aggression against one member would be considered as aggression against the other member states. In an apparent allusion to the Western Sahara conflict, member states pledged not to permit any activity or organization on their territory that could endanger the security or territorial integrity of another member state.

Relations between Algeria and Morocco had long been characterized by rivalry and occasional hostility. Immediately after Algerian independence, Morocco laid claim to stretches of southern and western Algeria that had been under Moroccan sovereignty before the French gained control over the area in the nineteenth century. In a series of sharp engagements in the disputed territory in October 1963, the professional Moroccan army consistently outperformed Algerian regulars and local guerrillas. Although OAU-sponsored mediation ended the fighting, the success of the Moroccans demonstrated

Algeria: A Country Study

the potential threat to Algerian security in the event of a more serious dispute.

In addition to fighting over borders, the two countries each sought primacy in the Maghrib. Their claims were rooted in part in ideology: Morocco's claim to regional leadership derived from its centuries-old national identity, whereas Algeria's stemmed from the prestige of winning its War of Independence. The ideological differences between the new socialist republic and the ancient kingdom were sharpened when, almost immediately after independence, Ben Bella began to trumpet his country's socialist-revolutionary doctrines and its opposition to conservative governments such as Morocco's. Relations improved after Boumediene came to power and as both countries concentrated on their domestic problems. In 1972 a treaty was signed defining the international border between them. The Moroccan government, however, deferred its official ratification of the treaty. Following the mending of differences over the Western Sahara question, Morocco's King Hassan II finally ratified the border treaty in May 1989.

The dispute over the Western Sahara had its origins in 1974 when Morocco began maneuvering to annex the territory, which was then under Spanish control and known as the Spanish Sahara. A series of Moroccan diplomatic initiatives—climaxed by a march of 350,000 Moroccans across the territory's northern border—resulted in a treaty by which Spain turned over the northern two-thirds of the Western Sahara to Moroccan administration and the rest to Mauritania (see Africa, ch. 4). By mid-1975 the Algerians were giving supplies, vehicles, and light arms to the Popular Front for the Liberation of Saguia el Hamra and Río de Oro (Frente Popular para la Liberación de Saguia el Hamra y Río de Oro—Polisario). The Polisario was the strongest of several indigenous national liberation movements active in the Western Sahara. Algerian authorities established refugee camps in the Tindouf area to house large numbers of Saharans, popularly known as Sahrawis, who abandoned the territory after the Moroccan takeover. Algeria thus became the principal foreign supporter of the Polisario in its long-running desert war to oppose Moroccan control of the disputed area.

Algeria gradually acquired a quantitative military superiority over Morocco with the introduction of large amounts of modern weaponry, mainly from the Soviet Union. Nevertheless, the Algerians avoided direct confrontation with the more experienced Moroccan troops. In January 1976, however, the Moroccans badly defeated two battalions of Algerian troops and took prisoners in clashes inside the Western Sahara. After that time, Algerian regulars did not venture into the Western Sahara despite Moroccan claims to the contrary. For their part, the Moroccans refrained from pursuing troops onto Algerian territory.

Initially, fighting in the Western Sahara featured attacks by the Polisario's light mobile forces against isolated Moroccan outposts. By 1982, however, the struggle had shifted in Morocco's favor. Morocco adopted a strategy of constructing fortified sand walls, mined and equipped with electronic warning systems. Enclosing progressively larger areas of the Sahara, Morocco was able to undercut the Polisario's ability to conduct hit-and-run attacks. The Moroccan military dominated the battlefield, effectively coordinating its modern ground and air firepower in spite of Algeria's deliveries of increasingly sophisticated arms to the Polisario guerrillas.

The success of Morocco's military strategy was one factor in the rapprochement between the two nations in 1988, following a twelve-year hiatus in diplomatic relations precipitated by Algeria's recognition of the Polisario government. Although the Polisario was able to mount an offensive against the sand wall in late 1989, breaking a truce that had held for nearly a year, Algeria—preoccupied by its own internal security problems—was no longer willing to devote enough arms and support to keep the independence movement alive. Algeria still provided refuge on its territory for about 10,000 guerrillas, but by the close of 1992 the Polisario's military defeats had nearly ended the insurgency.

Algeria's resumption of diplomatic relations with Morocco, accompanied by the opening of borders and a number of joint economic initiatives, eased the security situation on its western flank. Morocco's acceptance of the United Nations (UN) peace plan for the Western Sahara and the conclusion of the UMA treaty in 1989 further helped to abate remaining tensions.

Whereas Morocco had long been viewed as a potential threat, Muammar al Qadhafi's Libya was regarded as somewhat more friendly. The Algerian-Libyan security relationship was based on a common antipathy for the Western-dominated economic order and deep hostility toward Israel. This relationship, however, suffered several setbacks during the 1980s. In 1984 Morocco and Libya announced that they had secretly negoti-

Algeria: A Country Study

ated an alliance. Although the alliance's effect was short-lived, Algeria interpreted the agreement as upsetting the strategic balance in the Maghrib. Libya's unilateral annexation of a section of neighboring Chad and its military intervention in Chad hardened Algerian attitudes toward Libya, as did the suspicion that Libya was linked to unrest instigated by Islamist (also seen as fundamentalist) groups in Algeria. Libya's subsequent participation in the UMA, however, appeared to lay a foundation for more stable relationships with Algeria and the other states of the region.

Strategic Perspectives

In the early 1990s, among Algeria's neighbors, only Morocco and Libya could be viewed as potential military rivals. The active personnel strength of Morocco's armed forces was greater than the strength of Algeria's force, but its army was inferior in terms of armored vehicles and artillery. The Moroccan combat air force of French and United States fighter aircraft was smaller than the Soviet-equipped Algerian air force. Libya's equipment inventory—armor, artillery, and combat aircraft—was greater than either Morocco's or Algeria's, but its ground forces were much smaller. The Libyan navy was somewhat larger than that of Algeria (see fig. 9).

Unusual geographic features present Algeria's military leadership with special challenges in protecting the security of the country's borders. In 1993 most of the population of approximately 27.4 million was concentrated within 100 kilometers of the coast, with the density diminishing rapidly from north to south. The vast, unpopulated stretches of the Sahara Desert to the south would be difficult to defend against a strong and determined adversary. Algeria's western flank south of the Atlas Mountains would be especially vulnerable to a Moroccan attack, inasmuch as Moroccan forces would benefit from shorter communication and supply lines. Between Béchar and Tindouf, the strategic highway that roughly follows the Moroccan border could easily be severed, thereby breaking Algeria's only ground link to the mineral-rich Tindouf area and its connections with Western Sahara and Mauritania. In the northwest, however, the Atlas Mountains would act as a barrier discouraging invasion of the more populous parts of either country by the other.

The problems facing Algeria in the west are duplicated in the southeast, where the lengthy border area with Libya is isolated from the remainder of the country. A tenuous link to the region is provided by a road reaching the border town of Edjeleh, but it would be difficult to mount a defense of this remote area in the face of Libya's superiority in combat aircraft and armor.

In the far south, a trans-Saharan route branches before the border, connecting Algeria to Mali and to Niger. Fortunately, in view of the distances involved and the weak transport links, Algeria faces no serious threat from either country. Algerian border police have expelled nomadic Tuareg and black Africans who were refugees from the Sahel drought or engaged in black-market trading. Demarcation agreements were concluded with Mali and Niger in 1983.

Tunisia, with its small armed forces, has never presented a security problem for Algeria. A twenty-year disagreement over the border delineation with Tunisia was settled in 1983. Algeria and Tunisia have generally united when faced with Libyan bellicosity. When in 1985 Tunisia came under pressure from Libya in the form of border troop movements and violations of Tunisian air space, Algeria supported Tunisia by moving its troops to the border area. Algeria also signed a border agreement with Mauritania in 1985, after three years of negotiation.

Domestic Security Concerns

During the 1960s and 1970s, Ben Bella and Boumediene were primarily concerned with threats to their leadership from other figures who had been prominent in the struggle of the FLN against the French colonial presence. During the War of Independence, the FLN had never been a truly unified force; instead, it operated as a coalition of groups based on different ideological, personality, or ethnoregional considerations. As a result, first Ben Bella and then Boumediene were opposed by a range of individuals with strong revolutionary credentials. When Boumediene overthrew Ben Bella and assumed power in 1965, his tight grip on the military enabled him to dominate the opposition elements. After the abortive attempt in late 1967 by armed forces chief of staff Taher Zbiri to depose him, Boumediene's control appeared to be complete, and the opposition was forced either underground or abroad.

To maintain his hold on power, Boumediene relied heavily on the security forces—particularly the intelligence service of the ANP known as Military Security (Sécurité Militaire), which maintained strict surveillance within and beyond the national

Algeria: A Country Study

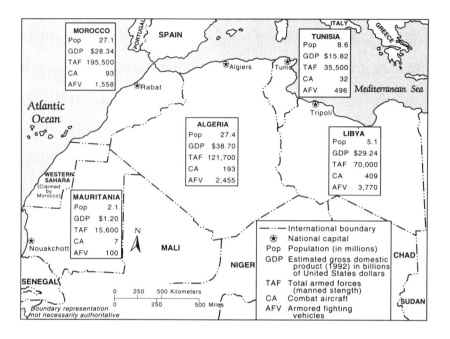

Source: Based on information from *The Military Balance, 1993–1994*, London, 1993, 111-12, 122–25, 131.

Figure 9. Balance of Power in the Maghrib, 1993

boundaries of people whose ideologies were considered questionable. All political organizations outside the FLN were considered illegal because the FLN was defined as representing all legitimate political tendencies. Open criticism of the regime was not permitted, and violators were subject to arrest and severe punishment. The murders in Europe of two former FLN leaders, Belkacem Krim and Mohamed Khider, were blamed on Algerian security forces. Many suspected that deaths of other well-known FLN personalities were linked to vengeance exacted through the Sécurité Militaire.

Benjedid, having been designated the FLN nominee for president at an FLN party congress in 1979, had greater legitimacy than his predecessors because of the wide support he enjoyed from fellow military officers. Reinforcing his position over time, he shunted his rivals and potential rivals into minor positions or out of the ruling apparatus altogether. By the mid-1980s, the government felt confident enough to release from prison or house arrest all political prisoners including Ben Bella, in detention at the time Benjedid assumed office.

Amnesties were also granted to those, among them Zbiri, who had been involved in the plots against Boumediene. Former FLN leaders living abroad were invited to return home.

Islamic Opposition

By the early 1980s, the Islamist movement provided a greater rallying point for opposition elements than did secular leftists. Although Islam was identified with the nationalist struggle against the French, the Algerian government had controlled its practice since independence through the Ministry of Religious Affairs and the Superior Islamic Council. The council maintained "official" mosques and paid the salaries of imams (religious leaders). Beginning in 1979, however, concurrent with the religious revolution that toppled the government of Iran, large numbers of young people began to congregate at mosques that operated beyond the control of the authorities. At prayer meetings, imams not paid by the government preached in favor of a more egalitarian society, against the arrogance of the rich, and for an end to corrupt practices in government, business, and religion.

In a pattern of escalating violence during the early 1980s, religious extremists became increasingly active, assaulting women in Western-style dress, questioning the legitimacy of the "Marxist" Algerian government, and calling for an Islamic republic that would use the Quran as its constitution. After a brutal confrontation between Marxist and Islamist demonstrators at the University of Algiers in November 1982, the authorities rounded up and prosecuted for subversion students, imams, and intellectuals linked with the Algerian Islamic Movement headed by Moustapha Bouyali. Bouyali himself remained at large, forming a guerrilla band that was involved in a number of clashes with security forces. He was killed in early 1987, and his group was disbanded.

Serious demonstrations to protest commodity shortages and high prices broke out in Algiers, Oran, and other cities in October 1988. When the police proved unable to curb the outbreak, troops supported by armored vehicles assumed responsibility for security. Large demonstrations were staged by Islamist groups inspired by the *intifada*, the uprising of Palestinians against Israeli rule on the West Bank of the Jordan River and in the Gaza Strip. It was estimated that more than 500 people were killed after ill-trained soldiers used automatic weapons against the demonstrators. More than 3,500 demonstrators were arrested, but most were released without charges before year's end. Allegations of arbitrary arrest, unfair trials, mistreatment, and torture compounded public anger against the government.

When Benjedid's reforms opened political life to wider public participation, the FIS emerged in 1989 as the primary instrument of the Islamic movement. The FIS achieved rapid success in local elections, especially in the working-class districts of Algiers and other cities. The FIS leaders, determined to remain a legitimate political party, did not acknowledge links with Islamist groups dedicated to violence. The party was banned in March 1992, however, and thousands of its officials and supporters were arrested under the state of emergency. After that time, the FIS appeared to have shifted to a policy of armed response, declaring that the "state violence" of the authorities justified recourse to "means other than dialogue."

Extremist branches of the Islamist movement engaged openly in violence against government targets after the cancellation of the elections. One of the most radical branches, Al Takfir wal Hijra (Repentance and Holy Flight), originally consisted of about 500 Algerian veterans of service in *mujahidin* (literally "holy warriors" or freedom fighters) forces in Afghanistan. Their acts of urban terrorism often were aimed against police and military posts in order to gather weapons and to demonstrate the government's inability to maintain control.

After the government's crackdown against the FIS in 1992, various other activist Islamist organizations sprang up, with units operating in groups of two to five, without apparent unified command. These groups, difficult to distinguish from each other, targeted police posts, courthouses and other public buildings, and selected public figures. In some cases, assassination targets were announced in advance.

Officials did not ascribe the June 1992 assassination of the chairman of the High Council of State, Mohamed Boudiaf, to terrorist groups, although Islamic activists welcomed the action. The assassin, a junior officer assigned to presidential security, was described as "motivated by religious convictions."

The government interned at least 9,000 persons, many of them elected FIS members of assemblies at the province (*wilaya*; pl., *wilayat*) and commune levels, at camps in the Sahara during the spring of 1992. Many of the urban terrorists waged guerrilla warfare from refuges in the mountainous areas adjacent to large cities. Large-scale gendarmerie actions hunted them down. Although the government claimed it had neutralized most terrorist groups, more rigorous measures were imposed in December 1992. These measures included a major sweep by 30,000 army and police personnel directed at every entity connected with the FIS, together with a strict curfew in Algiers and other localities.

After the banning of the FIS in Algeria, many FIS leaders escaped to France, where they reportedly continued to recruit new fighters and collect funds and supplies to pursue the armed struggle in Algeria. The FIS, as a foreign political party, was prohibited from operating on French soil; however, it was represented by the Algerian Brotherhood in France set up by Algerian students. Previously, the Movement for Democracy in Algeria of former President Ben Bella had used intimidation and violence in seeking the support of Algerians resident in France, but such intimidation was no longer considered necessary.

Berber Separatism

The Berbers, who constitute about one-fifth of the Algerian population, have resisted foreign influences since ancient times. They fought against the Phoenicians, the Romans, the Ottoman Turks, and the French after their 1830 occupation of Algeria. In the fighting between 1954 and 1962 against France, Berber men from the Kabylie region participated in larger numbers than their share of the population warranted.

Since independence the Berbers have maintained a strong ethnic consciousness and a determination to preserve their distinctive cultural identity and language. They have particularly objected to efforts to force them to use Arabic; they regard these efforts as a form of Arab imperialism. Except for a handful of individuals, they have not been identified with the Islamist movement. In common with most other Algerians, they are Sunni (see Glossary) Muslims of the Maliki (see Glossary) legal school. In 1980 Berber students, protesting that their culture was being suppressed by the government's arabization policies, launched mass demonstrations and a general strike. In the wake of riots at Tizi Ouzou that resulted in a number of deaths and injuries, the government agreed to the teaching of the Berber language as opposed to classical Arabic at certain universities and promised to respect Berber culture. Nevertheless, ten years later, in 1990, the Berbers were again forced to rally in large numbers to protest a new language law requiring total use of Arabic by 1997.

The Berber party, the Front of Socialist Forces (Front des Forces Socialistes—FFS), gained twenty-five of the 231 contested seats in the first round of the legislative elections of December 1991, all of these in the Kabylie region. The FFS leadership did not approve of the military's cancellation of the second stage of the elections. Although strongly rejecting the FIS's demand that Islamic law be extended to all facets of life, the FFS expressed confidence that it could prevail against Islamist pressure (see Role of Political Parties, ch. 4).

The Military Heritage

The People's National Army (Armée Nationale Populaire—ANP, known until 1962 as the Army of National Liberation—Armée de Libération Nationale—ALN) stems from a long military tradition in Algerian national life. Throughout their history, the peoples of North Africa have demonstrated a decided martial prowess, particularly when called upon to defend their independence. Berber tribesmen with a warlike reputation resisted the spread of Carthaginian and Roman colonization before the Christian era, and they struggled for more than a generation against the seventh-century Arab invaders who spread Islam to North Africa by military conquests mounted as jihads, or holy wars.

Tension, crisis, resistance, dissidence, and revolution have characterized Algeria's development, at times pitting Berbers against Arabs and during other periods uniting them in opposition to a common enemy. The people of the central Maghrib have also, on occasion, fought on the side of their foreign rulers; during the 132 years of colonial domination, the French augmented their pacification forces with Algerian recruits. During World War I, about 173,000 Algerians conscripted into service with the French army fought with valor against the Germans; 25,000 of the Algerians were killed in combat. Algeria also supplied France with soldiers in World War II, providing the Free French with men in the Italian campaign. The experience contributed to a growing dissatisfaction with the French presence in Algeria that in 1954 erupted in the eight-year struggle for independence.

At a meeting in 1954, the revolutionary leaders laid down the structure of the ALN. The six military regions, known at that time as *wilayat*, were subdivided into zones, areas, and sec-

National Liberation Army fighters during the War of Independence
Courtesy Algerian Ministry of Information

tors. Tactical units were assigned, commanders appointed, and a system of military ranks adopted; the designation of colonel was fixed as the highest officer grade.

In 1957 a coordinated campaign of strikes and violence in the cities triggered a brutally effective counterinsurgency campaign by the French that broke down FLN and ALN organizations inside Algeria, particularly in urban areas. The military and civilian revolutionary leadership took sanctuary in Tunisia and Morocco, leaving the "internal ALN"—composed of guerrillas that operated under autonomous local commanders—to continue the fight against the French. Largely unassisted by the revolutionaries outside Algeria, these internal forces—with a strong Berber component—suffered heavily. They were never completely destroyed, however, and their resistance succeeded in demoralizing the French, whose forces numbered 500,000 at their peak.

The regular ALN units, formed in Tunisia and Morocco with the tacit approval of the host countries, established bases near the Algeria border. Unlike the internal forces, the "external" ALN had a conventional organization and received training and modern equipment from sympathetic foreign sources. Although estimates of its size varied, a strength of 35,000 was claimed in 1960. Increasingly effective French measures to seal

Algeria: A Country Study

the borders hampered efforts to convey arms and supplies to the internal forces.

The external ALN was decisively defeated whenever it engaged the French directly. Nevertheless, it emerged as a central element among revolutionary forces, especially after the FLN leadership appointed Colonel Boumediene as ALN chief of staff in early 1960. Well before independence, regional factionalism and fierce personal rivalries raged among FLN internal and external military leaders and civilian politicians. Only six days before Algeria's formal independence on July 5, 1962, the civilian political faction controlling the Provisional Government of the Algerian Republic (Gouvernement Provisoire de la République Algérienne—GPRA) dismissed Boumediene and the rest of the general staff. Boumediene rejected their authority and instead supported the candidacy of Ben Bella, one of the "historic chiefs" of the War of Independence, against the GPRA. Boumediene led contingents of the external ALN and friendly guerrillas eastward to Algiers, overcoming resistance from other internal guerrilla leaders who felt that they had earned the right to shape the course of the revolution. Joining Ben Bella in the capital, Boumediene became minister of defense in the government formed in September 1962.

The failure of the GPRA to assert its supremacy over the external army's general staff constituted a turning point in Algerian military development. Thereafter, the political power of the ANP was firmly established. Several groups—mostly former internal leaders and politically motivated enemies of Boumediene—sought to preserve the Algerian armed forces' guerrilla traditions; they strongly opposed the creation of a strong, centralized military power under Boumediene's control. By contrast, according to Boumediene's philosophy, the security of a modern state required a well-equipped armed force trained and organized along conventional lines. The brief border war with Morocco in 1976, in which the conventional Moroccan army proved to be superior to the ANP, underscored the need to convert the ANP into a unified modern army.

The external forces were better organized, equipped, and trained and were not fractured by local *wilaya* loyalties as were the internal forces in the War of Independence. The internal guerrillas, who may have numbered no more than 25,000 at any one time, had, however, borne the brunt of the warfare. In addition, about 75,000 part-time irregulars carried out sabo-

Women's unit of People's National Army parading at ceremonies commemorating November 1, 1954, launch of Algerian War of Independence
Courtesy Embassy of Algeria, Washington

tage, acted as guides, supplied intelligence, and often took part in engagements near their own homes.

Boumediene vigorously undertook to reduce, consolidate, reorganize, and train the ANP's various elements. He purged most of the headstrong former guerrilla commanders. He retained professionals of the external army, as well as about 250 officers and noncommissioned officers (NCOs) with experience in the French army. The new ANP absorbed about 10,000 members of the internal guerrilla units; Boumediene discharged the rest, mostly Berbers.

In spite of his association with Boumediene, Ben Bella moved to gain control of the army in a series of efforts aimed at reducing the power of the defense minister. The new constitution of 1963 assigned the powers of commander in chief to Ben

Bella as head of state. Three weeks later, while Boumediene was in Moscow seeking arms, Ben Bella designated former *wilaya* leader Colonel Taher Zbiri as military chief of staff, further weakening the position of the minister of defense and the ANP. Boumediene met these threats by forging alliances with FLN leaders previously identified as his rivals. The coup d'état of June 19, 1965, which brought Boumediene to power, demonstrated his success in that Zbiri personally arrested Ben Bella.

Closely identified with the Boumediene government after the 1965 coup, the ANP exercised its influence through the country's supreme governing body, the Council of the Revolution. Of the council's twenty-six original members, twenty-two were military men with wartime or postwar service; twelve served at the time on the ANP general staff or as commanders of military regions.

In response to a failed coup attempt by chief of staff Zbiri at the end of 1967, Boumediene dissolved the general staff and solidified his control over the ANP by assuming personally many staff responsibilities. He excluded ANP leadership from day-to-day policy making but remained close to the army commanders whose support he needed to maintain political control.

Boumediene never considered himself a military professional, and he and his top aides never appeared publicly in uniform. He asserted that as a socialist state Algeria was not the instrument of a military regime or an officer caste. Nonetheless, the ANP was the best-organized and best-managed institution in the country, and many technically competent and experienced military personnel entered ministries and parastatal (partly government-owned and partly privately owned) corporations as part of the national economic elite.

Military management also undertook local civic-action and economic development projects. This role gave regional military commanders powers of patronage that further boosted their political influence. The regional commanders became more influential in local affairs than the governors of *wilayat*, who served under the Ministry of Interior, Local Communities, and Tourism (hereafter Ministry of Interior). The *wilayat* governors also frequently had military backgrounds.

After Boumediene was incapacitated by a fatal illness in late 1978, the Council of the Revolution assumed day-to-day political power on an interim basis. Only eight members of the council remained from the original twenty-six. Five were colonels;

they included Chadli Benjedid, who assumed responsibility for national defense matters. The nation's senior military officer, Benjedid was viewed as the ANP's candidate to replace Boumediene. He became president when the FLN Party Congress became deadlocked over two more prominent candidates.

Benjedid's Council of Ministers included strong ANP representation. Military men consistently made up half the membership of the FLN Political Bureau. Indeed, one observer described the FLN as a "screen" behind which the military exercised its influence as the real foundation of the regime. Many officers served in civilian posts; many observers believed, however, that their involvement in national decision making reflected Benjedid's confidence in their abilities and loyalty rather than an effort to impose direct military control.

The ANP's favorable image, based on its role in the War of Independence and in the creation of the postwar Algerian state, was badly tarnished by the ruthless way in which it suppressed the strikes and riots of "Black October" 1988. Troops deployed in the center of Algiers and other cities fired indiscriminately, with little regard for civilian casualties. Reacting to criticisms by human rights activists at home and abroad, Benjedid purged a number of military commanders and appointed younger, more professional officers with personal loyalty to him. Soon thereafter, all senior army officers resigned from the FLN Central Committee so as formally, if not actually, to distance themselves from civilian politics.

As the threat of Islamic militancy became more acute, the power of the army reemerged as the primary bulwark against religiously inspired violence. The role of the armed forces was legitimated by a four-month state of emergency declared after the May-June 1991 rioting. The military high command felt that the government's political liberalization measures and its lax attitude toward the Islamic threat were mistaken. When the first round of national election results of December 26, 1991, resulted in an overwhelming FIS victory, Benjedid was forced to resign as president. A five-member High Council of State soon assumed presidential powers. The council's only military representative was the minister of defense, Major General Khaled Nezzar, but the military exerted strong influence on the interim government. Troops and armored vehicles were deployed in the cities, military checkpoints were set up, and gatherings at mosques for political purposes were prohibited. The regime declared a one-year state of emergency, banned the FIS, and arrested thousands of its supporters. Convinced that the stability of the nation was at stake, the army clearly intended to crush the FIS. The militants' resort to terrorist attacks and the June 1992 assassination of Boudiaf, one of the original founders of the group that became the FLN, hardened the attitude of the military. Nezzar declared that the army would "conduct an implacable war until the total eradication of armed Islamic extremists who have soiled their hands with the blood of the defenders of order [is achieved]."

As 1992 drew to a close, the suppression of the Islamic political movement by the ANP and police appeared to be outwardly effective, although individual acts of violence continued. In spite of some desertions and arms thefts by sympathizers in the military, senior commanders asserted that the cohesion of the army was unaffected. The military leaders maintained that they had deemed it necessary to intervene only to head off an anarchic situation. Although the armed forces could have assumed power directly during the turmoil of 1992, they refrained from doing so. They continued to profess their intention of returning to their basic mission of providing for the defense and territorial integrity of the nation.

The Armed Forces

The armed forces consist of four branches: the army, the navy, the air force, and air defense (see fig. 10). They are augmented by the National Gendarmerie, which comes under the Ministry of Interior. According to *The Military Balance, 1993-1994*, the total strength of the active armed forces in late 1993 was 121,700, including the army, 105,000; the navy, 6,700; and the air force, 10,000. Air defense manning levels are not known, but one source estimates them as 4,000, included within the air force complement. The number of reserves is listed at 150,000, but their state of readiness is not known.

Under the constitution, the president is supreme commander of all the armed forces and is responsible for national defense. When Boumediene deposed Ben Bella in 1965, he eliminated the national defense portfolio to reinforce his own control over the ANP. In July 1990, Benjedid revived the position, appointing Nezzar to head the ministry. Nezzar had been chief of staff since he replaced Major General Abdallah Belhouchet in 1988. Belhouchet, who until that time had been considered the most important military figure after Benjedid, was dismissed as part of the wholesale removal of senior officers after the 1988 riots. After Benjedid's resignation as president in early 1992 and Nezzar's appointment as sole military representative on the High Council of State, the interim governing body, Nezzar was seen as the strong man of the regime.

Under the constitution, the head of state can turn for advice on national security matters to the High Security Council, which along with the Council of Ministers, is required to give its consent to the declaration of a state of emergency in the event the country faces imminent danger to its institutions, its independence, or its territorial integrity. The High Security Council must also be heard prior to a declaration of war by the president. The security council's members include the prime minister, the minister of national defense, the chief of staff of the armed forces, the minister of interior (an army officer), and the minister of justice. Upon Benjedid's resignation, the High Security Council assembled to cancel the second round of the general election and created the High Council of State to exercise interim presidential powers.

During the 1980s, Benjedid took a number of measures to reorganize the military high command so as to enhance the ANP's efficiency and military effectiveness. In 1984, after promoting eight colonels to become the first generals in independent Algeria, Benjedid announced the establishment of an ANP general staff. Previously, the armed forces had relied on the secretary general of the Ministry of National Defense to coordinate staff activities. The previous secretary general of the ministry, Major General Moustafa Benloucif, was named the first chief of staff. Benloucif had risen quickly in the ANP and was also an alternate member of the FLN Political Bureau. However, he was dismissed in 1986 without explanation; in 1992 the regime announced that Benloucif would be tried for corruption and the embezzlement of US$11 million, which had been transferred to European accounts.

The general staff had responsibility for operational planning for the integrated armed forces, budgeting, information and communications, logistics and administrative support, mobilization, and recruiting. It was not, however, part of the regular chain of command. In practice, the armed forces chief of staff dealt directly with the chiefs of the service branches and with the commanders of the six military regions. Along with Nezzar, the senior hierarchy of the armed forces included the chief of staff, Abdelmalek Guénaizia; the commander of the National Gendarmerie, Abbas Ghezaiel; the chief of military

Algeria: A Country Study

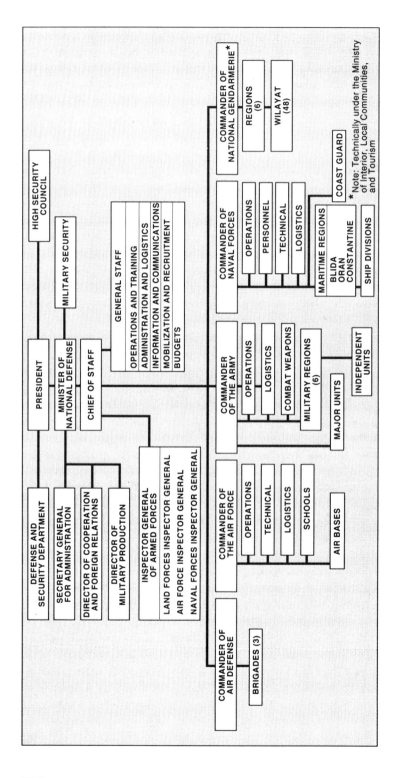

Figure 10. *Organization of National Defense, 1993*

security, Mohamed Médiène; and the inspector general of the land forces, Tayeb Derradji. Minister of Interior Larbi Belkheir, a major general who had been considered part of the collective military leadership, was replaced by a civilian minister after Boudiaf's assassination in mid-1992 and was no longer on active service.

Army

The army's personnel strength of 105,000 in late 1993 included 65,000 conscripts. The army's size nearly doubled after 1978, largely to prepare for possible hostilities with Morocco over the Western Sahara. After reaching a manpower strength of 120,000 in 1992 to deal with the pressures of domestic disturbances, financial considerations required a cutback in personnel. The army commander appointed in the spring of 1992 was Major General Khelifa Rahim, who also served as deputy chief of staff of the armed forces.

Territorially, Algeria is divided into six numbered military regions, each with headquarters located in a principal city or town (see fig. 11). This system of territorial organization, adopted shortly after independence, grew out of the wartime *wilaya* structure and the postwar necessity of subduing antigovernment insurgencies that were based in the various regions. Regional commanders control and administer bases, logistics, and housing, as well as conscript training. Commanders of army divisions and brigades, air force installations, and naval forces report directly to the Ministry of National Defense and service chiefs of staff on operational matters.

During the 1980s, most of the army's combat units were concentrated in Military Region II (Oran) and to a lesser extent in Military Region III (Béchar). Adjacent to Morocco, region III straddles the main access routes from that country. It is also near the troubled Western Sahara, embracing territory previously claimed by Morocco.

Much of the internal disorder and violence associated with economic distress and the Islamist movement has occurred in Military Region I (Blida), which includes the capital of Algiers, and Military Region V (Constantine). Army units have been strengthened in and near the cities where attacks against the government and security forces have occurred. Although regional commanders were originally all colonels, the commanders of region I (Mohamed Djenouhat) and region V (Abdelhamid Djouadi) were both promoted to major general

Algeria: A Country Study

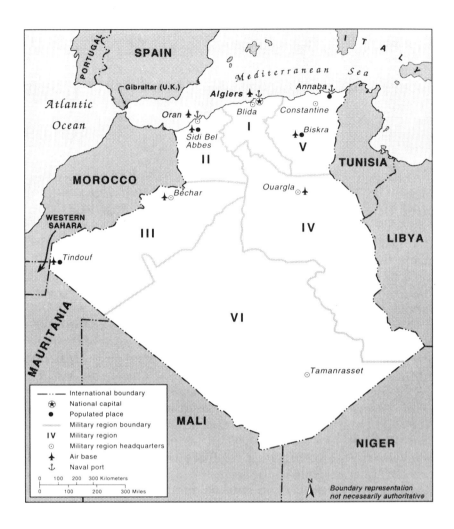

Figure 11. Military Regions, 1993

in 1992. The two southeastern jurisdictions—Military Region IV (Ouargla) and Military Region VI (Tamanrasset)—are sparsely populated tracts of desert where a limited number of combat troops carry out patrols and man small outposts. The Ouargla region assumed a measure of strategic importance after relations with Libya soured, but the military's main activities there and in Region VI are the construction and planting projects undertaken by conscript forces.

Originally organized as independent infantry battalions, the ANP decided in 1966, based on Soviet advice, to form four mechanized divisions. However, logistical problems and the high cost of associated heavy weaponry soon forced a reassessment of the plan. In 1992 the army again began to reorganize on a divisional basis; hence some units have been in a state of flux.

According to *The Military Balance, 1993–1994*, in 1993 the army's main combat units consisted of two armored divisions, each with three tank regiments and one mechanized regiment, and two mechanized divisions, each with three mechanized regiments and one tank regiment. Furthermore, in 1993 there were five motorized infantry brigades and one airborne special forces brigade. Each infantry brigade consisted of four infantry battalions and one tank battalion. In addition, in 1993 the army had seven independent artillery battalions, five air defense battalions, and four engineering battalions. The brigades had authorized personnel levels of 3,500 men, but all units were believed to be understrength.

Twelve companies of desert troops, each with about 400 men, functioned as border guards. Originally these troops patrolled on camels, but by the 1980s they relied extensively on light reconnaissance vehicles. Two special riot units, said to number about 15,000 men, were assigned to maintain civil order. In addition to other riot-control equipment, they reportedly were armed with shotguns.

The army was well equipped with both older and more up-to-date models of Soviet armor and artillery. In 1993 it had nearly 1,000 tanks, including more than 600 T–62s and late-model T–72s. About 200 T–72s had been delivered since 1990. Earlier versions of wheeled armored personnel carriers (APCs), the Soviet BTR–50 and BTR–60, had been supplemented by BMP–1 and BMP–2 tracked armored infantry fighting vehicles mounted with 73mm guns and a few with Sagger antitank missiles. The army's extensive artillery inventory was headed by Soviet 122mm and 152mm self-propelled howitzers. There were also more than 100 122mm, 140mm, and 240mm multiple rocket launchers in the inventory. The principal antitank weapons were the Soviet Sagger and the French Milan. In addition to a variety of towed and self-propelled air defense guns, the army had Soviet SA–8 and SA–9 vehicle-mounted surface-to-air missiles (SAMs) and SA–7 man-portable SAMs (see table 7, Appendix).

During the early years of the army's modernization in the 1960s and 1970s, thousands of ANP officers went to the Soviet

Algeria: A Country Study

Union for training. Since then, Algeria has established its own military academies, although Russian advisers were still attached to the ANP in 1993. Strategic and tactical doctrine continues to be based on Russian models. Basic army cadet training is conducted at the military academy at Cherchell, west of Algiers, the site of a French interservices military school taken over by the government in 1963. Officer candidates attend for three years, generally followed by a year of specialized training before being commissioned and assigned to field units. The Cherchell academy also includes a staff college for advanced training of a limited number of field-grade officers of all branches.

A number of other institutions are used to train army personnel. Among these are the school for technical, administrative, and logistical training at El Harrach, just southeast of Algiers; the school for armored units at Batna; the school for artillery units at Telerghma near Constantine; the school for infantry commandos at Biskra; the school for communications technicians at Bougara, on the outskirts of Algiers; and the school for desert cavalry units at Ouargla.

The army's NCOs are trained at Ksar el Boukhari, about 100 kilometers south of Algiers, where they receive instruction in leadership, principles of command and control, tactical deployment, and political indoctrination. The NCOs are often used in command positions in smaller tactical units.

Air Force

The Algerian air force, as of 1993 under the command of Colonel Mohamed Mokhtar Boutamine, has responsibility for defending the country's air space, supporting ground forces, supplying military transportation and cargo airlift, and carrying out land and maritime reconnaissance. In late 1993, the air force was equipped with some 193 combat aircraft and more than fifty attack helicopters, flying from about fifteen air bases. The service has expanded steadily since its inception in 1962, when Egypt donated five MiG–15 jet fighters and supplied a training mission. As more MiGs arrived, Algerian pilots were sent to Syria and Egypt and later to the Soviet Union for flight training. Others received flight training and technical schooling in France. With the help of Soviet advisers, a pilot training school was eventually established at Tafraoua near Oran. The Air Force Academy and a technical training school are also located at the Tafraoua complex.

According to *The Military Balance, 1993-1994*, in 1993 air force combat capabilities were built around three fighter/ground-attack squadrons and eight interceptor squadrons equipped exclusively with Soviet aircraft. The most advanced of these, although they had been in the inventory for more than a decade, were fourteen MiG-25s and three MiG-25Rs in a reconnaissance configuration. The fighter squadrons also included ninety-five MiG-21s and twenty MiG-23s. The fighter/ground-attack squadrons included forty MiG-23s and ten older Su-24s (see table 8, Appendix). The basic weapon of the fighter aircraft was the Soviet AA-2 (Atoll) and AA-6 air-to-air missiles.

The main pillar of the air force's transport capability in late 1993 was the fleet of sixteen Lockheed C-130 Hercules purchased from the United States. These were supplemented by six Soviet An-12s of comparable load capacity. Two Super King B-200s were outfitted for maritime reconnaissance.

The helicopter fleet in late 1993 comprised five squadrons of heavy- and medium-attack helicopters of Soviet manufacture, as well as a small number of transport helicopters. Air defense was under a separate command. It consisted of three brigades equipped with 85mm, 100mm, and 130mm (KS-12, KS-19, and KS-30) Soviet antiaircraft guns; and three SAM regiments, one equipped with Soviet SA-3, SA-6, and SA-8 SAMs.

Navy

With help principally from the Soviet Union, the Algerian Navy underwent considerable enlargement and modernization during the 1980s. Its ambition was to develop a fleet of well-armed vessels that would enable it to deal with the Moroccan or Libyan fleet and permit Algeria to project naval power beyond its own coastal waters. As of 1993, the navy was reportedly interested in acquiring surplus vessels from West European navies for patrolling its exclusive economic zone. These purchases, however, had not materialized by late 1993, probably owing to financial constraints.

In 1993 the naval complement of officers, enlisted personnel, and cadets was estimated at 6,700, with an additional 630 men in the coast guard. The latter group is part of the Ministry of Interior, although under the navy's operational control. All navy and coast guard personnel are volunteers. Previously, the commanding officer of the navy had held the rank of colonel;

in 1992, however, a brigadier general, Chaabane Ghodbane, was named to the post.

Algeria received its first two submarines, Romeo-class vessels, from the Soviet Union in 1983. In 1987 and 1988, the country acquired two Kilo-class submarines, quiet-running, high-speed vessels armed with both torpedoes and mines, from the Soviet Union. The Romeos were retired for use as training ships. Two additional Kilo-class submarines are reportedly on order (see table 9, Appendix).

The largest surface vessels are three Soviet Koni-class frigates commissioned between 1980 and 1985. With 1,440 tons displacement, each frigate is armed with Gecko SAMs and four 76mm guns. Three Soviet Nanuchka II–class corvettes of 850 tons were delivered between 1980 and 1982. They are armed with Gecko SAMs and four surface-to-surface missiles (SSMs). New diesel engines are reportedly being installed on the corvettes after problems were experienced with the performance and reliability of their propulsion mechanisms.

In addition to the larger combat vessels, in 1993 the naval forces operated a number of fast-attack craft and some smaller units for coastal patrols. They included eleven former Soviet Osa I– and Osa II–class missile boats, each mounted with four Styx SSMs. The navy also possessed twelve Kebir-class fast-attack craft, each mounted with a 76mm gun. The coast guard was temporarily operating six of these. Designed by Brooke Marine, the first two were built in Britain and the remainder were assembled or built at Mers el Kebir with assistance from Vosper Thornycroft.

The fleet in 1993 boasted a modest amphibious capability, based on a Polish LCT (landing craft, tank) and two larger British-built landing ships acquired in 1983 and 1984. A maritime reconnaissance squadron with two Super King 200Ts had been assigned to the navy, although the squadron's personnel and aircraft came from the air force.

Algeria's naval academy at Tamentfoust near Algiers provides officer training equivalent to that of the army and the air force academies. The navy also operates a technical training school for its personnel at Tamentfoust. Some higher-ranking naval officers have taken advantage of training in France, Russia, and the United States. Principal naval bases are located near Algiers, at Mers el Kebir, and at Annaba.

In addition to sixteen Italian-built light patrol craft, the coast guard in 1993 operated six Chinese patrol boats delivered in 1990; a seventh was delivered in 1992. In carrying out its coast guard duties, the navy coordinates its activities with elements of the Ministry of Interior, with the customs and immigration services, and the national police. Its goal is to prevent smuggling, the illegal entry of undesirable aliens, and other offenses in order to ensure the security of coastal areas.

Uniforms, Ranks, and Insignia

The army service uniform is of an olive drab shade similar in style to the uniform of the United States Army. Airborne troops wear camouflage material with distinctive boots. Air force uniforms are pale blue, and navy uniforms are dark blue. All services have winter, summer, and dress uniforms.

Insignia of rank are worn on shoulder straps by both officers and enlisted men of all services (see fig. 12). Rank designations are similar to those of the French military. There are no warrant officer grades, nor is there a grade corresponding to private first class. The ranks of senior commanders can be identified by a large wreath device with two swords plus one star (brigadier general) or two stars (major general).

Personnel and Recruitment

Independent Algeria has never experienced difficulty in meeting its military manpower needs. Its population is predominantly young. According to United States government data, of an estimated population in 1993 of 27.4 million, more than 6 million are males age fifteen to forty-nine. Of these, an estimated 3.8 million are considered fit for military service, and 293,000 reach the military age of nineteen annually. Accordingly, basic manpower resources are more than adequate to meet any foreseeable military needs.

Until mid-1967, the ANP relied entirely on volunteer manpower. Given the plentiful supply of young men, the economic attraction of the army compared with the difficulties of finding employment elsewhere, and the absence of aversion to military service, the ANP would seem to be able to depend on a voluntary system indefinitely. Algeria's commitment to Arab nationalism, however, caused a rethinking of recruitment policies after Arab forces were decisively defeated by Israel in the June 1967 War. By a 1968 decree, all Algerians were obligated to serve two years upon reaching the age of nineteen. The objective of this national service plan was to increase substantially the personnel strength of the army and, at the same time, to

Algeria: A Country Study

OFFICERS

ALGERIAN RANK*	MULAZIM	MULAZIM AWWAL	NAQIB	RAID	MUQADDAM	AQID	AMID	LIWA	NO RANK	NO RANK	NO RANK
ARMY, AIR FORCE, AND NAVY											
U.S. RANK TITLES FOR ARMY AND AIR FORCE	2D LIEUTENANT	1ST LIEUTENANT	CAPTAIN	MAJOR	LIEUTENANT COLONEL	COLONEL	BRIGADIER GENERAL	MAJOR GENERAL	LIEUTENANT GENERAL	GENERAL	GENERAL OF THE ARMY GENERAL OF THE AIR FORCE
U.S. RANK TITLES FOR NAVY	ENSIGN	LIEUTENANT JUNIOR GRADE	LIEUTENANT	LIEUTENANT COMMANDER	COMMANDER	CAPTAIN	REAR ADMIRAL LOWER HALF	REAR ADMIRAL UPPER HALF	VICE ADMIRAL	ADMIRAL	FLEET ADMIRAL

ENLISTED PERSONNEL

ALGERIAN RANK*	JUNDI	ARIF	ARIF AWWAL	RAQIB	RAQIB AWWAL	MUSAID	MUSAID AWWAL
ARMY, AIR FORCE, AND NAVY	NO INSIGNIA						
U.S. RANK TITLES FOR ARMY	BASIC PRIVATE	PRIVATE/ PRIVATE FIRST CLASS	CORPORAL/ SPECIALIST	SERGEANT	STAFF SERGEANT/ SERGEANT FIRST CLASS	MASTER SERGEANT/ FIRST SERGEANT	SERGEANT MAJOR/ COMMAND SERGEANT MAJOR
U.S. RANK TITLES FOR AIR FORCE	BASIC AIRMAN	AIRMAN/ AIRMAN FIRST CLASS	SENIOR AIRMAN/ SERGEANT	STAFF SERGEANT	TECHNICAL SERGEANT/ MASTER SERGEANT	SENIOR MASTER SERGEANT	CHIEF MASTER SERGEANT
U.S. RANK TITLES FOR NAVY	SEAMAN RECRUIT	SEAMAN APPRENTICE/ SEAMAN	PETTY OFFICER THIRD CLASS	PETTY OFFICER SECOND CLASS	PETTY OFFICER FIRST CLASS/ CHIEF PETTY OFFICER	SENIOR CHIEF PETTY OFFICER	MASTER CHIEF PETTY OFFICER

*Army shoulder boards are olive drab in color; air force shoulder boards are dark blue; navy shoulder boards are navy blue.

Figure 12. Commissioned Officer and Enlisted Personnel Ranks and Insignia, 1993

train a youth corps for national development. The first six months were to be spent in military training with the ANP and the rest in social and economic projects managed by the armed forces. National service was also intended to provide political education and indoctrination in the revolutionary socialist program of the government. As initially projected, an equal number of young men and women were to be inducted. In practice, far fewer than the originally intended numbers of men were called to duty, and the induction of women was never implemented. Some women were accepted as ANP volunteers, although fewer were serving in 1993 than in past years. Most of these women were in the lower grades and were limited to the military health service.

Conscription has remained in effect since 1969, although the period of compulsory service has been reduced to eighteen months. Those young men not conscripted by the end of the year in which they become eligible can obtain a certificate attesting to their exemption from future call-up so that they can continue their studies or work without further distraction.

After the national service program was introduced, conscripts generally were given civic-action assignments following their initial military training period of six months. In some cases, opportunities were offered for those with limited education to learn trades at various vocational schools, often connected with civil engineering and construction. Others learned to drive motor vehicles and to operate construction equipment. National service provided a ready source of workers for civic-action projects while freeing regular soldiers to concentrate on other military missions. Beginning in the 1980s, however, most conscripts appear to have been assigned to regular military units to complete their eighteen-month service obligation, and fewer were given nonmilitary assignments. Some conscripts, such as doctors who deferred their military service until completing their education, were allowed to fulfill their service obligation by occupying civilian posts in their special fields in rural areas or small towns.

In 1993 the top echelon of the Algerian officer corps, mainly men in their mid-fifties, included many veterans of the War of Independence. Most had served in the external ALN, a few had been guerrilla officers of the internal *maquis* (the French resistance during World War II), and others had experience in the French army. Some, like Nezzar, had served as NCOs with the French before defecting to the ALN.

The army's prestige—rooted in the revolutionary struggle against the French—was dimmed by its excessive use of force to control the mass demonstrations of 1988 and 1991. Most Algerian citizens were too young to recall the achievements of senior officers in the fight for independence. Moreover, much of the anger that had ignited demonstrations among the civilian population was directed against widespread corruption among highly placed officials. Although few of the senior military had been directly implicated, they tended to be regarded with the same suspicion as civilian officeholders.

Nevertheless, the newer military leadership was liberal in its outlook, associating itself with the forward-looking managerial class that welcomed the abandonment of the socialist experiment and favored political democratization and the adoption of a free-market system. Senior commanders were resolutely opposed to an Islamist-led state because they feared it would mean an end to the modernization movement.

Younger officers came from all walks of life. Because of the ANP's strict educational requirements, however, people raised in urban areas with greater educational opportunities were more strongly represented than those raised in rural Algeria. Generally, all officer candidates were expected to be eighteen to twenty-three years of age, to have completed twelve years of education and hold a baccalaureate certificate, to be unmarried, and to be in good health. Competitive written examinations were held for entry into the military academies.

Conditions of Service

The general environment of Algerian military life has long been of sufficiently high quality to make service in the ANP a reasonably attractive alternative to the deteriorating conditions found in the civilian sector. Most military personnel enjoy a higher standard of dignity and comfort than the average civilian in an economy struggling with unemployment and inflation. Food and pay compare favorably with that found in the civil sector. Other advantages, such as medical care, retirement benefits, and in-service training for later use in a civilian career, also make military service attractive. In principle, the armed forces do not constitute a privileged group insulated from the problems afflicting Algerian society as a whole. Nevertheless, the system is better organized and the standards of services provided tend to be superior to those available in civilian life. In a possible allusion to a decline of these standards, General

Nezzar spoke of the "Spartan" conditions of service life in discussing the problems of the armed forces in 1992.

After independence the government realized that the loyalty and morale of the armed forces were essential to its stability and from the start allocated the largest share of the military budget for personnel-related expenses: pay, allowances, rations, and clothing. The ANP operated post exchange and commissary systems, built holiday camps for dependents, and extended some opportunities for duty-free purchasing. Members of the armed forces also benefited from a social security program maintained by the ANP separately from the national program maintained by the government.

A political commissariat, set up by Boumediene in 1963 and patterned after similar groups in Soviet-type regimes, provided ideological indoctrination and oversight of the armed forces. Its officers reported directly to the FLN. The political commissariat provided political supervision, operated its own training school, and assigned graduates to all ANP units. Although apparently an influential agency in the 1970s, a decade later the commissariat served mainly as an instrument to provide goods and services to boost servicemen's morale.

In its earlier years, the ANP adopted a reserved and austere profile, dedicated to the national goals, exemplary in its conduct, and modest in its lifestyle. Differences between enlisted and officer pay, unlike those in some of the older armies of the Middle East and North Africa, did not reflect a class distinction in which a highly paid officer caste was separated from a mass of conscripts by a wide chasm of pay and privilege. Since the late 1970s, however, the officer corps has enjoyed comfortable living quarters and recreational facilities; had easy access to consumer goods, housing, and transportation; and been insulated from the sometimes overbearing state bureaucracy.

The officer corps is not characterized by elaborate ceremony, ostentatious attire, or an inflated rank structure. To maintain the revolutionary tradition of equality, the military hierarchy was deliberately limited to the rank of colonel. In 1984 this system was modified when the ranks of brigadier general and major general were created. A number of promotions in 1992 raised eight of some twenty brigadier generals to major general. The result was that commanders of similar rank often held vastly different command responsibilities. Seasoned and competent officers with relatively low ranks often held positions that in other armed forces would be associated with higher ranks.

The Defense Burden

Algerian military spending since independence has been relatively restrained. Despite the influence of the military establishment, the government on the whole has refrained from unduly favoring defense interests over other sectors; on the contrary, it has attempted to avoid burdensome military commitments. Algeria's outlays on its armed forces, both in terms of share of gross national product (GNP—see Glossary) and of total government budget devoted to defense, have been well below those of its North African neighbors, Libya, Morocco, and Tunisia.

The bulk of funding for the Ministry of National Defense is allocated annually from the country's current budget. In addition, an unknown amount is included in the country's capital budget. According to official Algerian statistics, funds allocated to the ministry measured in dinars (for value of the dinar—see Glossary) remained relatively constant through the early 1970s. Although this was a time when the country was still creating a professional military establishment and was developing its air and naval services, defense funding showed a substantial decline as a percentage of the central government's current budget, reflecting the government's preoccupation with domestic socioeconomic development.

By the mid-1970s, military spending began to rise as the country sought to improve its defensive posture and to achieve a higher level of military preparedness after the October 1973 War in the Middle East and Morocco's moves to annex the Western Sahara. According to data compiled by the United States Arms Control and Disarmament Agency (ACDA), defense expenditures continued to increase rapidly between 1978 and 1982, but fell slightly as a percentage of the government's current budget from 14.1 percent in 1978 to 13.0 percent in 1982. Military expenditures reached a high point in 1982, amounting to US$1.6 billion in constant 1991 dollars. Algeria's officially reported military expenditures consisted entirely of recurring or operating expenditures; all or most capital spending and overseas arms purchases were omitted from the reported figures. The ACDA studies added estimates covering these unreported items to the defense budget.

People's National Army officer lecturing on mechanical principles at the Combined Services Military Academy, Cherchell, west of Algiers
Courtesy Algerian Ministry of Information

ACDA's statistics indicated that military spending as a percentage of central government expenditures continued to decline after 1982, reaching a low of 6.3 percent in 1985, before rising again to nearly 10 percent in 1988. Military expenditures remained at 3 to 4 percent of GNP during most of the 1980s, but tapered off sharply to under 2 percent in 1991. Military expenditures per capita were US$50 annually in 1989 and US$28 in 1991. This sum was comparable to Morocco's expenditures, whereas Libya, with a much smaller population and an unusually large military sector financed by oil exports, spent US$613 per capita in 1991. A separate study, *World Military and Social Expenditures* by Ruth Leger Sivard, found that Algeria's military expenditures were proportionately lower than the average of all the countries of North Africa.

Algeria has no significant arms industry, and therefore valuable foreign exchange must be devoted to the purchase of imported weapons systems. To some extent, defense costs are offset by the contribution of the military to the civilian economy. Under both Boumediene and Benjedid, the government stressed the role of the armed forces in national development. Soldiers carried out public works projects that were often managed by officers. This aspect of the ANP's mission was emphasized in Article 82 of the 1976 constitution: "The People's National Army, instrument of the revolution, participates in the development of the country and in the construction of socialism." When a new constitution was adopted in 1989, the army's role was defined in a narrower traditional form as that of safeguarding national territory.

During the War of Independence, the FLN initiated a number of projects designed to achieve for the military a degree of self-sufficiency in producing food and other basic supplies. For example, at least fifty large farms were taken from French settlers and converted to army cooperatives after the war ended in 1962. These projects supplied some of the ANP's needs, and the military also profited from sales on the civilian market. The army was also involved in manufacturing and construction enterprises. Much of the construction and surfacing of a major road across the Sahara to the Niger border was the responsibility of the army, as was a notable planting project, the *barrage vert*, or green wall of trees, aimed at limiting the spread of the Sahara.

The army, furthermore, built low-income housing projects as well as barracks and housing for its own personnel. Since 1989, however, the army has discontinued civilian construction activities and a number of military enterprises. Some of these enterprises, including a brickworks, a wood-processing plant, and a poultry-raising business, have been transferred to public or private companies. Only certain road and railroad projects of a strategic nature have been retained.

Foreign Military Assistance

In spite of periodic reports that Algeria was negotiating with European manufacturers to produce weapons systems under license, the country continues to depend heavily on outsiders to supply the ANP. From independence through the 1980s, Algeria's most important supplier remained the Soviet Union. It was estimated that nearly 90 percent of the equipment in the

ANP inventory in 1993 was of Soviet origin. Algerian leaders have frequently stated their desire to diversify their sources of arms and to obtain access to up-to-date Western equipment, but the country's straitened economic circumstances have precluded a major shift to purchases from the West.

At independence the newly created ANP was using equipment from various sources. Some small arms had been delivered to the ALN during the war from China, Egypt, and other countries. The new force also benefited from some military supplies turned over by the French forces as they left the country and from Egypt's assistance to the air unit. Overall, however, the military was very poorly equipped; it lacked the heavy weapons associated with a modern military establishment.

Overtures to Western nations by Ben Bella and Boumediene resulted in lukewarm responses or, at best, offers on terms the Algerians considered too stringent. The French government of Charles de Gaulle, in particular, was reluctant to supply heavy items on concessional terms to the country it had so recently fought. The Soviet Union extended Algeria its first military credit, equivalent to about US$100 million, following an urgent visit by Boumediene to Moscow in late 1963 after a setback in the border war with Morocco. Soviet heavy arms and equipment soon began flowing into the country. After the June 1967 Arab-Israeli War, the Soviet Union stepped up arms deliveries and extended additional credits. Moroccan moves to annex the Western Sahara apparently provided a catalyst for further arms purchases. In 1980 the Soviet Union agreed to deliver an estimated US$3.5 billion in arms through 1985. Another agreement was signed in 1986 for a further US$2 billion in arms. These sales were on a credit basis highly favorable to Algeria, with repayment over an extended period at low interest rates. Nevertheless, Algeria was unwilling to enter into a close military relationship with the Soviet Union. It refused the Soviet Union basing rights at the large naval installation at Mers el Kebir, which the French had handed over in 1968, and the holding of joint military exercises.

Algeria received some of the most modern Soviet-made arms during the 1975 to 1985 period. The ANP was one of the first armies outside Eastern Europe to be equipped with the T-72 tank. It also received the BMP-1 and BMP-2 infantry fighting vehicle, MiG-23 and MiG-25 fighter aircraft, Mi-24 attack helicopters, modern rapid-firing artillery, and SA-2 and SA-3 air defense missiles. Although these were the "export" versions of various models, which lacked the capabilities of those in first-line Soviet units, they represented high-quality weaponry.

The Soviet Union also provided extensive training to ANP personnel. Between late 1963 and 1985, more than 3,500 officers and enlisted personnel received technical instruction in the Soviet Union. The number of Soviet military advisers assigned to Algeria to train and guide ANP personnel in the use of Soviet equipment as well as in tactical operations is estimated to have reached a high of 3,000, although by 1993 the number of Russians had fallen below 500.

During the 1980s, Algerian officials evinced a growing interest in ending the Soviet Union's almost complete monopoly in the sale of arms. The Benjedid government sought to practice strict nonalignment in its relations with the superpowers. The Algerians were impressed by the superior performance of Western equipment used by the Israelis during the 1982 invasion of Lebanon and by the more comprehensive training and support packages Western suppliers provided to their customers. Nonetheless, few negotiations with Western countries were actually consummated, presumably because of Algeria's tight budgetary and foreign-exchange limitations.

Available data reflected the continued predominance of the Soviet Union and Eastern Europe as sources of weaponry. According to ACDA, of a total of US$3.82 billion in arms imports during the period 1981 to 1985, about US$3.2 billion originated in the Soviet Union, US$170 million in the United States (primarily C-130 transport aircraft), US$100 million in France, US$160 million in Britain, and US$160 million in the Federal Republic of Germany (West Germany). During the period 1985 to 1989, Algerian arms imports totaled US$3.26 billion, of which US$2.7 billion originated in the Soviet Union, US$430 million in other East European nations, US$50 million in the United States, US$40 million in Britain, and US$20 million in France. Deliveries reached a peak of US$1.4 billion in 1981, representing 12.4 percent of all imports. By 1989 arms deliveries were down to US$600 million, only 6.8 percent of total imports, and continued to fall sharply in 1990 and 1991.

Under a set of agreements signed in 1963 and 1967, French military advisers maintained a permanent presence in Algeria after independence. A number of places at the French military academy at St. Cyr and the French gendarmerie school at Melun were allotted to Algerians. In 1969 about 340 French officers and NCOs were detached to work with the training ser-

Russian matériel of the type used by the Algerian Armed Forces: Mi–24 helicopter and T–55 tank

vices of the ANP. Relations chilled, however, after France escalated its military support for Morocco during the Western Sahara conflict; by 1981 only about twenty French advisers remained in Algeria.

The administration of the socialist François Mitterrand, who was elected president of France in 1981, was thought to be more attuned to Algerian interests than previous French governments had been. The French government increased the number of places in French military schools for Algerian cadets and extended additional credits. Algeria bought Panhard armored personnel carriers for the gendarmerie and Milan antitank missiles, but more extensive purchases, notably a national command-and-control radar network, failed to materialize.

From independence through the early 1980s, the ANP had purchased relatively small amounts of less sensitive military equipment from the United States such as several executive transport aircraft and unarmed primary trainers. Beginning in 1981, as part of a rapprochement that was kindled by Algeria's role as an intermediary in the release of the American hostages in Iran, Algerian requests for more sensitive military equipment were reviewed more favorably. In addition to the Lockheed C-130 transport aircraft, the United States furnished telecommunications equipment and military trucks during this period.

All of these sales were conducted on a commercial basis, and all of the equipment was classified as nonlethal. During Benjedid's 1985 visit to the United States, however, Washington approved Algeria's eligibility to purchase general defense equipment under the conditions of the Foreign Military Sales (FMS) program. Algerian arms requests were examined on a case-by-case basis. Direct purchases under FMS were minimal. They amounted to only US$2.2 million in fiscal year (FY—see Glossary) 1991 and were estimated to reach only $1 million in FY 1992 and FY 1993, although commercial transactions were somewhat larger. Since 1985, the United States Department of Defense has provided a small annual grant under the International Military Education and Training Program to provide professional military development courses and technical training for Algerian officers in leadership positions or deemed to be potential leaders.

Algeria purchased two tank landing ships from Britain in the early 1980s. In addition, the British undertook a joint project with the Algerian navy for the delivery of twelve fast-attack craft armed with Italian Otomat missiles. The first two of the attack craft were built in Britain, and ten others were built or assembled at the Mers el Kebir shipyard with British technical assistance.

Algeria has purchased some patrol craft from China, but there has been little other evidence of military cooperation between the two countries since the War of Independence. In 1991 it was disclosed that the Chinese were assisting in the construction of a nuclear reactor at Ain Oussera, about 140 kilometers south of Algiers. Subsequent reports stated that Iraq had sent scientists and some uranium to Algeria. Algerians asserted that the reactor was intended to produce only radioactive isotopes for medical research and to generate electric power. However, the secrecy surrounding the program, which had been initiated in 1986, raised suspicions. Algeria is not a signatory to the Nuclear Non-Proliferation Treaty, having rejected it on the principle that Algeria should not have to renounce a nuclear weapons program when other nations could continue with theirs. Algeria subsequently agreed to inspection of the site by the International Atomic Energy Agency.

Internal Security

Responsibility for maintaining law and order is shared by the Gendarmerie Nationale and the Sûreté Nationale. Operations against subversives are conducted by various civilian organizations as well as by Military Security (Sécurité Militaire—SM). The gendarmerie, active principally in rural areas and remote mountain and desert regions, and the Sûreté, an urban police force, were both formed after independence in 1962 and were patterned after their counterparts in metropolitan France. Both organizations carry out normal police duties, although they handle routine internal security functions as well. Military Security is responsible for foreign intelligence, military offenses, and civilian espionage and subversion, especially at times of a breakdown of public order.

The SM operates under the authority of the Ministry of Interior, as does the gendarmerie, although the latter is considered a paramilitary adjunct to the armed forces. In the early 1990s, the SM had about 6,000 to 10,000 military personnel equipped with shotguns and other small arms organized into counterterrorist brigades. SM personnel are commanded by an army general and report directly to the minister of national defense. Active in Algiers and the surrounding area, they have as their mission to investigate and respond to intelligence provided by the police and the gendarmerie. A Republican Guard Brigade of 1,200 persons is also available to deal with civil disturbances. It is equipped with light tanks and armored vehicles.

Gendarmerie Nationale

The Gendarmerie Nationale serves as the main rural police force. It was commanded in 1993 by Major General Abbas Ghezaiel, who reported directly to the minister of national defense. In 1993 gendarmerie personnel constituted a total force of 35,000. Although generally regarded as a versatile and competent paramilitary force, the gendarmerie since 1988 has been severely tested in dealing with civil disorder. It frequently has lacked sufficient manpower at the scene of disorder, and its units have been inadequately trained and equipped for riot control. The gendarmerie, however, has demonstrated the ability to root out terrorist groups operating from mountain hideouts.

The gendarmerie is responsible for maintaining law and order in villages, towns, and rural areas; providing security surveillance over local inhabitants; and representing government authority in remote regions, especially where tensions and conflicts have occurred in the past. The gendarmerie is organized in battalions, whose component companies and platoons are dispersed to individual communities and desert outposts. Its regional headquarters are in the same cities as the six military regional headquarters; it has subdivisions in the forty-eight *wilayat*. A highly mobile force, the gendarmerie possesses a modern communications system connecting its various units with one another and with the army. Gendarmerie equipment includes light armored weapons and transport and patrol vehicles. The force in 1993 had forty-four Panhard armored personnel carriers, fifty Fahd armored personnel carriers, and twenty-eight Mi–2 light helicopters. In addition to utilizing training provided by the French since independence, the gendarmerie operates its own schools for introductory and advanced studies. The gendarmerie's main training center is at Sidi Bel Abbes, the former headquarters of France's Foreign Legion. The academy for officers is at Isser, about 150 kilometers east of Algiers.

Sûreté Nationale

The Sûreté Nationale is the primary policing authority in Algeria's principal cities and other urban areas. Subordinated administratively to the Ministry of Interior, the Sûreté is charged with maintaining law and order, protecting life and property, investigating crimes, and apprehending offenders. In addition, it performs other routine police functions, including traffic control.

Under the direction of its inspector general, the Sûreté in 1993 consisted of a force of 16,000 and is believed to be organized along the lines of its French counterpart, with operational and investigative branches and supporting services. The judiciary police branch is responsible for criminal investigations, working in close coordination with the Office of the Public Prosecutor in the Ministry of Justice. Police elements assigned to the capitals of the *wilayat* are under the nominal control of the individual governors. A special riot police force is equipped with modern riot-control gear. Although the police were able to cope with urban disturbances and violence during the early and mid-1980s, the military had to be called in to help quell the severe riots in late 1988.

Elements of the Sûreté also play a role in countering threats to the government arising from political subversion. The Sûreté assigns police contingents to work with customs inspectors at legal points of entry to control illegal activities. Their main concerns are apprehending undesirable immigrants and contraband traffickers.

Intelligence Agencies

Military Security is the principal and most effective intelligence service in the country. Its chief in 1993, General Mohamed Médiène, was believed to number among the more influential officers of the ANP. After Boumediene took power in 1965, he relied on Military Security to strengthen his control over the ANP during the difficult process of amalgamating "external" and "internal" ALN personnel, some of whom were of questionable loyalty. Military Security became the dominant security service in the 1970s, responsible to the head of state for monitoring and maintaining files on all potential sources of opposition to the national leadership.

Although theoretically bound by the same legal restrictions as the Sûreté and gendarmerie, Military Security is less circumscribed in its operations. Frequent cases of incommunicado detention of suspects have been ascribed mainly to Military Security. An important role in the area of national security was later assumed by the General Delegation for Documentation and Security (Delégation Générale de Documentation et Sûreté—DGDS) as the principal civilian apparatus for conducting foreign intelligence and countering internal subversion. The security services are believed to infiltrate Islamist groups, to employ paid informers for monitoring opposition movements, and to practice extensive telephone surveillance without prior court authorization as required by law. During and after the riots of October 1988, widely published accounts told of torture and other human rights abuses of detainees. Both Military Security and the DGDS were implicated in the brutal treatment of detainees to obtain confessions or extract information on clandestine political activists. Government officials have acknowledged that individual cases of improper behavior by security forces occurred but stressed that torture was not sanctioned and that evidence of it would be investigated.

In September 1990, Benjedid announced the dissolution of the DGDS after criticism of its repressive role in the 1988 riots. The dissolution coincided with other government reforms to remove barriers to individual liberties. Informed sources believed, however, that this action did not represent an end to domestic intelligence operations but rather a transfer of DGDS functions to other security bodies. Surveying the intelligence picture in August 1992, the French periodical *Jeune Afrique* concluded that Military Security, with its abundant documentation on the leadership and organization of the violent Islamist groups, remained the senior intelligence body concerned with internal security. Other intelligence groups include a Coordinating Directorate of Territorial Security, an Antiterrorist Detachment, and a working group of the High Council of State charged with political and security matters. The precise functions and jurisdictions of these bodies remain fluid, according to *Jeune Afrique*.

Criminal Justice System

Ordinary criminal cases are heard in the regular civil court system by judges appointed by the Ministry of Justice through an independent board. Criminal cases are heard in forty-eight provincial courts, which have jurisdiction over more serious crimes as well as appellate jurisdiction over lower courts in local tribunals (*tribunaux*), which have original jurisdiction for less serious offenses. According to the United States Department of State's *Country Reports on Human Rights Practices* for 1992, the judiciary is generally independent of executive or military control, except in cases involving security or public order. During the period of martial law in 1991 and the state of emergency in 1992, this independence was largely circumvented.

In December 1992, special antiterrorist courts with civilian judges were established to try crimes specifically relating to terrorism. According to the Department of State, these courts are believed to have been formed so that the government might have greater influence over the outcome of security-related criminal cases. A State Security Court, which had previously tried cases involving endangerment of national security, had been abolished in 1989 as part of Benjedid's political reform program. Muslim sharia law predominated in local courts, but there were no Islamic courts as such. Military courts dealt with offenses by military personnel and all types of espionage cases. During the 1991 state of emergency, about 700 persons were tried in military courts whose jurisdictions had been widened to include acts endangering national security. The trials of seven FIS leaders in 1992 were among those heard by military courts. Some of the rights normally accorded in civil courts were ignored or circumscribed in the military courts.

Defendants in civil courts usually have full access to counsel who can function freely without governmental interference. The Algerian Bar Association provides *pro bono* legal services to defendants unable to pay for their own lawyer. In connection with criminal investigations, detention for questioning normally cannot exceed forty-eight hours, but an antiterrorist law issued in 1992 permits prearraignment detentions of up to twelve days.

Detainees must be informed immediately of the nature of charges against them. Once charged, a person can be held under pretrial detention indefinitely while the case is being investigated. No bail system exists, but provisional liberty may be granted if the detainee can demonstrate availability at all stages of the inquiry. Lawyers are entitled to have access to their clients at all times under visual supervision of a guard. Defendants have the right to confront witnesses and present evidence. Trials are public, and defendants have the right of appeal.

Prior to the civil unrest of 1991 and 1992, the government had introduced political reforms that liberalized the justice system with respect to actions deemed to threaten internal security. Previously, citizens could be arrested for expressing views critical of or different from those of the government, for disturbing the public order, for associating with illegal organizations, or, in extreme cases, for threatening state security. The new constitution of 1989 provides the right to form political parties and civic associations and to strike, and strengthens the right of freedom of expression and opinion. Nevertheless, under legislation introduced in 1990, persons convicted of publishing information endangering state security or national unity can be sentenced for a term of up to ten years. Criticizing Islam or another revealed religion can bring a penalty of up to three years' imprisonment.

According to Amnesty International, more than 100 persons were under sentence of death at the close of 1992. At least twenty-six Islamists were sentenced to death after the banning of the FIS in 1992, but no executions were actually carried out in 1992. More than 100 civilians and supporters of Islamic opposition groups were killed by security forces during 1992, and more than 1,000 people were in detention at the end of 1992 according to government sources.

The principal leaders of the FIS arrested in 1991—Abbassi Madani and Ali Belhadj (also seen as Benhadj)—were tried by a military court in mid-1992 for fomenting rebellion against the state. They could have been given the death sentence, but government prosecutors asked for life imprisonment. The court's sentence of twelve years was lighter than expected. Its leniency was construed as having been dictated by the government in an effort to ease tensions and improve the atmosphere for possible reconciliation with more moderate Islamic factions.

In 1987, reversing its previous policy, the government officially recognized a human rights group, the Algerian League of Human Rights. Legal status was subsequently accorded to the Committee Against Torture, which investigated allegations of government torture, as well as to a number of other human rights organizations. They have been permitted to lobby, publicize their findings, and publish reports on the treatment of detainees.

Under the 1991 state of emergency and the 1992 martial law decrees that gave military and security authorities wide latitude to enforce public order, large numbers of Islamists were detained. The government acknowledged that it detained 9,000 persons at eight desert camps without formal charges in 1992. By the end of the year, 1,000 were still held in four remaining camps, despite government plans to close them down. FIS leaders claimed that the number of those rounded up by the government had actually reached 30,000.

Prison Conditions

The prison system is operated as a separate function of the Ministry of Justice. The system includes many facilities established and operated by the French during their rule. Persons convicted of lesser crimes are sent to provincial civil prisons. Those found guilty of more serious crimes, including murder, kidnapping, or rape, which carry a potential death sentence, serve time in one of three penitentiaries. Persons convicted of treason, terrorism, and other crimes against the state are also sent to the penitentiaries.

According to the United States Department of State, conditions in both types of institutions range from primitive to modern. Conditions in the penitentiaries are said to be worse than in the more numerous civil prisons. At El Harrach, the main prison in Algiers, prisoners are often crowded together, and sanitary facilities are poor. Inmates at other prisons, especially those in outlying areas, are thought to live under better conditions. Prisoners are segregated according to the seriousness of their crimes and the length of their sentences.

Medical care is described as rudimentary in most cases, although a local doctor under contract visits each prison regularly to treat sick prisoners. Seriously ill prisoners are sent to local hospitals. Inmates of civil prisons can receive visits from their families once a week. It is more difficult to visit prisoners held in penitentiaries. Conjugal visits are sometimes permitted at the discretion of local prison authorities. The prison diet is described as bland and starchy. Visiting families may bring food to augment the inadequate prison fare.

Detainees in the Saharan security camps have been forced to contend with extreme heat, poor food, inadequate bedding, and overcrowding. Next of kin often have not been notified about inmates' detention, and many detainees have been released near the camps without transportation home. A medical team under the auspices of the Algerian League of Human Rights found no evidence of torture in the detention camps, however. The United States Department of State has observed that in 1992 there were fewer reports of torture and brutal treatment than in prior years. The government has responded to concerns that have been raised about conditions in prisons and desert internment camps by organizations such as Amnesty International and has promised to remind military commanders of their responsibility to safeguard the rights of internees.

* * *

Most of the data on the strength and equipment of the armed forces are based on *The Military Balance, 1993–1994*, and on *Jane's Fighting Ships, 1992–93*. Little detailed information has been disclosed by Algerian authorities on the structure and performance standards of the service branches. The role of the military in the political crisis of 1991–92 has been analyzed by several authorities, including Guy Mandron in *Jane's Intelligence Review* and John P. Entelis and Lisa J. Arone in *Middle East Policy*. Numerous articles in the French periodical, *Jeune Afrique*, have followed the efforts of the security forces to maintain order against violence by Islamic radicals.

Alastair Horne's *A Savage War of Peace* is a balanced and comprehensive account of the military and political aspects of the Algerian War of Independence. The functioning of the criminal justice system and the record of the police and the gendarmerie in the struggle against Islamic-inspired dissidence are summarized in the United States Department of State's annual *Country Reports on Human Rights Practices* and in annual reports by Amnesty International. (For further information and complete citations, see Bibliography.)

Appendix

1 Metric Conversion Coefficients and Factors
2 Students and Teachers by Education Level, Academic Year 1990–91
3 Gross Domestic Product by Sector, 1985, 1988, and 1990
4 Major Crops, 1986–91
5 Major Trading Partners, Selected Years, 1984–90
6 Balance of Payments, Selected Years, 1984–90
7 Major Army Equipment, 1993
8 Major Air Force and Air Defense Equipment, 1993
9 Major Navy Equipment, 1993

Appendix

Table 1. Metric Conversion Coefficients and Factors

When you know	Multiply by	To find
Millimeters	0.04	inches
Centimeters	0.39	inches
Meters	3.3	feet
Kilometers	0.62	miles
Hectares (10,000 m^2)	2.47	acres
Square kilometers	0.39	square miles
Cubic meters	35.3	cubic feet
Liters	0.26	pounds
Kilograms	2.2	pounds
Metric tons	0.98	long tons
	1.1	short tons
	2,204.0	pounds
Degrees Celsius (Centigrade)	1.8 and add 32	degrees Fahrenheit

Algeria: A Country Study

Table 2. Students and Teachers by Education Level, Academic Year 1990–91

Education Level	Males	Females	Total	Teachers
Basic education				
Years 1–6	2,312,412	1,876,740	4,189,152	151,262
Years 7–9	831,217	592,099	1,423,316	82,741
Total basic education	3,143,629	2,468,839	5,612,468	234,003
Secondary education				
General	296,043	302,861	598,904	37,965
Technical	105,666	47,694	153,360	6,318
Total secondary education	401,709	350,555	752,264	44,283

Source: Based on information from Leslie S. Nucho (ed.), *Education in the Arab World*, 1, Washington, n.d., 17, 19, 26.

Table 3. Gross Domestic Product by Sector, 1985, 1988, and 1990 (in billions of Algerian dinars)[1]

Sector	1985 Value	1985 Percentage	1988 Value	1988 Percentage	1990 Value	1990 Percentage
Agriculture	27.1	9.4	36.3	11.3	47.8	9.6
Hydrocarbons	64.0	22.3	42.0	13.1	115.0	23.1
Manufacturing ...	31.1	10.8	42.2	13.2	51.3	10.3
Public works and construction	41.7	14.5	51.2	16.0	75.8	15.3
Services	39.0	13.6	n.a.[2]	n.a.	91.2	18.4
Transportation and commerce ..	n.a.	n.a.	65.9	20.6	n.a.	n.a.
Other	84.5	29.4	82.4	25.8	115.9	23.3
TOTAL	287.4	100.0	320.0	100.0	497.0	100.0

[1] For value of the Algerian dinar—see Glossary.
[2] n.a.—not available.

Source: Based on information from Economist Intelligence Unit, *Country Profile: Algeria, 1991–92*, London, 1991, 16; and Economist Intelligence Unit, *Country Profile: Algeria, 1992–93*, London, 1992, 15.

Appendix

Table 4. Major Crops, 1986–91
(in thousands of tons)

Crop	1986	1987	1988	1989	1990	1991
Wheat	1,229	1,175	614	1,152	858	1,742
Barley	1,083	820	390	790	865	1,751
Citrus	253	277	312	268	281	n.a.[1]
Tomatoes	n.a.	193	255	212	168	n.a.

[1] n.a.—not available.

Source: Based on information from Economist Intelligence Unit, *Country Profile: Algeria, 1992–93*, London, 1992, 19.

Table 5. Major Trading Partners, Selected Years, 1984–90
(in percentages)

Country	1984	1986	1988	1990
Exports				
France	27.8	21.5	13.9	13.8
Germany[1]	2.9	3.2	10.3	7.4
Italy	17.7	19.9	17.8	19.2
Netherlands	11.7	14.2	6.3	7.4
Spain	n.a.	5.7	5.1	5.3
United States	21.2	17.4	22.1	21.0
Imports				
France	23.1	24.0	21.2	28.5
Germany[1]	10.5	11.1	10.6	9.8
Italy	8.6	12.9	10.9	12.3
Japan	n.a.	4.6	3.0	3.5
Spain	4.3	4.6	4.9	6.1
United States	5.5	7.7	9.9	10.0

[1] Includes former German Democratic Republic (East Germany) as of July 1990; earlier years include trade only with Federal Republic of Germany (West Germany).

Source: Based on information from Economist Intelligence Unit, *Country Profile: Algeria, 1990–91*, London, 37; Economist Intelligence Unit, *Country Profile: Algeria, 1991–92*, London, 1991, 40; and Economist Intelligence Unit, *Country Profile: Algeria, 1992–93*, London, 1992, 39.

Algeria: A Country Study

Table 6. *Balance of Payments, Selected Years 1984-90* [1]
(in millions of United States dollars)

	1984	1986	1988	1990[2]
Merchandise exports, f.o.b.[3]	12,792	8,065	7,620	10,150
Merchandise imports, c.i.f.[4]	–9,235	–7,879	–6,675	–9,160
Trade balance	3,557	185	946	990
Exports of services	599	549	470	n.a.[5]
Imports of services	–2,583	–2,035	–1,347	n.a.
Other income received	179	172	71	n.a.
Other income paid	–1,859	–1,865	–2,571	n.a.
Net private transfers	186	765	385	n.a.
Net official transfers	–5	–1	5	n.a.
Current account balance	74	–2,230	–2,040	–680
Direct investment	–14	11	8	n.a.
Portfolio investment	n.a.	n.a.	2	n.a.
Other capital	–197	579	734	n.a.
Capital account balance	–211	590	744	n.a.
Errors and omissions	–197	142	335	n.a.
Overall balance	–234	–1,498	–960	n.a.

[1] Figures may not compute to balances because of rounding.
[2] Estimated.
[3] f.o.b.—free on board.
[4] c.i.f.—cost, insurance, freight
[5] n.a.—not available.

Source: Based on information from Economist Intelligence Unit, *Country Profile: Algeria, 1991–92*, London, 1991, 41; "Algeria: Statistical Survey," in *Middle East and North Africa, 1992–93*, 1992, 326; and United States, Department of Commerce, *Foreign Economic Trends and Their Implications for the United States: Algeria*, Washington 1991, 2.

Table 7. Major Army Equipment, 1993

Type and Description	Country of Origin	In Inventory
Tanks		
T–72 main battle tank, 120mm gun	Soviet Union	300
T–62 main battle tank, 115mm gun	-do-	330
T–54/–55 main battle tank, 100mm gun	-do-	330
Armored vehicles		
BRDM–2 amphibious scout car	-do-	120
BMP–1/–2 infantry fighting vehicle	-do-	915
BTR–50/–60 armored personnel carrier	-do-	460
Artillery		
Towed		
122mm, various models	-do-	375
M–46, 130mm	-do-	10
ML–20 (M–1937), 152mm	-do-	20
Self-propelled		
2S 1, 122mm	-do-	150
2S 3, 152mm	-do-	25
Mortars		
M–37, 82mm	-do-	150
M–1943, 120mm	-do-	120
M–1943, 160mm	-do-	60
Antitank weapons		
Missiles		
AT–3 Sagger	-do-	40
Milan	France/ Germany	n.a.[1]
Guns		
D–44, 85mm	Soviet Union	80
SU–100, 100mm, self-propelled	-do-	50
Multiple rocket launchers		
BM–21, 122mm	-do-	48
BM–14/–16, 140mm	-do-	50
BM–24, 240mm	-do-	30
Air defense weapons		
Guns		
14.5, 20, 23, 37, and 57mm, various models	-do-	490
ZSU–23–4, 23mm, self-propelled	-do-	210
KS–12, 85mm; KS–19, 100mm; KS–30, 130mm	-do-	180

Appendix

291

Algeria: A Country Study

Table 7. Major Army Equipment, 1993

Type and Description	Country of Origin	In Inventory
Missiles		
SA–7 man-portable, surface-to-air (SAM).....	-do-	n.a.
SA–8 self-propelled SAM................	-do-	n.a.
SA–9 Gaskin, self-propelled SAM..........	-do-	n.a.

[1] n.a.—not available.

Source: Based on information from *The Military Balance, 1993–1994*, London, 1993, 111.

Appendix

Table 8. Major Air Force and Air Defense Equipment, 1993

Type and Description	Country of Origin	In Inventory
Fighter-ground attack craft		
MiG-23 BN	Soviet Union	40
Su-24	-do-	10
Fighter		
MiG-21 MF/bis	-do-	95
MiG-25	-do-	14
MiG-23 B/E	-do-	20
Reconnaissance		
MiG-25R	-do-	3
Super King Air B-200T (maritime)	United States	2
Transport		
C-130H and C-130H-30 Hercules	-do-	16
An-12	Soviet Union	6
Il-76	-do-	3
Helicopters		
Attack		
Mi-24	-do-	38
Mi-8/-17	-do-	20
Transport		
Heavy: Mi-8	-do-	15
Medium: Mi-17	-do-	12
Antiaircraft guns		
85mm, 100mm, 130mm	-do-	n.a.[1]
Surface-to-air missiles		
SA-3 low-to-medium range, fixed site	-do-	21
SA-6 self-propelled	-do-	2
SA-8	-do-	n.a

[1] n.a.—not available.

Source: Based on information from *The Military Balance, 1993–1994*, London, 1993, 111.

Algeria: A Country Study

Table 9. *Major Navy Equipment, 1993*

Type and Description	Country of Origin	In Inventory
Submarines		
Kilo-class	Soviet Union	2
Frigates		
Koni-class with SA–N–4 surface-to-air missiles (SAMs)	-do-	3
Corvettes		
Nanuchka II-class with SS–N–2C surface-to-surface missiles (SSMs) and SA–N–4 SAMs	-do-	3
Fast-attack craft, missile		
Osa I-class, Styx SSMs	Soviet Union	2
Osa II-class, Styx SSMs	-do-	9
Fast-attack craft, gun		
Kebir-class, 76mm gun	Britain/ Algeria	12[1]
Amphibious vessels		
Landing ship, logistic	Britain	2
Polnochny-class landing craft, tank	Soviet Union	1

[1] Six on loan to coast guard.

Source: Based on information from *Jane's Fighting Ships, 1992–93*, Alexandria, Virginia, 1992, 4; and *The Military Balance, 1993–1994*, London, 1993, 110.

Bibliography

Chapter 1

Abu-Nasr, Jamil M. *A History of the Maghreb.* Cambridge: Cambridge University Press, 1971.

———. *A History of the Maghrib in the Islamic Period.* Cambridge: Cambridge University Press, 1987.

Ageron, Charles-Robert. *Histoire de l'Algérie contemporaine.* (2 vols.) Paris: Presses universitaires de France, 1979.

Ahmedouamar, Mohamed Tahar. *Algeria, State Building: Through the Period of Instability, July 1962–December 1969.* Washington: Compasspoints, 1976.

Berque, Jacques. *French North Africa: The Maghrib Between Two World Wars.* New York: Praeger, 1967.

Brockelmann, Carl. *History of the Islamic Peoples.* New York: Capricorn Books, 1960.

Confer, Vincent. *France and Algeria: The Problem of Civil and Political Reform, 1870–1920.* Syracuse: University of Syracuse Press, 1966.

Danziger, Raphael. *Abd al-Qadir and the Algerians: Resistance to the French and Internal Consolidation.* New York: Holmes and Meier, 1977.

Gordon, David C. *North Africa's French Legacy, 1954–1962.* Cambridge: Harvard University Press, 1962.

Henissart, Paul. *Wolves in the City: The Death of French Algeria.* New York: Simon and Schuster, 1970.

Horne, Alistair. *A Savage War of Peace: Algeria, 1954–1962.* New York: Viking, 1977.

Hourani, Albert. *A History of the Arab Peoples.* New York: Warner Books, 1992.

Humbaraci, Arslan. *Algeria: A Revolution that Failed. A Political History since 1954.* New York: Praeger, 1966.

Jackson, Henry. *The F.L.N. in Algeria: Party Development in a Revolutionary Society.* Westport, Connecticut: Greenwood Press, 1977.

Julien, Charles-André. *Histoire de l'Afrique du nord: Tunisie, Algérie, Maroc.* Paris: Payot, 1966.

———. *Histoire de l'Algérie contemporaine: La conquête et les débuts de la colonisation (1827–1871).* Paris: Presses universitaires de France, 1964.

Lapidus, Ira M. *A History of Islamic Societies.* Cambridge: Cambridge University Press, 1988.
Laroui, Abdallah. *The History of the Maghrib: An Interpretive Essay.* Princeton: Princeton University Press, 1977.
Le Tourneau, Roger. *Évolution politique de l'Afrique du Nord musulmane, 1920–1961.* Paris: Armand Colin, 1962.
Merle, Robert. *Ahmed Ben Bella.* Paris: Gallimard, 1965.
"North Africa." Pages 904–33 in *The New Encyclopedia Britannica*, 24. Chicago: 1985.
Ottaway, David B., and Marina Ottaway. *Algeria: The Politics of a Socialist Revolution.* Berkeley: University of California Press, 1970.
Quandt, William B. *Revolution and Political Leadership: Algeria, 1954–1968.* Cambridge: MIT Press, 1969.
Rouvière, Jacques. *Le putsch d'Alger.* Paris: France-Empire, 1976.
Ruedy, John. *Land Policy in Colonial Algeria: The Origins of the Rural Public Domain.* Berkeley: University of California Press, 1967.
———. *Modern Algeria: The Origins and Development of a Nation.* Bloomington: Indiana University Press, 1992.
Soren, David, et al. *Carthage.* New York: Simon and Schuster, 1990.
Spencer, William. *Algiers in the Age of Corsairs.* Norman: University of Oklahoma Press, 1976.
Talbott, John. *The War Without a Name: France in Algeria, 1954–1962.* New York: Knopf, 1980.

Chapter 2

Algeria. *Annuaire statistique de l'Algérie.* (15th ed.) Algiers: 1991.
———. *Revue Économique et Sociale.* Algiers: 1991.
———. Agence nationale d'édition et de publicité. *Algérie, guide économique et social.* Algiers: 1989.
———. Office national des statistiques. *Recensement général de la population et de l'habitat du 20 mars 1987.* Algiers: 1989.
———. Office national des statistiques. *Recensement général de la population et de l'habitat, 1987: Résultats par agglomérations.* Algiers: 1989.
Allouche-Benayoun, Joelle. *Juifs d'Algérie hier et aujourd'hui: Mémoires et identités.* Toulouse: Éditions Privats, 1989.
Annuaire de l'Afrique du Nord. Aix-en-Provence: Centre de recherches et d'études sur les sociétés méditerranéenes, 1989.
Annuaire de l'Afrique du Nord. Paris: Centre nationale de la

recherche scientifique, 1990.
Annuaire de l'Afrique du Nord. Aix-en-Provence: Centre de recherches et d'études sur les sociétés méditerranéenes, 1991.
Annuaire de l'Afrique du Nord. Aix-en-Provence: Centre de recherches et d'études sur les sociétés méditerranéenes, 1992.
Boukhobza, M'Hamed. *Ruptures et transformations sociales en Algérie.* Algiers: Office des publications universitaires, 1989.
Carret, Jacques. "L'association des oulama: réformations sociales en Algérie," *L'Afrique et l'Asie moderne* [Paris], No. 43, 1958, 23-44.
Centre de recherches et d'études sur les sociétés méditerranéenes. *Développements Politiques au Maghreb.* Paris: Centre nationale de la recherche scientifique, 1979.
Chaker, Salem. *Berbères aujourd'hui.* Paris: Harmattan, 1989.
Chikh, Slimane. *L'Algérie en armes ou le temps des certitudes.* Paris: Economica, 1981.
Colonna, Fanny. "La Répétition: Les Tolba dans une commune rurale de l'Aurès." Pages 157-203 in *Annuaire de l'Afrique du Nord.* (18th ed.) Paris: Centre de recherches et d'études sur les sociétés méditerranéenes et Centre nationale de la recherche scientifique, 1979.
Deeb, Mary-Jane. "Islam and the State: The Continuity of the Political Discourse of Islamic Movements in Algeria from 1832 to 1992." (Paper delivered at conference on "Islam and Nationhood," Yale University, November 1992.)
———. "Radical Islam and the Politics of Redemption," *Annals of the Academy of Political and Social Sciences,* No. 548, November 1992, 52-65.
Demographic Year Book, 1990. New York: United Nations, Department of Economic and Social Affairs, Statistical Office, 1991.
Demographic Year Book, 1991. New York: United Nations, Department of Economic and Social Affairs, Statistical Office, 1992.
Economist Intelligence Unit. *Country Profile: Algeria, 1991-1992.* London: 1992.
Entelis, John P. *Algeria: The Revolution Institutionalized.* Boulder, Colorado: Westview Press, 1986.
Gellner, Ernest, and Charles Micaud (eds.). *Arabs and Berbers: From Tribe to Nation in North Africa.* Lexington, Massachusetts: Lexington Books, 1972.

Gendzier, Irene L. "Algeria and Modernization," *Government and Opposition* [London], No. 2, 1978, 247–58.

Gilette, Alain. *L'immigration algérienne en France.* Paris: Éditions Entente, 1984.

Gordon, David. *The Passing of French Algeria.* London: Oxford University Press, 1968.

Grimaud, Nicole. *La politique extérieure de l'Algérie.* Paris: Karthala, 1984.

Gruner, Roger. "La place de l'Islam dans les constitutions du Maghreb," *L'Afrique et l'Asie moderne* [Paris], No. 130, 1980, 39–54.

Harbi, Mohammed. "Nationalisme algérien et identité berbère," *Peuples méditerranéens* [Paris], No. 11, April–June 1980, 59–68.

Heggoy, Alf. "The Evolution of Algerian Women," *African Studies Review,* 17, No. 2, September 1974, 449–56.

———. *Insurgency and Counterinsurgency in Algeria.* Bloomington: Indiana University Press, 1972.

———. "Research Notes on the Evolution of Algerian Women," *African Studies Review,* 17, 1974, 228–35.

Hifi, Belkacem. *L'immigration algérienne en France: Origines et perspectives de non-retour.* Paris: Harmattan, 1985.

Hourani, Albert A. *History of the Arab Peoples.* New York: Warner Books, 1992.

Huzayyin, S.A., and T.E. Smith. Pages 397–425 in *Demographic Aspects of Socio-Economic Development in Some Arab and African Countries.* (Research Monograph Series, No. 5.) Cairo: Cairo Demographic Center, 1974.

Knauss, Peter R. *The Persistence of Patriarchy: Class, Gender and Ideology in Twentieth Century Algeria.* New York: Praeger, 1987.

Lawless, Richard I. "The Kabyles," *Family of Man,* No. 33, 1975, 1457–60.

Lawless, Richard, and Allan Findlay (eds.). *North Africa: Contemporary Politics and Economic Development.* New York: St. Martin's Press, 1984.

Leca, Jean. "Algerian Socialism: Nationalism, Industrialization, and State-Building." Pages 121–60 in Helen Desfosses and Jacques Levesque (eds.), *Socialism in the Third World.* New York: Praeger, 1975.

Leveau, Rémy, Catherine Wihtol de Wenden, and Gilles Kepel. "Les musulmans dans la société française: Introduction," *Revue française de science politique* [Paris], December 1987,

37, No. 6, 765–81.

Madani, Abbassi. *Mushkillat Tarbawiya fi al-Bilad al-Islamiya*. Algiers: Maktabat al Manara, 1989.

Micaud, Charles. "Bilingualism in North Africa: Cultural and Sociopolitical Implications," *Western Political Quarterly*, 27, No. 1, March 1974, 92–103.

Minces, Juliette. "Women in Algeria," Pages 159–71 in Lois Beck and Nikki Keddie (eds.), *Women in the Muslim World*. Cambridge: Harvard University Press, 1978.

Mortimer, Robert. "Algeria after the Explosion," *Current History*, 89, April 1990, 161–64, 180–82.

———. "Islam and Multiparty Politics in Algeria," *Middle East Journal*, 45, No. 4, Autumn 1991, 575–93.

Mouriaux, Catherine Wihtol de Wenden. "Syndicalisme français et l'Islam," *Revue française de science politique* [Paris], December 1987, 37, No. 6, 794–819.

Nucho, Leslie S. (ed.). *Education in the Arab World*, 1. Washington: AMIDEAST (America Mideast Education and Training Services), n.d.

Ollivier, Marc. "L'économie algérienne vingt ans après 1966: L'indépendance nationale en question." Pages 417–57 in *Annuaire de l'Afrique du Nord*. (24th ed.) Aix-en-Provence: Centre de recherches et d'études sur les sociétés méditerranéenes, 1985.

Ottaway, David B., and Marina Ottaway. *Algeria: The Politics of a Socialist Revolution*. Berkeley: University of California Press, 1970.

Ouerdane, Amar. *La question berbère dans le mouvement national algérien: 1926–1980*. Sillery, Quebec: Septentrion, 1990.

Quandt, William B. "The Berbers in the Algerian Political Elite." Pages 285–303 in Ernest Gellner and Charles Micaud (eds.), *Arabs and Berbers: From Tribe to Nation in North Africa*. Lexington, Massachusetts: Lexington Books, 1972.

Roberts, Hugh. "Radical Islamism and the Dilemma of Algerian Nationalism," *Third World Quarterly* [Abingdon, United Kingdom], 10, No. 2, April 1988, 556–89.

———. "Towards an Understanding of the Kabyle Question in Contemporary Algeria," *Maghreb Review* [London], 5, May–June 1980, 115–24.

Ruedy, John. *Modern Algeria: The Origins and Development of a Nation*, Bloomington: Indiana University Press, 1992.

Safran, William. *The French Polity*. (3d ed.) New York: Longman, 1991.

Sanson, Henri. "L'Algérie est-elle surpeuplée?" *Maghreb-Machrek* [Paris], No. 84, April–June 1979, 42–49.
Smith, Tony. "The Political and Economic Ambitions of Algerian Land Reform, 1962–1974," *Middle East Journal*, 29, No. 3, Summer 1975, 259–78.
Vallin, Raymond. "Fertility in Algeria: Trends and Differentials." Pages 131–51 in J. Allman (ed.), *Women's Status and Fertility in the Muslim World*. New York: Praeger, 1978.
Vatin, Jean-Claude. "Introduction à l'Islam, religion et politique: Communauté islamique et états musulmans, renaissance religieuse ou adaptations politiques?" *Revue de l'occident musulman et de la Méditerranée* [Aix-en-Provence], 29, 1980, 3–14.
———. "Popular Puritanism versus State Reformism: Islam in Algeria." Pages 98–121 in James P. Piscatori (ed.), *Islam in the Political Process*. Cambridge: Cambridge University Press, 1983.
———. "Religious Resistance and State Power in Algeria." Pages 119–57 in Ali Dessouki and Alexander Cudsi (eds.), *Islam and Power*. London: Croom Helm, 1981.
World Bank. *Healthcare Report on Algeria*. Washington: 1991.
———. *Report on Basic and Secondary Education*. Washington: 1993.
———. *Report on Higher Education*. Washington: 1990.
———. *Report on Housing in Algeria*. Washington: 1993.
———. *Social Indicators of Development, 1991*. Baltimore: Johns Hopkins University Press, 1991.
———. *World Debt Tables, 1991–92: External Debt of Developing Countries*. Washington: 1991.
———. *World Development Report, 1991: The Challenge of Development*. New York: Oxford University Press, 1991.
———. *World Development Report, 1992: Development and the Environment*. New York: Oxford University Press, 1992.
Zartman, I. William, "Algeria: A Post Revolutionary Elite." Pages 255–91 in Frank Tachau (ed.), *Political Elites and Political Development in the Middle East*. New York: Schenkman, 1975.
Zartman, I. William (ed.). *Man, State, and Society in the Contemporary Maghrib*. New York: Praeger, 1973.

(Various issues of the following publications were also used in the preparation of this chapter: *Annals of the Academy of Political and Social Sciences*; Foreign Broadcast Information Service, *Daily Report: Near East and South Asia*; Joint Publications

Research Service, *Near East/South Asia Report*; *Middle East Journal*; and *Third World Quarterly* [Abingdon, United Kingdom].)

Chapter 3

"Algeria." Pages 269-98 in *The Middle East and North Africa, 1993*. London: Europa, 1992.
Economist Intelligence Unit. *Country Profile: Algeria, 1990-91*. London: 1990.
———. *Country Profile: Algeria, 1991-92*. London: 1991.
———. *Country Profile: Algeria, 1992-93*. London: 1992.
———. *Country Report: Algeria* [London], Nos. 1-4, 1992.
Entelis, John P. *Algeria: The Revolution Institutionalized*. Boulder, Colorado: Westview Press, 1986.
Girardon, Jacques. "A Veiled Future for Algeria," *World Press Review*, August 1990, 32.
Lawless, Richard, and Allan Findlay (eds.). *North Africa: Contemporary Politics and Economic Development*. New York: St. Martin's Press, 1984.
The Middle East and North Africa, 1992-93. London: Europa, 1992.
Mortimer, Robert. "Algeria after the Explosion," *Current History*, 89, April 1990, 161-64.
———. "Islam and Multiparty Politics in Algeria," *Middle East Journal*, 45, No. 4, Autumn 1991, 575-93.
Ottaway, David B., and Marina Ottaway. *Algeria: The Politics of a Socialist Revolution*. Berkeley: University of California Press, 1970.
Parker, Richard B. *North Africa: Regional Tensions and Strategic Concerns*. New York: Praeger, 1984.
United States. Department of Agriculture. Economic Research Service. *Global Review of Agricultural Policies*. Washington: GPO, 1988.
———. Department of Commerce. *Foreign Economic Trends and Their Implications for the United States: Algeria*. Washington: GPO, March 1989.
———. Department of Commerce. *Foreign Economic Trends and Their Implications for the United States: Algeria*. Washington: GPO, February 1991.
———. Department of State. Embassy in Algiers. *The Telecommunications Equipment Market in Algeria*. Algiers: February 1992.
Wenner, Mark. "Algeria: A Difficult Adjustment." In *Agriculture in the Middle East and North Africa*. Unpublished. United

States Department of Agriculture, summer 1992.
World Bank. *World Debt Tables, 1991–92: External Debt of Developing Countries.* Washington: 1991.

———. *World Development Report, 1991: The Challenge of Development.* New York: Oxford University Press, 1991.

———. *World Development Report, 1992: Development and the Environment.* New York: Oxford University Press, 1992.

———. *World Tables, 1991.* Baltimore: Johns Hopkins University Press for World Bank, 1991.

(Various issues of the following publications were also used in the preparation of this chapter: *Current History, Economist* [London]; *Middle East Economic Digest* [London]; *Middle East International* [London]; *Middle East Journal*; and *Middle East Policy.*)

Chapter 4

Addi, Lahouari. "Dynamique et contradictions du système politique algérien," *Revue algérienne des sciences juridiques, économiques, et politiques* [Algiers], 26, June 1988, 495–508.

———. *État et pouvoir.* Algiers: OPU, 1990.

———. *Impasse du populisme.* Algiers: ENAL, 1990.

———. "Vers quel contrat social?" *Cahiers de l'Orient* [Paris], No. 23, 1991, 21–28.

Aghrout, Ahmed, and Keith Sutton. "Regional Economic Union in the Maghreb," *Journal of Modern African Studies* [Cambridge, United Kingdom], 28, No. 1, March 1990, 115–39.

Algeria. Ministry of Information and Culture. *The Agrarian Revolution.* (English ed.) (The Faces of Algeria, No. 23.) Algiers: 1973.

"Algeria's Facade of Democracy." Interview with Mahfoud Bennoune, *Middle East Report*, No. 163, March–April 1990, 9–13.

Almeyra, Guillermo M. "How Real Was Algeria's Agrarian Revolution?" *Cérès* [Tunis], 12, No. 2, 1979, 31–35.

Amrane, Djamila. "Algeria: Anticolonial War." Pages 123–35 in Nancy Loring Goldman (ed.), *Female Soldiers—Combatants or Non-combatants? Historical and Contemporary Perspectives.* Westport, Connecticut: Greenwood Press, 1982.

Anderson, Lisa. "Liberalism in Northern Africa," *Current History*, 89, No. 546, 1990, 145–75.

———. "The State in the Middle East and North Africa," *Comparative Politics*, 20, October 1987, 1–18.

Annuaire de l'Afrique du Nord (annuals 1982 through 1988–1989). Aix-en-Provence: Centre de recherches et d'études sur les sociétés méditerranéenes, 1982 through 1989.

Azarya, Victor. "Reordering State-Society Relations: Incorporation and Disengagement." Pages 3–21 in Donald Rothchild and Naomi Chazan (eds.), *The Precarious Balance: State and Society in Africa*. Boulder, Colorado: Westview Press, 1988.

Balta, Paul. 1986. "French Policy in North Africa," *Middle East Journal*, 40, Spring 1986, 238–51.

———. "La dynamique des relations intermaghrébines." Pages 217–32 in Bassma Kodmani-Darwish (ed.), *Maghreb: Les années de transition*. Paris: Masson, 1990.

Bedrani, Slimane. "Algérie: Une nouvelle politique envers la paysannerie?" *Revue de l'occident musulman et de la Méditerranée* [Aix-en-Provence], 45, 1987, 55–66.

Bekkar, Rabia. "Taking Up Space in Tlemcen: The Islamist Occupation of Urban Algeria," *Middle East Report*, No. 179, November-December 1992, 11–15.

Bennoune, Mahfoud. *The Making of Contemporary Algeria, 1830–1987: Colonial Upheavals and Post-Independence Development*. Cambridge: Cambridge University Press, 1988.

Burgat, François. *L'islamisme au Maghreb: La voix du sud*. Paris: Karthala, 1988.

———. "La mobilisation islamiste et les élections algériennes du 12 juin 1990, *Maghreb-Machrek* [Paris], No. 129, July-September 1990, 5–22.

———. "Les 'nouveaux paysans' Algériens et l'état," *Maghreb-Machrek* [Paris], No. 95, January–March: 1982, 56–65.

Charte d'Alger, 1964. Algiers: SNED, 1964.

Charte nationale, 1976. Algiers: Éditions populaires de l'armée, 1976.

Charte nationale algérienne, 27 juin 1976. (*Notes et études documentaires*, Nos. 4348–4350.) Paris: Documentation française, 1976.

Chaulet, Claudine. "Les ruraux algériens et l'état," *Revue de l'occident musulman et de la Méditerranée* [Aix-en-Provence], 45, 1987, 67–79.

Cheriet, Boutheina. "Islamism and Feminism: Algeria's 'Rites of Passage' to Democracy." Pages 171–215 in John P. Entelis and Phillip C. Naylor (eds.), *State and Society in Algeria*. Boulder, Colorado: Westview Press, 1992.

Chikh, Slimane. "La politique africaine de l'Algérie." Pages 1–54 in *Annuaire de l'Afrique du Nord*. (18th ed.) Paris: Centre de recherches et d'études sur les sociétés méditerranéenes et Centre national de la recherche scientifique, 1979.

Cody, Edward. "Reform Referendum Set in Algeria," *Washington Post*, October 13, 1988, A3.

Constitution of 1976. Algiers: Éditions populaires de l'armée, 1976.

Constitution of 1989. Algiers: SNED, 1989.

Daoud, Zakya. "La création de l'union du Maghreb arabe," *Maghreb-Machrek* [Paris], No. 124, April–June 1989, 120–38.

Dillman, Bradford. "Transition to Democracy in Algeria." Pages 31–51 in John P. Entelis and Phillip C. Naylor (eds.), *State and Society in Algeria.* Boulder, Colorado: Westview Press, 1992.

Djeghloul, Abdelkader. "Le multipartisme à l'algérienne," *Maghreb-Machrek* [Paris], No. 127, January–March, 1990, 194–210.

Duran, Khalid. "The Second Battle of Algiers," *Orbis*, 33, No. 3, Summer 1989, 403–21.

Economist Intelligence Unit. *Country Profile: Algeria, 1989–90.* London: 1989.

———. *Country Profile: Algeria, 1990–91.* London: 1990.

———. *Country Profile: Algeria, 1991–92.* London: 1991.

———. *Country Profile: Algeria, 1992–93.* London: 1992.

Écrement, Marc. *Indépendance politique et libération économique: Un quart de siècle du développement de l'Algérie, 1962–1985.* Algiers: Entreprise algérienne de presse, Office des publications universitaires, and Grenoble: Presses universitaires de Grenoble, 1986.

Entelis, John P. *Algeria: The Revolution Institutionalized.* Boulder, Colorado: Westview Press, 1986.

———. "Algeria: Technocratic Rule, Military Power." Pages 92–143 in I. William Zartman, et al. (eds.), *Political Elites in Arab North Africa: Morocco, Algeria, Tunisia, Libya, and Egypt.* New York: Longman, 1982.

———. "Algeria under Chadli: Liberalization Without Democratization, or Perestroika, Yes; Glasnost, No!" *Middle East Insight*, 6, No. 3, 1988, 47–64.

———. "Democratic and Popular Republic of Algeria." Pages 407–34 in David E. Long and Bernard Reich (eds.), *The Government and Politics of the Middle East and North Africa.* (2d ed. rev.) Boulder, Colorado: Westview Press, 1986.

———. "Elite Political Culture and Socialization in Algeria: Tensions and Discontinuities," *Middle East Journal*, 35, No.

2, Spring 1981, 191–208.

———. "Introduction: State and Society in Transition." Pages 1–30 in John P. Entelis and Phillip C. Naylor (eds.), *State and Society in Algeria*. Boulder, Colorado: Westview Press, 1992.

———. "Islam, Democracy, and the State: The Reemergence of Authoritarian Politics in Algeria." (Revised paper presented at Eighteenth Annual Symposium, Center for Contemporary Arab Studies, Georgetown University, on "Islamism and Secularism in North Africa," Washington, April 1–2, 1993.)

———. "U.S.-Maghreb Relations in a Democratic Age: The Priority of Algeria," *Middle East Insight*, 8, No. 3, January–February 1992, 31–35.

Entelis, John P., and Lisa J. Arone. "Algeria in Turmoil: Islam, Democracy, and the State," *Middle East Policy*, 1, No. 2, 1992, 23–35.

Entelis, John P., and Philip C. Naylor (eds.). *State and Society in Algeria*. Boulder, Colorado: Westview Press, 1992.

Fontaine, Jacques. "Les élections locales algériennes du 12 juin 1990: Approche statistique et géographique," *Maghreb-Machrek* [Paris], No. 129, July–September 1990, 124–40.

Gellner, Ernest, and Jean-Claude Vatin (eds.). *Islam et politique au Maghreb*. Aix-en-Provence: Centre de recherches et d'études sur les sociétés méditerranéenes, 1981.

Grimaud, Nicole. "Algeria and Socialist France," *Middle East Journal*, 40, No. 2, Spring 1986, 252–66.

———. "La France et le Maghreb: Vers un partenariat." Pages 323–40 in Bassma Kodmani-Darwish (ed.), *Maghreb: Les années de transition*. Paris: Masson, 1990.

———. "Nouvelles orientations de relations entre la France et l'Algérie," *Maghreb-Machrek*, No. 103, January–March 1984, 96–106.

———. *La Politique extérieure de l'Algérie*. Paris: Karthala, 1984.

———. "Prolongements externes des élections algériennes," *Cahiers de l'Orient* [Paris], No. 23, 1991, 29–40.

Harbi, Mohammed. *Aux origines du FLN: Le populisme révolutionnaire en Algérie*. Paris: Bourgois, 1975.

———. *Le FLN: Mirage et réalité—des origines à la prise du pouvoir, 1945–1962*. Paris: Éditions Jeune Afrique, 1980.

Hermassi, Elbaki. "State-Building and Regime Performance in the Greater Maghreb." Pages 75–88 in Ghassan Salamé (ed.), *The Foundations of the Arab State*. New York: Croom

Helm, 1987.
Hodges, Tony. "François Mitterrand, Master Strategist in the Maghreb." *Africa Report*, 28, May–June 1983, 17–21.
Humbaraci, Arslan. *Algeria: A Revolution that Failed. A Political History since 1954*. New York: Praeger, 1966.
Jones, Linda G. "Portrait of Rashid al-Ghannoushi," *Middle East Report*, No. 153, July–August 1988, 19–22.
Kapil, Arun. "Algeria's Elections Show Islamist Strength," *Middle East Report*, No. 165, September–October 1990, 31–36.
———. "Les partis islamistes en Algérie: Eléments de présentation," *Maghreb-Machrek* [Paris], No. 133, July–September 1991, 103–11.
———. "Portraits statistiques des élections du 12 juin 1990: Chiffres-clés pour une analyse," *Cahiers de l'Orient*, No. 23, 1991, 41–63.
Kielstra, Nico. "The Agrarian Revolution and Algerian Socialism," *MERIP Reports*, No. 67, 1987, 5–26.
Knauss, Peter R. "Algerian Women since Independence." Pages 151–69 in John P. Entelis and Phillip C. Naylor (eds.), *State and Society in Algeria*. Boulder, Colorado: Westview Press, 1992.
Kodmani-Darwish, Bassma. *Maghreb: Les années de transition*. Paris: Masson, 1990.
Korany, Bahgat. "Third Worldism and Pragmatic Radicalism: The Foreign Policy of Algeria." Pages 79–118 in Bahgat Korany and Ali E. Hillal Dessouki (eds.), *The Foreign Policy of Arab States*. Boulder, Colorado: Westview Press, 1984.
Laacher, Smain. *Algérie: Réalités sociales et pouvoir*. Paris: Harmattan, 1985.
Lassassi, Assassi. *Nonalignment and Algerian Foreign Policy*. Brookfield, Vermont: Avebury, 1988.
Lawless, Richard, and Allan Findlay (eds.). *North Africa: Contemporary Politics and Economic Development*. New York: St. Martin's Press, 1984.
Leca, Jean. "État et société en Algérie." Pages 17–58 in Bassma Kodmani-Darwish (ed.), *Maghreb: Les années de transition*. Paris: Masson, 1990.
Lewis, William. "Algeria and the Maghreb at the Turning Point," *Mediterranean Quarterly: A Journal of Global Issues*, 1, No. 3, Summer 1990, 62–74.
Mameri, Khalfa. *Citations du président Boumediene*. Algiers: SNED, 1975.
Marion, Georges. "'Ordre islamique' en Algérie," *Le Monde*

[Paris], July 17, 1990, 5.

Mitterrand, François. *Réflexions sur la politique extérieure de la France: Introduction à vingt-cinq discours, 1981–1985.* Paris: Fayard, 1986.

Mortimer, Robert A. "Algeria after the Explosion," *Current History*, 89, No. 546, April, 1990, 161–82.

———. "Algerian Foreign Policy in Transition." Pages 241–66 in John P. Entelis and Phillip C. Naylor (eds.), *State and Society in Algeria.* Boulder, Colorado: Westview Press, 1992.

———. "The Algerian Revolution in Search of the African Revolution," *Journal of Modern African Studies* [London], 8, No. 3, October 1970, 363–87.

———. "The Arab Maghreb Union: Political Economy and Geopolitics," *Relazioni Internazionali* [Naples], 12, December 1990, 14–24.

———. "Development and Autonomy: The Algerian Approach," *TransAfrica Forum,* Winter 1987, 35–48.

———. "Global Economy and African Foreign Policy: The Algerian Model," *African Studies Review,* 27, No. 1, March 1984, 1–22.

———. "Islam and Multiparty Politics in Algeria," *Middle East Journal,* 45, No. 4, Autumn 1991, 575–93.

———. "Maghreb Matters," *Foreign Policy,* 76, Fall 1989, 160–75.

———. "The Politics of Reassurance in Algeria," *Current History*, 84, No. 502, May 1985, 201–4, 228–29.

Mouhoubi, Salah. *La politique de coopération algéro-française: Bilan et perspectives.* Algiers: Office des publications universitaires, 1986.

Nacer, Abderrahmane Roustoumi Hadj (ed.). *Les cahiers de la réforme.* (5 vols.) Algiers: En.A.P., 1989.

Naylor, Phillip C. "French-Algerian Relations, 1980–1990." Pages 217–40 in John P. Entelis and Phillip C. Naylor (eds.), *State and Society in Algeria.* Boulder, Colorado: Westview Press, 1992.

Ottaway, David B., and Marina Ottaway. *Algeria: The Politics of a Socialist Revolution.* Berkeley: University of California Press, 1970.

Pfeifer, Karen. *Agrarian Reform under State Capitalism in Algeria.* Boulder, Colorado: Westview Press, 1985.

Projet de charte nationale, 1986. Alger: Parti du Front de Libération Nationale. Algiers: n.p., 1986.

Quandt, William B. "Can We Do Business with Radical Nationalists? Algeria: Yes," *Foreign Policy,* 7, 1972, 108–31.

――――. *Revolution and Political Leadership: Algeria, 1954–1968.* Cambridge: MIT Press, 1969.

Redjala, Ramdane. *L'opposition en Algérie depuis 1962*, 1. Paris: Harmattan, 1988.

Roberts, Hugh. "The Politics of Algerian Socialism." Pages 5–49 in Richard Lawless and Allan Findlay (eds.), *North Africa: Contemporary Politics and Economic Development.* New York: St. Martin's Press, 1984.

Shahin, Emad Eldin. "Algeria: The Limits to Democracy," *Middle East Insight,* 7, No. 6, July–October 1992, 10–19.

Smith, Tony. "The Political and Economic Ambitions of Algerian Land Reform, 1962–1974," *Middle East Journal,* 29, Summer 1975, 259–78.

Tahi, Mohand Salah. "The Arduous Democratisation Process in Algeria," *Journal of Modern African Studies* [Cambridge, United Kingdom], 30, No. 3, September 1992, 397–419.

Tlemcani, Rachid. "Chadli's Perestroika," *Middle East Report,* No. 163, March–April 1990, 14–17.

――――. *State and Revolution in Algeria.* Boulder, Colorado: Westview Press, 1986.

Tlemcani, Rachid, and William W. Hansen. "Development and the State in Post-Colonial Algeria," *Journal of Asian and African Studies* [Leiden], 24, Nos. 1–2, 1989, 114–33.

Yefsah, Abdelkader. *La question du pouvoir en Algérie.* Algiers: En.A.P., 1990.

Zartman, I. William. "L'élite algérienne sous la présidence de Chadli Benjedid," *Maghreb-Machrek* [Paris], 106, October–November 1984, 37–53.

――――. "The Military in the Politics of Succession: Algeria." Pages 21–45 in John W. Harbeson (ed.), *The Military in African Politics.* New York: Praeger, 1987.

――――. "Political Succession as a Conceptual Event: The Algerian and Tunisian Cases." (Paper presented at Fourteenth World Congress, International Political Science Association, Washington, September 23-25, 1988.)

(Various issues of the following publications were also used in the preparation of this chapter: *Africa Confidential* [London]; *Al Aqida* [Algiers]; *Al Chaab* [Algiers]; *Al Mazza* [Algiers]; *Al Salaam* [Algiers]; *Al Tadhkeer* [Algiers]; *Algérie Informations* [Algiers]; *Christian Science Monitor;* Economist, *Quarterly Economic Review: Algeria* [London]: *El Badil* [Algiers]; *El Khaban* [Algiers]; *El Moudjahid* [Algiers]; *El Mounqidh* [Algiers]; *El*

Watan [Algiers]; *Es Sahafa* [Algiers]; *Horizons* [Algiers]; *International Herald Tribune* [Paris]; *International Journal of Middle East Studies*; *L'Express* [Paris]; *Le Figaro* [Paris]; *Le Monde* [Paris]; *Le Monde Diplomatique* [Paris]; *Libération* [Paris]; *Middle East Studies Association Bulletin*; *Middle East Journal*; *New York Times*; *Révolution Africaine* [Algiers]; *Washington Post*; and *World Press Review*.)

Chapter 5

Air Forces of the World. (Ed., D.H. Chopping.) Geneva: Interavia Data, 1985.

Algeria. Ministry of Information and Culture. *De l'A.L.N. à l'A.N.P.* Algiers: Armée National Populaire, Commisariat Politique, 1974.

Amnesty International. *Amnesty International Report, 1992.* New York: 1992.

——. *Amnesty International Report, 1993.* London: 1993.

Damis, John. "Morocco and the Western Sahara," *Current History*, 89, No. 546, April 1990, 165–68, 184–86.

Deeb, Mary-Jane. "Inter-Maghribi Relations since 1969: A Study of the Modalities of Unions and Mergers," *Middle East Journal*, 43, No. 1, Winter 1989, 20–33.

Defense and Foreign Affairs Handbook, 1990–1991. (Ed., Gregory R. Copley.) Alexandria, Virginia: International Media, 1990.

de la Gorce, Paul-Marie. "Algérie: Un premier ministre de choc,"*Jeune Afrique* [Paris], No. 1645, July 16–22, 1992, 20–33.

——. "L'armée seule avec Dieu," *Jeune Afrique* [Paris], No. 1644, July 9–15, 1992, 59–62.

DMS Market Intelligence Reports: Foreign Military Markets: Middle East and Africa. Alexandria, Virginia: Jane's Information Group, 1989.

Duran, Khalid. "The Second Battle of Algiers," *Orbis*, 33, No. 3, Summer 1989, 403–21.

Dyer, Gwynne. "Algeria." Pages 10–14 in John Keegan (ed.), *World Armies*. Detroit: Gale Research, 1983.

Entelis, John P. "Democratic and Popular Republic of Algeria." Pages 407–34 in David E. Long and Bernard Reich (eds.), *The Government and Politics of the Middle East and North Africa.* Boulder, Colorado: Westview Press, 1986.

Entelis, John P., and Lisa J. Arone. "Algeria in Turmoil: Islam, Democracy, and the State," *Middle East Policy*, 1, No. 2, 1992, 23–35.

Gibbins, Penny. "Algeria's Trial of Strength," *Middle East* [London], No. 201, July 1991, 28–32.

Hermida, Alfred. "Death in Algiers," *Africa Report*, 37, No. 5, September–October 1992, 49–53.

———. "Democracy Derailed," *Africa Report*, 37, No. 2, March–April 1992, 12–17.

Horne, Alistair. *A Savage War of Peace: Algeria, 1954–1962.* New York: Viking, 1977.

Jane's Fighting Ships, 1992–93. (Ed., Richard Sharpe.) Alexandria, Virginia: Jane's Information Group, 1992.

Kaidi, Hamza. "La guerre civile est déjà là," *Jeune Afrique* [Paris], No. 1624, February 20–26, 1992, 19–21.

"The Maghreb: The Rise of Radical Islam." Pages 109–15 in Sidney Bearman (ed.), *Strategic Survey: 1991–1992.* London: Brassey's for the International Institute for Strategic Studies, 1992.

Mandron, Guy. "The Algerian Confrontation." *Jane's Intelligence Review* [Coulsdon, United Kingdom], 4, No. 7, July 1992, 321–24.

The Middle East and North Africa, 1993. London: Europa, 1992.

The Middle East Military Balance, 1989–1990. (Ed., Joseph Alpher.) Boulder, Colorado: Westview Press for Jaffee Center for Strategic Studies, 1990.

The Military Balance, 1992–1993. London: International Institute for Strategic Studies, 1992.

The Military Balance, 1993–1994. London: International Institute for Strategic Studies, 1993.

Milivojevic, Marko. "Algeria's National Popular Army," *Armed Forces* [Shepperton, United Kingdom], 8, No. 4, April 1989, 158–63.

Mortimer, Robert A. "Algeria after the Explosion," *Current History*, 89, No. 546, April 1990, 161–82.

———. "Islam and Multiparty Politics in Algeria," *Middle East Journal*, 45, No. 4, Autumn 1991, 575–93.

Quandt, William B. *Algerian Military Development: The Professionalization of a Guerrilla Army.* Santa Monica, California: Rand, 1970.

Roberts, Hugh. "Radical Islamism and the Dilemma of Algerian Nationalism," *Third World Quarterly* [Abingdon, United Kingdom], 10, No. 2, April 1988, 556–89.

Sivard, Ruth Leger. *World Military and Social Expenditures, 1991.* Washington: World Priorities, 1991.

United States. Arms Control and Disarmament Agency. *World*

Military Expenditures and Arms Transfers, 1990. Washington: GPO, 1991.

———. Department of State. *Country Reports on Human Rights Practices for 1990.* (Report submitted to United States Congress, 102d, 1st Session, Senate, Committee on Foreign Relations, and House of Representatives, Committee on Foreign Affairs.) Washington: GPO, 1991.

———. Department of State. *Country Reports on Human Rights Practices for 1991.* (Report submitted to United States Congress, 102d, 2d Session, Senate, Committee on Foreign Relations, and House of Representatives, Committee on Foreign Affairs.) Washington: GPO, 1992.

———. Department of State. *Patterns of Global Terrorism: 1991.* Washington: 1992.

———. Department of State and Defense Security Assistance Agency. *Congressional Presentation for Security Assistance, Fiscal Year 1993.* Washington: 1992.

"World Defence Almanac: Algeria," *Military Technology* [Bonn], 1, January 1992, 153.

Yared, Marc. "La deuxième guerre d'Algérie: A-t-elle commencée?" *Jeune Afrique* [Paris], Nos. 1649–50, August 13–26, 1992, 38–48.

Zartman, I. William. "The Algerian Army in Politics," Pages 224–49 in Claude E. Welch, Jr. (ed.), *Soldier and State in Africa.* Evanston, Illinois: Northwestern University Press, 1970.

———. *Political Elites in Arab North Africa.* New York: Longman, 1982.

(Various issues of the following publications were also used in the preparation of this chapter: *Africa Confidential* [London]; *African Defence Journal* [Paris]; *Economist* [London]; Economist Intelligence Unit, *Country Reports: Algeria* [London]; Foreign Broadcast Information Service, *Daily Report: Middle East and Africa; Facts on File; Jeune Afrique* [Paris]; Joint Publications Research Service, *Near East/South Asia Report; Keesing's Record of World Events* [London]; *Marchés tropicaux et méditerranéens* [Paris]; *Middle East Insight; New York Times; Washington Post;* and *Washington Report on Middle East Affairs.*)

Glossary

autogestion—Self-management system. Originated in takeover of management functions by farm and industrial workers after Algerian independence.

barrels per day (bpd)—Production of crude oil and petroleum products is frequently measured in barrels per day and often abbreviated as bpd. A barrel is a volume measure of forty-two United States gallons. Conversion of barrels to tons depends on the density of the specific product. About 17.3 barrels of average crude oil weigh one ton. Light products such as gasoline and kerosene average close to eighteen barrels per ton.

dinar (DA)—Unit of Algerian currency since 1964; divided into 100 centimes. The average exchange rate was DA9.0 in 1990, DA18.5 in 1991, DA21.8 in 1992, DA24.5 in 1993, and DA40.7 in October 1994.

European Community (EC)—*See* European Union (EU).

European Union (EU)—Until November 1993, the EU was known as the European Community (EC). The EU comprises three communities: the European Coal and Steel Community (ECSC), the European Economic Community (EEC), and the European Atomic Energy Community (Euratom). Each community is a legally distinct body, but since 1967 they have shared common governing institutions. The EU forms more than a framework for free trade and economic cooperation: the signatories to the treaties governing the communities have agreed in principle to integrate their economies and ultimately to form a political union. Belgium, France, Italy, Luxembourg, the Netherlands, and the Federal Republic of Germany (West Germany) were charter members of the EU; Britain, Denmark, and Ireland joined on January 1, 1973; Greece became a member on January 1, 1981; and Portugal and Spain entered on January 1, 1986.

GDP (gross domestic product)—A value measure of the flow of domestic goods and services produced by an economy over a period of time, such as a year. Only output values of goods for final consumption and investment are included because the values of primary and intermediate production are assumed to be included in final prices. GDP is sometimes aggregated and shown at market prices, meaning that indirect taxes and subsidies are included; when these have been eliminated, the result is GDP at factor cost. The word *gross* indicates that deductions for depreciation of physical assets have not been made. *See also* GNP.

GNP (gross national product)—The gross domestic product (*q.v.*) plus the net income or loss stemming from transactions with foreign countries. GNP is the broadest measurement of the output of goods and services by an economy. It can be calculated at market prices, which include indirect taxes and subsidies. Because indirect taxes and subsidies are only transfer payments, GNP is often calculated at factor cost by removing indirect taxes and subsidies.

Hanafi—One of four major legal schools in Sunni (*q.v.*) Islam, the Hanafi school makes substantial use of reason in legal opinions. Named for Ali Numan Abu Hanifa (ca. 700–67), a leading theologian in Iraq.

Ibadi—From Abu Allah ibn Ibad (ca. 660–ca. 715), a moderate Kharijite who spent considerable time in Basra, Iraq. The Kharijites were members of the earliest sect in Islam that left the followers of Ali or Shia (*q.v.*) because of Shia willingness to allow human arbitration of Ali's dispute with the caliph, Uthman, rather than divine judgment.

imam—A word used in several senses. In general use, it means the leader of congregational prayers; as such it implies no ordination or special spiritual powers beyond sufficient education to carry out this function. It is also used figuratively by many Sunni (*q.v.*) Muslims to mean the leader of the Islamic community. Among Shia (*q.v.*) the word takes on many complex meanings; in general, however, and particularly when capitalized, it indicates that particular descendant of the Party of Ali who is believed to have been God's designated repository of the spiritual authority inherent in that line. The identity of this individual and the means of ascertaining his identity have been major issues causing divisions among Shia.

International Monetary Fund (IMF)—Established along with the World Bank (*q.v.*) in 1945, the IMF is a specialized agency affiliated with the United Nations and is responsible for stabilizing international exchange rates and payments. The main business of the IMF is the provision of loans to its members (including industrialized and developing countries) when they experience balance of pay-

Glossary

ments difficulties. These loans frequently carry conditions that require substantial internal economic adjustments by the recipients, most of which are developing countries.

London Club—An informal group of commercial banks that come together to negotiate a debt rescheduling agreement with a country. The group has two committees, an economics committee that develops economic data projections and a negotiating committee. Committee members usually come from the five principal banks that hold the largest amounts of a country's debt.

Maghrib—The western Islamic world (northwest Africa); distinguished from the Mashriq, or eastern Islamic world (the Middle East). Literally, "the time and place of the sunset—the west." For its Arab conquerors, the region was the "island of the west" (*jazirat al maghrib*), the land between the "sea of sand" (the Sahara) and the Mediterranean Sea. Traditionally includes Morocco, Algeria, Tunisia, and Tripolitania (in Libya); more recently some sources have treated Mauritania as part of the region. Also transliterated as Maghreb.

Maliki—Named for Malik ibn Anas (ca. 710–95), a leading jurist from Medina. The Maliki school is one of four major legal schools in Sunni (*q.v.*) Islam, which recorded the Medina consensus of opinion, using tradition as a guide.

Paris Club—The informal name for a consortium of Western creditor countries (Belgium, Britain, Canada, France, Germany, Italy, Japan, the Netherlands, Sweden, Switzerland, and the United States) that have made loans or guaranteed export credits to developing nations and that meet in Paris to discuss borrowers' ability to repay debts. Paris Club deliberations often result in the tendering of emergency loans to countries in economic difficulty or in the rescheduling of debts. Formed in October 1962, the organization has no formal or institutional existence. Its secretariat is run by the French treasury. It has a close relationship with the International Monetary Fund (*q.v.*), to which all of its members except Switzerland belong, as well as with the World Bank (*q.v.*) and the United Nations Conference on Trade and Development (UNCTAD). The Paris Club is also known as the Group of Ten (G–10).

Shia (from Shiat Ali, the Party of Ali)—A member of the smaller of the two great divisions of Islam. The Shia supported the claims of Ali and his line to presumptive right to the caliphate and leadership of the Muslim community, and on this issue they divided from the Sunni (*q.v.*) in the major schism within Islam. Later schisms have produced further divisions among the Shia over the identity and number of imams (*q.v.*). Most Shia revere Twelve Imams, the last of whom is believed to be hidden from view.

Sunni—The larger of the two great divisions of Islam. The Sunni, who rejected the claims of Ali's line, believe that they are the true followers of the sunna, the guide to proper behavior set forth by Muhammad's personal deeds and utterances.

World Bank—Informal name used to designate a group of four affiliated international institutions: the International Bank for Reconstruction and Development (IBRD), the International Development Association (IDA), the International Finance Corporation (IFC), and the Multilateral Investment Guarantee Agency (MIGA). The IBRD, established in 1945, has the primary purpose of providing loans to developing countries for productive projects. The IDA, a legally separate loan fund but administered by the staff of the IBRD, was set up in 1960 to furnish credits to the poorest developing countries on much easier terms than those of conventional IBRD loans. The IFC, founded in 1956, supplements the activities of the IBRD through loans and assistance specifically designed to encourage the growth of productive private enterprises in the less developed countries. The MIGA, founded in 1988, insures private foreign investment in developing countries against various noncommercial risks. The president and certain senior officers of the IBRD hold the same positions in the IFC. The four institutions are owned by the governments of the countries that subscribe their capital. To participate in the World Bank group, member states must first belong to the International Monetary Fund (IMF—*q.v.*).

Index

Abbas, Ferhat, 37, 39, 40, 41, 45; head of government-in-exile, 53; head of National Assembly, 57; placed under house arrest, 59
Abbasid caliphate, 15
Abbasids, xxvii, 12
Abd Allah ibn Yasin al Juzuli, 14
Abd al Mumin, 15, 16
Abd al Qadir, 25–27
Abd ar Rahman ibn Rustum, 12
Abd ar Rahman II, 26
Abdessalam, Belaïd, 190, 191
Abduh, Muhammad, 37
Abu al Muhajir Dina, 12
Abu Bakr ibn Ibrahim al Jaddali, 15
Abu Bakr ibn Tufayl, 16
Abu Nidal Organization, 240
Abu Yaqub Yusuf, 16
Ach Chaab (The People), 220
acquired immune deficiency syndrome (AIDS), 119
Africa, sub-Saharan: refugees from, 245; relations in, 226–27
African Development Bank, 161
Agency for Development and Promotion of Investment, 140
agrarian reform, 80, 156, 158
agrarian revolution (1971), 61, 123, 158
agricultural: exports, 152, 170; imports, 157, 181; infrastructure, 156; production, 61, 156–57; workers, 98
agricultural products (*see also under individual crops*): grain, 157; imports of, 157; tree crops, 157, 158
agriculture (*see also under agrarian*), 132, 152–160; under Almohad rule, 16; areas for, 72; of Berbers, 93; under Ben Bella, 178; under Benjedid, xxix, 131; under Boumediene, 61, 179; under French rule, 33; government role in, 178, 203; investment in, 139; nationalized, 130, 179, 213; as percentage of gross domestic product, 134, 152–53; privatization in, 63, 69, 130; under Roman rule, 8

Agriculture and Rural Development Bank (Banque de l'Agriculture et du Développement Rural), 142
Ahaggar highlands, 73, 81; Berbers in, 82, 84
Ahmad ibn Muhammad, 25
Ahmed, Mourad Sid (*see also* Djafar al Afghani), xxxii
AIDS. *See* acquired immune deficiency syndrome
Aïn el Hanech: prehistoric inhabitants of, 5
Air Algérie, 166
air defense, 256
Aire Liquide (France), 168
air force, 256, 262–63; aircraft of, 238, 262, 263; insignia, ranks, uniforms, 265
Air Force Academy, 262
Air France, 166
airports, 161, 164–66
Air Products Company, 168
AIS. *See* Islamic Salvation Army
Ait Ahmed, Hocine, 42, 43, 44, 91; opposition of, to Ben Bella, 58, 59
Al Aghlab, Ibrahim ibn, 12
Al Badil (The Alternate), 220
Algerian Assembly: abolished, 47
Algerian Association for the Emancipation of Women, 218
Algerian Brotherhood, 249
Algerian Communist Party (Parti Communiste Algérien—PCA), 38, 214; opposition of, to Ben Bella, 58
Algerian Confederation of Employers, 214
Algerian Development Bank (Banque Algérienne de Développement), 142
Algerian General Workers' Union (Union Générale des Travailleurs Algériens—UGTA), 211–12
Algerian Islamic Movement, 247
Algerian League of Human Rights, 182, 282, 283
Algerian Muslim Congress, 38

Algeria: A Country Study

Algerian National Assembly, 32
Algerian socialism. *See* nationalization
Algiers, 3; airport of, 164; captured by Almohads, 15; electricity generation at, 149; European migration to, 23; founded, 13; French administration of, 29; French blockade of, xxviii, 22; invasion of, xxviii, 22-23; under Khair ad Din, 19; migration to, 46, 79; population of, 79-80; port of, 163; subway system, 162; uprisings in, 54
Algiers Charter (1964), 178
Al Jazair, 69
Al Joumhouria (The Republic), 220
Almohad rebellion (1125), 15
Almohads, xxvii, 3, 11, 15-16; conquests by, 15
Almoravids, xxvii, 3, 14-15; activities of, 14-15
Al Moudjahid (The Fighter), 220
Al Muizz, 13
ALN. *See* National Liberation Army
Al Qayrawan: established, 11; sacked, 14
Al Qiyam, 110, 215
Alrar gas field, 147, 148
Amis du Manifeste et de la Liberté. *See* Friends of the Manifesto and Liberty
AML. *See* Friends of the Manifesto and Liberty
Amnesty International, 282, 284
Amour massif, 72
Anadarko Petroleum Corporation, 168
Anatolia, 19-20
Andalus (*see also* Spain): influence of, 15; refugees from, 92
Anglo-Suez Campaign (1956), 48
Angola: support for revolutionaries in, 226, 239
Annaba, 73; airport of, 164; electricity generation at, 149; population of, 80; port of, 163
An Nasr (The Victory), 220
ANP. *See* People's National Army
Antiterrorist Detachment, 280
APC. *See* Communal Popular Assembly
APN. *See* National People's Assembly
APW. *See* Popular Wilaya Assembly
Arab countries: economic aid from, 138; relations with, 227-28
Arabic language, 86-87, 89; broadcasts in, 90, 167; education in, 112; instruction in, 90; introduction of, 3; newspapers in, 220; as official language, 25, 43, 90, 221; spread of, 14
Arab League. *See* League of Arab States
Arab-Israeli dispute, 227-28
Arab-Israeli wars: of 1967, 240, 229, 273; of 1973, 240, 270
arabization, 11-17, 87-91, 220-21, 232; of Berbers, 14, 62, 221; under Boumediene, 220; in education, 112-13, 115, 220, 221; impact of, xxvii; opposition to, 62, 89, 90, 249-50; political aspects of, 90-91, 221
Arab Organization for Space Communications (Arabsat), 167
Arab rule: opposition to, 12; slavery under, 12
Arabs, xxvii, 11-17; alienation of Berbers by, 12, 250; identification with, 82; as percentage of population, 82; social structure of, 82, 91; and women, 102
Arabsat. *See* Arab Organization for Space Communications
Arafat, Yasir, 227
Aragon: trade with, 17
armed forces, 237-38, 250, 256-70; anti-Islamist actions of, xxxii-xxxiii; attitudes toward, 255; civic action role of, 238, 254, 260, 267, 272; commander in chief, 194, 256; general staff, 257; high command of, 257-59; ideological indoctrination in, 269; internal security by, 184, 187, 255, 268; manpower resources, 265; matériel of, 238, 240, 261, 262, 263, 264, 272-74, 276, 277; missions of, 272; modernization of, 252; number of personnel in, 252, 256; as political elite, 205; political role of, 177, 180, 205, 206, 237, 252, 254; purged, 253, 255; under Roman rule, 8; reserves, 256; restructuring of, 253; self-sufficiency of, 272; social security program of, 269; uniforms, ranks, and insignia of, 265; women in, 102, 267
Armed Islamic Group (Groupe Islamique Armé—GIA), xxxi; government activities against, xxxii
Armed Islamic Movement (Mouvement Islamique Armé—MIA) (*see also* Islamic Salvation Army), xxxi-xxxii, 191
Armée de Libération Nationale. *See*

National Liberation Army
Armée Islamique du Salut. *See* Islamic Salvation Army
Armée Nationale Populaire. *See* People's National Army
army, 256, 259–62; deployment of, 237, 259–60; insignia, ranks, and uniforms, 265; matériel of, 261; number of personnel in, 256, 259; organization of, 260–61; political power of, 176, 193; restructuring of, 238, 261; territorial organization of, 259–60; training of, 261–62
Arslan, Shakib, 36
Aruj, 19
Arzew gas plant, 148
Assemblée Populaire Communale. *See* Communal Popular Assembly
Assemblée Populaire de Wilaya. *See* Popular Wilaya Assembly
Assemblée Populaire Nationale. *See* National People's Assembly
Association des Uléma Musulmans Algériens. *See* Association of Algerian Muslim Ulama
Association of Algerian Muslim Ulama (Association des Uléma Musulmans Algériens—AUMA), 37, 41–42, 45; French view of, 38; outlawed, 42
Atlas mountains, 72; Berbers in, 82, 93
Augustine of Hippo, 10
AUMA. *See* Association of Algerian Muslim Ulama
Aurès Mountains, 73; Berbers in, 82, 83, 93; population in, 81
autogestion, 58, 61, 153, 178
Averroes. *See* Ibn Rushd

Baader-Meinhof Gang: military support for, 240
balance of payments, 170
Bani Abd el Wad, 16
Bani Merin (Zenata Berbers), 16
banking, 142; under French rule, 142; and investment, 142; privatization in, 63, 69; reform, 142
Bank of Local Development (Banque de Développement Local), 142
Bank of Manufacturing and Services (Banque des Industries de Transformation et des Services), 142
banks: foreign, 134; privatized, 63, 69

Banque Algérienne de Développement. *See* Algerian Development Bank
Banque Centrale d'Algérie. *See* Central Bank of Algeria
Banque de Développement Local. *See* Bank of Local Development
Banque de l'Agriculture et du Développement Rural. *See* Agriculture and Rural Development Bank
Banque des Industries de Transformation et des Services. *See* Bank of Manufacturing and Services
Banque Extérieure d'Algérie. *See* Foreign Bank of Algeria
Banque Nationale d'Algérie. *See* National Bank of Algeria
Banque Nationale de Paris: loan from, 137
Banu Hilal tribe, 14
Banu Sulaym tribe, 14
baraka, 17
Barbarossa. *See* Khair ad Din
barrage vert (green barrier), 160, 272
Batna: population of, 80
Battle of Algiers (1956), 49, 50
Battle of Sedan (1870), 30
Béchar oasis, 72
beduin: arrival of, 14; sedentarization of, 94–95; social structure of, 91
Bejaïa, 13, 73; port of, 163
Bejaïa Plain, 72
Belgium: bilateral credit lines with, 137
Belhadj, Ali, xxx, xxxi, 63, 209; arrested, 64, 187, 282
Belhouchet, Abdallah, 256
Belisarius, 11
Belkheir, Larbi, 188, 259; in coup d'état of 1992, 64
Ben Ali, Zine el Abidine, 225
Ben Badis, Abd al Hamid, 37–38
Ben Bella, Ahmed, 43, 44, 256; as commander in chief, 253–54; deposed, 60; external security under, 139; foreign policy of, 130–31; nationalist activities of, xxviii, xxix, 56–57; opposition to, 58, 59, 60, 245; as president, 59, 177, 178; in War of Independence, 46, 47–48
Ben Bella government, 59, 177–78; economy under, 129; education under, 100
Ben Boulaid, Moustafa, 44
Bendjelloul, Mohamed, 39

Benhadj, Ali. *See* Belhadj, Ali
Benjedid, Chadli: forced to resign, 64, 188, 255, 257; politics of, 61; as president, xxviii–xxiv, 61, 99, 180–81, 237, 255
Benjedid government, 61–64, 204–5, 255; amnesties under, 246–47; anticorruption campaign under, 182; economic reforms under, xxix, 61, 129–30, 131, 156, 175, 181–84, 205, 229, 248; education under, 100; family code under, 200; foreign policy under, 227, 241; Islam under, 107, 209; manufacturing under, 151; military assistance under, 240; opposition to, 62; political reforms under, 175, 176, 181–84, 192, 196, 200, 229, 248; press under, 219; social reforms under, 129–30
Benloucif, Moustafa, 257
Ben M'Hidi, Larbi, 44
Berber kingdoms, 7–8
Berber language, 81, 86–87, 249; broadcasts in, 90; dialects of, 87, 221
Berber question, 89–90
Berber separatism, 249–50
Berbers, xxvii, 11, 81; arabization of, 14, 62, 221, 249–50; under Arab rule, 12; blood revenge among, 100; under Carthaginian rule, 7–8; geographic distribution of, 82–83; identification with, 82; Islamist attacks on, xxxii; military heritage of, 250; origins of, 3, 5, 81–82; percentage of, in population, 82, 249; political parties of, xxix, 91, 186, 250; political protests by, 62; religions of, 10, 107, 108, 249; under Roman rule, 8; social structure of, 91, 93; taxes on, 12; and women, 102
Berbers, Chaouia, 72; anti-French uprisings by, 38–84; dialect of, 87, 221; and women, 102
Berbers, Kabyle, 59, 82, 83; antiarabization demonstrations by, 90; anti-French uprisings by, 38–84; cultural movement of, 89–90; dialect of, 87, 116, 221; as *évolués*, 88; migration by, 83, 92, 93–94, 124; villages of, 93
Berbers, Kutama: converted to Islam, 13
Berbers, Mzab, 74, 82, 84; dialect of, 87, 221
Berbers, Tuareg, 81, 82, 84–86, 245; dialect of, 87, 221; occupations of, 86; population of, 84
Berbers, Zenata, 16
bidonvilles. *See* shantytowns
biens vacants. *See* housing, abandoned
birth control. *See* family planning
Biskra oasis, 72
Bitat, Rabah, 44, 56
Black October riots, 130, 132, 183, 184, 196, 213, 247–48, 257,268, 280
Black Panthers: military support for, 240
Blida: population of, 80
Blum, Léon, 38
border problems: with Mali, 226; with Mauritania, 226, 245; with Morocco, 222, 242, 252; with Niger, 226; with Tunisia, 222, 245
border security, 244–45
Boudiaf, Mohamed, 44; assassinated, xxx, 190, 248, 256, 259; as head of state, xxx, 64, 189, 207; opposition of, to Ben Bella, 58
Boumediene, Houari, 56–57, 97, 177; as ALN chief of staff, 252; coup by, 60, 131, 178, 192, 256; death of, xxviii, 61, 131, 180; opposition to, 61, 245; politics of, 60–61; as president, 61, 237; support for, 180
Boumediene government, 60–61, 178–81; agrarian reform under, 156, 213; arabization under, 89, 220; education under, 100; elite under, 205; external security under, 239; foreign policy under, 242; industrialization under, 97; Islam under, 107; legal system under, 199; local government under, 202; political parties under, 195, 204; political reform under, 194
Bourguiba, Habib, 225
Boutamine, Mohamed Mokhtar, 262
Bouyali, Moustapha, 247
Britain: matériel from, 264, 274, 276–77; trade with, 18
Brooke Marine, 264
budget, 135–36
budget deficit: efforts to limit, 136
Bugeaud, Thomas, 25; military strategy of, 26
bureaucracy. *See* civil service
Bureau Politique. *See* Political Bureau
bureaux arabes, 27
Byzantine rule, 3

Byzantines, xxvii, 11

Cairo: established, 13
Caisse Nationale d'Épargne et de Prévoyance. *See* National Fund for Provident Savings
Cambon, Jules, 34
Capsian culture, 4–5
Carthage, 7–8; destroyed, 7, 11
Carthaginian rule, 3; Berbers under, 7–8, 250; opposition to, 250; towns established under, 7
Catholicism, Roman: introduction of, 111
Catholic missions. *See* missions
Catroux, Georges, 41
CCE. *See* Committee of Coordination and Enforcement
CCN. *See* National Consultative Council
censorship, 219
census, 76, 77
Central Bank of Algeria (Banque Centrale d'Algérie), 134; established, 142; exchange rate under, 137, 171; financial management by, 135
Chabaani, Mohamed, 59
Chad: Libya's invasion of, 244
Challe, Maurice, 51
Charles X: deposed, 23
Chelif River valley, 72
children: custody of, 105
China, People's Republic of: matériel from, 264, 273, 277
Christianity (*see also under individual denominations*): conversion to, 10; heresies of, 10; introduction of, 10, 111
Christians: under Islam, 11, 110
civil aviation, 164
civil service: under Almohad rule, 16
Classical period, 7–11
Claudius, 8
Clauzel, Bertrand, 23–24, 25
Clemenceau, Georges, 32–33, 35
climate, 74–75, 157; rainfall, 74, 153
CNDR. *See* National Committee for the Defense of the Revolution
CNRA. *See* National Council of the Algerian Revolution
CNT. *See* National Transitional Council
Coast Guard, 263, 264–65
Colonial Bank of Algeria, 142
colonial rule. *See* French rule

colonists. *See* colons
colons (*see also* European settlers): conservatism of, 38, 39, 44; exodus of, 57, 122, 130; hegemony of, 32–34; origins of, 24; property abandoned by, 121–22, 153; uprising of 1960 by, 54; vigilante units of, 46
Comité de Coordination et d'Exécution. *See* Committee of Coordination and Enforcement
Comité National pour la Défense de la Révolution. *See* National Committee for the Defense of the Revolution
Comité Révolutionnaire d'Unité et d'Action. *See* Revolutionary Committee of Unity and Action
Commissariat aux Énergies Nouvelles. *See* Commissariat for New Energy
Commissariat for New Energy (Commissariat aux Énergies Nouvelles), 149
Committee Against Torture, 282
Committee for the Legal Equality of Men and Women, 218
Committee of Coordination and Enforcement (Comité de Coordination et d'Exécution—CCE), 47
Committee of Public Safety, 51–52
Communal Popular Assembly (Assemblée Populaire Communale—APC), 203
communications. *See* telecommunications
concentration camps, 51, 56, 84, 95
Congo: military support for, 239
Conquest of Literacy program, 116–18
Conseil National de la Révolution Algérienne. *See* National Council of the Algerian Revolution
Conseil Consultatif National. *See* National Consultative Council
Conseil National de Transition. *See* National Transitional Council
Constantine, 10; airport of, 164; French administration of, 29; migration to, 79; population of, 80
Constantine Plan (1954), 112
constitution of 1963, 59, 178; political parties under, 195; president under, 194; suspended, 60, 179, 192
constitution of 1976, 180, 192–93; armed forces under, 272; freedom of expression under, 219; judiciary under, 200;

321

political parties under, 195; promulgated, 61; revisions to, 193
constitution of 1989, xxix, 63, 185, 192, 193; divisive issues in, 193; labor under, 282; political parties under, 196–97, 282; president under, 194, 257; suspended, 206; women under, 63
construction industry, 151–52; neglect of, 136
consumer goods: imports of, 138, 169; shortages of, 62, 247
Coordinating Directorate of Territorial Security, 280
cotton: production of, 24
Coty, Réné, 52
Council of Carthage (256), 10
Council of Ministers, 60, 255, 257
Council of the Revolution, 60, 178–80, 194, 195, 204, 254; eliminated, 204; members of, 60, 254–55
coups d'état: of 1958, 52; of 1965, 60, 131, 178, 192, 254; of 1992, xxx, 64, 175, 176, 188, 196, 198, 237, 206, 230
coups d'état, attempted, 179, 245, 254
courts, 280–81; antiterrorist, 281; Chamber of Accusation, 201; military, 189, 201, 281; provincial, 201; secular, 198–99; sharia, 91, 198–99; state security, 281; tribunal, 201
Couscous Revolt. *See* Black October
Crédit Populaire d'Algérie. *See* Popular Credit of Algeria
Crémieux, Adolphe, 30–31
Crémieux Decrees (1870), 31, 111
criminal justice system (*see also* judicial system; courts), 280–83
crops, 157–58
CRUA. *See* Revolutionary Committee of Unity and Action
cultural revolution (1970), 99
currency, 137–38; devaluation of, xxxiv, 138, 171

Dahra massif: Berbers in, 82
Darlan, Jean Louis, 40
debt, external, 136–37, 171; amount of, xxxv, 136, 137; attempts to reschedule, xxxv
debt payments, xxxiv, 136–37
debt rescheduling, 137; with London Club, xxxv; with Paris Club, xxxv

debt servicing, 136–37, 170, 171
Decatur, Stephen, 22
defense spending, 136, 270–72
de Gaulle, Charles, 41, 51, 52–54
de Lamoricière, Louis, 26
Délégation Générale de Documentation et Sûreté. *See* General Delegation for Documentation and Security
Democratic Union of the Algerian Manifesto (Union Démocratique duManifeste Algérien—UDMA), 42; support for, 45
democratization, 184–88
demonstrations. *See* political demonstrations
Denmark: war with, 22
Derradji, Tayeb, 259
dey, 20
DGDS. *See* General Delegation for Documentation and Security
Didouch, Mourad, 44
Diocletian, 10
Directions des Infrastructures de Base. *See* Directorates for Basic Infrastructures
Directorates for Basic Infrastructures (Directions des Infrastructures de Base), 163
Distrigaz, 147
divorce, 105
Djafar al Afghani (*see also* Mourad Sid Ahmed), xxxii
Djanet oasis, 86
Djendjene: port of, 163
Djenouhat, Mohamed, 259
Djouadi, Abdelhamid, 259
Donatist controversy, 10
drought, 153; of 1866, 31; of 1994, xxxiv

earthquakes: of 1989, xxxiv
EC. *See* European Community
economic austerity measures, xxxvii, 132, 136
economic development, 132; plans, 129–30
economic plans, 130–31; First Five-Year (1980–84), 61, 131, 151–52, 156; First Four-Year (1970–73), 131; First Three-Year (1967–69), 131; Second Five-Year (1985–89), 122, 131, 151–52, 156–57; Second Four-Year (1974–77), 118, 131; Third Five-Year (1990–94), 131

Index

economic policy: factors influencing, 132

economic reform, xxix, xxxiv, 132–34; under Benjedid, 61, 62–63, 130, 183, 184, 229

economy: under Ben Bella, 129; decline of, 62; liberalization of, xxviii–xxiv, 131, 132, 139, 175, 181–84, 205, 223; prehistoric, 5; role of government in, 131–34; socialist, 129, 130

Edjeleh oil fields, 145

education (*see also* schools), 112–18; Arabic in, 90, 112, 116; arabization in, 112–13, 115, 220, 221; of elite, 96–97; French as language of, 90, 112, 116, 232; under French rule, 33–34, 88, 112, 215; of girls, 100, 115; government responsibility for, 203; government spending on, 34, 69, 113, 136; importance of, 96–97, 100; postsecondary, 100, 115–16, 215; qualification for military officers, 268; reorganization of, 112–14; technical, 115; track system in, 114; vocational, 115; of women, 115, 215

Égalité, 41

Egypt: matériel from, 273; military training in, 262; relations with, 227

Eisenhower, Dwight D., 40

elections: candidates in, 194–95; of 1947, 43; of 1948, 43; of 1951, 43; of 1962, 177; of 1963, 178; of 1976, 180; of 1977, 180; of 1979, 180–81; of 1990, xxix, xxxv, 186, 196, 210, 248; of 1991, xxxv, 175, 188, 196, 197–98, 250, 255; postponed, 186, 188; rigged, 43; voter turnout at, 202

electoral law of 1990, 64

electoral system, 198

electric power, 149; hydro, 149; investment in, 139, 140; nuclear, 149; in rural areas, 149; solar, 149; subsidies for, 138

El Harrach prison, 283

elite class, 88, 175, 205–6; Berbers in, 88; education of, 96–97; factionalism in, 205; under French rule, 94; members of, 205; as percentage of population, 96; role of, in government, 196, 204

employment, 143–45; in agriculture, 152; growth of, 144; of women, 104, 143, 216

Enagas, 147

energy resources (*see also* electricity; *see also under individual energy sources*), 145–50; exports of, 179; hydroelectric, 149; nuclear, 149; solar, 149

English: broadcasts in, 167

Enterprises for Cement and Derivatives (Entreprises des Ciments et Dérives), 152

entrepreneurial class, 214

Entreprise Nationale de Production de Produits Pharmaceutiques. *See* National Enterprise for Production of Pharmaceuticals

Entreprises des Ciments et Dérives. *See* Enterprises for Cement and Derivatives

Entreprises Publiques Économiques. *See* Public Economic Enterprises

EPÉs. *See* Public Economic Enterprises

Erem mineral research, 148

Europe: guestworkers in, 143–44; health care professionals from, 120; relations with, 229; university study in, 116

Europe, Eastern: trade with, 168; university study in, 116

European Community (EC): economic aid from, 138; imports from, 157; loan from, 137; trade with, 168

European influence, 37

European settlers (*see also* colons), 23, 29, 93–94; exodus of, 86, 96, 129, 177; land owned by, 33; number of, 86, 93; origins of, 24, 31

European Union: loans from, xxxv

Évian Accords (1962), 54–55, 230

évolués, 34, 94; politics of, 45

exchange rate, 137–38, 139, 171

executive branch (*see also* president), 193–94

Exmouth, viscount, 22

exports (*see also under individual products*), 169–70, 224; of crops, 152, 170; to France, xxxvi, 167, 231; to Greece, 233; of hydrocarbons, 145, 167, 169, 170, 181, 229–30, 231, 233; to Italy, 233; of minerals, 149, 170; of natural gas, 134; to Turkey, 233; to United States, 229–30

External Delegation: formed, 44

"Face the Press" (*Face à la Presse*), 220

323

Algeria: A Country Study

families, 100–101; extended, 100, 121; kinship units in, 92; in War of Independence, 95
family code, 104–5, 111, 200, 209, 216–18
family planning, 105–6
family status law, 199; women under, 62, 199
famine, xxxiv, 31–32
Fanon, Frantz, 45–46
FAO. *See* United Nations Food and Agriculture Organization
farmers: urban migration by, 46; social structure of, 91
farming: changes in, 95
farms: cooperative, 61; state, 153–56
Fatimids, 13–14
Fédération des Élus Indigènes. *See* Federation of Elected Natives
Federation of Elected Natives (Fédération des Élus Indigènes—FÉI), 36, 38
FÉI. *See* Federation of Elected Natives
feminist groups, 111, 215
Ferphos iron and phosphate company, 148
Ferry, Jules, 32
FFS. *See* Front of Socialist Forces
finance, public, 134–42; decentralization of, 135; reform of, 25, 135
FIS. *See* Islamic Salvation Front
fishing, 160
flag, 26–27
FLN. *See* National Liberation Front
floods, 153
FMS. *See* United States Foreign Military Sales Program
food: imports of, 134, 169, 181; prices, 181; shortages of, 62, 132, 134, 181, 183, 247; subsidies for, 157
foreign assistance, 138; from Arab countries, 138; from European Union, xxxv; from France, xxxv, 138; from Italy, 138; from London Club, xxxv; from Paris Club, xxxv; from Spain, 138; from the United States, 230
Foreign Bank of Algeria (Banque Extérieure d'Algérie), 142
foreign debt. *See* debt, external
Foreign Legion, 54; atrocities committed by, 50; established, 25; number of troops in, 50
foreign military assistance, 272–77

foreign policy, 221–33
forestry, 153, 160; area of, 160; reforestation schemes in, 76, 160
forests: reduction of, 75
France: bilateral credit lines with, 137; blockade of Algiers by, xxviii, 22; café wars in, 45; dependency on, 230; economic aid from, xxxv, 138, 231; exports to, xxxvi, 149, 167, 231; guest-workers in, xxxvi, 35, 78, 143–44, 231–32; health care professionals from, 120; immigrants in, 78–79; influence of, xxxv–xxxvi; invasion by, xxviii, 22–23; intervention of, in Western Sahara, 231; Islamists in, 232, 249; matériel from, 273, 276; migration to, 78, 83, 93–94, 124, 231–32; military advisers from, 274–76; military training in, 262, 264, 274–75, 278; opposition in, to War of Independence, 53; refusal of, to recognize government-in-exile, 54; relations with, xxxvi, 230–33, 276; settlers from, 24, 94; terrorism in, 45, 53, 54; trade with, 18, 168; troops of, in War of Independence, 50
Free French, 40, 250
French citizenship, 86; conditions for, 30, 34; for *évolués*, 34; for Jews, 31, 40; for Muslims, 39
French Colonial Bank of Algeria, 134
French Communist Party, 36, 37
French language: broadcasts in, 90, 167, 232; education in, 112, 115, 116, 232; newspapers in, 220, 232
French rule (*see also* colonists), 3–4, 22–56, 93–94; administration under, 27; banking under, 142; colonization by, 27; education under, 33, 88, 112, 215; influence of, 3–4; judicial system under, 198; land distribution under, 23–24, 29–30; legacy of, 210–11; military rule under, 27–32; Muslims under, 29–30, 110; opposition to, xxviii, 24–25, 83–84, 249; rationale for, 23, 24; reform under, 41; social organization under, 96; taxes under, 33; tribal structure under, 29–30; urban migration under, 93; veiling under, 102, 215; women under, 215
Friends of the Manifesto and Liberty (Amis du Manifeste et de la Liberté—AML), 41

Index

Front des Forces Socialistes. *See* Front of Socialist Forces
Front de Libération Nationale. *See* National Liberation Front
Front Islamique du Salut. *See* Islamic Salvation Front
Front of Socialist Forces (Front des Forces Socialistes—FFS), xxix, xxx, 91, 186, 187, 250; in elections of 1990, 197; in elections of 1991, 188, 197, 250; formed, 59

gas, natural: export of, 134, 229–30, 231, 233; income from, xxix, 134–35, 147–48; liquefied, 147–48; prices, 231; reserves, 129, 147; subsidies for, 138
Gassi Touil gas field, 147
Gaz de France, 147
GDP. *See* gross domestic product
Gendarmerie Nationale. *See* National Gendarmerie
General Confederation of Algerian Economic Operators, 214
General Delegation for Documentation and Security (Delégation Générale de Documentation et Sûreté—DGDS), 280
generals' putsch (1961), 54–56
General Union of Algerian Merchants and Artisans, 214
General Union of Algerian Workers (Union Générale des Travailleurs Algériens—UGTA), 58, 144, 189
Genoa: raiders from, 14
geographic regions, 72–74; High Plateaus, 72; northeast, 73; Sahara, 73–74; Saharan Atlas, 72; the Tell, 72
geostrategic situation, 244–45
gerrymandering, 186–88, 198
Ghardaïa oasis, 84
Ghezaiel, Abbas, 257
Ghodbane, Chaabane, 264
Ghozali, Sid Ahmed, xxx, 64; in coup d'état of 1992, 64; as prime minister, 187, 188; resignation of, 190
Ghozali government, 187
GIA. *See* Armed Islamic Group
Giraud, Henri, 40
GNP. *See* gross national product
gold: trade in, 17
Gouvernement Provisionel de la République Algérienne. *See* Provisional Government of the Algerian Republic
government: Arabic as language of, 90, 221, 221; decentralization of, 69; crackdown on Islamists, 110–11, 208, 248–49; press under, 219; role of, in economy, 131–34, 177; structure of, 176, 193–95, 204–5; women in, 218
government, local, 202–3; under Boumediene, 202; commune, 203; *dawair*, 203; decentralization of, 202; in Kabylie, 83; municipal, 203; *wilayat*, 202–3
government revenue, 135–36; from hydrocarbons, 135
government spending, 69, 136; on agriculture, 156; on defense, 270
GPRA. *See* Provisional Government of the Algerian Republic
grain: imports, 157; production, 157
Grand Erg Oriental (Great Eastern Erg), 73, 74
Grand Erg Occidental (Great Western Erg), 74
Grande Kabylie, 72
Grand Mosque of Córdoba, 15
Grand Mosque of Tilimsan, 15
Greater Maghrib, 223
Great Eastern Erg. *See* Grand Erg Oriental
Great Western Erg. *See* Grand Erg Occidental
Greece: relations with, 233
gross domestic product (GDP): growth rate, xxxiv
gross domestic product fractions: agriculture, 134, 152–53; health care, 119; hydrocarbons, 145; industry, 151; manufacturing, 134
gross national product (GNP): defense spending as percentage of, 270, 271
Groupe Islamique Armée. *See* Armed Islamic Group
Guénaizia, Abdelmalek, 257
guestworkers, xxxvi, 35, 78, 224, 231–32; remittances by, 143, 144, 170
Guinea-Bissau: support for revolutionaries in, 226

Hafsids, 16, 19
Hammadids, 13
Hamrouche, Mouloud, 187
harkis, 50, 78
Hasfids, 17

325

Hassan ibn Khair ad Din, 19
Hassan II, 242
Hassi Messaoud oil field, 145, 147, 148
Hassi R'Mel gas field, 147, 148
Haut Conseil de Sûreté. *See* High Security Council
Haut Conseil d'État. *See* High Council of State
Hauts Plateaux. *See* High Plateaus
HCÉ. *See* High Council of State
health, 118–21
health care: access to, 118–19; spending on, 69, 119
health care professionals, 18; in armed forces, 267; foreign, 120–21; number of, 120; training of, 120
health care system: organization of, 119; reorganization of, 118
health facilities, 119
High Council of State (Haut Conseil d'État—HCÉ), xxvii, 192, 200, 206–7, 255, 257; formed, 64, 189, 237, 257; intelligence activities of, 280
High Judicial Council, 194, 200, 201–2
High Plateaus (Hauts Plateaux), 72, 75
High Security Council (Haut Conseil de Sûreté), xxvii, xxx, 188, 207, 257
hijackers: landing clearance for, 229
Hilton Hotels, 143
Hippo Regius, 7, 10, 11
Horizons, 220
Horne, Alistair, 56
hotels, 143
Houari Boumediene University of Science and Technology, 115–16
households, 100–101
housing, 121–24; in abandoned properties, 121–22, 151; construction, xxxv, 122–23, 272; demand for, 152; under economic plans, 122; investment in, 123; in Kabylie region, 124; policies, 151–52; in rural areas, 80, 123, 124; shortage, xxxv, 69, 94, 121, 122–23, 136, 151, 152; in urban areas, 81, 94, 123–24
Hussein Dey, 23
hydrocarbon industry (*see also* oil; petroleum), 129, 145–48, 164; attempt to diversify, 135; exports by, 145, 167, 169, 170, 170, 181; investment in, 139; nationalized, 230; as percentage of gross domestic product, 145; prices in,
134; processing, 150; restructuring of, 147; revenue from, 135

Ibero-Maurusian culture, 5
Ibn Rushd (Averroes), 16
imams, 12–13, 208
Imazighen. *See* Berbers, Kabyle
IMET. *See* International Military Education and Training
IMF. *See* International Monetary Fund
imports: agricultural, 157; of consumer goods, 138, 169; controls on, 169; demand for, 170; of food, 134, 169, 181; of industrial goods, 169; liberalization of, 139–40, 170
income: per capita, 69
independence, 55, 56–57, 129, 175, 177; interest in, 41
indigenization: in education, 112–13
industrialization, 181; under Boumediene, 97, 179, 205
industry, 150–52; under Ben Bella, 178; under Boumediene, 179; emphasis on, 131, 132, 136; government role in, 177–78, 203; imports by, 169; nationalized, 130, 179; as percentage of gross domestic product, 151; prehistoric, 5; restructuring in, 151
infant mortality, 118
inflation, xxxiv, 196
infrastructure: development of, 136, 238
intelligence agencies (*see also under individual agencies*), 189, 245–46, 279–80
Inter-Air Services, 166
internal security, 277–84
Intelsat. *See* International Telecommunications Satellite Corporation
International Atomic Energy Agency, 277
International Finance Corporation: membership in, 140
International Military Education and Training (IMET), 276
International Monetary Fund (IMF): loans from, xxxiv–xxxv; standby agreement with, 137, 138, 170
International Telecommunications Satellite Corporation (Intelsat), 167
International Women's Day, 215
investment, 139–42; and banking, 142; liberalized, 139, 182; in manufacturing, 151; priorities for, 139; spending,

Index

136; in tourism, 139, 143
investment, foreign, 132, 140, 171, 182; objectives of, 140; regulation of, 140–42
Iran: release of hostages from, 207, 230
Iran-Iraq War, 228
Iraq: invasion of Kuwait by, 222, 228, 241; support for, 228
irrigation, 33, 153, 157
iron, 129; deposits, 148; exports of, 169, 170; mines, 149; mining, 148
Islam, 11–17, 106–11; conversion to, 12–13, 107; government role in, 209, 247; history of, 107–8; identification with, 107, 207; impact of, xxvii; introduction of, 3, 108; legal schools of, 91; mystical, 17; proselytizing in, 109–10; role of, xxxiii, 178; as state religion, xxxiii; tenets of, 108–9; worship in, 109
Islam, Ibadi, 12, 84, 91, 108
Islam, Ibadi Khariji, 12; refugees, 13
Islam, Ismaili Shia, 13
Islam, Shia, 108
Islam, Sufi, xxxiii
Islam, Sunni, 107–8, 249
Islamic brotherhoods, 108
Islamic fundamentalists. *See* Islamists
Islamic Jihad, 241
Islamic law, Maliki, 16, 91, 249
Islamic reform movement, 37
Islamic schools, 37, 91
Islamic Salvation Army (Armée Islamique du Salut—AIS), xxxi–xxxii
Islamic Salvation Front (Front Islamique du Salut—FIS), xxvii, xxix, 187; agitation by, 64; banned, xxx, 64, 189, 207, 248, 249, 255–56; in elections of 1990, 186, 197, 210, 248; in elections of 1991, 188, 237, 197, 255; founded, 63; origins of, 110; platform of, xxxiv, 209–10; role of, 209–10; support for, 99, 175
Islamism, 207–10; rise of, xxxvi, 207–8, 232, 255
Islamist groups: appeal of, xxix, xxxiii, 175, 208–9; attacks by, on Berbers, xxxii; counterattacks on, xxxii; distribution of, 259; government crackdowns on, 110–11, 189–90, 237, 208, 232, 248–49, 256, 282; Libyan support for, 244; origins of, 110; political opposition by, 247–49; proliferation of, xxxiv, 110, 208, 248; social programs of, 208; terrorist activities of, xxxii, 189, 190, 191, 237, 247, 256
Islamists, xxvii, 191; arrested, xxx, 187, 189, 200, 248, 282, 283; in elections of 1990, xxxv, 175; in France, 232; goals of, 69; influence of, 62; number of, xxxiii; opposition to, 189, 224, 268; protests by, 62
Islamization, 11–17
Israel, 240
Italy: bilateral credit lines with, 137; economic aid from, 138; exports to, 233; matériel from, 264–65; relations with, 233; settlers from, 24, 94; trade with, 18, 168

janissaries, 19–20
Japan: bilateral credit lines with, 137
Jaurès, Jean, 33
Jeune Afrique, 280
Jeunesse Algérienne. *See* Young Algerians
Jews (*see also* Judaism): arrival of, 10; exodus of, 55, 86, 111–12; French citizenship for, 31, 40; under Islam, 11, 110; number of, 111; as refugees, 55; from Spain, 17
jihad: of Abd al Qadir, 25–26
joint ventures, 132, 139, 168
Jonnart, Charles: as governor general, 35
Jonnart Reforms (1919), 35–36
Jordan: relations with, 227
journalists (*see also* media; press): arrested, 220; role of, 219, 220
journalists' associations, 63, 219
Journal Officiel, 135
Judaism (*see also* Jews): Berber conversion to, 10, 108
judges, 200
judicial system, 198–202
Justinian, 11

Kabyle language, 87, 116; broadcasts in, 167
Kabyle people. *See* Berbers, Kabyle
Kabylie Mountains, 73; Berbers in, 82; population in, 81
Kabylie region, 16, 249; electricity generation in, 149; French administration of, 32; housing in, 124; migrants from,

327

78; villages in, 83; and War of Independence, 83
Kabylie revolts, xxviii, 31-32, 83-84
Kafi, Ali, xxx, 207; as head of state, 190, 207
Khair ad Din (Barbarossa), xxvii, 19
Khalid ibn Hashim, 36
Kharijites, 12
Khemisti, Fatima, 215
Khemisti Law (1963), 215-16
Khider, Mohamed, 44, 56; corruption by, 58; exiled, 58; murdered, 246
Krim, Belkacem, 44; murdered, 246
Ksour massif, 72
Kusayla, 12
Kuwait: Iraq's invasion of, 222, 241

labor movement: growth of, 212
labor unions, 45, 145, 171, 211-12
Lacoste, Robert, 47; new administrative structure under, 47
Laghouat oasis, 72
Lamari, Mohamed, 190
Lamtuna tribe, 14
land: abandoned, 153; arable, 129, 153; area, 69, 129; erosion, xxxiv; French acquisition of, 23-24, 32, 93, 153; legislation, 123; nationalized, 213; ownership, 30, 93, 153; privatized, 182; redistribution of, 61, 98, 153, 156, 214
land reform, 153-57; under Tripoli Program, 56
land tenure, 153-57; under French rule, 29-30
land use, 81, 153
language (*see also under individual languages*): dual system of, 87
law: secular, 201; sharia, 201, 281
Law on Money and Credit (1990), 135, 139
Law on Trade Union Activity (1990), 145, 171
Law Relative to Political Associations (1989), 197
lawyers, 281
lawyers' associations, 63
lead, 148; mines, 149
League of Arab States (Arab League), 227
Lebanon: relations with, 227
legal system: defendants in, 200; revised, 199

legislative branch, 194-95; reforms in, 194
Le Soir d'Algérie (Algerian Evening), 220
Libya: disputes with, 241; matériel of, 244; as member of Union of the Arab Maghreb, xxxvi, 223, 241; invasion by, of Chad, 244; navy of, 244, 263; relations with, 225-26, 243-44, 260; support by, for Islamist groups, 244; trade with, 168-69
literacy: programs, 116-118; rate, 87, 116, 118
livestock, 93, 158-60; cattle, 158; goats, 158; grazing, 153; poultry, 158; sheep, 158
Loi d'Orientation Foncière (land legislation) (1990), 123
London Club: loan from, xxxv
Louis Napoleon (*see also* Napoleon III), 26
Louis Philippe: accession of, 23

Madani, Abbassi, xxx, xxxi, 63, 209; arrested, 64, 187, 282
Maghrib, 3, 69; Islamism in, xxxvi; migration to, 17; prehistoric inhabitants of, 4-5; relations within, 222-26; role in, xxxvi; Spanish influence on, 18
Maghrib, Greater, 223
Maghrib Permanent Consultative Committee, 223
Malek, Redha, xxvii, xxx, 191, 207
Malek government, xxx; anti-terrorist activities of, xxxii; talks by, with terrorists, xxx
Mali: border conflicts with, 226
Maliki law. *See* Islamic law, Maliki
Manifesto of the Algerian People (1943), 40-41
manufacturing, 132, 148, 151; under French rule, 33; government emphasis on, 134; investment in, 151; as percentage of gross domestic product, 134
marabouts, 17, 25, 93, 108; cults of, 17; influence of, xxxiii, 17
March Decrees (1963), 57-58
Marrakech, 15
marriage: age for, 102, 216-18; agreements, 101; contracts, 101; laws, 101; women in, 105

Index

martial law, xxvii, xxx, 176, 186, 282–83; individual freedom under, 200
Masinissa, 7
mass associations, 63, 211
Massu, Jacques, 50, 52
matériel, 238; air force, 262, 263; army, 261; from Britain, 264, 274, 276–77; from China, 264, 273, 277; diversity of, 274; from Eastern Europe, 274; from Egypt, 273; from France, 273, 274, 276; from Germany, 274; from Italy, 264; navy, 264; procurement of, 272; from the Soviet Union, 238, 240, 261, 262, 263, 264, 272–74; from the United States, 263, 274, 276
Maternal and Infant Protection Centers (PMICS), 106
Mauritania, 7; border dispute with, 226, 245; as member of Union of the Arab Maghreb, xxxvi, 223, 241; relations with, 224; as signatory of Treaty of Fraternity and Concord, 223; trade with, 168–69
May Day demonstrations (1945), 41–42
MDA. *See* Movement for Democracy in Algeria
Medeghri, Ahmed, 60
Médéa: founded, 13
media (*see also* journalists; press): restrictions on, 220
Médiène, Mohamed, 279
men, 101–4; in population, 76, 77; social organization of, 100
Mendès-France, Pierre, 44–45
merchant class, 94
Merinids, 17
Mers el Kebir: Spanish conquest of, 18
Messadia, Mohamed Cherif, 185
Messali Hadj, Ahmed, 36–37; arrested, 43; French view of, 38; opposition of, to Ben Bella, 58; political parties of, 39, 41, 45
MIA. *See* Armed Islamic Movement
middle class: members of, 97–98; as percentage of population, 96
Middle East affairs, 227–28
migration, 78–79; to France, 78, 231–32; to urban areas, 46, 79
Miliana: founded, 13
military: academies, 262; advisers, 274–76; conscription, 240, 265–67; conscripts, 238, 259; heritage, 250–56; regions, 259; strategy, 26
military officers, 267; educational requirements of, 268; purge of, 256–57; ranks of, 269–70; reorganization of, xxxii, 257; training of, 261–62
military personnel, 265–68
military rule, 27–32, 206–7
Military Security (Sécurité Militaire), 245–46, 277–78, 279–80
military training, 264; of foreign soldiers, 239; in foreign countries, 261–62, 264, 274–76
millet system, 20
minerals, 148–49; investment in, 139
Minimum Activity Wage (Salaire Minimum d'Activité), 144
mining, 148–49; under French rule, 33
Ministry of Agriculture and Fishing, 116, 213
Ministry of Algerian Affairs (France), 29
Ministry of Energy and Petrochemical Industries, 116
Ministry of Finance, 135
Ministry of Higher Education, 114
Ministry of Information, 219
Ministry of Interior, Local Communities, and Tourism, 163, 254, 264, 279
Ministry of National Defense, 270
Ministry of National Education, 114
Ministry of Planning: abolished, 131
Ministry of Public Health, 105
Ministry of Public Works, 163; Airport Directorate, 164
Ministry of Religious Affairs, 110, 208, 247
Ministry of Transport, 161, 163
minorities, religious, 111–12
missions, Christian, 111; schools of, 114
Mitidja Plain, 72
Mitterrand, François, 44, 276
MNA. *See* National Algerian Movement
modernization, 98; cultural conflict caused by, 98
Money and Credit Council: duties of, 139; financial management by, 135; members of, 139
Moors, 92
Morice, André, 50
Morice Line, 50–51
Morocco: air force of, 244; army of, 244; attempt by, to annex Western Sahara, 270, 273, 276; border disputes with,

329

Algeria: A Country Study

222, 252; border treaty with, 242; captured by Almohads, 15; disputes with, 241; as member of Union of the Arab Maghreb, xxxvi, 223, 241; military support for, 239; navy of, 263; relations with, 222, 224–25, 241–43; trade with, 168–69; war with, 22, 252
mosques: government-controlled, 110
Mostaganem: port of, 163; Spanish conquest of, 18
Mouvement Islamique Armée. *See* Armed Islamic Movement
Mouvement National Algérien. *See* National Algerian Movement
Mouvement pour la Démocratie en Algérie. *See* Movement forDemocracy in Algeria
Mouvement pour le Triomphe des Libertés Démocratiques. *See* Movement for the Triumph of Democratic Liberties
Movement for Democracy in Algeria (Mouvement pour la Démocratie en Algérie—MDA), xxix, 186, 228, 249
Movement for the Triumph of Democratic Liberties (Mouvement pour le Triomphe des Libertés Démocratiques—MTLD), 42; end of, 45
Mozambique: support for revolutionaries in, 226, 239
MTLD. *See* Movement for the Triumph of Democratic Liberties
Mubarak, Husni, 227
Muhammad (prophet), 108–9
Muhammad ibn Abdallah ibn Tumart, 15
Muhyi ad Din, 25
Muslims (*see also* Islam): conversion of, in Spain, 17; definition of, 108; duties of, 109; under French rule, 29–30, 49; suffrage of, 52; taxes on, 109; worship by, 109
Muslim courts. *See* courts, sharia
Mzab, 74

Namibia: support for revolutionaries in, 226
Naples: war with, 22
Napoleon III (*see also* Louis Napoleon), 29–30; decree of 1863, 29–30; decree of 1865, 30
Nasser, Gamal Abdul, 44

National Algerian Movement (Mouvement National Algérien—MNA), 45
National Assembly: dissolved, 57, 60, 64, 179
National Association of Cork and Wood Industries (Société Nationale des Industries des Lièges et du Bois), 160
National Bank of Algeria (Banque Nationale d'Algérie), 142
National Charter (1976), 61, 179, 192–93, 195, 204; foreign policy under, 222; gender equality under, 216
National Committee for the Defense of the Revolution (Comité National pour la Défense de la Révolution—CNDR), 59
National Committee on Population, 106
National Company for Electricity and Gas (Société Nationale de l'Électricité et du Gaz—Sonelgaz), 149
National Company for Mechanical Construction (Société Nationale de Constructions Mécaniques), 151
National Company for Mineral Research and Exploration (Société Nationale de Recherches et d'Exploitations Minières), 148
National Company for Research, Production, Transportation, Processing, and Commercialization of Hydrocarbons (Société Nationale pour la Recherche, la Production, le Transport, la Transformation, et la Commercialisation des Hydrocarbures—Sonatrach), 147, 148, 168; formed, 132; joint ventures of, 139
National Consultative Council (Conseil Consultatif National—CCN), 192, 207
National Corporation for Maritime Transport and the Algerian National Navigation Company (Société Nationale de Transports Maritimes et Compagnie Nationale Algérienne de Navigation—SNTM-CNAN), 163
National Council of the Algerian Revolution (Conseil National dela Révolution Algérienne—CNRA), 47
National Enterprise for Production of Pharmaceuticals (Entreprise Nationale de Production de Produits Pharmaceutiques), 168
National Fund for Provident Savings

Index

(Caisse Nationale d'Épargne et de Prévoyance), 142
National Gendarmerie (Gendarmerie Nationale), 238, 256, 257, 274–76, 277, 278
National Guaranteed Minimum Wage (Salaire National Minimum Garanti), 144
national identity, 88
nationalism, 34–39
nationalist movement, 34–39; leaders of, 34–35
nationalization: of abandoned property, 153; of agriculture, 130, 179; under Benjedid, 130; under Boumediene, 179; of industry, 130, 179; in March Decrees, 57–58; of news media, 219; under Tripoli Program, 56
National Liberation Army (Armée de Libération Nationale—ALN), 250; areas controlled by, 49; chief of staff of, 252; creation of, xxviii; factions in, 49; guerrilla warfare by, 48–49, 53; matériel of, 251; number of troops in, 251; organization of, 48, 250–51; training of, 251
National Liberation Front (Front de Libération Nationale—FLN), 44, xxx, 45–46, 55, 131; armed forces in, 237; under Benjedid, 196; under Boumediene, 179, 204; under constitution of 1989, 196; creation of, xxviii; in elections of 1990, 196; in elections of 1991, 188, 196; factions in, 49, 56, 187, 195; government-in-exile of, 52–53, 177; labor unions under, 212; as political elite, 205; political power of, 176, 178; popular aversion to, 195–96; role of, 195–97; in War of Independence, 44, 49, 195; workers under, 212
National Liberation Front Central Committee, 193, 205–6
National Liberation Front Party Congress, 61, 205
National Office to Promote Prefabricated Construction (Office National de la Promotion de la Construction en Préfabriqué), 152
National People's Assembly (Assemblée Populaire Nationale—APN), 104, 180, 194–95; suspended, 189, 195; women in, 216

National Railroad Transportation Company (Société Nationale des Transports Ferroviaires—SNTF), 161
National Transitional Council (Conseil National de Transition—CNT), xxxii
National Union of Algerian Farmers (Union Nationale des Paysans Algériens—UNPA), 213–14
National Union of Algerian Students (Union Nationale des Étudiants Algériens—UNÉA), 212; dissolved, 213
National Union of Algerian Youth (Union Nationale de la Jeunesse Algérienne—UNJA), 213
National Union of Algerian Women (Union Nationale des Femmes Algériennes—UNFA), 215
NATO. *See* North Atlantic Treaty Organization
natural resources, 145–50
naval academy, 264
navy, 256, 263–65; bases of, 264; fleet of, 238, 263; insignia, ranks, and uniforms, 265; matériel, 264; modernization of, 263; training, 264
Neolithic civilization, 5
Nerva, 8
Netherlands: trade with, 18; war with, 22
newspapers (*see also* journalists): banned, 188
Nezzar, Khaled, xxx, 255, 256, 256, 257, 267, 269; in coup of 1992, 188
Niger: border conflicts with, 226; military support for, 239
North Atlantic Treaty Organization (NATO), 53
Nuclear Non-Proliferation Treaty, 277
Numidia, 7, 10

OAS. *See* Secret Army Organization
oases, 72
OAU. *See* Organization of African Unity
Occidental Petroleum Corporation, 168
Office National de la Promotion de la Construction en Préfabriquée. *See* National Office to Promote Prefabricated Construction
oil (*see also* hydrocarbons; petroleum), 145–47; exploration, 146–47; exports of, 229–30; income from, xxix, 134–35; price crash, xxix, 62, 69, 132, 135,

331

170, 181, 184, reserves, 129, 146
ojaq. See janissaries
One Thousand Socialist Villages program, 123, 156
OPEC. *See* Organization of the Petroleum Exporting Countries
Operation Torch (1942), 40
Oran: airport of, 164; electricity generation at, 149; French administration of, 29; migration to, 79; population of, 80; port of, 163; Spanish conquest of, 18
Oranian culture, 5
Organic Statute of Algeria (1947), 43
Organisation de l'Armée Secrète. *See* Secret Army Organization
Organisation Spéciale. *See* Special Organization
Organization of African Unity (OAU), 225, 226, 239
Organization of the Petroleum Exporting Countries (OPEC): production quotas, 146
OS. *See* Special Organization
Ottoman rule, xxvii, 3, 19–21; massacre of 1860 under, 26; social organization under, 91–93; opposition to, 249
Ouarsenis massif: Berbers in, 82
Oujda Group, 57, 60
Oulad Naïl massif, 72
Overseas Private Investment Corporation, 140

PAGS. *See* Socialist Vanguard Party
Palestine Liberation Organization, 227, 241
Palestinian nationalists, 227, 240
Palestinian terrorists, 240–41
Panhandle, 147
Paris Club: debt rescheduling with, xxxv
Parti Communiste Algérien. *See* Algerian Communist Party
Parti de la Révolution Socialiste. *See* Socialist Revolution Party
Parti de l'Avant-Garde Socialiste. *See* Socialist Vanguard Party
Parti du Peuple Algérien. *See* Party of the Algerian People
Party of the Algerian People (Parti du Peuple Algérien—PPA), 37, 41–42; formed, 39
PCA. *See* Algerian Communist Party

People's National Army (Armée Nationale Populaire—ANP). *See* armed forces
Pfizer, 168
Philippeville massacre (1955), 46–48
Phoenicians, 7, 249
phosphate, 129, 149; exports of, 149, 169, 170
physicians' associations, 63
pieds noirs. See colonists
Pisa: raiders from, 14
PLO. *See* Palestine Liberation Organization
PMICS. *See* Maternal and Infant Protection Centers
Polisario. *See* Popular Front for the Liberation of Saguia el Hamra and Río de Oro
political: activity, 216, 218; associations, 182; culture, 176–77; elite, 175; liberalization, 132, 175, 181–84, 200, 223, 229, 282; movements, 35–38; participation, 184; reform, 63, 175, 176, 184, 192, 282; unrest, xxix, 132; violence, xxxi, 212
Political Bureau (Bureau Politique), 56–57; abolished, 60; formed, 56, 195; members of, 255
political demonstrations, 247–48; of 1945, 41–42; of 1952, 43; of 1990, 64; of 1991, 186, 268; of 1992, xxx; by students, 62, 90, 213, 247; by women, 104, 216, 218
political parties (*see also under individual parties*): of Berbers, xxix; under Boumediene, 195; under constitution of 1963, 195; legalized, 90–91, 186, 193, 196–98, 200, 208, 209, 211, 214, 282; proliferation of, xxix, 193, 197, 208, 211, 214; role of, 195–98
political power: contention for, 177; distribution of, 176
political protest, 38; against Islamists, 189; by women, xxxii
politics: postindependence, 176–77
Popular Credit of Algeria (Crédit Populaire d'Algérie), 142
Popular Front for the Liberation of Saguia el Hamra and Río de Oro—Polisario), 224, 242; support for, 225–26, 242
Popular Wilaya Assembly (Assemblée

Populaire de Wilaya—APW), 202–3
population, 76–81; age distribution in, 77; of Algiers, 79–80; of Annaba, 80; of Batna, 80; of Berbers, 84; of Blida, 80; class distribution in, 96; of Constantine, 80; density, 79–81; distribution of, 81, 244; of European settlers, 86, 93; of Jews, 111; of men, 76, 77; in 1954, 76; in 1966, 76; in 1990, 76; in 1993, 76, 129; projected, 76; of Sétif, 80; urban, 91; of women, 76, 77
population fractions: in agriculture, 153; Berbers, 82, 249; elite class, 96; middle class, 96; Roman Catholics, 111; rural, 153
population statistics: birth rate, 77; death rate, 77; fertility rate, 77; growth rate, xxxv, 76–77, 80, 105, 106, 121, 132, 134, 157, 181; infant mortality rate, 118; life expectancy, 77
ports, 161, 162–63; improvements in, 163
Portugal: trade with, 18
PPA. *See* Party of the Algerian People
prehistory, 4–5; people in, 5
president (*see also* executive branch), 193–94; as commander in chief, 256
press (*see also* journalists; media; newspapers), 189, 218–20; censorship of, 219; function of, 219; government control of, 219; nationalization of, 219; restrictions on, 220
prices: controls on, 69, 182–83; food, 181; increases in, xxxiv, 132, 247
prisoners, 283; escape by, xxxii
prison camps, 189, 283–84
prisons: conditions in, 283–84
privateering, 17, 18–19; organization of, 18–19; purposes of, 18
privateers, xxvii–xxviii, 18–19, 92; income of, 19; influence of, 19, 20; tribute demanded by, 21
private sector: trade, 170
privatization, 182, 214
Programme d'Emploi des Jeunes. *See* Youth Employment Program
professional associations, 45
Provisional Government of the Algerian Republic (Gouvernement Provisionel de la République Algérienne—GPRA), 52–53, 177, 252; recognition of, 53, 54

PRS. *See* Socialist Revolution Party
Prussia: war with, 22
Public Economic Enterprises (Entreprises Publiques Économiques—EPÉs), 131
Punic Wars, 7

radio, 167; censorship of, 219
Rahim, Khelifa, 259
railroads, 161–62; investment in, 139
Rally for Culture and Democracy, 91
Red Beard. *See* Khair ad Din
Red Brigades: military support for, 240
reform: under French rule, 41
refugees: from Andalus, 92; under Fatimids, 13; under French, 31; from sub-Saharan Africa, 245; from War of Independence, 55
regroupement program, 51, 56, 84, 95
religion (*see also under individual sects*): of Berbers, 10
religious brotherhoods, 25
religious minorities, 111–12
religious unrest, 37
Republican Guard Brigade, 278
Revolt of the Mercenaries (341–238 B.C.), 7
revolutionaries: support for, 222, 226, 237, 239, 242–43
Revolutionary Committee of Unity and Action (Comité Révolutionnaire d'Unité et d'Action—CRUA) (*see also* National Liberation Front), 44
Rhourd en Nous gas field, 147
Rida, Muhammad Rashid, 37
riots: of 1988, 130
Road of African Unity, 164
roads, 161, 163–64
Roman Catholic Church. *See* Catholic Church, Roman
Roman rule, xxvii, 3, 8–10; decline of, 8, 11; opposition to, 8, 249, 250
royaume arabe, 29–30
Ruedy, John, 24, 56
rural areas: electricity in, 149; families in, 101; under French rule, 24; housing in, 80, 123, 124; kinship units in, 92; police in, 238; population in, 153; religion in, 17; social organization in, 91, 92, 96; taxes in, 21; women in, 104; workers in, 98
Russia (*see also* Soviet Union): health

Algeria: A Country Study

care professionals from, 120; military training in, 264; war with, 22
Rustumid imamate, 12

Saddam Husayn, 228
SADR. *See* Saharan Arab Democratic Republic
Saharan Arab Democratic Republic (SADR) (*see also* Western Sahara), 225
Sahara Atlas range, 72, 75
Sahara Desert, 73; Berbers in, 82; *erg*, 73
Sahnoun, Ahmed, 62
Salaire Minimum d'Activité. *See* Minimum Activity Wage
Salaire National Minimum Garanti. *See* National Guaranteed Minimum Wage
Salan, Raoul, 50–51, 52
Sanhaja, 13, 14
SAS. *See* Special Administration Section
schools: enrollments in, 112, 114–5; under French rule, 33; Islamic, 37; mission, 114; number of, 115; private, 114; religious, xxxiv, 33, 87, 91; technical, 115; vocational, 115
Second Republic, 179–81, 193
Secretariat of State for Planning, 131
Secret Army Organization (Organisation de l'Armée Secrète—OAS), 54, 55
Secret Organization for Safeguarding the Algerian Republic, xxxii
Section Administrative Spécialisée. *See* Special Administration Section
Sécurité Militaire. *See* Military Security
security concerns: global, 239–41; and individual freedom, 200
security, domestic, 245–50
security, external, 238–45; under Ben Bella, 239; under Boumediene, 239–40
service sector, 142–43
Sétif: population of, 80
shantytowns, 122, 124
shipping, 162
shurfa, 92–93
Sicily: raiders from, 14
Sifi, Mokdad, xxvii
Sivard, Ruth Leger, 271
Skikda, 73; port of, 163
slavery: under Arab rule, 12, 92; of foreign sailors, 21, 92
slaves: trade in, 17
SNTF. *See* National Railroad Transportation Company
SNTM-CNAN. *See* National Corporation for Maritime Transport and the Algerian National Navigation Company
social classes (*see also under individual classes*): formation of, 3; system of, 96–97
socialism, 131–32, 175, 176–77, 178–81
Socialist Revolution Party (Parti de la Révolution Socialiste—PRS), 58
Socialist Vanguard Party (Parti de l'Avant-Garde Socialiste—PAGS), 214
social services, 136; by Islamist groups, 208
social structure, 91–99, 210–11
social unrest, 63
Société Nationale de Constructions Mécaniques. *See* National Company for Mechanical Construction
Société Nationale de l'Électricité et du Gaz—Sonelgaz. *See* National Company for Electricity and Gas
Société Nationale de Recherches et d'Exploitations Minières. *See* National Company for Mineral Research and Exploration
Société Nationale des Industries des Lièges et du Bois. *See* National Association of Cork and Wood Industries
Société Nationale des Transports Ferroviaires. *See* National Railroad Transportation Company
Société Nationale de Transports Maritimes et Compagnie Nationale Algérienne de Navigation. *See* National Corporation for Maritime Transport and the Algerian National Navigation Company
Société Nationale pour la Recherche, la Production, le Transport, la Transformation, et la Commercialisation des Hydrocarbures. *See* National Company for Research, Production, Transportation, Processing, and Commercialization of Hydrocarbons
Sofitel hotel chain, 143
Sonatrach. *See* National Company for Research, Production, Transportation, Processing, and Commercialization of Hydrocarbons
Soustelle, Jacques, 46, 52
Soustelle Plan (1955), 46

South Africa: support for revolutionaries in, 226, 239, 240
Southern Rhodesia: military support for, 240
South Vietnam. *See* Vietnam, Republic of
Soviet Union (*see also* Russia): matériel from, 238, 240, 261, 262, 263, 264, 272–74; military training in, 262
Spain (*see also* Andalus): bilateral credit lines with, 137; Christian reconquest of, 17; conquests by, 18; economic aid from, 138; exports to, 149; influence of, on Maghrib, 18; relations with, 233; settlers from, 24, 94; trade with, 18; war with, 22
Spanish Inquisition, 17
Spanish language: broadcasts in, 167
Special Administration Section (Section Administrative Spécialisée—SAS), 50
Special Organization (Organisation Spéciale—OS), 42–43; broken up, 44
Star. *See* Star of North Africa
Star of North Africa (Étoile Nord-Africain), 36, 39; banned, 36, 39; demands of, 36–37
state enterprises, 177–78, 203, 205; broken up, 61, 64, 182; privatized, 182, 214
state farms. *See* farms, state
state of emergency: of 1988, 184; of 1991, 64, 282–83; of 1992, 64, 176, 189, 192, 248, 255–56, 257
State Security Court, 281
steel: investment in, 139; production, 151
strikes, xxix, 145, 212, 121, 282; of 1988, 63, 183
strikes, general: of 1957, 49–50; of 1980, 90, 249; of 1990, 64, 187
student associations, 45, 63
student demonstrations, 62, 213, 247, 249–50; proarabization, 90
student unions, 212–13
students: increase in, xxxv; study abroad by, 116
subsidies: for food, 157; reduction of, 138, 182–83
suffrage. *See* voting
Süleyman the Magnificent, 19
Sultani, Abdelatif, 62
Superior Islamic Council, 247
Supplementary Finance Law (1990), 139–40
Supreme Court, 200–201
Sûreté Nationale, 277, 279
Sus, 15
Syria: military training in, 262; relations with, 227

taifa. *See* privateers
Takfir wal Hijra (Repentance and Holy Flight), 248
Tamanrasset, 81, 86
Tassili-n-Ajjer, 73; Berbers in, 84; cave paintings in, 4–5
taxes: under Almohad rule, 16; under Arab rule, 12; forms of, 135–36; under French rule, 33; Muslim, 109; revenues from, 136; in rural areas, 21
teachers, 114, 115
telecommunications, 166–67; international, 166–67; investment in, 140
telephones, 166, 167
television, 166, 167; censorship of, 219
Tell Atlas range, 72, 75; Berbers in, 82
Ténès: Spanish conquest of, 18
terrain, 75–76
terrorism, 229; casualties from, xxxi; in France, 45, 53, 54; government activities against, xxxii, 50, 191, 248–49; Islamist, xxx, xxxi–xxxii, 189, 190, 191, 237, 247, 256; pro-independence, 43, 47, 55; and veiling, xxxii
Tlemcen: Spanish conquest of, 18; under Zayanids, 16, 17
torture, 189, 280, 284
tourism, 142–43; decentralized, 143; government role in, 203; investment in, 139, 143
Tousmi, Cherif, xxxii
trade (*see also* exports; imports), 167–70, 231; account, 170; attempts to open, 132; deficit, 181; domestic, 84; European merchants in, 18; under French rule, 33; in gold, 17; liberalization of, 171, 182; partners, 168–69; private-sector, 170; in slaves, 17
Trajan, 8
transit, 3
transportation, 160–66; airports, 161; government role in, 203; infrastructure, 160–61; investment in, 140; modernization of, 161; ports, 161; railroads, 161; roads, 161; urban, 162

335

Treaty of Fraternity and Concord (1983), 223, 225, 226
treaty of 1797, 21
treaty of 1837, 25; broken, 25-26
treaty of 1989, 237
Treaty of Oudja (1984), 223, 226
tribes, 121; under French rule, 29-30; structure of, 29-30, 92-93
Tripoli: war with, 22
Tripoli Program (1962), 56, 58, 99, 177
Tunis: war with, 22
Tunisia: border dispute with, 245; as member of Union of the Arab Maghreb, xxxvi, 223, 241; relations with, 222, 225; as signatory of Treaty of Fraternity and Concord, 223; trade with, 168-69
Turkey: relations with, 233
Turkish language, 19

UDMA. See Democratic Union of the Algerian Manifesto
UNÉA. See National Union of Algerian Students
UGTA. See General Union of Algerian Workers
UMA. See Union of the Arab Maghrib
Umayyads, xxvii, 11, 12
underemployment, 144
unemployment, xxix, 57, 62, 69, 98, 99, 132, 144, 181, 182, 183, 196; compensation, 144
UNESCO. See United Nations Educational, Scientific, and Cultural Organization
UNFPA. See United Nations Fund for Population Activities
Union Démocratique du Manifeste Algérien. See Democratic Union of the Algerian Manifesto
Union du Maghreb Arabe. See Union of the Arab Maghrib
Union Générale des Travailleurs Algériens. See General Union of Algerian Workers
Union Nationale de la Jeunesse Algérienne. See National Union of Algerian Youth
Union Nationale des Étudiants Algériens. See National Union of Algerian Students
Union Nationale des Femmes Algériennes—UNFA. See National Union of Algerian Women
Union Nationale des Paysans Algériens. See National Union of Algerian Farmers
Union of Algerian Workers (Union Syndicale des TravailleursAlgériens), 45
Union of the Arab Maghrib (Union du Maghreb Arabe—UMA), xxxvi; formed, 241, 223-24, 226; members of, xxxvi, 138, 241; trade in, 168-69
Union Syndicale des Travailleurs Algériens. See Union of Algerian Workers
United Nations: and War of Independence, 48, 53; and Western Sahara, 224
United Nations Educational, Scientific, and Cultural Organization (UNESCO), 118
United Nations Food and Agriculture Organization (FAO), 158
United Nations Fund for Population Activities (UNFPA), 106
United States: aid from, 230; exports to, 229-30; imports from, 157; matériel from, 263, 276; military training in, 264; relations with, xxxvi, 21-22, 229-30; trade with, 168; university study in, 116; war with, 22
United States Foreign Military Sales Program, 276
universities, 115; enrollment in, 112, 116; women in, 100
University of Algiers, 115; Islamist movement at, 110-111, 247; system of, 116
University of Annaba, 115
University of Batna, 116
University of Blida, 116
University of Constantine, 115
University of Oran, 115
University of Science and Technology, 115
University of Sétif, 116
University of Sidi Bel Abbes, 115
University of Tizi Ouzou, 116, 221, 249
University of Tlemcen, 115
UNJA. See National Union of Algerian Youth
UNPA. See National Union of Algerian Farmers
Uqba ibn Nafi, 11

urban areas: families in, 101; housing in, 81, 123–24; Islam in, 108; organization of, 91–92; percentage of population in, 91
urbanization, 69, 79–81; and families, 101; pace of, 80; under Roman rule, 8
urban migration, 79, 157; under French rule, 93, 94; and housing shortage, 121, 124, 151; in War of Independence, 46
Vandals, xxvii, 10–11
V-E Day revolt, xxviii, 42
veiling, 96, 102, 111; and terrorism, xxxii
Vichy regime, 40
Vietnam: health care professionals from, 120
Vietnam, Republic of: military support for, 240
villages, 93; industrial, 122
Viollette, Maurice, 38
Viollette Plan, 38–39
Vosper Thornycroft, 264
voting: eligibility, 32, 52; turnout, xxxv; by women, 43, 52

wage, 144; minimum, 144; negotiation process, 145; scale, 144
Warnier, Auguste, 32
War of Independence, 4, 26, 44–46, 129, 251–53; begun, xxviii, 44; 251–53; casualties in, xxviii, 49, 55, 76; conduct of, 48–51; ended, xxviii; families in, 95; generals' putsch in, 54–56; impact of, 95–96; in Kabylie region, 83; leaders of, 44; opposition to, in France, 53; *quadrillage* in, 50–51; refugees from, 55; United Nations pressure in, 48; urban migration in, 46; women in, 95, 102, 215
water: distribution losses, xxxiv; investment in, 140
welfare system, 121, 184
West: relations with, 228–33
Western influence, xxxv–xxxvi, 97
Western Sahara (*see also* Saharan Arab Democratic Republic), 241; dispute over, 224, 242–43; French intervention in, 231; Morocco's attempt to annex, 270, 273; nationalist insurgency in, 237
wheat, 31
Wilaya Charter (1969), 202
wine: exports of, 158, 169, 170; production, 158
women, 101–4; Arab, 102; in armed forces, 102, 267; Berber, 102; conduct of, 101; demonstrations by, 104; deprived of civil rights, 62, 63, 104; education of, 115; employment of, 104, 143, 216; feminist, 111; marriage of, 105, 216; political influence of, 216, 218; political protest by, xxxii; in population, 76, 77; rights of, 199; roles of, 97, 100, 215; rural, 104; seclusion of, 100; status of, 104; terrorist killings of, xxxii; veiling of, 96, 102, 111; voting by, 43; in War of Independence, 95, 102, 215
women's associations, 45, 218
women's movement, 215–18
workers' committees, 130
work force, 143–45; age of, 143; education of, 143; growth of, 144; size of, 129, 143; women as percentage of, 104, 143
working class, 98
World Bank: aid from, 69, 114; loans from, 138, 151, 162, 163; structural adjustment loan from, 137
World Military and Social Expenditures (Sivard), 271
World War I, 250
World War II, 40, 250

Yahya ibn Ibrahim al Jaddali, 14, 15
Yaqub al Mansur, 16
Young Algerians (Jeunesse Algérienne), 35–36
Youth Employment Program (Programme d'Emploi des Jeunes), 144
youth groups, 212–13
Yusuf ibn Tashfin, 15

Zarzaïtine oil fields, 145
Zayanids, xxvii, 16–17
Zbiri, Taher, 247; coup attempt by, 245, 254; as military chief of staff, 254
Zenata, 14
Zeroual, Lamine: as president, xxvii, xxxi
Zimbabwe: support for revolutionaries in, 226
zinc, 129, 148; mines, 149
Zirids, 13
Zouaouah dialect, 116, 221

Contributors

Lisa J. Arone is a research assistant at Princeton University, who has collaborated in the past with John P. Entelis in writing about the Maghrib.

Mary-Jane Deeb, Academic Director, The Omani Program, School of International Service, the American University, is the author of numerous articles on North Africa for scholarly journals.

John P. Entelis, Professor of Political Science and Co-Director of the Middle East Studies Program at Fordham University, has published extensively on North Africa.

Boulos A. Malik has served in North Africa and the Middle East for the United States Department of State and has also written for the Voice of America and Reuters.

Helen Chapin Metz is Supervisor, Middle East/Africa/Latin America Unit, Federal Research Division, Library of Congress.

Jean R. Tartter is a retired Foreign Service Officer who has written widely on the Middle East and Africa for the Country Studies series.

Anthony Toth, an expert on Middle East affairs, has written on the area for a number of publications.

Published Country Studies

(Area Handbook Series)

550–65	Afghanistan	550–28	Ethiopia
550–98	Albania	550–167	Finland
550–44	Algeria	550–173	Germany, East
550–59	Angola	550–155	Germany, Fed. Rep. of
550–73	Argentina	550–153	Ghana
550–169	Australia	550–87	Greece
550–176	Austria	550–78	Guatemala
550–175	Bangladesh	550–174	Guinea
550–170	Belgium	550–82	Guyana and Belize
550–66	Bolivia	550–151	Honduras
550–20	Brazil	550–165	Hungary
550–168	Bulgaria	550–21	India
550–61	Burma	550–154	Indian Ocean
550–50	Cambodia	550–39	Indonesia
550–166	Cameroon	550–68	Iran
550–159	Chad	550–31	Iraq
550–77	Chile	550–25	Israel
550–60	China	550–182	Italy
550–26	Colombia	550–30	Japan
550–33	Commonwealth Caribbean, Islands of the	550–34	Jordan
550–91	Congo	550–56	Kenya
550–90	Costa Rica	550–81	Korea, North
550–69	Côte d'Ivoire (Ivory Coast)	550–41	Korea, South
550–152	Cuba	550–58	Laos
550–22	Cyprus	550–24	Lebanon
550–158	Czechoslovakia	550–38	Liberia
550–36	Dominican Republic and Haiti	550–85	Libya
550–52	Ecuador	550–172	Malawi
550–43	Egypt	550–45	Malaysia
550–150	El Salvador	550–161	Mauritania

550–79	Mexico	550–179	Spain
550–76	Mongolia	550–96	Sri Lanka
550–49	Morocco	550–27	Sudan
550–64	Mozambique	550–47	Syria
550–35	Nepal and Bhutan	550–62	Tanzania
550–88	Nicaragua	550–53	Thailand
550–157	Nigeria	550–89	Tunisia
550–94	Oceania	550–80	Turkey
550–48	Pakistan	550–74	Uganda
550–46	Panama	550–97	Uruguay
550–156	Paraguay	550–71	Venezuela
550–185	Persian Gulf States	550–32	Vietnam
550–42	Peru	550–183	Yemens, The
550–72	Philippines	550–99	Yugoslavia
550–162	Poland	550–67	Zaire
550–181	Portugal	550–75	Zambia
550–160	Romania	550–171	Zimbabwe
550–37	Rwanda and Burundi		
550–51	Saudi Arabia		
550–70	Senegal		
550–180	Sierra Leone		
550–184	Singapore		
550–86	Somalia		
550–93	South Africa		
550–95	Soviet Union